A COMPANION TO THE BRITISH ARMY

1660-1983

DAVID ASCOLI

BOOK CLUB ASSOCIATES
LONDON

CAROLO SECUNDO REGI
EXERCITUS JURE CONSTITUTI
CONDITORI

This edition published 1984
by Book Club Associates
by arrangement with HARRAP LIMITED

Designed by Michael R. Carter

Printed and bound in Great Britain
by R. J. Acford, Chichester

CONTENTS

ACKNOWLEDGMENTS

In compiling this *Companion* I have received unstinted help from so many quarters that it is impossible to list the roll of honour in detail. Regimental Secretaries and Curators of Regimental Museums have been generous with their time and patience in answering my questions and correcting my inadequacies, and if in crossing this military minefield I have inadvertently touched off any detonators, my resulting injuries are entirely self-inflicted. Any errors of omission or commission will be noted and subsequently corrected. I would, however, like to record here some individual and personal expressions of appreciation.

Lieutenant Colonel Sir Colin Cole, Garter Principal King of Arms and Inspector of Regimental Colours, for his advice and help in several matters which lie within his special parish; and Roy Field of Hobson and Sons (London) Ltd, who is a walking encyclopaedia on the subject of Regimental Colours and associated militaria.

Lieutenant Colonel Jim Kelly and my many old friends at the Royal Hospital, Chelsea, for keeping me on the straight and narrow path of military orthodoxy. If in doubt go to the horse's mouth, always mindful that horses can both bite and kick.

John Andrews, Chief Librarian of the Ministry of Defence and, especially, the late Stephanie Glover, who was, over many months, a tireless helper and a very present help in trouble. I would like to pay my own tribute to her here. In a sense, this is her book.

David Smurthwaite, Keeper, Books and Archives at the National Army Museum and his cheerful staff who have delved and spun for me, Adam and Eve personified.

Brigadier Roy Thurburn, formerly Secretary to the Battle Honours Committee, who has kindly given me the benefit of his special knowledge and experience of a difficult and complex field.

Matthew Little of the Royal Marines Museum at Eastney who has awakened some happy memories of that incomparable Corps.

Finally, I would like to record my gratitude to my publisher, Richard Butterworth, who has dictated the strategy and let the tactics look after themselves, as a good general should; to my editor, Roy Minton, who has constantly reminded me of the old Army adage that 'time spent on reconnaissance is seldom wasted'; and to my designer, Michael Carter, who has brought me to book.

The First Mutiny Act, 3 April 1689, 1 Will. and Mar. Sess 1, No. 7 is in the custody of the House of Lords Records Office, and the Preamble is reproduced here by kind permission of the Clerk of the Records.

The illustrations in Section D are reproduced by kind permission of the National Army Museum and the Parker Gallery, 12A and B, Berkeley Street, London, W.1.

PREFACE

The British Army is a very singular institution.

A foundling child, begotten in 1660 in the long shadow of Cromwell's New Model (for twenty-five years it was never referred to as an 'Army', and for twenty-nine was held to be constitutionally illegal), it has survived political prejudice, parliamentary antipathy, Treasury parsimony and, for much of its existence, public hostility. It has been bravely, but sometimes indifferently, led: in war *fortiter in re*, always; in peace *suaviter in modo*, seldom. As an institution rooted, however precariously, in the people it has long reflected the highest virtues and the worst vices of the British character. Small wonder, for it seems often to have had more dedicated opponents at home than abroad.

This long-standing love-hate relationship is reflected in a profound aversion, both public and political, to compulsory service. Except for two brief periods — 1916–19 and 1939–60 — the Army, unlike those of other great powers, has been in principle a volunteer organization. I say in principle since the word 'volunteer' is capable of some very nice distinctions.[1] The crimping establishments of the eighteenth century were little more than forced-labour exchanges. The old recruiting sergeants, wily confidence tricksters to a man, resorted to the simple expedients of bribery and beer; and both worked like a charm. Free will, the essence of volunteering, was the exception and not the rule.

Until this century very few men enlisted for purely altruistic reasons. For the most part they joined on other grounds: unemployment, boredom, a taste for adventure, an emergency exit from sexual indiscretions or from the law, even — though their pay was derisory and often in arrears — for money. If Army life was spartan, it was no more so than that which they had left behind them. If Army punishment was savage, it was consistent with a social system which, even at the time of Waterloo, tolerated a legal code under which there were 223 crimes which carried the death penalty.[2]

Yet the brutal and licentious soldiery were not, in Wellington's much-misquoted words, 'the scum of the earth'. Most of them, to be sure, came from brutal and licentious backgrounds, for society gave them no other option; but their record, emblazoned on countless regimental colours, testifies to the

---

[1]'Impressment' was authorized by an Act of 1702 when imprisoned debtors were released in return for agreeing to enlist 'for the duration', or provided that they could find a suitable substitute. The same Act permitted the conscription of unemployed men and paupers. The practice was revived briefly in 1756. (Clode, *Military Forces of the Crown*.)

[2]There were occasional concessions. In 1810 the death penalty was abolished for the curious crime of 'begging by soldiers and sailors without the permission of their commanding officers'.

9

character and fortitude of simple men, united in a common purpose and a fierce regimental pride, who when called upon to do their duty did it without much question and often little understanding. They were — and are — formidable soldiers; and for far too long they were greatly ill used by politicians and public alike.

The hostility to compulsory military service — even to the very idea of a standing army in time of peace — was a direct consequence of Cromwell's military dictatorship; and a nation ready to embrace the challenge of foreign wars was all too easily persuaded that the same soldiers were an expensive luxury and a 'Grievance and Vexation to the People'[3] in times of tranquillity.

For two hundred years, except in time of war and until the Army Service Act of 1847 and Cardwell's Short Service Act of 1870, men enlisted for life,[4] a contract broken only by desertion, disbandment, infirmity or death, a circumstance illuminated by a Minute in the proceedings of the Chelsea Board at the Royal Hospital:

> Hugh Brown of Capt d'Arboledo's Independent Company at Jersey submits a petition representing that after 35 years service in Sir Bevill Greenville's Regt. he was ordered to be taken into the said Company in which he has served 25 years and being now discharged from thence after sixty years service in the Army and 87 years of age, prays to have the benefit of the Out-Pension.

Until the wars of this century, the strength of the Army has never exceeded 250,000 men, and successive governments, quick to recruit in times of emergency, were quicker still to disband when danger had passed. Yet what this modest instrument achieved is well illustrated by a simple example.

During the twenty-two years of the Revolutionary and Napoleonic Wars — that is to say, from 1793 to 1815 — the British Army was variously engaged in Holland, France, Flanders, the Peninsula, the Mediterranean, Italy, Egypt, Arabia, India, Nepal, Ceylon, the Indian Ocean, the Dutch East Indies, South Africa, the West Indies, South America, North America and — rather improbably — Fishguard, to say nothing of four naval actions. The list of battle honours from 1662 to 1902 alone reads like a world gazetteer, while still leaving room to add Korea and the Falkland Islands in our own day.

It is instructive, too, to note the number of established British regiments engaged in some of the more celebrated battles and campaigns. For example:

Blenheim (1704)	21
Dettingen (1743)	26
Quebec (1759)	7
Minden (1759)	6
Emsdorff (1760)	1
Assaye (1803)	3
Peninsula (1808-14)	71
Waterloo (1815)	37
Aliwal (1846)	4
Crimea (1854-5)	61
Omdurman (1898)	9

[3]Commons Journals, 1 April 1679
[4]Clode *op.cit.*

In the Second Boer War (1899-1902) every regiment of the Regular Army was engaged[5] with the exception of 4th Dragoon Guards, 4th Hussars, 15th Hussars and 21st Lancers. In addition, detachments of 43 Yeomanry regiments and 50 Militia battalions were present.

Across two hundred and fifty years, only once — in South Africa — did the British Army outnumber its opponents.

This is neither a history of the British Army nor a chronicle of battles and campaigns. It would be a bold author, and an even braver publisher, who presumed to offer a Roland to Sir John Fortescue's magisterial, if occasionally eccentric, Oliver. I have neither the wit nor knowledge, nor thirty years to spare. There is a whole library of conventional histories, some of which cover the long chronicle in the sweep of a single volume, others which deal with different aspects and different periods; for excepting the brief interlude between the Treaty of Utrecht and the battle of Dettingen there has been scarcely a year in which the Army has not seen active service on one continent or another. I have included in the bibliography a select, and admittedly subjective, list of accessible, informative, occasionally contentious books and journals (no reader with a taste for polemics should miss *Fifteen Years of "Army Reform"*, published anonymously in 1884); but it is a necessarily modest catalogue.

It has long seemed to me that the Army is its own best historian. From the beginning, from the raising of the first six Standing Regiments, it has written its own record in the long march of events. In a little over 300 years it has won 1003 battle honours on five continents. In sporting terms it has suffered fewer than fifty defeats away from home, and one honourable draw — at Fontenoy. Its achievements are more vividly displayed on its standards, guidons and colours and in its regimental badges and devices than in any history book. And yet, while it brought honour and greatness to the nation and maintained the 'Pax Britannica' in spite of, rather than with the ungrudging support of, its political masters, few trumpets sounded for it. 'Two centuries of persecution could not wear out its patience,' wrote Fortescue. 'Two centuries of thankless toil could not abate its ardours. Two centuries of conquest could not awake its insolence.' It was left to the new century to redress the balance of the old.

There is a curious anachronism. We have a Royal Navy. We have Royal Marines and a Royal Air Force.[6] But we have no Royal Army. Certainly, until the reorganization and the amalgamations which followed the Second World War and the retreat from Empire, there had been 78 individual Regiments and Corps which bore a 'Royal' title; but no Royal Army. As we shall see, from the Restoration of 1660 and again from the Mutiny Act of 1689 Parliament was engaged in a relentless (and often ridiculous) battle to limit the military prerogative of the Crown, as witness John Dunning in the Commons in April 1780 (while an inept Government was busy losing the American Colonies): 'It is necessary to declare that the influence of the Crown has increased, is increasing, and ought to be diminished.' The chief target was the Standing Army, effectively controlled by Parliament through its statutory right to vote supplies and limit the establishment, while conceding to the Crown 'the Government, Command and Disposition of the Forces'[7]. It was not until the creation of the Army Council in

---

[5]Some infantry regiments with both or even three battalions.
[6]Its predecessor, the Royal Flying Corps formed in 1912, was granted its distinction before it had ever been in action.
[7]The office of Commander-in-Chief was not put on a statutory footing until 1793.

1904 that the semantic arguments were resolved. Meanwhile, to the great good fortune of both Parliament and people, the Army soldiered on.

I have confined this book to the Regular Army, and have referred to the Volunteers, the Militia and the Territorials only where — as, for example, in the Militia Acts of the Restoration, in the Cardwell and Haldane reforms, in the Second Boer War, and in the post-1946 period — they illustrate political rather than military attitudes. Similarly, I have omitted all but passing references to the Indian Army and to the former Colonial regiments.

I have called this a Companion; that is to say, a vade-mecum to the constant, and often bewildering, changes in the anatomy of the Army. There are, as I believe, a number of key dates in the mainstream of our military development — for instance: 1661, 1685, 1689, 1751, 1782, 1858, 1870, 1881, 1904, 1922, 1948, 1968 — and these are reflected in the reference tables and in the introductory notes to the different sections of the book. I have sought to provide the reader with a broad spectrum of information about the rise — and sometimes the fall — of this unique institution. In compiling this Companion I have been given unstinted help by an 'army' of experts at every level. Any errors or inaccuracies are my own, and I would welcome comment and corrections; for the Army is an elusive quarry.

Finally, I would add two words of explanation. After much consideration, I have chosen to present the central section — the detailed anatomy — alphabetically, and cross-referenced to the 'spinal column' on pages 61-5. Within each table and elsewhere I have shown Regiments and Corps in their official order of precedence.

Secondly, a matter of nomenclature. In the Infantry of the Line, the titles 'regiment' and 'corps' are interchangeable. The same is true of the titles 'regiment' and 'battalion', with certain exceptions. Fifteen regiments of Foot each raised a second battalion during the mid-eighteenth century, after which these were disbanded or re-formed as new regiments. The twenty-five senior corps again raised second battalions in 1857 and 1858, and these were left intact by Cardwell when the remaining Line regiments were linked in pairs.[8] The one exception to this far-reaching change was The Queen's Own Cameron Highlanders (79th Foot), which remained the only single-battalion regiment until 1897.

In 1948 all infantry corps, other than the three senior regiments of Foot Guards, were reduced to a single battalion — but not for long. Today, after further reorganization, five of the six 'large' regiments formed between 1964 and 1968 consist each of three battalions, and the sixth of two.[9]

It is unlikely that the last chapter has been written.

---

[8]The following Line regiments at various times raised four Regular battalions: The Royal Fusiliers, The Worcestershire Regiment, The Middlesex Regiment, The King's Royal Rifle Corps and The Rifle Brigade (see individual entries).

[9]The Parachute Regiment, the youngest infantry corps, consists of three battalions. Two regiments of the Brigade of Gurkhas have two battalions.

INTRODUCTION

Britain is an island. From this remote and improbable base, perched on the shoulder of Europe, she created and sustained an Empire unexampled both in its size and in its authority, and founded, like its Roman model, on the principles of law, order, commercial enterprise and self-interest. But contrary to conventional wisdom, the British Empire grew and prospered by the reverse premise that the flag followed trade. Only a nation of shopkeepers would have thought of embarking on a colonial venture by forming, under a Royal Charter of 31 December 1600, a joint-stock company to promote its interests in India.

We are thus, by a natural conjunction of temperament and geography, a maritime people. From the earliest time to the present day, our history has been dominated by a single unrelenting element. Without command of the sea Britian would long since have been reduced to a rural irrelevance in the great passage of world affairs.[1]

The sea has played two different, but complementary, roles in British history: first, 'as a moat defensive to a house', it has served as a bastion against all would-be invaders since William of Normandy; secondly, it has been a highway, a summons to Empire. Without the Fleet and the authority of naval power, the imperial dream would never have become reality. Armies, however small, cannot be transported and sustained without command of the sea. Without the Royal Navy, the conquest of India or Canada, to take but two examples, would have been impossible, while nearer home Britain would never have been able to influence the balance of power in Europe as she did. It has been said by some historians that the battle of Leipzig in 1813 marked the final decline of Napoleon. That is not so. Eight years earlier at Trafalgar French sea-power was destroyed, and with it the power to interfere with the movement of troops and supplies to the Peninsula. Isolated and blockaded, France went down to inevitable defeat. The battle of Waterloo was won not on the playing-fields of Eton but in the Mediterranean and in the Western Approaches.

From feudal times the Navy was virtually a law unto itself, and this was in marked contrast to the obsessive hostility of Parliament to the existence of a Standing Army in time of peace. The reasons, however prejudiced, are understandable.

The Navy, removed in its coastal bases from the seat of government and for long periods at sea, did not represent a threat to the internal security of the State

---

[1] The Battle of Britain was as much about control of the Channel as of the skies above it.

13

other than by mutiny or disaffection; and Blake's[2] Articles of War, framed in 1652 and elaborated by the Convention Parliament of 1660, were designed 'for the better ordering and government of the said fleet'.

The special status of that fleet had been underlined as far back as 1415, when the Commons recorded their opinion that 'la dit Naveye est la griendre substance du bien, profit, et prosperitee du vostre dit Roialme'.[3] This wording was repeated almost exactly in the preamble to the Naval Discipline Act of 1661,[4] the first measure by which the constitutional position of the Royal Navy (unlike that of the Army) was established by permanent Statute: 'His Majesty's Navies, ships of War, and forces by Sea, wherein, under the good Providence and Protection of God, the wealth, safety, and strength of this kingdom *is so much concerned*'. No government has seen fit to pay any such tribute to the Army. Indeed, the future Duke of Wellington, no great advocate of the senior service, had this to say: 'The Navy was the characteristic and constitutional force of Britain, but the Army was a new *[sic]* force arising out of the extraordinary exigencies of modern times', while Clode wrote: 'The Navy and the Militia were the Constitutional forces which Parliament encouraged — at the *expense* of the Army.' Thus the Navy continued on its separate way, immune from Parliamentary interference, secure in its public image, seldom short of money, and giving a wide berth to those with inquisitive minds and critical intentions. Not for nothing has it been called the silent service. The Army was to be less fortunate and a great deal less privileged.

'OUR GUARDS AND GARRISONS'

On 29 May 1660, his thirtieth birthday, Charles II returned to London and to the throne denied to him for eleven years. John Evelyn watched his triumphant progress: 'I stood in the Strand and beheld it, and blessed God. And all this was done without one drop of blood shed, and by that very army which rebelled against him.' To match the occasion, the sun shone brilliantly. It had been a long, dark night.

Evelyn could not then have foreseen the significance of that day. The 'army' to which he referred — the New Model — had been an oppressive instrument of political power, led by a military junta without public approval or constitutional authority. The nation was sullen and resentful; and Parliament, after a brief flicker of euphoria, determined never again to abrogate its constitutional authority over the Army to any third party, whether he be King or Lord Protector. At once it found itself faced by a dilemma.

The first action of the Convention Parliament was to disband the army of the Commonwealth. The King, mindful of his father's abuse of the royal prerogative and of the Petition of Right, offered no objection, and the view of the Commons was summed up by the Secretary of State who during the debate on the Act[5]

---

[2]Blake, and before him naval commanders such as Frobisher and Drake, bore the title of 'General at Sea'. The ancient office of 'Lord High Admiral' (to distinguish the service from the Army) was revived by Charles II in 1660 and conferred on his brother, the Duke of York.
[3]Parliamentary Rolls, 3 Hen. V.
[4]This Act remained in force, with minor amendments, until 1749 and again until 1866 when the final words of the preamble were changed significantly to '...the wealth, safety, and strength of the Kingdom *chiefly depend*'. The Naval Discipline Act of 1955, mindful perhaps of the not insubstantial achievements of the Army in two World Wars, watered down the last phrase to '*so much depend*'.
[5]*The Act for Speedy Disbanding.* The cost to the Exchequer for implementing the Act was £835,819 8s. 10d.

observed that 'so long as the soldiery continued, there would be a perpetual trembling in the nation, for they are inconsistent with the happiness of any Kingdom'. So the process of disbanding continued by lot, and by Christmas 1660 there remained only General Monk's Coldstream Regiment (the military instrument of Restoration) and his own regiment of Horse.

But there also remained the questions of the security of the realm and the personal safety of the Sovereign; and here history took a hand. In January 1661 there occurred a minor insurrection in the City of London by an eccentric sect called the Fifth Monarchists. It was quickly suppressed by Monk's troops and by the King's personal guards who had returned with him from exile; but the occasion provided Parliament with a warning, and Charles with an excuse. The final disbandment of the Army was halted, and on 14 February, in a symbolic gesture, Monk's Coldstream Regiment laid down its arms on Tower Hill and took them up again as the Lord General's Regiment of Foot in the service of the Crown.

It is from this date that the Regular Army may be said to have its origin; but as early as August the previous year Charles and his Chancellor, Clarendon, had discussed the creation of a personal bodyguard.[6] This was to consist of two regiments of horse and two of foot, and was to be raised from men who had served the King during his exile in France and the Low Countries, and whose loyalty could therefore be assumed. They were, however, not sufficiently numerous to form four regiments, and accordingly Charles, on the pretext provided by the Fifth Monarchists, announced on 26 January 1661 a draft establishment of the Life Guards, His Majesty's Regiment of Horse, and two regiments of Foot Guards, consisting of Royalists and 'safe' Parliamentarians, at an annual cost of £122,407 15s. 10d. These, his Household troops, were solely for his personal protection, to carry out police duties, and to serve as a trained nucleus for expansion in the event of war. There is no evidence that at any time during his reign did Charles intend to use the Standing Army to frustrate the will of Parliament or to suppress civil liberties, and at his death the Army numbered fewer than 7,000 men. But he had reckoned without his contentious Lords and Commons, and without the memory of Cromwell.

So much for the personal safety of the Sovereign; there remained the security of the kingdom against its enemies from without. At the date of the Restoration there were twenty-eight key points, or fortresses, in England, and these were manned by independent companies consisting of former Parliamentary soldiers. These troops were excluded from the provisions of the Disbandment Act, and after the replacement of their officers by Royalists they were continued in the King's service — and charged to the King's account. In June 1661 they were added to the establishment of what were strictly termed 'Our Guards and Garrisons'. Not for another twenty-eight years (by when their strength had been substantially increased) could Parliament bring itself to call them 'the Army', and then only as a term of ill-concealed abuse.

Parliament at once found itself caught in a constitutional quandary. Since the existence of a Standing Army in time of peace had, Charles I and Cromwell notwithstanding, been held to be against the law, how was it to reconcile the Guards and Garrisons with the existing legal force for the defence of the realm?

The Assize of Arms of 1181 had required all freemen over the age of fifteen to keep weapons in their homes, in quality and number according to their rank and

[6]There were many historical precedents, notably the creation of the Yeomen of the Guard by Henry VII, and the Gentlemen Pensioners by Henry VIII.

station. Originally intended as a purely civil measure to 'abate the power of felons' and keep the peace, the system developed on the appointment of Lords-Lieutenant into a primitive 'territorial Army' charged, together with the Trained Bands in towns and cities, not only with maintaining public tranquillity, but with ensuring the security of the kingdom against foreign aggression. Further statutes defined the obligations for service of this essentially civilian force — for example, its members were protected from having to leave their county or shire 'save upon the coming of strange enemies into the realm', or for the suppression and defeat of any insurrection. Not for over a century was any provision made for their embodiment in time of war, for only the Crown could make war and peace. But by firmly placing this citizen force under the authority of Lords-Lieutenant and the local gentry of the shires, and not under the Crown, Parliament ensured sovereignty over it, and thus over the internal security of the kingdom.

The first use of the title 'Militia' appears in the Commons Journal of 31 January 1641, which prompted the agitated Member for Great Marlow to declare: 'I do heartily wish that this great word — this new word — the Militia — this harsh word might never have come within these walls.' What may have been his opinion of the ruthless use of a far harsher military instrument soon to subvert the Constitution, and eventually parliamentary democracy itself, is not recorded. But the historic necessity for this citizen army in time of peace was not easily to be set aside, so that two hundred years later Clode could write without equivocation: *'The Constitutional Force for the Defence of the realm is the Militia'*, adding:

> The army became as dependent on the Crown as the Crown was on the army, and the Militia became a counterpoise to the Standing Army and a National Security. Parliament, therefore, firmly held the Militia within its own control, as a protection against the encroachments alike of the Crown and the Standing Army upon the Liberties of the People.

And therein lay the seeds of confrontation.

Parliament's honeymoon with the King was short-lived. Charles was every inch a Stuart, and as adamant concerning his Divine Right as his royal prerogative. But he had before him the example of his father's fate, and had no wish to go upon his 'travels' again. Parliament was no less jealous of its own rights and privileges. Thus the scene was set for a curious running battle during which an often resistible force came into collision with a by no means immovable object. Repeatedly during the next twenty-five years, as the Standing Army set out upon its long and stony road, both sides for different reasons were driven to compromise. At Charles's death it could be said that honours were even. Not so with his intolerant brother James; and it was not until the Declaration of Rights in 1689 that Parliament could rightly say that it had gained statutory, if not undisputed, control over the nation's military forces.

Scarcely had Charles made known his intention of forming a permanent military force of Guards and Garrisons than the Commons took up the challenge, and in July 1661 brought forward a short Bill to establish and settle the Militia of the kingdom on a constitutional basis. This measure was designed to indemnify persons acting under Royal Commissions of Lieutenancy and to forbid the Crown to compel any subjects 'to march out of the kingdom otherwise than by the laws of England ought to be done'. It then proceeded in its preamble to declare that the supreme command not only of the Militia but of 'all Forces by Land and Sea and of all Forts and places of strength' was vested solely in the King.

Charles might be forgiven for wondering whether his 'faithful Commons' had decided to forgive and forget. On his return to England they had agreed to a modest annual supply of £1,200,000, out of which he must find the money to support his Guards and Garrisons.[7] But the wording of this Bill, while carefully avoiding any reference to a Standing Army, conferred on him — or so it seemed — Cromwellian powers over all the armed forces of the State.

But in the following year Parliament went further, and in a second Militia Act it declared: 'Within all his realms and dominions, the *sole supreme Government, Command and Disposition* of the Militia, and of all Forces by sea and land, and of all Forts and places of strength, is, and by the laws of England ever was, the undoubted right of His Majesty; and that both or either of the Houses of Parliament cannot nor ought to pretend to the same.'

In fact this apparent act of submission to the Crown set down, even if it did not forthwith establish, a major constitutional principle; and the wording was by no means so imprecise (or generous) as it might seem. The intention of the Act may be summarized thus: only the King had the right to make war (a privilege which Parliament was happy to 'delegate' to the Crown), and to exercise that right it was obvious that he must have control of all available resources. But — and here the Act is specific in its omission — Parliament retained the sole right to regulate the *size* of any Standing Army in time of peace (its *legality* was curiously not challenged here) and to limit its money supply (which amounted to the same thing). A later, contradictory, clause in the Act placed the Militia of each county under the 'Government and Command' of a Lieutenant to be appointed by the Crown, while continuing the system of local financing of all territorial forces, without limit on their size. Parliament may have thus congratulated itself on its ingenuity; but history has a way of embarrassing clever politicians.

What were the 'Forces by land' so vaguely specified in the Acts as distinct from the Militia? Before the Civil War, the profession of arms was practised on a casual level, with little opportunity for either officers or men to learn their trade except in routine suppression of domestic disorder in Scotland and Ireland and in ill-conceived ventures such as Buckingham's expedition to La Rochelle. But it was a mercenary age, and the Thirty Years' War provided an inviting stage for soldiers of fortune.

As early as 1572 an English brigade and four Scottish regiments had been formed for service in the Dutch Republic, and by Royal Warrant of 1633 Sir John Hepburn had been granted permission to raise a Scottish regiment for service under the French Crown.[8] Thus at the Restoration there existed these mercenary units in foreign pay, the discredited army of the Commonwealth, and a garrison of 6000 Parliamentary troops which had occupied Dunkirk since the battle of the Dunes in 1658, and which was now enlarged by the addition of a

---

[7]The cost in 1661 was £189,724 11s. 4d.; but Charles had learned that these matters were better arranged in France by his cousin, Louis XIV; and accordingly he enlisted the aid of his wealthy Paymaster, Sir Stephen Fox, who underwrote Army pay through his own credit while retaining a commission of a shilling in the pound.

[8]As Le Régiment d'Hébron.

small number of Royalist exiles.[9]

But by 1662 (when the new Cavalier Parliament passed its second Militia Bill with the express purpose of limiting the King's power to rule by the threat of military force) much had happened, and already the battle-lines were being drawn for the long and bitter conflict between Crown and Parliament, at the heart of which was — and long would so remain — the Standing Army.

At the outset the conduct of that Army did little to recommend it. The Royal Guard, beholden to no one except the King, behaved with an insolence all too reminiscent of its predecessors, not least in the exercise of its assumed police duties. For — 'it caused more trouble by way of riots and disorders than it ever helped to solve; it frequently [and illegally] housed itself on civilians under free quarter; and it attracted some of the worst dregs of society into its ranks'.[10] In so doing it set a pattern for the future which all its bravery in battle and patience in adversity would not erase for two centuries to come. Within a year it contrived to earn a double and equally disabling distinction: the pathological hostility of Parliament and the hatred of the public.[11]

It also began to grow. The increase in numbers was very modest, and except during three short periods of emergency the strength of the Standing Army barely doubled during Charles's reign. The process was not entirely of the King's own making, but it was enough to inflame the passions of a Parliament as obsessed with a fear of Popery as with the abuse of the prerogative, and persuaded that constitutional rectitude rested solely in the Militia. It is a fact that after the final Dissolution in 1681 and during his last four years, when he was literally monarch of all he surveyed, Charles did not add a single regiment to the ten then on foot on the English establishment and in Tangier. It may be argued that to the end he was short of money, but that disability did not deter his arrogant and bigoted brother. Charles felt secure with what he had, and it is to the credit of this complex but compassionate man that he left only one more military memorial, a Hospital at Chelsea to serve as a retreat for soldiers grown old and infirm in the service of the Crown. There is no doubt that his peevish Commons, had they not been sent packing at Oxford, would have loudly condemned that act of charity.

The military pattern of Charles's reign ran its course against a continuous counterpoint of political and religious ferment, fuelled by the King's ambivalent conduct of foreign affairs. Not without reason, Parliament distrusted him. Not without reason, he became exasperated by what he believed to be an organized conspiracy against his prerogative. Yet by the end he succeeded in laying the foundation of the Regular establishment. How this was achieved may be summarized under three heads.

First, the Standing Army. It did not take Charles long to decide that, while the four regiments of Household troops were enough to protect his person, they were too few to ensure the defence of the realm, let alone provide an expeditionary force in the event of war. Accordingly in 1661 he persuaded Louis XIV to return to him on temporary loan the Régiment de Douglas (formerly Hepburn's Scots; see p.17, footnote 8). This decision, in apparent breach of the

---

[9]In addition, there were the separate garrison companies of the Scottish and Irish establishments which were charged to the revenues of those two kingdoms.
[10]Childs, *The Army of Charles II.*
[11]A wiser man than Charles would have avoided the provocation of putting his private army in the same red coats as Cromwell's soldiers.

tacit agreement with Parliament, offered a dangerous hostage to fortune, and so the regiment went back to France in the following year. Not until 1673 did it take its place on the permanent English establishment and claim its precedence as The Royal Regiment of Foot (and, in due course, The Royal Scots, the senior infantry regiment of the Line by virtue of Charles I's Warrant of 1633).[19]

Next, in October 1664, the King directed by Order in Council that 'twelve hundred land souljers be forthwith raysed to be in readiness to be distributed into his Majestie's Fleets prepared for sea service' under the title of The Admiral's, or Duke of York's Maritime Regiment of Foot. This was an astute move, for by specifying the words 'sea service' Charles neatly pre-empted any Parliamentary objections. This corps took its place among the original six Standing Regiments, but it was not until 1755, after many vicissitudes, that it was placed under Admiralty control as the forerunner of the Royal Marines. And in 1665, with the end of the Second Dutch War, the King recalled the one remaining corps of the English Brigade in the service of the Republic, which took its place on the permanent establishment as The Holland Regiment (and in due course the 3rd Foot, or The Buffs).

So much for the domestic scene; but Charles also had a foreign commitment. Under the terms of the marriage settlement with Catherine of Braganza in 1661, he had received a dowry of £500,000, and the trading posts of Bombay and Tangier. The money was a welcome subvention, the colonial acquisitions less so, for Parliament cynically left the King to maintain the latter out of the former.

Bombay provided its own solution. A small and unenthusiastic body of disbanded soldiers was dispatched there, but disease and disaffection soon took their toll, and Charles, without benefit of foresight, was happy to lease the place to the East India Company at an annual rent of £10.

Tangier was a different matter, for it offered a safe harbour and, with a military presence in the town, a valuable base for naval operations in the western Mediterranean. Accordingly an expeditionary force was raised in January 1662, recruited from disbanded troops at home and from the garrison at Dunkirk,[13] and formed into two new regiments, The Tangier Horse (to become the Royal Dragoons) and The Tangier Regiment (to become the 2nd Foot, or Queen's Royal (West Surrey). It proved to be a singularly unattractive station for the soldiery (Pepys on a visit recorded his distaste at the lack of discipline — 'nothing but vice in the whole place ... swearing, cursing, drinking, and whoring') and a serious drain on the Privy Purse. When in 1680 the depleted garrison was faced by a full-scale Moorish offensive it was reinforced by a composite battalion of Foot Guards, four companies of The Royal Regiment, and a newly raised second Tangier Regiment (the Earl of Plymouth's, or Duchess of York's) which was duly to take its place in the Standing Army as The King's Own Royal Regiment (Lancaster). Eventually, in 1684, Charles decided to cut his losses. The garrison was evacuated and the three Tangier regiments were taken on to the English establishment. It had been an expensive wedding present.[14]

---

[12]The 'rank' or precedence of Regiments and Corps of the Regular Army does not date from their original raising but from their entry on to the British establishment. Predictably, there are anomalies and exceptions.

[13]Later in the year the remainder of this garrison was withdrawn, the Royalist element joining the King's Guards and the remainder being dispersed at home or to foreign service. The town itself was sold in October to Louis XIV for £200,000.

[14]Nevertheless, Tangier has a special distinction for it is the first in the long line of battle honours of the British Army, even though the qualifying regiments had to wait 250 years for the privilege (but see p.179).

Meanwhile, nearer home Charles had been living dangerously. The three crises which resulted from his deceitful foreign policy need not concern us here, for they served only to widen the rift between King and Parliament. The Second and Third Dutch Wars were strictly naval affairs, although that did not deter Charles from misappropriating funds specifically voted for the Fleet. Twenty-two new regiments were raised in 1665 and 1672, but only a small part of these were actively engaged, and then as marines, a duty second only in unpopularity to colonial service. All had been disbanded by 1674. Four years later, twenty regiments were raised for war with France (at least, an anti-Catholic crusade was more palatable to Parliament). Fourteen of these were sent to Flanders to support the Prince of Orange, but before they were ready for action a peace treaty had been concluded and they returned to England. Parliament, in rebellious mood, demanded that the Army at once be reduced to its pre-1665 size; and in a heated debate in the Commons Colonel Birch provided a prophetic footnote to history. 'Keep up the army for fear of France', he declared, 'and keep it up for ever!' The future would prove him wiser than he knew.[15]

Charles bowed before the storm. The new regiments were disbanded. Only the Standing Army remained.

In 1681,[16] when Charles by distancing himself from Parliament had reached calmer waters, the strength of 'Our Guards and Garrisons,' including the Tangier regiments, was 6,872 and their cost £201,358 1s. - 0¼d.[17] It is hard to believe that this modest military presence could have generated such irrational hostility; but the times were irrational, and it is not easy to understand today the depth of political suspicion and anti-Catholic hysteria which then gripped the country.

It is to Charles's determination to ride out this storm that the Regular Army owes not only its continued existence but also, by a curious irony, the key to its future survival: the regimental system. Ironic, because for many years the abuse of that system came close to destroying it.

While jealously preserving his supreme command of 'all Forces by Land', Charles left their 'furnishing and sustenance' to individual regimental Colonels. Given the spirit of the times, this was a hazardous decision and a licence for malpractice, for in effect Colonels literally owned their regiments and, with very few exceptions, made a handsome profit out of their investment. But for all its defects, the system stamped a seal of individuality on the constituent parts of the Army. If the men in the ranks were in every sense 'private' soldiers, they also acquired a sense of belonging and, however shabbily they were treated, a corporate, almost tribal, pride. Fortescue expressed it thus:

> It was in virtue of this independence that the little group of regiments called the Standing Army was able to withstand for two centuries the hatred, malignity and stinginess of Parliament, and the contempt and scorn of every citizen.... The persecution of the soldier continued unrelentingly. Against such an Army as that of Cromwell it might have succeeded. Against a collection of proprietary regiments it failed.[18]

[15]Of the 100 battle honours awarded for actions between 1695 and 1815, 75 were won against the French.
[16]For comparative figures in 1781, 1881 and 1981, (see pp.27, 46 *fn.* and 57).
[17]Public Record Office. AO1/52/33.
[18]Fortescue, *A History of the British Army*, Vol xiii, Epilogue.

If Charles had painfully learnt the art of political compromise, his brother needed no such exemplar. James was an experienced soldier (and sailor). He was also a bigoted Catholic, and was well aware of Parliament's efforts to exclude him from the succession. If he was fated to be the victim of his own arrogance and (curiously) cowardice, he also began with the luck of the damned.

Within weeks of his accession, Charles's natural son, the Duke of Monmouth, landed at Lyme Regis and raised his standard in the West Country. James at once set out with the seasoned veterans of Tangier, and at the night battle of Sedgemoor on 6 July defeated Monmouth and crushed the rebellion. Just as Venner's minor insurrection had played into Charles's hands, so Monmouth's ill-judged demonstration gave James a decisive argument for a substantial increase in the Standing Army, for the rebellion had created a degree of panic unequalled since de Ruyter's foray up the Medway, and the Militia, the darling of Parliament, had shown itself to be a toothless and unreliable watchdog.

James was a man to act first and argue later. Two weeks after the battle of Sedgemoor he ordered home the six regiments still serving in Holland after the late Flanders campaign. Of these two took their place on the permanent establishment as the 5th and 6th Regiments of Foot.[19]

Next he addressed himself to a modest reorganization of the Board of Ordnance,[20] a civilian body of great (and patently rusty) antiquity which was responsible for artillery and engineer services, commissariat duties (under such euphonious titles as 'The Office of Tents and Toils'), and the provision of weapons and ammunition for both Army and Navy. To provide an escort for artillery trains James raised 'Our Ordnance Regiment' or Royal Regiment of Fuzileers (7th Foot); and by the autumn he had raised six regiments of Horse and two of Dragoons (to become the 1st to 6th Dragoon Guards and the 3rd and 4th Hussars) and a further eight of Foot (8th to 15th). At the same time he formed the independent Garrison Companies of the Irish establishment into nineteen new regiments, but of these only one survived into the next reign as the Royal Regiment of Ireland or Royal Irish Regiment (18th Foot). By one of the many curiosities which occur throughout the history of the Regular Army, it was this now-disbanded Irish regiment which was to receive the first reward for distinguished conduct in battle when, after the siege of Namur in 1695, William III conferred upon it a Royal title, the badge of the Lion of Nassau, and the motto *Virtutis Namurcensis Praemium*.

Thus by the summer of 1687 James's proselytizing zeal was backed by an army half as large as that of the Commonwealth, and his intention was plain. If he could not convert the country to Catholicism by persuasion he would do so by intimidation, and to make that intention clearer still he assembled his troops in a great encampment at Hounslow. On 3 July he faced an apprehensive Commons and demanded a supply of £1,400,000. The future Earl of Peterborough was under no illusion when he declared that the sole purpose of the Standing Army — 'this very present evil' — was to subvert the laws and establish arbitrary power. The Commons, in an attempt at compromise, offered £700,000, with the proviso that it should be spent only on the discredited Militia. The King's uncompromising answer was to dissolve Parliament the following day. It did not meet again during his reign.

---

[19]These, and subsequent, numbers of Line regiments are those authorized by the Royal Warrant of 1751. For their territorial or regional designations, see Section A.
[20]Abolished as such in 1855.

Even then James might well have made a virtue out of Parliament's irresolution. Instead he chose further provocation by conferring high military and political office on Roman Catholics and by forming a seventh regiment of Horse, twelve new regiments of Foot (of which only the 16th and 17th survived), and by bringing on to the English establishment a regiment of Scottish Dragoons, the future Royal Scots Greys.[21]

Too late the King read the danger signals and sought safety in conciliation. But by the autumn the summons had gone out to the Protestant Prince of Orange, and on 22 December, deserted by his own unenthusiastic soldiers, James signed an order to disband the Army and made good his escape to France at — as a suitable touch of black humour — the second attempt.

It is probable that the bloodless revolution prevented a bloody civil war. It is quite certain that, by his arbitrary pursuit of power, James ensured that never again would Parliament abdicate control over the Regular Army.

The Convention of Estates of the Realm, summoned by William III on his arrival in London, presented him with the Declaration of Rights. It was in effect a very explicit service contract setting out the terms under which the Lords Spiritual and Temporal were prepared to offer him and Mary the Crown; and it contained these words:

> The raising and keeping a Standing Army within the Kingdome in time of peace, unless it be with the consent of Parliament, is against Law.

Thus after twenty-nine years the constitutional principle which had stood between King and Parliament was established; but like many principles enunciated before and since, it contained a seed of future argument.

'In time of peace'? When the first Parliament of the new reign met it found itself faced by a problem of some difficulty. Before his flight James had signed an instrument of disbandment, but Parliament now hesitated. France was already at war again in Flanders, and there was the threat of a Jacobite rebellion in Ireland. Both put at risk the Protestant faith which William had been called to defend. The disbanding of the Army was therefore halted, and while the Commons debated the niceties of their new-found constitutional rights, events took an unexpected turn.

In March ten battalions were ordered to Holland — ironically under the terms of Charles II's treaty with the man who now occupied his throne. One regiment, Dumbarton's (The Royal Scots), with many Jacobite sympathizers in its ranks, mutinied on reaching Ipswich and marched north towards the border, but overtaken near Lincoln by a strong posse of Dutch Guards, it surrendered. And in doing so it created a Gilbertian situation.

Since it had long been argued that the Army (being illegal in time of peace) did not in fact exist, soldiers were not governed by any special code of law (when embodied for active service they became subject to Articles of War which were issued and enforced only for the duration of hostilities). But mutiny was not a civil crime. How then could the mutinous Royal Scots be punished?

In some confusion Parliament brought forward a Bill 'for punishing officers and soldiers who shall mutiny or desert Their Majesties service', and on 3 April

---

[21]One of James's last acts was to advance the precedence of this regiment to 1681 by a Royal Warrant dated 1 November 1688.

1689 the first Mutiny Act[22] became law.

The Mutiny Act (which specifically excluded the Militia until amended in 1756) did not seek to legalize the Army in time of peace, although it justified its purpose by quoting that constitutional principle as expressed in the Declaration of Rights. It was designed to provide the first disciplinary code governing the punishment (and rights) of officers and men *in their capacity as soldiers and without prejudice to their civil liberties and obligations*; and its preamble runs thus:

> WHEREAS the raising or keeping a Standing Army within this Kingdome in time of Peace unless it be with consent of Parliament is against Law AND WHEREAS it is judged necessary by their Majesties and this present Parliament That during this time of danger severall of the forces which are now on foot should be continued and others raised for the safety of the Kingdome for the common defence of the Protestant Religion and for the reduceing of Ireland AND WHEREAS no man may be forejudged of Life or Limb or subjected to any kind of Punishment by Martiall Law or in any other manner than by the Judgement of his Peers and according to the known and established Laws of this Realme yet nevertheless it being requisite for retaining such forces as are or shall be raised during this Exigence of Affaires in their duty an exact discipline be observed AND THAT Souldiers who shall mutiny or stirr up Sedition or shall desert their Majesties service be brought to a more exemplary and speedy Punishment than the usuall forms of Law will allow BE it therefore ENACTED...

The Act shows every sign of hasty drafting, and it was not long before Parliament seized upon the first phrase of this preamble to apply the measure for purposes quite other than those of 'punishing officers and soldiers'. At its first passage it was given statutory effect for six months, and was thereafter required to be renewed annually (in fact between 1689 and 1712 it lapsed on ten occasions, once for a period of two years when, after the Peace of Ryswick, the Commons in a moment of lunacy moved to disband the entire Army). As for the concept of even-handed justice, the inequity and savagery of punishment which persisted for nearly two centuries reflected little credit on Parliament and none at all on the average regimental officer.[23]

Yet for all its abuse, the Mutiny Act is of historic importance. For 167 years after 1712 it was renewed annually, often after frequent amendment and partisan opposition, until in 1879 a permanent Army Discipline and Regulation Act was passed; but even at that date it was provided that in order to secure the right of Parliament to give or withhold its consent to a Standing Army the permanent Act was inoperative unless brought into force by an annual Act.

The 1879 measure was replaced two years later by the Army Act, and this continued in force until, with the adoption of the new 'joint services' structure in 1964, it was in turn replaced by the present quinquennial Armed Services Act, with which there passed into history the famous preamble of 1689.

---

[22]On 23 December a second Mutiny Bill was passed which differed in that its title added the words 'for punishing false musters', an ineffective attempt to stop the time-honoured practice by which Colonels drew pay for fictitious soldiers.

[23]An amendment to the Mutiny Act of 1713 gave regimental officers the power to inflict corporal punishment *of up to 1000 lashes* 'for immorality, misbehaviour, or dereliction of duty'. In 1811 this power was restricted to offences committed 'upon active service or in the field'. Flogging was not finally abolished until the Army Act of 1881 (Section 44).

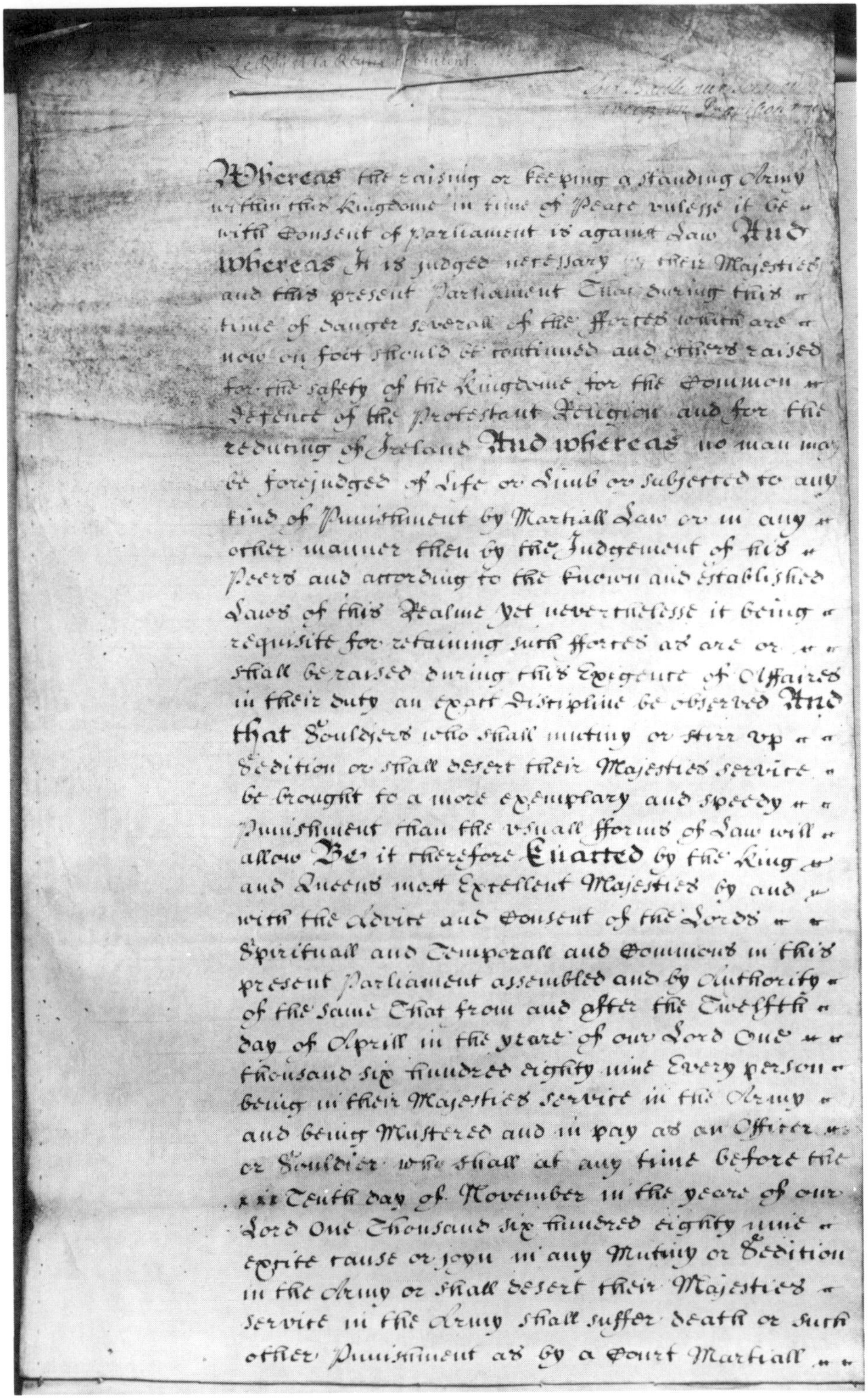

Le Roy et la Reyne le veulent.

Whereas the raising or keeping a standing Army within this Kingdome in time of Peace unlesse it be with Consent of Parliament is against Law And Whereas It is judged necessary by their Majesties and this present Parliament That during this time of danger severall of the fforces which are now on foot should be continued and others raised for the safety of the Kingdome for the Common Defence of the Protestant Religion and for the reduceing of Ireland And whereas no man may be forejudged of Life or Limb or subjected to any kind of Punishment by Martiall Law or in any other manner then by the Judgement of his Peers and according to the knowne and established Lawes of this Realme Yet neverthelesse it being requisite for retaining such fforces as are or shall be raised during this Exigence of Affaires in their duty an exact Discipline be observed And that Souldiers who shall mutiny or stirr up Sedition or shall desert their Majesties service be brought to a more exemplary and speedy Punishment than the usuall fformes of Law will allow Be it therefore Enacted by the King and Queens most Excellent Majesties by and with the advice and Consent of the Lords Spirituall and Temporall and Commons in this present Parliament assembled and by authority of the same That from and after the Twelfth day of Aprill in the yeare of our Lord One thousand six hundred eighty nine Every person being in their Majesties service in the Army and being Mustered and in pay as an Officer or Souldier who shall at any time before the Tenth day of November in the yeare of our Lord One Thousand six hundred eighty nine excite cause or joyn in any Mutiny or Sedition in the Army or shall desert their Majesties service in the Army shall suffer death or such other Punishment as by a Court Martiall

The Preamble to the first Mutiny Act of 3 April, 1689

An Act to continue for Three Months the Act of the Session of the forty-first and forty-second years of the reign of Her present Majesty, chapter ten, intituled " An " Act for punishing Mutiny and Desertion, and for the " better Payment of the Army and their Quarters."

[21st March 1879.]

WHEREAS the raising or keeping a standing army within the United Kingdom of Great Britain and Ireland in time of peace, unless it be with the consent of Parliament, is against law :

And whereas it is adjudged necessary by Her Majesty and this present Parliament that a body of forces should be continued for the safety of the United Kingdom, and the defence of the possessions of Her Majesty's Crown, and that the whole number of such forces should consist of one hundred and thirty-five thousand six hundred and twenty-five men, including those to be employed at the depôts in the United Kingdom of Great Britain and Ireland for the training of recruits for service at home and abroad, but exclusive of the numbers actually serving within Her Majesty's Indian possessions :

Number of men to consist of 135,625, including those employed at depôts in United Kingdom, but exclusive of those actually serving in India.

And whereas no man can be forejudged of life or limb, or subjected in time of peace to any kind of punishment within this realm by martial law, or in any other manner than by judgment of his peers, and according to the known and established laws of this realm ; yet nevertheless it being requisite, for the retaining all the before-mentioned forces and other persons specified in the Act next herein-after mentioned in their duty, that an exact discipline be observed, and that soldiers who shall mutiny or stir up sedition, or shall desert Her Majesty's service, or be guilty of crimes and offences to the prejudice of good order and military discipline, be brought to a more exemplary and speedy punishment than the usual forms of the law will allow :

And whereas the Act of the session of the forty-first and forty-second years of the reign of Her present Majesty, chapter ten, intituled "An Act for punishing mutiny and desertion, and for the " better payment of the army and their quarters," will be in force only in Great Britain until the twenty-fifth day of April one thousand eight hundred and seventy-nine, and elsewhere until the several dates in the said Act mentioned.

41 & 42 Vict. c. 10.

And whereas a Bill has been introduced into Parliament to amend the law relating to the discipline and regulation of the army, and it is expedient to continue the above-mentioned Act until other provisions can be brought into force for the government of the army.

The Preamble to the transitional Act of 1879 which bridged the phasing out of the Mutiny Act and the introduction of the Army Act of 1881. Compare the wording with that of the first Mutiny Act of 1689 on p. 23.

Had half as much time and heat been spent over the years on improving the status, pay and conditions of soldiers as on vilifying and abusing them, Fortescue would have had less cause for anger.

Parliament had shown rare foresight in judging it necessary 'that severall of the forces now on foot should be continued and others raised'; for before the year was out England was faced by rebellion in Ireland and Scotland and by war with France. Of the 35 regiments hurriedly raised to meet these successive emergencies, only 17 were to survive, and they are of particular interest since they included 9 from the Scottish and Irish establishments, the first to be transferred before the Acts of Union of 1707 and 1800. The surviving English and Welsh regiments were to become the 19th, 20th, 22nd, 23rd, 24th, 28th, 29th and 30th Foot.[24] The Scottish corps were those which would become 7th Hussars, The Scots Guards, and three Lowland regiments, The Royal Scots Fusiliers (21st), The King's Own Scottish Borderers (25th) and The Cameronians (26th); while the Irish regiments were the 5th, 6th and 8th Dragoons (to become 5th Royal Irish Lancers, 6th (Inniskilling) Dragoons and 8th King's Royal Irish Hussars) and the future Royal Inniskilling Fusiliers (27th).

In Flanders the campaign was distinguished more for the administrative shambles on both sides than for any particular military skill, with the British able to match only a single victory at Namur against defeats at Steinkirk and Landen; and with the signing of the Treaty of Ryswick in 1697 the war stumbled to an end. When five years later Britain next entered the European lists it would be with a very different Army and under a commander of genius.

With the end of the war abroad and national bankruptcy at home, Parliament took leave of its senses and a resolution was moved in the Commons that every regiment raised since 1660 should be disbanded. There ensued an all too familiar running battle which culminated in the King's threat to abdicate and Parliament's refusal to renew the Mutiny Act. Finally the Commons agreed to maintain a token force of 7,000 men at home and a further 12,000 for the policing of Ireland. Fortunately for the country and for the future peace of Europe, the Regular Army survived, albeit with the standing regiments reduced to little more than cadres; for on 16 September 1701 James II died in France and Louis XIV's action in recognizing his son as King of England made war inevitable.

The new century was to be one of spectacular naval and military achievement. It began with the defeat of one French attempt to dominate Europe. It ended with Britain, now a great colonial power, facing a no less daunting challenge from the same quarter.

Between the years 1700 and 1800 the Regular Army grew dramatically as the nation's overseas commitments increased; and as it grew it changed. During this period 11 new cavalry and 67 new infantry regiments were added to the permanent establishment, while The Royal Regiment of Artillery and the Corps of Royal Engineers replaced the old civilian improvisations of the Ordnance Board. By mid-century regiments of the Line were no longer known by their Colonels' names but by consecutive numbers and (from 1782) by the addition of territorial titles. In 1781, at the height of the American War of Independence,

---

[24]Temporarily disbanded in 1698 and re-formed as a regiment of Marines in 1702.

the strength of the Regular Army stood at 80,579, at an annual cost of £3,609,532 10s. 10d.[25]

It would be reasonable to think that the nation had at last come to terms with its Army. Marlborough's brilliant campaigns had proved what British soldiers, properly led and efficiently administered, could achieve against the most professional military power in Europe. But the contradictions remained, prejudice proved stronger than pride, and the old hostility to a Standing Army now acquired a new dimension with the rise of party politics. Marlborough's reward was summary dismissal, and scarcely was the ink dry on the peace treaty when a major part of the Army which had served Parliament and people so well was disbanded or, in the inelegant contemporary word, 'broke'.[26] It had happened before, and it would happen again with monotonous and perilous regularity down the years. Indeed, between the Peace of Ryswick in 1697 and the present day there have been fourteen major reductions in the effective size of the Regular Army; and even when the irrational fear of military tyranny had ceased to obsess the country successive governments took refuge behind another political smoke-screen called money. Peace can be as dangerous an enemy of the profession of arms as war.

Throughout the eighteenth century politicians and pamphleteers pursued the same vendetta, but with different degrees of sophistry and malice. There was a comfortable assumption that the Navy would ensure the nation's security. Thus one Honourable Member:

> I beg it may not be taken for granted that, if we dismiss our soldiers, we shall therefore leave ourselves naked .... No, Sir, Providence has given us the best Protection .... Our Situation, that is our natural Protection; our Fleet is our Protection.

And thus Jonathan Swift, Whig turned Tory, at his most cynical:

> A standing army in England, whether in time of Peace or War, is a direct absurdity for it is no part of our business to be a warlike nation, otherwise than by our fleets. In foreign wars we have no concern, further than in conjunction with allies, whom we may either assist by sea, or by foreign troops paid with our money.[27]

The true absurdity of this quaint observation is quite otherwise. When Swift was writing the nation of shopkeepers was already on the march building a great commercial empire, peacefully where possible but by military means where necessary. Before the century was out this 'unwarlike' nation would have broken the colonial power of France, defeated her in two critical campaigns in Europe and but for political ineptitude have kept the richest prize of all, the American colonies. Certainly it was the Navy which made possible and which sustained the Empire, but it was Swift's 'absurd' Army which sealed the victories and secured the far horizons.

---

[25]Of this total £1,166,409 16s. 10d. represented what were called 'Extraordinaries'. These were sums expended but not sanctioned by Parliament, and they were a fertile field for dishonest practices. They were not abolished until 1836.
[26]The Mutiny Act of 1716 fixed the strength of the Army at the purely arbitrary figure of 18,000.
[27]Swift, *Of Public Absurdities in England.*

To underline the hypocrisy of the national character in its attitude to any form of military presence, it is interesting to reflect that 1715, the year of Sheriffmuir, also saw the passing of the Riot Act. The English have long confused liberty with licence and have rioted happily under slogans as various as 'No Popery!' and 'No Gin!' Before the existence of an effective police force the distasteful duty of acting in aid of the civil power to suppress public disorder fell to the Army, an invasion of licence which the riotous citizens neither forgave nor forgot.[28]

The soldiers themselves contributed to these strained relations, for they were as licentious as their fathers who had so shocked the broadminded Pepys on his visit to Tangier. The practice of billeting troops on private householders as well as innkeepers (legalized by the Second Mutiny Act) did little to endear the men to a resentful public. Discipline at home was lax (it had been a different story under Marlborough abroad), and was not improved by officers who purchased their commissions as status symbols, and many of whom indeed were little more than boys.[29]

With the increase in the establishment during Queen Anne's reign an attempt was made to remove what had become a serious public grievance, and by 1714 a modest number of barracks had been built in forts and garrison towns. They were administered (if that is the correct word) by the Board of Ordnance acting in the capacity of property agents, and provided accommodation somewhere between that of a prison and a workhouse. They also provided Parliament with an improbable new stick with which to beat the Army, and the Commons Journals of the period are peppered with sanctimonious complaints that 'they isolated the soldiers from the people' and thus, by a curious kind of logic, made possible a surreptitious increase in the size of the Standing Army; ergo, the building of barracks should be discontinued. It was; and it was not resumed until the appointment of a Barrackmaster-General in 1792.

Yet throughout the years of Walpole's 'long peace' the Army continued to increase in size. Its opponents at home could not, or would not, see that the growth of commerce entailed the expansion of military forces, for trading communities needed protection which only the Army could provide; and it was the power and influence of the commercial lobby which led, against every odd, to the steady development of an institution feared and traduced by the governments which paid it, and hated and abused by the very people from whose ranks it came. Unloved, unhonoured, underpaid and ill-housed, the Regular soldier served out his time.

A WIND OF CHANGE

The end of the long peace found the Army, in Granard's phrase, 'growing old in idleness and routine'. It would not long be so; for within twenty years, at Dettingen and Plassey, Minden and Quebec, Warburg and Wandewash, it had served notice on its enemies at home and abroad that the spirit and tradition of Marlborough still burned strong. Wherever it was called upon to serve it carried

---

[28]It needs little imagination to guess that the formation of the Metropolitan Police in 1829 was bitterly opposed on the grounds that it was a 'military', and therefore unconstitutional, body.

[29]Sir George Howard, who commanded The Buffs at Fontenoy and Culloden, was commissioned into the Army at the age of six, while Colonel Luttrell's Regiment of Foot included two ensigns aged fourteen and twelve respectively.

with it the characteristics of the breed: good humour, bad language, stubborn courage, bloody-mindedness, patience in adversity, a passion for strong drink, pride. Many years later, at a moment of crisis, Sir John French (a man not quick to praise) confided to his diary: 'Half a million of these would walk over Europe.' It took one-tenth as many to build half an Empire.

An army is the sum of its parts. The parts of an army are its regiments. And the parts of a regiment are its soldiers. That knowledge was at the heart of Marlborough's genius, as it was of Wellington's. And the men knew this too. In a motley world a red coat isolated soldiers from civilians (the word 'civvie' to this day still has an undertone of *apartheid*) more effectively than any barracks, even though public contempt may often have concealed a touch of public envy.[30] Thus as with enduring British institutions, there grew from unlikely beginnings 'the regiment', a close-knit freemasonry bound by shared adversity, by a common purpose, and by mutual pride. Now, in the years which followed Dettingen, this unique system experienced something of a sea-change. It happened in this fashion.

At the Peace of Aix-la-Chapelle in 1748 the British Regular establishment, apart from Household troops, consisted of 21 cavalry and 49 infantry regiments, to which had been added in 1716 the embryo Royal Regiment of Artillery. Line regiments were still, as Fortescue described them, 'proprietary',[31] belonging to the Crown only in the sense that the sovereign had the statutory 'Government, Command and Disposition of the Army', their titles (with eleven exceptions) changing with those of their successive Colonels, their uniforms subject to sartorial whim, their *company* colours charged with the armorial bearings of their respective owners. Thus by the middle of the eighteenth century the Army was the sum of its private parts, its anatomy a loose association of *disjecta membra*. It was in urgent need of plastic surgery.

The surgeon was now at hand. George II, his Hanoverian blood stirred perhaps by the growing reputation of his Prussian neighbour Frederick, if not by his own unmemorable presence on the field of Dettingen, addressed himself to the operating table.

He started with the heart — the Colours, which since ancient times had been the rallying-point in battle and the visible symbol of corporate identity. Since the first days of the Standing Army units had varied in size according to the depredations of Parliament and the rise and fall in the recruiting exchange-rate. Regiments had dwindled to fewer than a hundred men (in 1698 three such were considered too small to justify a muster-roll), and had grown in times of emergency to eight or even twelve companies, each with its separate Colour, as if the limbs owed nothing to the body of which they were a part. This excess of individuality did not commend itself to the King, and three successive Royal Warrants illustrate his determination first to establish the *Regiment* as the true corporate unit, as Charles II had intended, and secondly to abolish the primacy of individual Colonels in the style and designation of their proprietary corps. It is from these three Warrants that the Regular Army assumed much of the unique character which, *mutatis mutandis*, has survived to the present day.

The first Warrant of 1743 dealt with 'Our *[the word is important]* Marching

---

[30]When James encamped his Army at Hounslow the citizens of London, far from being intimidated, flocked to enjoy the colourful spectacle.
[31]Commission by purchase was not abolished until 1871.

Regiments of Foot', that is to say, Infantry Regiments of the Line; and its chief directive was to replace the proliferation of company devices with two, and only two, Colours thus:[32]

> The King's, or first Colour of every Regiment is to be the Great Union throughout.
> The Second Colour to be the Colour of the Faceing of the Regiment [*viz: blue for Royal Regiments, buff, green, white etc.*] with the Union in the upper Canton [*viz: next to the staff*]

This Warrant[33] remains with subsequent amendments, such as the addition of Royal and Ancient Badges and battle honours and distinctions, the Royal authority for Colours. The correctness of the heraldic and other details of the composition and design of a Colour is the responsibility under the Crown of the Inspector of Regimental Colours, an Office held by Garter Principal King of Arms, to whom all proposals for new colours and any alterations in old ones are first submitted for the Sovereign's approval.

The second Royal Warrant, issued in 1747, dealt with clothing regulations, and its purpose was to give some substance and detail to the loosely applied word 'uniform'. And it included this instruction:

> In the centre of each colour is to be painted or embroidered in gold Roman characters the *number* of the rank of the Regiment within a wreath of roses and thistles.

Thus was laid down the first attempt to standardize the 'regimental' system and to depersonalize the old order which had existed for nearly a century, by giving a numerical 'rank' or precedence to the various corps.[34] Perhaps because the Army was engaged in more urgent matters abroad, the Warrant seems largely to have been ignored, and Colonels continued to decorate their Colours with their personal crests and armorial bearings.[35] But not for long.

On 1 July 1751 the King issued his third Royal Warrant. It opened with the words: 'Regulations for the Colours, cloathing, etc., of the Marching Regiments of Foot, and for the Uniform Cloathing of the Cavalry, their Standards, Guidons etc.' And it proceeded with these unequivocal instructions:

> No Colonel to put his Arms, Crest, Device or Livery on any part of the Appointments of the Regiment under his Command.
> No part of the Cloathing or Ornaments of the Regiments to be Allowed after the following Regulations are put into Execution, but by Us, or our Captain General's Permission.

The Warrant — plainly the work of an advisory team with an eighteenth-century preference for elegance rather than functionalism — goes into a fastidious detail

---

[32]Regiments of Household Cavalry and Horse carried Standards; Regiments of Dragoons, Guidons. Where Infantry regiments consisted of two battalions both carried colours.
[33]It did not apply to the King's personal troops, the regiments of Foot Guards. These not only bear a Sovereign's Colour and a Regimental Colour for each battalion, but still have separate Company Colours.
[34]For the rules of Precedence as earlier laid down in 1715, see Section A.
[35]Until their amalgamation in 1922, the 7th Dragoon Guards continued to use the crest of their old Colonel, Earl Ligonier, as their headdress badge.

which need not concern us here; but a number of the instructions are of particular historical importance, for they provide the origins of future regimental designations and distinctions.

In 1686 James II had introduced Grenadier Companies into each Line regiment. These were formed of the tallest men, and wore a distinctive mitre cap (redesigned in 1768 in black bearskin similar in pattern to the modern headdress of the Foot Guards). The 1751 Warrant laid down that the front of the cap was to be the distinguishing colour of the regimental facing, and these were listed in an accompanying 'General View ... of the Several Marching Regiments of Foot'. It then added that the cap would bear the King's Cypher and Crown with the Hanoverian motto *Nec Aspera Terrent* on 'the little flaps', and on the back 'the Number of the Regiment'. By this simple expedient the King impressed his Royal authority on the principle of 'uniformity', while creating the precedent from which were to develop the modern symbols of individuality — the distinctive headdress badges of regiments and corps.

Predictably, there were exceptions to the above directive, for the Warrant then adds: 'The Royal Regiments and the Six Old Corps differ from the foregoing Rule.' And this requires an explanation.

It has been noted earlier that the Army is the only service which does not bear the title 'Royal', and it is curious that George II, with his constant references to 'Our Army', did not carry his decision to abolish the proprietary system to this logical conclusion. However, since the creation of 'Our Guards and Garrisons' in 1661, it had become the practice to confer a Royal title on selected regiments as a mark of long and distinguished service or, as in the case of the 18th, or Royal Irish, for particular gallantry in action. The result has been an apparently arbitrary system of awards, as, for random example, the 21st and 23rd Foot in 1712, the 60th (Royal Americans) on its formation in 1755, the 25th in 1805, the 6th and 35th in 1832, the 49th/66th in 1885, the 3rd, 5th and 9th in 1935, and the 10th, 17th and 37th/67th in 1946. Much the same pattern has applied to the Cavalry.[36]

The 1751 Warrant which was addressed to a Regular Establishment of 70 cavalry and infantry Line regiments and the Royal Regiment of Artillery listed 14 infantry regiments as 'differing from the foregoing Rule' in that they were entitled to wear 'Royal Devices and Ancient Badges' on their Colours and appointments. Of these corps eight were 'Royal' (1st, 2nd, 4th, 7th, 8th, 18th, 21st and 23rd Foot), and each bore a special device on its Colours, such as the Cross of St Andrew, the Paschal Lamb, the Lion of England, the Rose and Crown, the Harp, the Thistle, the crest of the Prince of Wales, while common to each was the White Horse and motto of the House of Hanover borne with the regimental number on the back of the grenadier caps. The 'exceptional' rule did not apply to the remaining Royal regiment, the Artillery, which did not — and does not — carry Colours.[37]

The 'Six Old Corps', referred to for the first time in the 1743 Warrant, were of more arcane origin, and had ceased to be so called or exceptionally treated by the end of the eighteenth century. It has been suggested[38] that the name was derived from the six regiments raised in France during the reign of Henri II as

---

[36]For a complete list, with date of original honour, see Section B.

[37]All Royal regiments were — and are — distinguished by blue facings with the exception of five of the six regiments awarded the honour since 1935 and granted special permission to retain their original facings.

[38]*JSAHR*, Vol 13, 1934 (270).

the *Vieux Corps,* but given the antipathy to all things French in eighteenth-century England this seems improbable. A more likely explanation is to be found in the schedule to the 1751 Warrant, which lists the 'Ancient Badges' carried on the Colours of these select regiments, as distinct from those which hitherto had borne the arms or badges of their Colonels. Thus the Six Old Corps were as follows: 3rd, 5th, 6th, 27th, 41st and 42nd Foot (the latter, The Highland Regiment, formed from Independent Companies in 1725, regimented in 1739, and numbered in 1751). The 3rd Foot, or The Buffs, was the old Holland Regiment; the 5th and 6th Foot had joined the English establishment from Dutch service in 1688; the 27th, or Inniskilling Regiment, was raised in 1689; and the 41st, or The Invalids, was formed from Independent Companies of 'emerited souldiers' in 1719. All, except the last (to become The Welch Regiment), have since been awarded a Royal title.

This then was the Army which embarked on the victorious battles of the Seven Years' War, on the conquest of Canada, the defeat of French colonial power in India, and the American disaster, neatly numbered and dressed to kill. 'Yet despite these unparalleled exertions, which did so much towards the foundation and expansion of the modern British Empire, the Army remained an object of suspicion.'[39] Even though it was now, as never before, the sum of its parts, no interest was taken in improving either the efficiency or the lot of what Junius called 'a gallant army, which never fought unwillingly but against their fellow-subjects, mouldering away for want of the direction of a man of common abilities and spirit'. One such man was long since dead. It was to take a moment of supreme crisis to find another.

The thirty years which followed the 1751 Warrant were a singular period in the development of an Army not unused to cavalier treatment before or since. Each emergency saw the raising of new regiments which were committed to battle with scant concern for training, and even less for medical or administrative care. Each peace treaty saw Parliament hasten to wield the axe to old and new alike. The result is to be seen in the bewildering changes in the anatomy of the Army during this time of military achievement and political vandalism. To take one example, the new Highland regiments, the brain-child of William Pitt, were raised, disbanded, re-formed, renumbered, retitled, disbanded again, and were not to find a safe and abiding home on the Regular establishment until the last years of the century, when, with the second Act of Union of 1800, they were joined by the first of the new Irish regiments. One other example will serve to illustrate the wantonness of political prejudice. In 1757, with a large part of the Army engaged overseas, Parliament introduced a new Militia Act[40] designed not to provide a necessary force for home defence but as a long-term substitute for the Regular establishment, 'a good resource', observed one comfortable Member, 'in case of general danger'. To ensure the same political control that it had won over the Standing Army, Parliament made the Militia subject to an annual measure to regulate its pay and clothing. The ranks were to be filled by Protestants and raised by ballot, an ill-concealed form of conscription which received a predictable response. It is not without irony that the resulting indiscipline and riots had to be suppressed by the only disciplined alternative, the Regular soldiers.

[39]Omond, *Parliament and the Army, 1642-1904.*
[40]In the previous year the Militia had, with doubtful constitutional propriety, been made subject to the Mutiny Act.

By 1780, a year of up-swing in the fluctuating size of the Army, there were 28 cavalry[41] and 70 infantry Line regiments. The American War and the threat of hostilities with Spain had roused the country to one of its periodic bouts of patriotic zeal, and while some counties raised corps of volunteers, others applied their efforts towards recruiting men for particular Regular regiments.

The 'territorial' idea was not a new one, for Sir George Howard, the former child-ensign in the Buffs and by now the revered Governor of the Royal Hospital, informed the Commons that twenty years earlier the late Duke of Cumberland had proposed 'that each county should have one or more regiments of its own, such as the Middlesex Regiment, the Essex Regiment or the Surrey Regiment ....', and he went on to describe how, during his own active service, certain regiments had always raised their recruits from particular towns or districts. It seems that while the Army was busy digesting the novelty of consecutive numbering, this practice of local recruitment was not generally followed, and the Duke of Cumberland's prophetic plan was not pursued.

Now, however, in the summer of 1782, the following circular was sent out from the office of the Adjutant-General to the 'Agents of the Infantry Regiments as far as 70 inclusive,[42] excepting those in Ireland':

> I am to desire that you will signify to the Colonels of the ..... Regiments of Foot to which you are Agents that General Conway [Commander-in-Chief] wishes to be informed if they have any particular connexion or Attachment to a particular County, or any reason to wish for bearing the name of any particular County, and if so to name the County.

The Colonels, perhaps with the memory of the 1751 Warrant's invasion of their privacy still fresh, received this vague inquiry with mixed feelings.[43] For example, General Hodgson of the 4th Foot replied in some dudgeon:

> I am to acquaint you [the Adjutant-General] that during the time I had the honour to be Colonel of *The King's Own Regiment of Foot*, I never heard anything mentioned on the subject as that Corps never had the smallest conception it could forfeit the respectable name it now bears. I presume and hope the plan in contemplation is only meant to extend to those Regiments which have no distinction but that of a number.

Earl Percy, on the other hand, was enchanted:

> I have This Instant received your letter of the 27th of July, and cannot hesitate One Moment in wishing that the 5th Regt. of foot may bear the name of the County of Northumberland, with which I have the Pleasure to be so nearly connected.

Few Colonels shared Earl Percy's enthusiasm, and many either ignored the circular or nominated areas in which recruiting was traditionally strong, but with

---

[41]This, apart from a shuffling of the pack after Waterloo, was to remain the maximum number of cavalry Line regiments until the first amalgamations in 1922.
[42]The 70th Foot (to become the 2nd Battalion, East Surrey) was at that date the junior regiment on the infantry establishment. The 71st, the first of the new Highland regiments (to become the 1st Battalion, Highland Light Infantry), was not added to the establishment until 1786.
[43]*JSAHR*, March 1958, pp 34-8.

which their regiments had no particular connection.[44] Accordingly the Commander-in-Chief, this time with the King's personal authority, issued another and more stiffly worded circular on 31 August accompanied by two lists which directed 'the Rank of Regiments as attached to Counties' and 'Counties as assigned to Regiments'. Excluded were twelve regiments, including the Six Old Corps, which already had distinctive titles such as '1st, or Royals', 2nd, or Queens', 4th, or King's Own', '21st, or Royal North British Fuziliers'. The less privileged remainder were allocated territorial titles on a more or less arbitrary basis, and these were to remain unchanged for almost a century until the equally arbitrary game of musical chairs following Cardwell's localization scheme to link infantry regiments in pairs which was put into effect on 1 July 1881.

In 1785, a century after the death of Charles II, the military organization of the country was in disarray. There were in effect four separate 'armies': the Regular establishment, reduced in size by nearly half since the Treaty of Versailles in 1783; the predominantly civilian establishment of the Board of Ordnance, which included the Royal Artillery and the officer Corps of Engineers (re-formed in 1787 as the Corps of Royal Military Artificers); the Militia, under the control of the Home Department; and the Volunteers, who existed as a series of private 'clubs'. The office of Commander-in-Chief was vacant, and the military adviser to the Cabinet was the Master-General of the Ordnance, with the absurd anomaly of having no responsibility for the advice he gave. The political control of the Regular Army was vested in name, if not in fact, in the Secretary-at-War,[45] who by 'custom and practice', though without constitutional authority, was the accepted channel of communication between the King and the Army. The absurdity of the position had been illustrated in 1779 when the then Secretary, Charles Jenkinson, refused to answer a question put to him in the Commons on the ground that he was not a Minister and therefore could not be expected 'to have a competent knowledge of the destination of the army, and how the war was to be carried on'.[46] It was against such a background of ineptitude that the American colonies were lost; and such was the situation on the outbreak of war with France in 1793.

When, on 7 July 1815, the Allies entered Paris they were led by the 2nd Battalion, The 95th (Rifle) Regiment.[47] The occasion was a small but significant one in the historical context of the British Army. The 95th was an innovation in an Army not greatly attached to novelty.[48] The idea was not entirely new, for Line regiments had included light infantry companies since the mid-eighteenth

[44]The Colonel of the 20th Foot, long associated with Devon and formerly known as The Exeter Regiment, picked 'Lancashire'. Allotted the title 'East Devonshire' instead, his nose for a strong recruiting area was rewarded 99 years later when the regiment was renamed The Lancashire Fusiliers.

[45]For the origins — and manifest defects — of this office, which was not finally abolished until 1863, see Section F.

[46]Burke's celebrated Act for Economical Reform (1783) not only made the Secretary-at-War responsible to Parliament but also for the financial administration of the Army.

[47]On 16 February 1816, on Wellington's recommendation, the Prince Regent ordered that the 95th should be taken out of the numbered line and renamed The Rifle Brigade. It accordingly took 'the left of the line', a privilege still held by the Regiment today as a constituent part of The Royal Green Jackets.

[48]Since the first of George II's Royal Warrants, cavalry of the line had adopted a new style. The seven regiments of Horse had become Dragoon Guards, and all but three regiments of Dragoons (to become famous as the Union Brigade at Waterloo) had been restyled 'Light Dragoons'.

century, but these had gone into the discard at each successive reduction or disbandment. To explain the revival, it is necessary to take a largely forgotten figure off the shelf of history and dust down a reputation which deserves better than two lines in a popular ditty.

The 'Grand Old Duke of York', second son of George III, became, effectively, Commander-in-Chief[49] in 1795, two years after the office had been revived in the ageing and discredited person of Lord Amherst. He was to preside over the 'Horse Guards' for thirty-two years, except for a brief period when a public scandal obliged him to withdraw into the wings. He was the first great Army reformer since Marlborough, and the last until Edward Cardwell nearly eighty years later. 'It was he more than any other man who moulded the existing British Army into an improved and improving force.'[50]

While Wellington was still making his way as a young Lieutenant-Colonel in the Mahratta and Mysore campaigns, the Duke of York went to work on the ramshackle organization which he had inherited,[51] and on the serious weaknesses which had emerged from the Flanders campaign of 1793-4. In one sense he was fortunate, for in William Pitt he had a man whose political will matched his own military resolve. Both men foresaw the scale and duration of the conflict with France, and both understood, as Kitchener and Churchill would later understand, that victory would demand the total mobilization of all national resources. Neither could have foreseen at the outbreak of war that the time of crisis would bring forth two men, a sailor and a soldier, to match the hour; and it is an interesting reflection that Nelson had been dead three years when Wellington arrived in Lisbon with the short and unequivocal order to achieve 'the final and absolute evacuation of the Peninsula by the troops of France'.

The Duke of York's reforms touched the Army at nearly every point except — and it was an important exception — in the one area over which he did not exercise direct authority, for the Board of Ordnance continued (especially in its supply and medical departments) to demonstrate a lack of organization and efficiency which constantly prejudiced the operations of the Army in the field.

The Commander-in-Chief began with the officer corps, riddled as it was with patronage[52] and by ten years of malpractice by Sir George Yonge, the most venal and corrupt of all Secretaries-at-War. The C-in-C, for all his royal authority, could not break the system of commission by purchase, but he set limits on the rate of advancement from the most junior ranks, and transferred from the Secretary-at-War to his own Military Secretariat the supervision and approval of all promotions. The result may be seen in the character and quality of so large a proportion of Wellington's senior officers.

The Duke of York's concern to improve the quality of leadership was reflected in a more radical way. For years little had been done to train officers in any but the most elementary duties, and the trade in commissions had served as a positive deterrent to professionalism. More seriously, the relationship between officers and soldiers existed tenuously across a deep social divide bridged by a savage and brutalizing disciplinary code. That the Army not only survived such

---

[49]His title on appointment was Field-Marshal on the Staff, and changed in 1799 to Captain-General.
[50]Glover, *Wellington's Army in the Peninsula*.
[51]By the date of his death the Regular establishment was complete except for the three cavalry and nine infantry regiments which were transferred from the East India Company to the Crown in 1861.
[52]By a fortunate irony, Wellington's greatly accelerated promotion to Lieutenant-General was largely due to the efforts of an influential brother in high places.

treatment but conducted itself so notably in action is a tribute to the men themselves, to a minority of conscientious officers, but above all to the mystique of 'the regiment'.

To this critical problem the C-in-C addressed himself by instituting what was, in the context of the time, a revolutionary programme of training in man-management.[53] He understood, as did such convinced disciples as Sir John Moore, that true discipline proceeds from trust, and that the King's commission was an honour and not a social privilege — 'the timely interference of the officer', he wrote, 'his personal intercourse and acquaintance with his men (which are sure to be repaid by the soldiers' confidence and attachment) and, above all, his personal example ...'[54] This was an entirely novel sentiment, and it was to lie at the heart of Wellington's personal popularity with the rank and file. The puritan in Wellington could never stomach the licentious conduct of his men — 'no soldier,' he wrote, 'can withstand the temptation of wine.... They are constantly intoxicated when absent from their regiments, and there is no crime they will not commit to obtain it' — but the leader in him stood in awe at their obedience to orders, their steadiness under fire, and their impetuous ardour in attack. The respect was mutual, the combination irresistible.

But there was another innovation in the Duke of York's programme of reform — the tactical training of troops and their deployment on battlefields not greatly larger than those of Marlborough's campaigns, but on which the geometry of battle had altered significantly with the development of more sophisticated weapons. History has dwelt on the infantry squares at Waterloo, but the essence of British tactics during this period was linear — two ranks of a single regiment able to deliver a volume of fire twice as great as that from a French division attacking in solid columns; and training had also produced a standard of musketry which was to be so signal a feature of another expeditionary force a century later.

The anatomy of the Army did not greatly change, for Parliament ensured that it would not provide the means for it to do so. But two examples will show how military ingenuity could defeat disabling budgets. They may best be explained by what was then the new tactical doctrine of 'fire and movement'.

Ever since its formation in 1716 as a branch of the Ordnance Board, the Royal Artillery had been an 'infantry' arm, in the sense that it was known as 'Foot Artillery', moving at a foot's pace and manned by civilian drivers.[55] Now, in 1793, a new branch of the arm was formed with the title of The Royal Horse Artillery, in which all personnel were mounted, and thus able to move at the pace of cavalry (to emphasize their role, RHA units were described as 'Troops' instead of 'Companies'). The true novelty of these 'galloper guns' was to underline the concept of mutual interdependence between assaulting arms. It would be many years before the military hierarchy recognized the natural corollary that an army in the field is as good as its supporting and supply services.

The second innovation was a revival of the tactical use of light infantry. As we have noted, the victory parade in Paris in July 1815 was led by the 95th (Rifle) Regiment. This young corps — then only fifteen years old — had a curious origin.

---

[53] A Royal Military College for training junior officers was opened at High Wycombe in 1802.
[54] The story is told of the Duke of York that, on hearing that a footman had refused access to a woman visitor on the grounds that she was 'just some old soldier's wife' he replied: 'Pray tell me who else is Her Royal Highness the Duchess of York other than an old soldier's wife?'
[55] In 1794 civilian drivers were replaced by a 'Corps of Captains Commissaries and Drivers'.

In 1797 a special Act of Parliament authorized the raising of a fifth battalion of the 60th (Royal American) Regiment[56] for service in America. The battalion, recruited entirely from foreigners, was, unlike its four sister battalions, dressed in green jackets and armed with the comparatively new 'rifle'.

In the following year a submission was made to the Horse Guards that the home establishment should have a regiment of its own, armed with the rifle and trained in light-infantry skirmishing tactics. Thus at the instance of the Duke of York there came about the 'Shorncliffe experiment' and the formation of an 'Experimental Corps of Riflemen' or 'Rifle Corps'. The raising of this regiment was itself a new departure, for its ranks were filled by carefully selected drafts from fourteen Line regiments. Thus it was from the outset a *corps d'élite;* and élitist it has remained.[57]

The presiding genius of the Shorncliffe experiment was Sir John Moore, a man whose tactical skills were matched by an acute perception of the Duke of York's humanizing attitude to discipline and man management. To the new Corps at Shorncliffe he added — although the reasons for his particular choice are not recorded — a battalion each of the 43rd (Monmouthshire) Regiment and the 52nd (Oxfordshire) Regiment, both of which were converted to Light Infantry in 1803.[58] Thus was created the nucleus of the Light Division which was to serve with such distinction from Corunna to Waterloo. 'Proper saucy fellows we were,' wrote the archetypal light-infantryman, Sir Harry Smith, whose Spanish child-bride was to give her name to a small township in Natal where a century later the 95th was to win two of its many battle honours.

Throughout this time of change, and for much of the long war, one thing did not alter. The Regular Army remained essentially a volunteer institution, and the traditional hostility to any form of compulsory service ensured that while the Army was never short of overseas commitments, it was always short of men. It was not until the year of Trafalgar that the picture improved.

The absurdity of the situation lay in Parliament's insistence on the special status of its own 'constitutional' Army, the Militia, controlled by the Home Office and confined strictly to home defence. Indeed, Parliament took legal steps to limit recruitment by making any militiaman who joined the Regular Army liable to six months' imprisonment. The disincentive to regular recruitment was actively encouraged by the passing of a Ballot Act in 1802 which laid down that all men between the ages of eighteen and forty (with a predictable quota of 'reserved occupations') were liable for Militia service, the charge of 'conscription' being answered by the lame device that, in the words of earlier Militia Acts, such men could not be compelled 'to march out of the Kingdom'. Any man could obtain immunity from the draft; for life, by providing a suitable substitute, or for five years by paying a 'fine' of £15. Thus when Wellington embarked on his Peninsula campaign with fewer than 26,000 men, the privileged Militia, exempt from service overseas, numbered 86,788. It took a Bonaparte to break this mould of political folly.

From the early months of 1807 militiamen were permitted to transfer to

---

[56]Renamed the 60th, or King's Royal Rifle Corps in 1830.

[57]So popular was the new Rifle Corps that within five years three battalions had been raised and further volunteering was forbidden. It entered the numbered list of Line regiments as the 95th in 1802.

[58]The historic association of Shorncliffe was perpetuated in 1958 with the formation of The Green Jackets, which became in 1966 The Royal Green Jackets.

Regular regiments of their choice. There was still no element of compulsion, and so the government could — and did — salve its public conscience. Even then the strength of the Regular Army did not exceed 250,000. Certainly the numbers were swelled by mercenaries and allied troops, but the victories — from Java to Niagara, and from the Cape of Good Hope to Waterloo — were made possible by the irresistible conjunction of British naval power and British soldiers. It is not without interest that the first battle honour awarded to the fledgling 95th was for service as marines at the battle of Copenhagen in 1801.

When the long war ended, so too did an era in the development of an army which had contrived, in spite of the best endeavours of Parliament and people to blunt its cutting edge, to become the most formidable military power among all nations. Not for a hundred years would it return to an European battlefield; and by then much had happened to it.

THE REMODELLED ARMY

In 1852 the Duke of Wellington died. During half a century he had dominated the military scene, for the last ten years as the Commander-in-Chief whose personal prestige ensured his public veneration if not his immunity from political criticism.

It has been said that the neglect of the Army in the years between Waterloo and the Crimean War was the direct result of Wellington's Olympian detachment and his ultra-conservatism, but this is only partially true. The answer lay far back in history, and history was now repeating itself. During the Napoleonic Wars England had indeed saved Europe by her example, but had bankrupted herself by her exertions. It was a familiar situation to which the politicians addressed themselves with equally familiar zeal and disastrous effect; for this was no longer the old agrarian England but a new industrial society, and the disbandment of the victorious army threw thousands of men on the labour market. The Militia laws were held in abeyance; the Volunteers raised during the crisis of the 1780s disappeared; and with a shrunken Regular Army fully absorbed in colonial commitments, the defence of the realm devolved on 10,000 service pensioners.

Like many soldiers before and since, Wellington was politically innocent. His conservatism was underlined, even during his brief Premiership, by his insistence on keeping the office of the Commander-in-Chief, the 'Horse Guards', totally divorced from the civilian 'War Department'; his refusal to modernize the inefficient administrative structure of the Army; and his determination to preserve the old order by perpetuating the separate Board of Ordnance and the proprietary system of commissions by purchase.

But even his unique authority could not influence Parliamentary control of the military purse-strings, and the sharpest weapon in Parliament's armoury remained the Mutiny Act. The new Radical Left still believed in the eighteenth-century views about the Standing Army and the iniquity of barracks. To the Duke's concern in 1842 at the state of the nation's defences, his own colleague Robert Peel (whose police experience should have taught him better) replied airily:

> We should best consult the true interests of the country by husbanding our resources in time of peace and, instead of lavish expenditure on all the

means of defence, by placing some trust in the latent and dormant energies of the nation (to) enable us to defy the menaces of any foreign power.

There was more than an echo of Jonathan Swift in so complacent an assumption, and a still louder reverberation in Cobden's public speeches with their strident references to 'aristocratic privilege' and 'the degradation of the masses', and their dangerous revival of the old heresy that an efficient Navy was an adequate defence for the country without the assistance of land forces. It was as if Napoleon had been no more than a figment of history.

But the mood of complacency was now rudely disturbed. In 1848 Europe — and Britain — were in political ferment, and a reluctant Parliament was compelled by its own political master, public opinion, to re-examine the crumbled ramparts of defence. In 1852 it brought forward a new Militia Act, which made the revived force liable for service in any part of the United Kingdom, recruited by voluntary enlistment, but with the unpopular ballot system retained as a last resort in the event of an emergency. There was no reference to any increase in the strength of the Regular Army — indeed, the Mutiny Act of that year actually reduced the size by 4,000 men, and the estimate by £212,000. The tired old Duke accepted defeat. In his last speech in the House of Lords on 15 June he agreed to the new measure, saying that since the country had never had a proper peace establishment it was now necessary to turn to the Militia as an alternative. And he ended with one final — and devastating — aside: 'As to the Regular Army, there have not been, for the last ten years, more men than enough to relieve the sentries on duty at your stations in different parts of the world.'

In all the long march of the British Army towards political respectability and public acceptance, there are two particular events which mark what may properly be called the change from evolution to revolution.

By one of the many ironies of politics, it was Palmerston, that improbable paradox of a sabre-rattling Liberal, who manoeuvred the country into an unnecessary and ineptly conducted war. The expeditionary force which was dispatched to the Crimea in 1854 was in every essential, other than uniform appearance, identical to the Army which had fought in the Peninsula more than forty years earlier. The story of the ill-fated campaign[59] — the exemplary conduct of the soldiers in conditions of appalling severity, the incompetence of leaders whose chief qualifications for command were wealth and social standing, the complete breakdown of the administrative services — is well known. More importantly, it was described in chilling detail at the time in the despatches of William Russell. The public was deeply shocked, as well it might be, for it was a chief accessory to the crime. For nearly two centuries it had treated the Army with insolent contempt, celebrating victories to which it could lay no title, deriding and vilifying an honourable calling. Now the Army was once more called upon to pay the price.

While the war was still in progress the Government moved cautiously to place the governance of the Army on a footing comparable with that of the Board of Admiralty, and to end the absurdity by which the military forces of the Crown

---

[59]It is a measure of the shortage of regular troops available that ten battalions of Militia volunteered for garrison duties in the Mediterranean, for which service they were duly awarded a 'battle honour'.

were split between three separate and autonomous offices — those of the Commander-in-Chief, the Board of Ordnance and the Home Department. The most important of several political decisions was to divest the old office of Secretary of State for War and the Colonies of all responsibility for colonial affairs and to subordinate to the new Minister the ill-defined functions of the Secretary-at-War, who had existed in a self-perpetuating and non-statutory limbo since the days of the Restoration.[60] Three more major changes followed in quick succession: the Board of Ordnance was abolished, and its duties were divided between the Secretary of State and the Commander-in-Chief; the Militia was transferred from Home Office control to the War Department;[61] and in 1856 the historically inefficient Commissariat was prised out of the clutches of the Treasury and transferred to the new Department.

Thus what Lord Panmure, Secretary of State during the war, described as 'the old-fashioned departmentalism' began to disappear; but traditional attitudes are not easily changed by cosmetic surgery. While the superstructure of the antique edifice had lost some of its gargoyles, the foundations remained untouched. In Pall Mall sat the new political head of the Army. In Whitehall sat a formidable traditionalist, the Queen's cousin, the Duke of Cambridge, as General Officer Commanding, a position he was to hold under different titles for thirty-eight years. Between the two offices there existed variously a state of undeclared war and an uneasy truce; but by the time of the Duke's resignation in 1895 the politicians had won the day. The War Office reigned supreme, and the Army had undergone — the diehards would have said 'suffered' — its greatest transformation in two hundred years.

The Crimea alone was not the catalyst, for with the end of the bleak campaign Parliament reverted to type and, bravely brandishing the Mutiny Act, reduced the Army to a skeleton of its wartime size. With hindsight — and history had provided a library of past lessons — it should have known better, for in the prosperous Britain of Victoria's high noon the idea of armed tyranny could no longer be treated as a serious threat to civil liberty. In the process of remodelling the Army the refusal to foot the necessary bill was now to be the root of lasting evil, and there is a sombre note, at once prophetic and pathetic, in the words of Sidney Herbert, one of the ablest of administrators:

> It is the fault of all Parties, all Administrations, every Parliament. At the commencement of the War we had to make means, and to create an Army and to use it at the same time. It is a difficulty which you have to encounter when you have to make an Army at the same time you are to use it.

There was no 'difficulty'; simply a pathological distaste for soldiers.

It is probable that the changes in the superstructure would have been the limit of any expression of a guilty conscience in high places — indeed, the report of the Committee of Inquiry into the conduct of the Crimean War is a classic example of the art of whitewashing in public — but this time history was to prove less accommodating. There now occurred the second event which would convert the process of rehabilitation into full-blooded reform.

Since the final defeat of the French in Bengal and the Carnatic in 1764, British

[60]The office of Secretary-at-War was abolished in 1863.
[61]In 1857 the War Department was renamed the 'War Office'.

authority in India had been established through a unique consortium of Cabinet and Company. The growth of the East India Company's power and its annexation of the several states of the sub-continent had led to a gradual extension of parliamentary control over its affairs. An Act of 1784 had brought all the Company's military and political activities under a Board of Control which was in fact, if not yet in name, the India Office.

There is no historical parallel for this partnership, built as it was on the twin pillars of patronage and maritime power. India attracted to it many of the outstanding merchant and military venturers of the age, even if it broke as many reputations as it made, and there was a comfortable assumption that distance lent security as well as enchantment to the view (in the early years of the nineteenth century as much as two years could pass between the sending of a letter from Calcutta to London and the receipt of a reply[62]). The Sikh Wars of 1845 and 1848 had completed the conquest of the Punjab, and except on the volatile Frontier where Asia shaded into Europe, British sovereignty — the Raj — seemed undisputed.

The Mutiny of 1857 affected public opinion even more profoundly than the scandals of the Crimea, for it called in question the very nature of a complacent sovereignty, and of the future of the old 'Governor and Company of Merchants of London trading to the East Indies'. The Government at home was faced by two decisions. Its political answer was to wind up the Company and to transfer its servants, powers and territories to 'the Crown in India'.[63] Its military option was complicated by the novel constitutional situation thus created. Would the royal prerogative be infringed if a new British Army was established in India separate from and independent of the existing Regular Army? The solution, reached after a deal of semantic argument, was a compromise. The European troops in the service of the Company were absorbed into the Regular establishment,[64] the Indian native regiments were reorganized under their own Commander-in-Chief answerable to the Crown through the Governor-General, while the British force to be kept in India (and charged against the revenues of that country) was fixed at a maximum of 80,000 officers and men. This last decision was soon to have interesting consequences.

The momentum of Army reform, reluctantly forced on successive governments by events in the Crimea and in India, soon foundered in a welter of words. In the ten years after the Mutiny there were convened 'seventeen Royal Commissions, eighteen Select Committees, nineteen Committees of Officers within the War Office, besides thirty-five Committees of Military Officers'.[65] The main stumbling-block was the refusal of the military left hand to accept the political authority of the right. The Duke of Cambridge, with the full (and sometimes wilful) support of the Queen, stood firm on the royal prerogative as defined in the preamble to the 1662 Militia Act; indeed, the exact wording of that preamble was repeated in the Statute Law Revision Act of 1863. But the political counter was to interpret the wording of the preamble to mean that the right of the Crown to command and administer the Army was not an actual *personal* right but

---

[62]Heathcote, *The Indian Army*
[63]Not until the Royal Titles Act of 1877 did Parliament authorize the Queen to assume the additional title of 'Empress of India'.
[64]Thus in 1861 there were transferred 12 cavalry and infantry regiments, 4 batteries of Royal Horse Artillery, and the European element of the Engineer services.
[65]Clode, *op.cit.*

'a part of that State authority which appertains indeed to the Crown, yet must only be exercised through Ministers, through advisers responsible to Parliament'. The Duke of Cambridge would have been on stronger ground if he had applied his powers of patronage to improve the administrative structure and service conditions of the Army for which he claimed, with doubtful constitutional propriety, the sole military responsibility. The trouble with democracy is that it prefers the soft option to the hard decision; and the impasse between Pall Mall and Whitehall could only be resolved by a tribune rather than a tinker. The tribune was now at hand.

Edward Cardwell was appointed Secretary of State for War in Gladstone's first administration of 1868; and it may rightly be said that his assumption of office marked the making of our modern Army. If it is possible to sum up his achievement in a single phrase, it was the victory of professionalism over patronage. It has been claimed that in the process he destroyed the regimental system which alone had preserved the Army as the sum of its parts; on the contrary, it was the very strength of that system which he seized upon as the essential framework of his own 'new model'. The main thrust of all his own — and, indeed, of all subsequent — reforms was to create, within the financial limits set by political parsimony, an army fit to fight a war rather than play at peace. This unexceptionable object was to be achieved not without dust and heat, for there are no trenches defended more stoutly than those occupied by privilege and prejudice.

The situation which Cardwell inherited was briefly thus: a War Office at loggerheads with the Commander-in-Chief; a Regular Army stretched beyond its means by the aftermath of the Mutiny; a Reserve available for duty overseas of 3,117 men; a separate Militia tightly restricted to home defence; a ramshackle, largely civilian disorganization of supply and administrative services, the disjointed tail of a disembodied dog; and the emergence of a formidable new military menace in the shape of Bismarck's Prussia.

The new tribune discarded the familiar woodman's axe in favour of the welder's torch, and his programme of reform was dictated by a single purpose: the integration of all the military resources of the nation. He started at the top, with a resolute disregard of royal sentiment and eighteenth-century attitudes:

> I contend, [he wrote to Gladstone] for the principle of plenary responsibility to Parliament on the part of the Parliamentary head of the Department; and, consequently, for the absence of all reservations expressed or implied from the authority of that officer.[66]

Accordingly the War Office Act of 1870 brought the Horse Guards under the same roof as the Secretary of State and reorganized it into three departments:

1 Military — under the Commander-in-Chief.
2 Supply — under the Surveyor-General.
3 Finance — under the Financial Secretary.

The C-in-C remained the chief military adviser to the Secretary of State, and

[66]Biddulph, *Cardwell at the War Office.*

responsible for the administration and discipline of the Army,[67] but the Act established once and for all the authority of the Minister as, for want of a better word, the 'head' of the Army. To his credit, the Duke of Cambridge accepted the inevitability of change. He growled in public and sulked in private — 'the removal of the Commander-in-Chief to the office at Pall Mall...would place him in a position of subordination which would virtually deprive him of all his specific [sic] attributes... This would be a degeneration which would altogether alter his status.' Precisely. Cardwell could not have put it better himself. Hence the War Office Act of 1870.

Cardwell's reforms may be summarized thus.

He started with the problem that the existing regimental system and the practice of enlistment for life had meant that the Regular Army had never possessed a reserve of trained men, with the result that each successive emergency had been met by a matching measure of improvisation. This situation had been aggravated by the reorganization of the Indian Army, and of what came to be known as 'the Army in India' after the Mutiny. To meet this problem he made colonial territories largely responsible for their own security, thus releasing to the home establishment a significant number of overseas garrison troops; and in 1870 he introduced the Army Enlistment Act by which men could join the Regular Army on a short-service engagement of twelve years, of which six would be spent with the colours and six on the reserve[68] (men were still permitted to re-engage for a maximum service of twenty-one years).

The next measure of reform, the Regulation of the Forces Act of 1871, transferred the Militia from the control of Lords-Lieutenant to that of the War Office; and, by Royal Warrant signed by the Queen on 17 July, abolished the purchase of commissions. This, as we have seen, had been a contentious issue ever since the creation of the Standing Army. Wellington had defended the system on the curious ground that 'promotion by purchase exempts the British army from the character of a mercenary army', yet he seems to have found no anomaly in his own criticism of many of his regimental officers. Cardwell was concerned not only to create out of the different military strands 'one harmonious whole' but to make the profession of arms truly professional. And this was the purpose of his third and most far-reaching reform.

In 1872 he announced his 'localization' scheme. The underlying object of this radical restructuring of the existing regimental system was to stimulate recruitment in the wake of the earlier Enlistment Act; for while this would within a measurable period create the trained reserve which Cardwell considered vital to the country's present and future military needs, it would also reduce the effective strength of men serving with the colours. The solution, he decided, lay in the 'territorial' idea which had been superimposed on unenthusiastic regimental commanders a century earlier.

At the time of the new reforms the Regular Army consisted of 141 battalions/regiments of infantry independently organized and administered through the office of the Commander-in-Chief.[69] Cardwell's new plan was as follows. The country was divided into 66 Brigade Districts based on county boundaries and allocated according to the size of local population centres (The

---

[67]In 1872, control of the Militia was transferred from Lords-Lieutenant to the Commander-in-Chief.
[68]The Act aimed to create a Reserve of 80,000 men.
[69]The 25 senior Line regiments had been authorized to raise second battalions after the Mutiny, although there is no documentary evidence why this cut-off point was chosen.

King's Royal Rifle Corps and The Rifle Brigade, each with four Regular battalions, were treated as a separate case). Within each District, Regular and auxiliary units were organized as follows, around a regimental depot which acted as an administrative headquarters and a basic training centre for recruits: infantry regiments from the 26th to the 109th Foot (the 60th and 79th excepted) were linked in pairs (though at this stage still retaining their existing numbers and titles), and were brigaded with two Militia battalions and local volunteer groups, thus forming a new 'territorial force'.[70] In presenting his scheme Cardwell explained that his primary purpose was to rationalize the country's military resources, and by concentrating on local association to encourage recruiting through a sense of 'family' affiliation. Of the two Regular battalions, one would serve abroad while the other would act as a feeder to replace casualties and wastage through reversion to the new reserve. The Militia, he hoped, would be trained and organized to provide a second-line reserve in case of a national emergency.

The scheme had many virtues. It was economical in terms both of men and of money. For the first time in two hundred years, it provided a flexible framework for peacetime soldiering or, if the necessity arose, a trained nucleus for a wartime army. And predictably it aroused a storm of hostility. This is not to be wondered at, for monoliths do not care for the mason's chisel; still less do they like seismic disturbance. The real opposition was not to the reform itself but to the fact that it was initiated by, as one opponent put it, 'wanton amateurs overriding the advice of dedicated and experienced professionals' — the same professionals who had demonstrated their dedication to such disastrous effect in the Crimea. Expressions of dismay abounded — 'this baneful transmutation'; 'the destruction of our regiments'; 'the reformers [are] dull-witted, stupid, or in short, fools'; 'a sacrilegious assault on our entire military system'. The Duke of Cambridge's opinion of the new scheme provided Cardwell with all the justification he needed. 'It is not necessary. All that is required can be done without it, and therefore, if that is the case [sic], WHY DO IT?' It was left to an anonymous 'military man'[71] to utter the final fatuity.

> Seldom has more signal proof been afforded than by some of the measures in question of the truth of the proposition that "Reform" does not always mean improvement, but that on the contrary it sometimes means deterioration, damage and failure.... The main lines of policy, having been entered upon hastily and without due appreciation of the consequences involved, have ended in miserable failure.

Yet not one of Cardwell's critics offered a single constructive or alternative proposition. All the dozens of committees which sat between 1858 and 1868 had been stifled by the drifting aura of incense from the altars of the Peninsula and Waterloo. No one seemed to notice the ominous smoke rising from the camp-fires of the newly militant Prussia.

Inevitably there were defects in Cardwell's measures. For example — and it is a fact not often remarked upon — they applied almost exclusively to Regular and auxiliary infantry units. Virtually nothing was done to improve the machinery by which the Army at home and in the field was serviced and

[70]Not to be confused with the Territorial Army created by Richard Haldane on 1 April 1908.
[71]*Fifteen Years of "Army Reform"*.

supplied, although it is from this period that serious attention was first paid to commissariat and medical organization.[72] Secondly, the short-service and localization schemes depended heavily — in the event, too heavily — on a steady supply of recruits of an adequate standard (the minimum age for enlistment was eventually fixed at nineteen, or – with a wink in the direction of recruiting sergeants — 'the physical equivalent of nineteen'). Not only was there a shortage of recruits, but more seriously, an unexpected wastage of non-commissioned officers choosing to transfer to the reserve after completing six years' colour service.[73] Yet the new measures were in the process of improvement by much trial, and some error, when in 1874 the political pendulum swung, and Cardwell was out of office.

The new administration had different priorities, among which Army reform did not rate highly. Fortunately, in the light of subsequent events, the new reforms were accepted as at best a necessary evil — until 1879, when a committee was convened to inquire into defects in the short-service system and the localization scheme. Its terms of reference stated that 'there is no intention ... to depart from the general principles of reorganization which have been accepted by the country [if not by the Army] since 1870', and confirmed the linked-battalion idea as the basic principle of regimental structure. In fact, the Airey Committee thought otherwise, and its main recommendation was that the best means of improving the contentious short-service system was the unlinking of battalions and the creation of large depots. There was loud cheering in the last ditch; but by the time the Committee reported the political pendulum had swung again, and the reformers were back in office.

The new Secretary of State was Hugh Childers, rudely described as 'a successful colonist in Australia who, on his return to this country had become a successful politician ... who never had had anything to do with the army, and presumably knew nothing whatever about it before he came into the War Office'.[74] If the diehards thought that salvation was now at hand they were swiftly disabused of any such notion. Not only did Childers reject the recommendations of the Committee in detail but he decided that the main defect in Cardwell's reforms was that they did not go far enough. This he proceeded, in his own word, to 'rectify'.

General Order 41 of 1 May 1881 opened thus:

> The following changes in the organization, titles, and uniform of the regiments of the Infantry of the Line and Militia...will come into effect on July 1st, 1881.
> The Infantry of the Line and Militia will in future be organized in Territorial Regiments, each of four battalions for England, Scotland, and Wales, and of five battalions for Ireland: the 1st and 2nd of these being Line battalions,[75] and the remainder Militia. These regiments will bear a territorial designation corresponding to the localities with which they are connected; and the words 'Regimental District' will in future be used...

[72]In the Army Estimates for 1879 there is this quaint item: 'Pay, etc of Establishment of Instructors in Cookery — £110'.
[73]In 1881 the period of enlistment was altered to seven years with the colours and five on the reserve.
[74]*Fifteen Years of "Army Reform"*.
[75]The exceptions were the 60th and 79th, and The Rifle Brigade.

Curiously enough, the Order omitted to add that consecutive numbering, introduced by the Royal Warrant of 1751, would cease to apply. Regiments would now be known solely by their territorial and/or distinctive title. The welder's torch had done its work.

It is difficult to appreciate today the sense of shock which this decision generated throughout the Army and within the regimental system; and Appendix A to the Order (hurriedly amended two months later to correct some of the more manifest anomalies and absurdities) is a monument to the proposition that the road to Hell is paved with good intentions. Here are some examples.[76]

The 'territorial' obsession threw up such novelties as The Kentish Regiment (The Buffs); The York Regiment (King's Own Borderers); The Halifax Regiment (Duke of Wellington's); the two Staffordshire regiments titled in the wrong order of seniority. The 28th (North Gloucestershire) and the 61st (South Gloucestershire) married logically as The Gloucestershire Regiment, as did the 37th (North Hampshire) and the 67th (South Hampshire) as The Hampshire Regiment. But what logic was there in such unions as the 30th (Cambridgeshire) and 59th (2nd Nottinghamshire) as first The West Lancashire and then The East Lancashire Regiment, or the 63rd (West Suffolk) and the nomadic 96th as The Manchester Regiment?

Many of the new second battalions found themselves junior in rank or precedence to corps far younger than themselves. As much salt was rubbed into wounds as balm, and not even a review of battle honours and the direction that 'all distinctions, mottoes, badges or devices appearing hitherto in the "Army List" or on the colours, as borne by either of the Line battalions of a Territorial Regiment, will in future be borne by both those battalions' did much to soften the blow to injured pride and bruised tradition.

In the light of history, both Cardwell and Childers were right, but the old Army[77] neither forgave nor forgot. A century later the new Army would find itself travelling back along much the same road.

It is a measure of Cardwell's judgment that his restructured regimental system survived for so many years, in spite of a generation of hostility within the Army itself. It would take two World Wars, an irreversible shift in the balance of power, and the retreat from Empire to create out of the old anatomy something leaner, and with more muscle and stronger sinews.

But for all Cardwell's reforming energy (and the Prussian model was there to see), the crucial weakness still lay in the head and not the limbs; and the old antagonism between Whitehall and Pall Mall was now ruthlessly exposed in South Africa. The Second Boer War, a classic example of the sledgehammer-and-nut syndrome, revealed chronic defects in the command and administrative structure of the War Office. In a grandiose gesture 387,500 troops were committed over a period of two and a half years to the reduction of a small, skilful and highly mobile army of irregulars. The maintenance of such a force — infinitely the largest that Britain had yet put into the field — proved to be far beyond the capabilities of commanders and their staffs, and the result was a shambles on a Crimean scale.

In 1903 a Royal Commission reported on the conduct of operations in the late

[76]See also Order of Precedence on pp. 84-9.
[77]In 1881 the strength of the Army was 189,133, at a cost of £5,129,000.

war. At least it avoided the laughable exercise in whitewashing in which the 1857 Committee had indulged, but its conclusions were evasive, unconstructive and irrelevant to the future. And it was to this problem — the future — that the Government at last addressed itself. On 6 November 1903 a new Committee was set up under Lord Esher to examine 'the reconstitution of the War Office'. The first part of its report, published in less than three months, was to have a profound — and profoundly important — influence on the structure of the British Army.

The Committee made three main recommendations: first, the abolition of the office of Commander-in-Chief (the last incumbent was Lord Roberts); second, the creation of a Committee of Defence,[78] chaired by the Prime Minister; and third, the formation of an Army Council, chaired by the Secretary of State and consisting of four military and three civilian members. All these recommendations were accepted by the Government, and the Army Council came into formal existence on 10 August 1904. With its creation ended 250 years of controversy, acrimony and often semantic argument which had existed since the Militia Acts of the Restoration. The Esher recommendations carried to a logical conclusion one of Cardwell's reforms which, largely because of the special status of the Duke of Cambridge and his manipulation of the royal prerogative, had been left in limbo — namely, the constitutional principle that Parliament's will is sovereign, and that the primacy in the control of the armed forces of the Crown is vested in the government of the day acting through an appointed Minister answerable for the conduct of his office — and therefore for the Army itself — to the elected representatives of the people. In all the years of political and military confrontation the chief victim had been the Army itself.

The report of the Esher Committee had, by its terms of reference, concentrated on the War Office, and had ignored the wider question of the structure of the Army and of its constituent parts, although the South African War had all too clearly demonstrated the lack of administrative organization in the field. There was a reason for this. The Committee was concerned solely with home defence.[79] It therefore left the matter of anatomy to the new surgical team of professionals and laymen on the Army Council. There followed a pause for refreshment.

But in 1906 the political pendulum swung again and the British people voted into power, with a landslide majority, a party whose roots were strongly pacifist, anti-military, non-interventionist, Swift-like in its reliance on the politics of absurdity. In such a party there was no stampede to occupy the office of Secretary of State for War; yet by one of the many ironies of history it was such a party which now discovered in its ranks perhaps the greatest of all Army reformers.

Richard Haldane was an academic and a man of peace, with a passion for German philosophy and a deep distrust for German nationalism. In his memoirs he recalled a meeting with the Prime Minister. 'Nobody', said Campbell-Bannerman, 'will touch the War Office with a pole.' 'Then give it to me,' replied Haldane.

He began by asking himself a pragmatic question which Cardwell had side-stepped and which Esher had by-passed. What was the purpose and function of the British Army? It was a question which no one in high places had

[78]Renamed the Committee of Imperial Defence in 1908.
[79]Among other of its proposals was the setting up (shades of Cromwell!) of seven Home Commands.

seriously considered before: the politicians, because of historic prejudice and pro-naval complacency; the soldiers, because of pride, pique and public hostility. Haldane accepted the premise that, as an imperial power, the government must provide the military capacity to police its overseas territories. But what of the Regular Army and the auxiliary forces at home? History had repeatedly shown, for reasons which require no rehearsing, that war, like peace, is indivisible, and that for more than two hundred years the country had been unready — some might also say unwilling — to meet successive emergencies, whether in Europe or further afield. He recognized that a nation (and indeed his own party) firmly wedded to the principle of voluntary service[80] would neither tolerate — nor pay for — a Standing Army comparable in size to those of other great continental powers. But he also recognized the growing threat of German imperialism, and foresaw with chilling accuracy the nature of the conflict ahead and the inevitability of British involvement.

Haldane's reforms, carried out between 1906 and 1912, were therefore designed — within very narrow parameters — to equip the country for a continental war. He proceeded with a lawyer's logic, and his five main lines of action may be summarized thus:

1   The creation of a General Staff under a Chief of Staff, with three Directors of (a) Military Operations, (b) Staff Duties and (c) Military Training.

2   The formation of an Expeditionary Force of six infantry divisions and one cavalry division, complete — and not before time — with supporting arms and services, and ready for dispatch overseas within twelve days of mobilization.

3   The Regular Army was to conform to Cardwell's scheme, except that the periods of service with the colours and on the reserve were varied in length, particularly in regard to supply and service Corps.

4   The Militia was reorganized as the Special Reserve with the function of supplying drafts to the Expeditionary Force in the event of war.

5   The Volunteers and the Yeomanry were reorganized into a Territorial Army of fourteen infantry divisions and fourteen cavalry brigades, with a primary responsibility for home defence, but with a secondary role of relieving Regular overseas garrisons and of providing a trained reservoir of manpower in the event of a major conflict.

Thus, due largely to the vision and resolution of this most unmilitary of men, there sailed for France in August 1914 what has been described as 'the best-trained, best-organized and best-equipped British Army that ever went forth to war.[81] Those words conceal a greater truth. The British Expeditionary Force was in fact the *first* such Army; and it was to pay a terrible price for that signal honour.

It would be reasonable to suppose that an event as convulsive as the First World

---

[80]In 1902 Lord Roberts had strongly argued the case for conscription or 'national service'.
[81]*Military Operations, France and Flanders, 1914*, Vol.I.

War would have radically altered the form and face of the Regular Army; but that did not happen. To compare the Army List of 1914 with that of 1919 is to compare, in virtually every respect, a like anatomy with like. Indeed, the order of battle of Line regiments remained unchanged. The sole addition to the Regular establishment was a fifth regiment of Foot Guards, the Welsh, formed in 1915.

There were certainly a number of temporary additions — for example (curiously) six regiments of cavalry, and an Army Cyclist Corps — but none of these survived the subsequent process of demobilization. There were, however, two revolutionary developments which were fundamentally to change the whole concept of warfare.

The first was what may be called the introduction of a third dimension. As early as 1878 military experiments had been conducted with observation balloons, and in 1890 the first Balloon Section was added to the establishment as a unit of the Royal Engineers.[82] In 1911 balloons and dirigibles were combined to form an Air Battalion, and by Royal Warrant of 13 April 1912 — a date of profound significance — the Royal Flying Corps was created, consisting, in operational terms, of a Naval Wing and a Military Wing. The Military Wing remained an adjunct of the Royal Engineers, and the five squadrons which accompanied the BEF to France were designated as 'Army Troops' under the direct control of the Commander-in-Chief.

By the end of 1917 the number of aircraft on the Western Front had risen to 1,580 and the Corps had far outgrown its primitive purpose of observation and reconnaissance and had become a strategic rather than a tactical weapon. Accordingly on 1 April 1918 a new service, the Royal Air Force, came into existence under the direct control of an Air Council. Little more than a hundred years had passed since the changing geometry of the battlefield had resulted in 'galloper guns' and 'an Experimental Corps of Riflemen'; the third dimension now extended the conduct of warfare far beyond the immediate battlefield.

The impact of air power was slow to find acceptance among the traditionalists of the two other services (it is interesting to speculate how it might have influenced the thinking of innovatory minds like those of Cardwell and Haldane, working as they were in a two-dimensional field). The Army had long since learned that military operations could only be conducted on the back of naval supremacy, and had resigned itself to the historic political and public prejudice against soldiers and in favour of sailors. Amphibious warfare was a *sine qua non* for an island race with imperial pretensions. But the emergence of a 'third force' had implications not easily grasped by a generation wearied by the seemingly insuperable deadlock in the static landscape of trench warfare. The Royal Air Force, the pristine plumage of its 'young eagles' carefully protected by Trenchard, followed a detached existence, literally in its own element; and it was not until the Second World War and the arrival of Winston Churchill as *genius loci* and inspiration of a 'nation in arms' that the process of assimilation was set in train with the establishment of a Joint Chiefs of Staff Committee. Even then it would take nearly twenty years after the defeat of Germany for inter-service rivalries to be resolved, when on 1 April 1964, sixty years after the creation of the Army Council, the three separate Ministries were amalgamated as a single Ministry of Defence. It was almost exactly three hundred years since Parliament had vested supreme command of 'all Forces by Land and Sea' in the Crown.

---

[82]Until the formation of properly organized service Corps, the Royal Engineers were the repository of almost every technical function, from railway construction to communications.

Charles II would not have understood, but he would have greatly approved.

Yet while the third dimension was being filled, the second radical change in the anatomy of the Army was taking place. It had its roots in the stalemate on the Western Front; but its origins go far back in time.

The history of warfare has been the history of two irreconcilable opposites: defence and attack. For more than six hundred years after the battle of Adrianople in A.D. 378 the dominant arm had been the cavalry, and the irresistible weapon of attack the armoured knight. For the next six hundred years science and ingenuity had sought to return to the foot soldier the primacy he had enjoyed as Greek hoplite and Roman legionary. The invention of gunpowder and the development of artillery and firearms progressively swung the balance of power on the battlefield, so that by the nineteenth century the geometry of the killing-ground had been decisively altered. Ney's cavalry was destroyed on the rampart of the British infantry squares at Waterloo; the Prussian Guard foundered on the fire-power of four French battalions at St Privat in 1870.

By 1915 the killing-ground was dominated by the machine-gun, 'the concentrated essence of infantry', in Liddell Hart's striking phrase. 'No-Man's-Land' had become an impassable barrier to the attacker, and such successes as were achieved were measured in yards and at intolerable cost. It was to break this deadlock and to restore to the attacker freedom of movement and protection against an entrenched defender that the ghost of the armoured knight was summoned up.

On 16 February 1916 the first six companies of tanks were formed. For security reasons they were known as the Heavy Branch of the Machine Gun Corps[83] — an ironic cover-name, since they were designed as a counter-measure to the very weapon by which they were described. On 27 July 1917 the new 'cavalry' was renamed the Tank Corps.[84] The old power of the horse was thus replaced by horse-power, and with the advent of mechanization the science of warfare would be transformed from the static battles of attrition to a fluid war of movement. Together the aeroplane and the armoured fighting vehicle would combine to eliminate No-Man's-Land and restore to the attacker much of the power he had surrendered in the recent past. The anatomy of the Army would now assume a radical new structure. The change was slow, the gradualness inevitable.

With the end of the First World War the great citizen armies were dispersed and the Regular Army, in keeping with historical precedent, reverted to its former estate, short of men and short of money. The parallel with 1815 was almost exact. But between 1918 and 1923 a number of important changes took place, and these may be summarized as follows.

The infantry continued as it had been since Cardwell's time, for the imperial commitments remained and the two-battalion regimental system had long since been accepted (despite some residual opposition) as having the virtues of simplicity and economy, even if in the aftermath of war most units were at little more than half their established strength. There were two changes reflected in the Army List, one cosmetic and one political: Line regiments, given the option of changing their titles to conform with their 'territorial' rather than their

[83]Formed in 1915 and disbanded in 1922.
[84]Royal Tank Corps, 1923; Royal Tank Regiment, 1939.

'honour' designations, largely chose to do so (for example, Princess Charlotte of Wales's Royal Berkshire Regiment became The Royal Berkshire Regiment (Princess Charlotte of Wales's), while others assumed new titles in line with their historic associations (for example, The Royal Scots (The Lothian Regiment) became The Royal Scots (The Royal Regiment)). And in 1922, with the establishment of the Free State, five Irish regiments were disbanded.[85]

With the cavalry, untouched by the Cardwell and Haldane reforms, it was otherwise. With the reduction of the Army to — and even below — its pre-war strength, room had to be found for the new Tank Corps, and money for starting the general process of mechanization. Thus there began a series of amalgamations similar to, but more logical than, the infantry scheme of 1881. The first such was an internal marriage between the 1st and 2nd Life Guards. It was followed thus in 1922: 3rd and 6th Dragoon Guards; 4th and 7th Dragoon Guards; 5th Dragoon Guards and (an exception to the rule of 'like with like') 6th (Inniskilling) Dragoons; 5th and 16th Lancers;[86] 13th and 18th Hussars; 14th and 20th Hussars; 15th and 19th Hussars; and 17th and 21st Lancers. By the end of the year the cavalry of the Line had been reduced from 28 to 20 regiments. At the same date the Tank Corps consisted of 6 Battalions and 12 Armoured Car Companies.

In the post-war reorganization there is an odd anomaly. Despite their outstanding record across four and a half years, not one single Line regiment was accorded a 'Royal' title (in 1946 three infantry corps — Lincolnshire, Leicestershire and Hampshire — were to be so honoured). In contrast, five service Corps[87] — Chaplain's Department, Ordnance, Pay, Service and Veterinary — with tenuous origins and brief traditions, were awarded the distinction. All had served with exemplary devotion, but none could match the record of such as the old Holland Regiment or the 'Fighting Fifth'.[88] Truly, the British Army is a very singular institution.

It is from this post-1914-18 period that it is possible to date the significant change of heart of the British public towards the British soldier, for it is here that past and present meet. There are veterans of the old Edwardian Army who remember the notices in public-houses which said: NO DOGS. NO SOLDIERS — in that order. It had then still been possible for a mother to write scathingly to a future Chief of the Imperial General Staff: 'What cause have you for such a Low Life? The Army is a refuge for all Idle people. I would rather Bury you than see you in a red coat.'

But the First World War changed both hearts and minds. It had reached out, as had no war before, into every home in the land. It had left no village without its memorial, no family without its private wounds. The Army had come to the people, and the people now came out to meet its Army, whether in annual

---

[85]The Royal Irish (18th), The Connaught Rangers (88th/94th), The Leinster (100th/109th), The Royal Munster Fusiliers (101st/104th), and The Royal Dublin Fusiliers (102nd/103rd).

[86]The new regiment was numbered *16th/5th* Lancers, and this has a curious history. In 1799 the 5th Royal Irish Dragoons were disbanded for, among other naughty deeds, 'seditious and outrageous proceedings' and 'atrocious acts of disobedience'. In 1858 the regiment was re-formed as the 5th Royal Irish Lancers, and was permitted to resume its old precedence (1689) and its former battle honours. It was not, however, permitted to forget; and on amalgamation with the 16th Lancers, seventy years its junior, it was ranked in its later line of succession.

[87]In 1920 the Signals branch of the Royal Engineers was separated from its parent Corps and provided with its own identity — and a Royal title.

[88]Both awarded a Royal distinction in 1935.

Remembrance or in the pageantry of Tournament or Tattoo. It had not been so before. There are no cenotaphs to celebrate the great wars of the eighteenth and nineteenth centuries, and very few memorials to mark the South African War. So careless are the British people of their own heroic past.

The Regular Army which went to war in 1939 was not greatly different in size from that of 1914 (a reduction of nine cavalry regiments by amalgamation and ten infantry battalions by disbandment). On paper at least, it was fully mechanized except for the Household Cavalry and the two surviving regiments of Dragoons, unlike the German Army which, even as late as the Normandy landings, still retained a surprisingly high proportion of horse-drawn transport. But the years of peace had been largely locust years, and recession and appeasement had combined to stifle the development of the one weapon of the First World War which had shown how the initiative in land battles could be restored to the attacker. In 1939 there were only eight battalions of the Royal Tank Regiment and the recently converted regiments of mechanized cavalry, all both ill-equipped and under-equipped. There had been prophets in the land like Fuller and Liddell Hart advancing the theory and practice of armoured warfare, but, like Mitchell and Hamley and Henderson a century earlier, they were voices in the wilderness. So too with the third dimension, and the military implications of air power. Thus it was that the British Army was once again committed to fight a new war with many of the arms and attitudes of the old.[89]

The Second World War marked the full development of the two great innovations of twenty years earlier — air power and armour. The first, exploiting the third dimension, created the concept of total war, waged without discrimination between military and civilian objectives; the second eliminated the static battlefield and enlarged the geometry of the killing-ground to the point where the only limitation was that of supply and reinforcement. No longer could the three services function independently of each other, and no longer did they. The supreme example of a combined operation — imperfectly understood and expensively learned at Gallipoli — was the Normandy landing, the Air Force preparing and supporting the assault, the Army delivered on the beaches by the Navy. Not until the twentieth day did casualties reach the British losses sustained on a single morning on the Somme.

There were, as in the First World War, temporary additions to the peacetime establishment: the Reconnaissance Corps, disbanded in 1946; six armoured cavalry regiments, disbanded in 1948; a Lowland and a Highland Regiment, both disbanded in 1949. The geography of the European theatre, however, produced a very British innovation, the Commandos, raised as highly trained specialist units by both the Army and the Royal Marines, and it is a curious twist of history that the Maritime Regiment of 'sea-souljers' raised by Charles II in the service of the Fleet should find its post-war salvation in another element.

The fusion of elements produced another — and permanent — innovation with the formation in 1942 of The Parachute Regiment and The Glider Pilot Regiment under the administrative control of The Army Air Corps. In 1950 the Corps was temporarily disbanded and The Parachute Regiment transferred to

[89]The disease was contagious. The French Army sheltered behind its Maginot Line, as if the Schlieffen Plan had never existed. In 1940 it took the Germans 42 days to achieve what Schlieffen had aimed to do in 39.

the Infantry of the Line with precedence after The Argyll and Sutherland Highlanders. In 1957, on the re-forming of the Corps in a combatant role, The Glider Pilot Regiment was officially dissolved and the Corps reconstituted into Divisional regiments of squadrons which carry out the functions of the war-time Air Observation Post Squadrons, and in addition Army transport and helicopter missions.

'I think', said a 1918 veteran, 'that the Great War just died of old age.' That was not true of the Second World War. It ended not with a whimper but with a bang, the echoes of which still fill the corridors of political and military power. A single second on the morning of 6 August 1945 wiped out a great deal more than Hiroshima. It erased a whole concept of warfare, and effectively created a new, gigantic No-Man's-Land precariously poised between two new super-powers; and it gave an entirely new meaning to the word 'deterrent'. Henceforth war would be defined in two categories: the ultimate, or nuclear; the limited, or conventional.

With the end of the Far East War, the emergence of the super-powers and the political decision to withdraw from Empire, the future organization of the Regular Army was subjected to the most fundamental reassessment since the time of Cardwell's reforms, its primary function 'conventional' within the framework of the new North Atlantic Treaty Organization. There followed a period of rationalization (a new euphemism for 'reduction') which created as many anomalies as it solved, and as much dust and heat as had the celebrated General Order 41 of 1881. That the marching and counter-marching of the period to 1970 was necessary is no longer a matter for argument; that it was conducted with much misgiving reflects the historic divide between political expediency and military imperatives. How the Regular Army was transformed during this period is shown in the table on pp.102-10. Why this process happened is a fascinating commentary on the British genius for ambivalence.

In 1945 the Regular Army (service Corps apart) consisted as follows: 2 regiments of Household Cavalry; 5 regiments of Foot Guards; 20 regiments of mechanized Cavalry; The Royal Tank Regiment; 64 regiments of Infantry, to which had been added during the war The Parachute Regiment and The Special Air Service Regiment. By 1970 rationalization had slimmed this establishment to: 2 regiments of Household Cavalry; 5 regiments of Foot Guards; 14 armoured regiments of Cavalry and Tanks; and 33 regiments of Infantry, to which had been added in 1948 the Brigade of Gurkhas. Thus in unit terms, if not in established strength, the anatomy of the Regular Army, by a curious historical statistic, was almost exactly half that authorized by General Order 41 of 1881. The process, infinitely complicated, can only be summarized here.

Special Army Order 165 of 1946 reorganized the Foot Guards and the Infantry of the Line into 15 administrative Corps, grouped on a regional or, in the case of Guards, Light Infantry and Rifle Regiments, 'category' basis, and lettered consecutively from A to P. It was an anonymous and unimaginative arrangement which ran counter to the long-accepted territorial structure, and it contained some strange anomalies. Accordingly the Warrant was amended by Army Order 61 of 1948, and the new corps were restyled to form a Brigade of Guards, a Light Infantry Brigade, a Green Jacket Brigade and eleven 'regional' Brigades.[90]

[90]For detailed composition of these Brigades, see individual entries in Section C.

Here the planners paused and the politicians took over.

The India Independence Act of 1947[91] had brought to an end two centuries of British rule in the sub-continent, and with it a reassessment of the Regular Army's overseas commitments. Ever since the Mutiny there had existed side by side the Indian Army and 'the Army in India', the latter 'garrison' element provided through Cardwell's system of linked battalions. The withdrawal of a British presence from so large a part of the old imperial territories east of Suez was at once reflected in the decision to reduce — precipitately, as events in Malaya and elsewhere presently proved — all infantry corps except the three senior regiments of Foot Guards and The Parachute Regiment to single battalions. The effect — even if the irony was not recognized — was to march the Line regiments back to the *status quo ante* Cardwell's localization scheme of 1872; nor was it to be by any means the end of that road. One link, however, was preserved with the imperial past. On 1 January 1948 four Rifle Regiments of Gurkhas (2nd, 6th, 7th and 10th), together with supporting elements of Engineers, Signals and Transport, were transferred to the British establishment as The Brigade of Gurkhas. It was the most imaginative decision in a period short on imagination and long on confusion.

Thus by the early 1950s the infantry of the Line had been, with the exceptions noted above, reduced to 64 single-battalion regiments; nor was the cavalry of the Line, standard-bearer of the new technology of armoured warfare, left unscathed in the slimming process. It entered the 1950s with the 20 regiments which had formed, with the Royal Tank Regiment, the new Royal Armoured Corps of 1939. By 1971 the total had been further cut to 13 by the following amalgamations: The Royal Horse Guards and The Royal Dragoons (Blues and Royals); The King's Dragoon Guards and The Bays; The Carabiniers and The Royal Scots Greys; the 3rd and 7th Hussars; the 4th and 8th Hussars; the 9th and 12th Lancers; and the 10th and 11th Hussars. By then there remained no regiment of Dragoons. Ponsonby's famous Union Brigade of Waterloo was gone beyond recall.

Scarcely had the Regular Army learned to live with the problems of rationalization than the politicians cried havoc and let loose an awkward, if inevitable, dog of peace.

In 1957 the Government decided to suspend conscription and to phase out National Service by 1 January 1960. With hindsight it may be argued that it was an injudicious hostage to fortune in an unstable world; but that is not of consequence here. When times are out of joint *vox populi* is not to be gainsaid. At that juncture another tribune — a Cardwell or a Haldane — might have tilted the scales. But this time there were no tribunes.

The effect of ending National Service was to create a crisis of manpower in the Regular Army. Even the modest establishment of 20 cavalry and 64 single-battalion infantry regiments, not to mention supporting arms and services, could not be sustained by voluntary enlistment and penny-pinching pay. The planners returned to the drawing-board.

In the autumn of 1957 a Committee was set up to consider the best method of reducing the infantry establishment by 17 battalions (since the 1946 rationalization this effectively meant that many regiments would lose their individual identity). For the basis of reorganization the Group/Brigade system of 1946-8

[91]Separate Acts in the same year gave independence to Burma and Ceylon.

was selected, and by 1958 — after much lobbying and agonizing — 15 pairs of battalions were chosen for amalgamation within 14 Brigades, each consisting of three or four battalions.[92] Unlike the 1872 localization scheme, the 1957 'linking' process produced new single-battalion regiments, as, for example, The Devonshire and Dorset Regiment, and The Duke of Edinburgh's Royal Regiment (Berkshire and Wiltshire). It was at best a cosmetic exercise, even to the introduction of 'anonymous' Brigade cap-badges which owed nothing to the component corps, and which were a negation of the very essence of the infantry arm — the regimental system. More importantly, it shirked the wider issue of creating an organization tailored to the Army's new role, at once compact and flexible. Indeed, the Army Council largely ignored the Committee's recommendations, for by 1958 the idea of the 'large' regiment — a natural modern corollary to Cardwell — already commanded considerable support among those who had done their sums and had reconciled the equation of manpower to military capability.[93] Thus — and not for the first time — the Army found itself with the worst of two worlds.

With two exceptions,[94] no major changes in infantry organization took place in the four years after 1958; but in 1962 a new Committee was set up to implement the Army Council's decision 'that the Infantry shall be organized into large regiments'. In fact the process had already started with the conversion of the East Anglian Brigade into The East Anglian Regiment, and since this was the vanguard of reform it may conveniently be taken to illustrate the hesitant steps by which nine pre-Cardwell regiments of Foot were reduced to three battalions of a new corps, The Royal Anglian. In the process nine celebrated regiments dropped their former territorial designations. It was in a sense Cardwell in reverse. Had the Army Council pressed ahead with its plan there would have emerged from the former Brigade system twelve 'large' regiments of three or four battalions; but it did not, preferring rather to encourage corps 'to move voluntarily towards the Large Regiment'. By no means all accepted the invitation, so that by 1971 (when the cycle of change had run its course) there were six 'large' regiments, eleven amalgamated in pairs, and eleven which still retained their independent identity. In the process two — The Cameronians and The York and Lancaster — opted for disbandment. But in the meantime the prototype had evolved thus.

In 1958 (the new battalions would be numbered according to the seniority of component regiments) The Bedfordshire and Hertfordshire amalgamated with The Essex to form the 3rd East Anglian Regiment (16th/44th Foot).

In 1959 The Royal Norfolk and The Suffolk amalgamated as the 1st East Anglian (Royal Norfolk and Suffolk).

In 1960 The Royal Lincolnshire (from the Forester Brigade) amalgamated with The Northamptonshire as the 2nd East Anglian (Duchess of Gloucester's Own Royal Lincolnshire and Northamptonshire).

In 1963 The Royal Leicestershire was transferred on the dispersal of the Forester Brigade.

---

[92]A Fusilier Brigade was formed in 1957. In 1962 the Midland Brigade was renamed the Forester Brigade, but this in turn was dispersed the following year with the decision to create 'large' regiments.

[93]It was at this period that the idea of a single Royal Corps of Infantry was first promoted.

[94]The Highland Light Infantry was transferred to the Lowland Brigade on amalgamation with The Royal Scots Fusiliers (1959); The Oxford and Bucks L.I. from the Light Infantry Brigade to the Green Jackets Brigade (1958).

Thus at this stage the new regiments at least retained territorial suffixes, but with the final conversion to a 'large' regiment in 1964 the territorial links were dropped and the corps retitled The Royal Anglian Regiment.

It was not quite the end of the affair, for in 1970 with another round of infantry cuts, the new regiment was reduced to three battalions by the process of 'assimilating' The Royal Leicestershire.

There is no obvious explanation why the Army Council — and the subsequent Army Board — did not carry the 1962 proposal through to its logical conclusion. In spite of early antagonism and growing pains, the new 'large' regiments settled down to a peaceful co-existence. If it was not always a marriage of true minds, the system worked well, and, within the new-style regimental system, provided a flexibility which had not previously been a signal feature of Army organization. Indeed, with the removal of the much-criticized Brigade cap-badges, the new regiments demonstrated considerable ingenuity in devising insignia and appointments which incorporated the historic traditions of all their component parts. The explanation of the curiously hybrid establishment which took root after 1968 would seem to lie in the 'voluntary option' offered by the Army Council six years earlier. The old Wessex Brigade is a case in point. Originally it had consisted of six regiments reduced to four by the amalgamation of The Devonshire and Dorset (1958) and The Royal Berkshire and Wiltshire (1959). These, with The Gloucestershire and The Royal Hampshire, would have fitted conveniently into the 'large' regiment pattern; but it did not happen, and indeed The Royal Hampshire's brinkmanship brought it perilously close to disbandment. The Fusilier Brigade, on the other hand, embraced the new theology with the enthusiasm of kindred spirits, even if one component regiment — the Royal Warwickshire Fusiliers, restyled as such in 1963 — had, so to speak, side-stepped out of the Forester Brigade.

With the phasing out of Brigades a new administrative superstructure was introduced in 1968 with the formation of six Divisions, ranking thus by order of precedence of their senior corps: Guards, Scottish, Queen's, King's, Prince of Wales's and Light.[95] Of these, two — Queen's and Light — included five out of the six 'large' regiments. Since then, while there have been further reductions within regiments, the planners have left the Army in peace; but in the light of past history this singular and honourable institution would do well to keep its powder dry.

It is a far cry from the time, three hundred years ago, when in the face of every political and public obstacle, Charles II ensured the survival of his ten Standing Regiments, and thus, through many vicissitudes, the very existence of the small, professional Army of today. That the money to maintain his Guards and Garrisons, so painfully prised from a resentful Parliament, was less than one-seventh of the cost of a single Challenger tank would have both amazed and amused the King. Since then Parliament and public have made their peace with their soldiers, and for that the soldiers, by their patience and by their achievements, may rightly take the credit. The rough redcoat of the Tangier garrison has become a craftsman in a world of technology; and not until our own day has he received the reward of technical skill. In 1981 the average strength of

---

[95] The Parachute Regiment and the Brigade of Gurkhas remained outside the Divisional organization.

the Regular Army was 167,000, at an estimated cost of £1,384,072,000. Such a figure may be more easily comprehended by a simple comparison. A 'private man' in Charles's Army would have needed to serve for over four hundred years to earn the annual pay of a young soldier today. That would also have amazed — and greatly gratified — the King.

THE SPINAL COLUMN

The following table lists in alphabetical order the Regular Regiments, Corps, Brigades and Divisions of the British Army. Also included are The Royal Marines to underline their historic and (increasingly) modern 'military' role, together with certain of the original regiments of the Army of Charles II (e.g. The Tangier Regiment). Following the end of the First World War there began a radical restructuring of the Army, with a steady process of amalgamation (and disbandment) of Regiments, the addition of new Corps to the permanent establishment, and as a result many changes in style and designation. To distinguish between what may be called the 'old' and the 'new' Army, Regiments and Corps which predate 1918 are shown in roman type; subsequent changes and additions in bold. Regiments of Dragoon Guards, Dragoons, Hussars and Lancers are grouped together in order of precedence. Page references are to individual entries in Section C, *The Anatomy of the Army,* and in Section E, *Regimental and Corps Headdress Badges.* With one exception, Regiments and Corps raised for war service and subsequently disbanded, such as the Army Cyclist Corps (1914) or the Reconnaissance Corps (1942), have been omitted. The exception is the Machine Gun Corps (raised in 1915 and disbanded in 1922), which was the improbable parent of the sibling Royal Tank Regiment.

	Hussars, 10th Royal (Prince of Wales's Own)	133,**273**
	Hussars, 11th (Prince Albert's Own)	133,**273**
	Hussars, The Royal	133,**273**
	Hussars, 13th	134,**273**
	Hussars, 13th/18th Royal	134,**273**
	Hussars, 14th (King's)	134,**274**
	Hussars, 14th/20th King's	134,**274**
	Hussars, 15th (The King's)	134,**274**
	Hussars, 15th/19th The King's Royal	135,**274**
	Hussars, 18th Royal (Queen Mary's Own)	135,**273**
	Hussars, 19th Royal (Queen Alexandra's Own)	135,**274**
	Hussars, 20th	136,**274**
	Intelligence Corps	136,**290**
	Irish Guards	136,**276**
	King's	137,**279**
8th	King's (Liverpool)	137,**279**
	King's Own Royal Border	137,**278**
4th	King's Own Royal (Lancaster)	138,**278**
25th	King's Own Scottish Borderers	138,**283**
51st and 105th	King's Own Yorkshire Light Infantry	138,**281**
60th	King's Royal Rifle Corps	139,**288**
53rd and 85th	King's Shropshire Light Infantry	139,**281**
	Lancashire	139,**285**
20th (XXth)	Lancashire Fusiliers	140,**279**
	Lancers, 5th (Royal Irish)	140,**275**
	Lancers, 9th (Queen's Royal)	141,**274**
	Lancers, 12th Royal (Prince of Wales's)	141,**274**
	Lancers, 9th/12th Royal	141,**275**
	Lancers, 16th (The Queen's)	141,**275**
	Lancers, 16th/5th The Queen's Royal	142,**275**
	Lancers, 17th (Duke of Cambridge's Own)	142,**275**
	Lancers, 21st (Empress of India's)	142,**275**
	Lancers, 17th/21st	142,**275**
17th	Leicestershire **(Royal, 1946)**	161,**280**
100th and 109th	Leinster (Royal Canadians) **(disbanded 1922)**	148,**292**
	Life Guards (1st and 2nd)	143,**270**
	Light Infantry	143,**282**
10th	Lincolnshire **(Royal, 1946)**	161,**280**
47th and 81st	Loyal North Lancashire	144,**285**
	Machine Gun Corps **(disbanded 1922)**	144,**293**
63rd and 96th	Manchester	145,**279**
57th and 77th	Middlesex	146,**278**
	Military Police, Corps of **(Royal, 1946)**	119,**290**

	Military Provost Staff Corps	146,**290**
9th	Norfolk **(Royal, 1935)**	163,**279**
48th and 58th	Northamptonshire	147,**280**
64th and 98th	North Staffordshire	147,**285**
5th	Northumberland Fusiliers **(Royal, 1935)**	163,**278**
43rd and 52nd	Oxfordshire and Buckinghamshire Light Infantry	148,**288**
	Parachute Regiment	148,**287**
	Pioneer Corps **(Royal, 1946)**	163,**290**
	Prince of Wales's Own Regiment of Yorkshire	149,**282**
	Queen's	150,**278**
	Queen Alexandra's Imperial Military Nursing Service	149,**291**
	Queen Alexandra's Royal Army Nursing Corps	149,**291**
	Queen's Lancashire	150,**285**
	Queen's Own Buffs, Royal Kent	150,**277**
79th	Queen's Own Cameron Highlanders	150,**286**
	Queen's Own Highlanders	150,**287**
50th and 97th	Queen's Own Royal West Kent	151,**277**
	Queen's Royal Surrey	151,**277**
2nd	Queen's Royal (West Surrey)	151,**277**
	Rifle Brigade	152,**288**
	Royal Anglian	152,**280**
	Royal Armoured Corps	152,**270**
	Royal Army Medical Corps	153,**289**
49th and 66th	Royal Berkshire	156,**286**
	Royal Corps of Signals	156,**276**
	Royal Corps of Transport	156,**289**
102nd and 103rd	Royal Dublin Fusiliers **(disbanded 1922)**	157,**293**
	Royal Electrical and Mechanical Engineers, Corps of	118,**289**
	Royal Engineers, Corps of	119,**276**
	Royal Flying Corps (Military Wing)	157,**293**
7th	Royal Fusiliers (City of London)	157,**279**
	Royal Green Jackets	158,**288**
	Royal Highland Fusiliers	158,**283**
	Royal Horse Artillery	158,**270**
	Royal Horse Guards (The Blues)	159,**270**
27th and 108th	Royal Inniskilling Fusiliers	159,**283**
18th	Royal Irish **(disbanded 1922)**	159,**292**
87th and 89th	Royal Irish Fusiliers	160,**284**
	Royal Irish Rangers	160,**284**
83rd and 86th	Royal Irish Rifles	160,**284**
	Royal Marines	162,**286**
101st and 104th	Royal Munster Fusiliers **(disbanded 1922)**	162,**292**
	Royal Regiment of Artillery	164,**276**

	Royal Regiment of Fusiliers	164,**279**
	Royal Regiment of Wales	164,**283**
1st	Royal Scots	165,**277**
21st	Royal Scots Fusiliers	165,**282**
35th and 107th	Royal Sussex	165,**278**
	Royal Tank Regiment	166,**276**
83rd and 86th	**Royal Ulster Rifles**	166,**284**
6th	Royal Warwickshire **(Fusiliers, 1963)**	166,**278**
23rd	Royal Welsh Fusiliers **(Royal Welch Fusiliers, 1920)**	167,**283**
	Scots Guards	167,**276**
72nd and 78th	Seaforth Highlanders	168,**286**
45th and 95th	Sherwood Foresters	168,**284**
13th	Somerset Light Infantry	169,**281**
	Somerset and Cornwall Light Infantry	169,**281**
40th and 82nd	South Lancashire	169,**285**
38th and 80th	South Staffordshire	170,**285**
24th	South Wales Borderers	170,**283**
	Special Air Service Regiment	170,**288**
	Staffordshire	171,**286**
12th	Suffolk	171,**279**
	Tangier Horse	19,**120**
	Tangier Regiment	19,**151**
	Tangier Regiment, 2nd	19,**138**
	Tank Corps **(Royal, 1923)**	166,**275**
41st and 69th	Welsh **(Welch, 1920)**	171,**283**
	Welsh Guards	172,**277**
14th	West Yorkshire	172,**282**
62nd and 99th	Wiltshire	173,**286**
	Women's Royal Army Corps	173,**291**
29th and 36th	Worcestershire	173,**284**
	Worcestershire and Sherwood Foresters	174,**284**
65th and 84th	York and Lancaster **(disbanded 1968)**	174,**292**
19th	Yorkshire **(Green Howards, 1920)**	174,**282**

A

ORDERS OF PRECEDENCE

As the Standing Army began to expand it became necessary to establish rules governing the seniority of regiments. Accordingly, on 12 September 1666, Charles issued a Royal Warrant setting down the first Order of Precedence:

> For the preventing of all Questions and Dispute that might arise for and concerning the Ranks of the several Regiments, Troops and Companies which now are or at any time hereafter shall be employed in our Service. We have thought good to issue out these following Rules and Directions.
>
> First, as to the Foot, that the Regiment of Guards [*Grenadier*] take place of all other Regiments ... the General's Regiment [*Coldstream*] to take place next, the Admiral's[1] immediately after, and all other Regiments and Colonels to take place according to the Date of their Commissions.
>
> 2nd. As to the Horse, that the three Troops of Guards [*Life Guards*] take place before all others ... That the King's Regiment of Horse [*Royal Horse Guards*] take place immediately after the Guards...[2]

With the evacuation of the Tangier garrison and the addition of the three Tangier Regiments to the English establishment, the King issued a further Warrant on 6 February 1684:

> ... concerning the Ranks of the several Regiments of Foot, That Our Own Regiment of Guards [*Grenadier*] take place of all other Regiments of Foot, that our Coldstream Regiment of Guards take place next. After which our Scotch Regiment [*Royal Scots*] and Tanger Regiment [*Queen's*]. Our Brother James Duke of Yorkes Regiment[3] are to have precedency as they are here ranked ... All other Regiments of Foot take place according to their respective Seniorities from the time they were *raised*[4] so as that no Regiment is to loose its Precedency by the Death of their Colonell.

By the following year, after Monmouth's rebellion, there had been a significant increase in the Standing Army, and in a Warrant of 3 August James confirmed his brother's general ruling, and fixed the infantry Order of Precedence thus: Grenadier Guards, Coldstream Guards; 1st, 2nd, Prince George of Denmark's, 3rd, 4th, and 7th to 15th Regiments of Foot (the 5th and 6th were still in Dutch service); and to these had been added by the end of the reign the 16th, 17th, 19th and 20th, and early in 1689 the 22nd, 23rd and 24th.

It is clear that the constant raising and disbanding of new corps at this date led to much confusion and dispute, not least in regard to the regiments of the Irish and Scottish establishments lately taken onto the English establishment.[5] Accordingly, on 10 June 1694 King William issued a Royal Warrant at 'our Camp at Roosbeck in the Low Countrys'. This Warrant is of special importance, since it laid down the principle which, despite the meddlesome interference of Queen Anne, was to govern the whole future question of regimental precedence, and largely explains the bewildering changes in numerical designations

[1]Disbanded in 1689 as Prince George of Denmark's Regiment, and raised again in 1755 as 'The Marines'.
[2]For purposes of clarity, here and below, regiments are shown by their subsequent distinctive or numerical designations.
[3]The Admiral's Regiment.
[4]A ruling not finally countermanded until 1718.
[5]Namely, The Royal Irish and The Royal Scots Fusiliers (18th and 21st).

during the latter part of the eighteenth century. The essential change was the dating of a regiment's seniority *not from that of its original raising, but from its entry onto the English establishment,*[6] thus:

> 1st.   That an English Regiment shall take place of all other regiments, being otherwise in the same circumstances.
>
> 2nd.   That an Irish Regt. shall have rank from the Day it comes on the English Establishment...
>
> 3rd.   That a Scots Regiment coming upon the English Establishment shall take rank with other Regiments from that time.

The Warrant then proceeded to confirm that 'the English Regts. that have lately served in Holland [*5th and 6th*] take their Rank immediately after the Queen's Regiment of Foot [*4th, or King's Own Royal Regiment*]'.

With the end of the war in 1712, however, and the inevitable decision to disband a large part of Marlborough's army, William's ruling on regimental seniority was reversed, to the accompaniment of much argument and discontent. On 28 July Queen Anne addressed herself to the Board of General Officers through the Secretary-at-War:

> Her Majesty having been moved upon the Affair relating to the Ranks of Sevl. Regiments now settling by the Board of General Officers, I am to signify you Her Pleasure That Regard is to be had to the Date of Raising the said Regimts, and not to the time of their coming upon the English Establishment.

This new ruling raised several anomalies, and accordingly the Board, finding that 'Inconveniences did Arise', made representations to the Queen on 23 September:

> The Board ... foresee great Difficultys in relation to Her Majt's Horse and Foot Guards with those of Scotland;[7] for that by Her Majt's said Orders, the Scots Regimt of Foot Guards [*Scots Guards*] and the Coldstream Regimt.[8] will take place of Her Majt's first Regimt. (*Grenadier*); The Scots Troops of Guards, and the Earl of Stair's Scots Regimt. of Dragoons [*Royal Scots Greys*] have precedency of Her Majt's. Own Royl. Regimt. [*Royal Dragoons*] and the Other Two English Regimts. of Dragoons [*3rd and 4th Hussars*] ...

To this the Secretary-at-War replied a week later:

> I am to acquaint you that her Majty ... has Commanded Me to Acquaint the Board that it is her Pleasure that the said Rule do not extend to alter the present Rank of any of Her Guards, nor of any other Regimt. that was Raised before the last Warr.

This may have satisfied the Queen, but not her Colonels, who submitted 'a

---

[6]Predictably, as is noted below, there were and are exceptions; as for example, the ranking of Regiments of Horse (Dragoon Guards) above the historically senior Regiments of Dragoons.
[7]The Act of Union had been passed in 1707.
[8]Both raised before the Restoration.

petition of Claims'.[9] The baffled Board reshuffled the pack, and eventually on 23 April 1713 a Royal Warrant was issued which laid down the following Order of Precedence: Life Guards; Royal Horse Guards; Horse *[Dragoon Guards]*, 1st to 7th; Dragoons, 1st to 8th; Foot Guards, 1st, 2nd, 3rd; Foot, 1st to 18th, 21st, 25th, 20th, 19th, 22nd, 23rd, 24th, 27th, 26th, 35th, 36th, 28th, 39th, 29th, 30th, 31st, 32nd, 37th, 33rd, 34th and 38th. This arbitrary register can only be explained by the fact that some Colonels carried more clout than others. It had no historical validity, not even by the Queen's reckoning.

With the accession of George I, the Board lost no time in reopening negotiations, and on 11 January 1715 the Secretary-at-War informed them thus:

> Rank of the Regiments to be adjusted according to King William's Rules [*the 'Roosbeck' Warrant of 1694*]. His Majty ... is pleased to Order and Direct (Disapproving of all Retrospects) that the Rules settled by King William which have Governed during the Two late Wars shall remain and be Established as a Regulation for the settling the Rank and Seniority of the sevl. Regimts which now do or lately did serve in the army ...

A month later the Board submitted the following list (updated on 24 May 1718 by the addition of the 9th to 14th Dragoons[10] and the 40th Foot *[1st Bn, The South Lancashire Regiment]*: Life Guards; Royal Horse Guards; Horse *[Dragoon Guards]*, 1st to 7th; Dragoons, 1st to 8th; Foot Guards, 1st, 2nd, 3rd; Foot, 1st to 39th. An interesting omission was the new Royal Regiment of Artillery, established in 1716.

The regulation of 1718 governing the Order of Precedence remained the official authority until the numbering of regiments in 1751, by when a further nine regiments of Foot had been added to the establishment, although the Royal Artillery still ranked last until in 1756 — without explanation — it was promoted above not only the 'Marching Regiments' but also the Foot Guards. Thereafter, during the second half of the eighteenth century, with the raising and disbanding of new corps in confusing sequence, there were inevitable anomalies, but 'King William's Rule' was still applied, and seniority granted only on permanent entry onto the establishment, until the final addition of the nine regiments of Foot transferred from the East India Company in 1861.

The rule continued to apply — although deeply resented — when the numbered corps were replaced by territorial regiments in Cardwell's localization scheme, and many regiments of venerable antiquity found themselves relegated to second battalions. Nor did it end there; for the process was extended even further with the wholesale amalgamations which followed the Second World War.[11]

There remain two 'special cases'.[12] First, the right of the line. On 22 June 1857

---

[9]The Queen was not amused, for she 'would not suffer the same to be Read; Resented the Proceedings; and declared She expected her Orders should be obeyed'.

[10]Subsequently Lancers and Hussars.

[11]The same process of seniority was applied to the previously civilian service Corps as they came onto the Regular establishment, ranking after the Infantry of the Line.

[12]And two marginal glosses. Until April 1939 the Royal Tank Corps took precedence after the Infantry of the Line. Then, on the formation of the Royal Armoured Corps, the new Royal Tank Regiment was promoted to rank after 17th/21st Lancers; and The Royal Marines, formed in 1755, takes precedence after The Duke of Edinburgh's Royal Regiment (Berkshire and Wiltshire) when parading with the Army.

the Duke of Cambridge made the following humble submission to Queen Victoria:

> In the year 1756 precedence was given to the Royal Artillery before all Infantry including the Regiments of Foot Guards.
>
> The Regiments now designated Life Guards and Royal Horse Guards were formed in 1660 and 1661, at which period there was no Horse Artillery.
>
> As therefore the Foot Artillery [*sic*] have precedence of all Infantry including Your Majesty's Regiments of Foot Guards and dismounted Cavalry, it is submitted to Your Majesty that it would be consistent with this Regulation that the Royal Horse Artillery should take precedence of all Cavalry including Your Majesty's Regiments of Life Guards and Royal Horse Guards.
>
> It is therefore submitted that the Royal Horse Artillery shall take precedence accordingly of all Cavalry Regiments including Your Majesty's Regiments of Life Guards and Royal Horse Guards.

To this submission the Queen gave her approval; but plainly the Household Cavalry did not take kindly to losing pride of place to a regiment whose seniority dated only from 1793, for the following compromise was made in Queen's Regulations of 1873:

> *Order of Precedence*
> 1. The Regiments of Life Guards and The Royal Regiment of Horse Guards.
> 2. The Royal Horse Artillery, but on parade *with their guns*, this Corps will take the Right and march at the head of the Household Cavalry.

And so it is to-day.

Secondly, the left of the line. In 1816, on the authority of the Prince Regent, The Rifle Brigade — then the 95th Foot — was taken out of the numbered line and took position on the left. This was a signal privilege, and although never subsequently ratified by General Order or similar directive it has become part of the regiment's custom and tradition. With the transfer of the East India Company's much more junior regiments to the British establishment, and again after the formation of territorial corps in 1881, The Rifle Brigade continued to occupy its privileged position. To-day the privilege has been assumed by The Royal Green Jackets, even though the new 'large regiment' contains the older and more senior 43rd/52nd Foot and the 60th, or King's Royal Rifle Corps.

The following tables show the Order of Precedence of the British Army at five particular stages of its development: *1684*, when the first ten regiments had taken their place on the permanent English establishment; *1751*, following upon the numbering of Line regiments in accordance with George II's Royal Warrant; *1861*, after the transfer of regiments from the East India Company; *1881*, as a result of General Orders 41 and 70; and *1983*.

1

ORDER OF PRECEDENCE, 1684

(by Royal Warrant of February 6th)

*The Life Guards
- King's Troop
- Duke of York's Troop
- Queen's Troop

*The Royal Regiment of Horse Guards (The Earl of Oxford's)

*1st, or Royal Regiment of Foot Guards (*to become* The Grenadier Guards)

*2nd Foot Guards, The Coldstream Regiment (*to become* The Coldstream Guards)

The Royal (Scotch) Regiment of Foot (*to become* The Royal Scots)

The Queen's Regiment of Foot (*formerly* The Tangier Regiment)

*The Admiral's, or Duke of York's Regiment of Foot (*to become* The Royal Marines)

*The Holland Regiment of Foot (*to become* The Buffs)

The King's Own Royal Regiment of Dragoons (*formerly* The Tangier Horse)

The Duchess of York and Albany's Regiment of Foot
   (*to become* The King's Own Royal Regiment (Lancaster))

*The six original Standing Regiments

2

ORDER OF PRECEDENCE, 1751

(by Royal Warrant of July 1st)

Life Guards[5]
Royal Horse Guards (The Blues)[5]

1st, or King's Regiment of Dragoon Guards[5]
2nd or Queen's Regiment of Dragoon Guards[5]
3rd Regiment of Dragoon Guards
1st Horse
2nd Regiment of Horse
3rd Regiment of Horse or The Carabineers
4th Regiment of Horse
1st or Royal Dragoons[5]
2nd or Royal North British Dragoons[5]
3rd or King's Own Regiment of Dragoons[1/5]
4th Regiment of Dragoons[1]
5th or Royal Irish Dragoons[4/5]
6th or The Inniskilling Dragoons
7th or The Queen's Regiment of Dragoons[1/5]
8th Regiment of Dragoons[1]
9th Regiment of Dragoons[1/2]
10th Regiment of Dragoons[1]
11th Regiment of Dragoons[1]
12th Regiment of Dragoons[1/3]
13th Regiment of Dragoons[1]
14th Regiment of Dragoons[1]

1st Foot Guards[5]
2nd Foot Guards[5]
3rd Foot Guards[5]

1st or Ye Royal Regiment of Foot[5]
2nd or The Queen's Royal Regiment of Foot[5]
3rd Regiment of Foot or The Buffs[6]
4th or The King's Own Regiment of Foot[5]

2

ORDER OF PRECEDENCE, 1751

1918 SHORT TITLE	PRESENT SHORT TITLE
1st Life Guards	The Life Guards
2nd Life Guards	
Royal Horse Guards	Blues and Royals
1st King's Dragoon Guards	1st Queen's Dragoon Guards
2nd Dragoon Guards (Queen's Bays)	1st Queen's Dragoon Guards
3rd Dragoon Guards	Royal Scots Dragoon Guards
4th Dragoon Guards	4th/7th Royal Dragoon Guards
5th Dragoon Guards	5th Royal Inniskilling Dragoon Guards
6th Dragoon Guards	Royal Scots Dragoon Guards
7th Dragoon Guards	4th/7th Royal Dragoon Guards
1st (Royal) Dragoons	Blues and Royals
2nd Dragoons (Royal Scots Greys)	Royal Scots Dragoon Guards
3rd Hussars	Queen's Own Hussars
4th Hussars	Queen's Royal Irish Hussars
5th Lancers	16th/5th Lancers
6th (Inniskilling) Dragoons	5th Royal Inniskilling Dragoon Guards
7th Hussars	Queen's Own Hussars
8th Hussars	Queen's Royal Irish Hussars
9th Lancers	9th/12th Lancers
10th Hussars	Royal Hussars
11th Hussars	Royal Hussars
12th Lancers	9th/12th Lancers
13th Hussars	13th/18th Hussars
14th Hussars	14th/20th Hussars
Grenadier Guards	Grenadier Guards
Coldstream Guards	Coldstream Guards
Scots Guards	Scots Guards
Royal Scots	Royal Scots
Queen's	Queen's
Buffs	Queen's
King's Own	King's Own Royal Border

5th Regiment of Foot[6]
6th Regiment of Foot[6]
7th or Ye Royal Fusiliers[5]
8th or The King's Regiment of Foot[5]
9th Regiment of Foot
10th Regiment of Foot
11th Regiment of Foot
12th Regiment of Foot
13th Regiment of Foot
14th Regiment of Foot
15th Regiment of Foot
16th Regiment of Foot
17th Regiment of Foot
18th Regiment of Foot or The Royal Irish[5]
19th Regiment of Foot
20th Regiment of Foot
21st Regiment of Foot or Ye Royal North British Fusiliers[5]
22nd Regiment of Foot
23rd Regiment of Foot or The Royal Welch Fusiliers[5]
24th Regiment of Foot
25th Regiment of Foot
26th Regiment of Foot
27th or The Inniskilling Regiment of Foot[6]
28th Regiment of Foot
29th Regiment of Foot
30th Regiment of Foot
31st Regiment of Foot
32nd Regiment of Foot
33rd Regiment of Foot
34th Regiment of Foot
35th Regiment of Foot
36th Regiment of Foot
37th Regiment of Foot
38th Regiment of Foot
39th Regiment of Foot
40th Regiment of Foot
41st Regiment of Foot or The Invalids[6]
42nd Regiment of Foot[6]
43rd Regiment of Foot
44th Regiment of Foot
45th Regiment of Foot

1918 SHORT TITLE	PRESENT SHORT TITLE
Northumberland Fusiliers	**Royal Regiment of Fusiliers**
Royal Warwickshire	**Royal Regiment of Fusiliers**
Royal Fusiliers	**Royal Regiment of Fusiliers**
King's (Liverpool)	**King's**
Norfolk	**Royal Anglian**
Lincolnshire	**Royal Anglian**
Devonshire	**Devonshire and Dorset**
Suffolk	**Royal Anglian**
Somerset L. I.	**Light Infantry**
West Yorkshire	**Prince of Wales's Own Yorkshire**
East Yorkshire	**Prince of Wales's Own Yorkshire**
Bedfordshire	**Royal Anglian**
Leicestershire	**Royal Anglian**
Royal Irish	**(Disbanded)**
Yorkshire	**Green Howards**
Lancashire Fusiliers	**Royal Regiment of Fusiliers**
Royal Scots Fusiliers	**Royal Highland Fusiliers**
Cheshire	**Cheshire**
Royal Welsh Fusiliers	**Royal Welch Fusiliers**
South Wales Borderers	**Royal Regiment of Wales**
King's Own Scottish Borderers	**King's Own Scottish Borderers**
1st Bn, Cameronians	**(Disbanded)**
1st Bn, Royal Inniskilling Fusiliers	**Royal Irish Rangers**
1st Bn, Gloucestershire	**Gloucestershire**
1st Bn, Worcestershire	**Worcestershire and Sherwood Foresters**
1st Bn, East Lancashire	**Queen's Lancashire**
1st Bn, East Surrey	**Queen's**
1st Bn, Duke of Cornwall's L. I.	**Light Infantry**
1st Bn, Duke of Wellington's	**Duke of Wellington's**
1st Bn, Border	**King's Own Royal Border**
1st Bn, Royal Sussex	**Queen's**
2nd Bn, Worcestershire	**Worcestershire and Sherwood Foresters**
1st Bn, Hampshire	**Royal Hampshire**
1st Bn, South Staffordshire	**Staffordshire**
1st Bn, Dorsetshire	**Devonshire and Dorset**
1st Bn, South Lancashire	**Queen's Lancashire**
1st Bn, Welsh	**Royal Regiment of Wales**
1st Bn, Black Watch	**Black Watch**
1st Bn, Oxford and Bucks L. I.	**Royal Green Jackets**
1st Bn, Essex	**Royal Anglian**
1st Bn, Sherwood Foresters	**Worcestershire and Sherwood Foresters**

46th Regiment of Foot
47th Regiment of Foot
48th Regiment of Foot
49th Regiment of Foot
Royal Regiment of Artillery[5]

[1]Between 1775 and 1818 converted to Light Dragoons, and between 1805 and 1861 to Hussars.
[2]Converted to Lancers 1816.
[3]Converted to Lancers 1816.
[4]Disbanded 1799. Re-embodied as Lancers 1858.
[5]The Royal Regiments.
[6]The 'Six Old Corps'.

1918 SHORT TITLE	PRESENT SHORT TITLE
2nd Bn, Duke of Cornwall's L. I.	Light Infantry
1st Bn, Loyal North Lancashire	Queen's Lancashire
1st Bn, Northamptonshire	Royal Anglian
1st Bn, Royal Berkshire	Duke of Edinburgh's Royal
Royal Regiment of Artillery	Royal Regiment of Artillery

3

ORDER OF PRECEDENCE, 1861

(including the Cavalry* and Infantry Regiments transferred from the East India Company to the British establishment which entered the Army List for the first time in this year. From the 1st to the 70th Regiments of Foot the territorial titles, with minor variations, are those adopted in 1782)

Royal Horse Artillery (*see page 71*)
1st Life Guards
2nd Life Guards
Royal Horse Guards
1st The King's Dragoon Guards
2nd Queen's Dragoon Guards
3rd (Prince of Wales's) Dragoon Guards
4th (Royal Irish) Dragoon Guards
5th (Princess Charlotte of Wales's) Dragoon Guards
6th Dragoon Guards (Carabiniers)
7th (The Princess Royal's) Dragoon Guards
1st (Royal) Dragoons
2nd Royal North British Dragoons (Scots Greys)
3rd (King's Own) Hussars
4th (The Queen's Own) Hussars
5th (Royal Irish) Lancers
6th (Inniskilling) Dragoons
7th (Queen's Own) Hussars
8th (The King's Royal Irish) Hussars
9th (Queen's Royal) Lancers
10th The Prince of Wales's Own Royal Hussars
11th Prince Albert's Own Hussars
12th (Prince of Wales's Royal) Lancers
13th Hussars
14th (King's) Hussars
15th (King's) Hussars
16th (The Queen's) Lancers
17th Lancers
18th Hussars
19th Hussars*
20th Hussars*
21st Hussars* (Lancers, *1897*)
Royal Regiment of Artillery (*RHA excepted*)

Corps of Royal Engineers
Grenadier Guards
Coldstream Guards
Scots Fusilier Guards
 1st, or The Royal Regiment
 2nd, or Queen's Royal Regiment
 3rd (East Kent – The Buffs) Regiment
 4th, or The King's Own Regiment
 5th, or Northumberland Fusiliers
 6th (Royal 1st Warwickshire) Regiment
 7th (Royal Fusiliers)
 8th (The King's) Regiment
 9th (East Norfolk) Regiment
10th (North Lincolnshire) Regiment
11th (North Devonshire) Regiment
12th (East Suffolk) Regiment
13th (1st Somersetshire) (Prince Albert's Light Infantry) Regiment
14th (Buckinghamshire) Regiment
15th (Yorkshire, East Riding) Regiment
16th (Bedfordshire) Regiment
17th (Leicestershire) Regiment
18th (The Royal Irish) Regiment
19th (1st Yorkshire, North Riding) Regiment
20th (East Devonshire) Regiment
21st (Royal North British) Fusiliers
22nd (Cheshire) Regiment
23rd (Royal Welsh) Fusiliers
24th (2nd Warwickshire) Regiment
25th (King's Own Borderers) Regiment
26th Cameronian Regiment
27th (Inniskilling) Regiment
28th (North Gloucestershire) Regiment
29th (Worcestershire) Regiment
30th (Cambridgeshire) Regiment
31st (Huntingdonshire) Regiment
32nd (Cornwall) Light Infantry
33rd (Duke of Wellington's) Regiment
34th (Cumberland) Regiment
35th (Royal Sussex) Regiment
36th (Herefordshire) Regiment
37th (North Hampshire) Regiment
38th (1st Staffordshire) Regiment
39th (Dorsetshire) Regiment

40th (2nd Somersetshire) Regiment
41st (The Welsh) Regiment
42nd (The Royal Highland) Regiment (The Black Watch)
43rd (Monmouthshire Light Infantry) Regiment
44th (East Essex) Regiment
45th (Nottinghamshire Regiment) Sherwood Foresters
46th (South Devonshire) Regiment
47th (Lancashire) Regiment
48th (Northamptonshire) Regiment
49th Princess Charlotte of Wales's Hertfordshire Regiment
50th (The Queen's Own) Regiment
51st (2nd Yorkshire, West Riding), (The King's Own Light Infantry) Regiment
52nd (Oxfordshire Light Infantry) Regiment
53rd (Shropshire) Regiment
54th (West Norfolk) Regiment
55th (Westmoreland) Regiment
56th (West Essex) Regiment
57th (West Middlesex) Regiment
58th (Rutlandshire) Regiment
59th (2nd Nottinghamshire) Regiment
60th, or The King's Royal Rifle Corps
61st (South Gloucestershire) Regiment
62nd (Wiltshire) Regiment
63rd (West Suffolk) Regiment
64th (2nd Staffordshire) Regiment
65th (2nd Yorkshire, North Riding) Regiment
66th (Berkshire) Regiment
67th (South Hampshire) Regiment
68th (Durham - Light Infantry) Regiment
69th (South Lincolnshire) Regiment
70th (Surrey) Regiment
71st (Highland) Light Infantry
72nd (Duke of Albany's Own Highlanders) Regiment
73rd (Perthshire) Regiment
74th (Highlanders) Regiment
75th (Stirlingshire) Regiment
76th Regiment
77th (East Middlesex) Regiment
78th (Highland) Regiment, or The Ross-shire Buffs
79th Regiment, or Cameron Highlanders
80th (Staffordshire Volunteers) Regiment
81st (Loyal Lincoln Volunteers) Regiment
82nd (The Prince of Wales's Volunteers) Regiment

83rd (County of Dublin) Regiment

84th (York and Lancaster) Regiment

85th (Bucks Volunteers) (The King's Light Infantry) Regiment

86th (Royal County Down) Regiment

87th (The Royal Irish Fusiliers) Regiment

88th (Connaught Rangers) Regiment

89th Regiment

90th Perthshire Light Infantry

91st (Argyllshire) Regiment

92nd (Gordon Highlanders) Regiment

93rd (Sutherland Highlanders) Regiment

94th Regiment

95th, or Derbyshire Regiment

96th Regiment

97th (The Earl of Ulster's) Regiment

98th Regiment

99th (Lanarkshire) Regiment

100th (Prince of Wales's Royal Canadian) Regiment

101st Royal Bengal Fusiliers

102nd Royal Madras Fusiliers

103rd Royal Bombay Fusiliers

104th Bengal Fusiliers

105th Madras Light Infantry

106th Bombay Light Infantry

107th Bengal Infantry Regiment

108th Madras Infantry Regiment

109th Bombay Infantry Regiment

The Prince Consort's Own Rifle Brigade

NOTE

The Order of Precedence for 1861 does not include any service or ancillary Corps. Virtually none had been formed by this date and since most of those which did exist, even in embryonic form, were civilian organizations, they did not rank in the establishment of the Regular Army. After the Royal Engineers (1787) the first Corps, as such, was the Royal Corps of Waggoners, formed in 1794, but it was not taken on the establishment as the Army Service Corps until 1888. The first Order of Precedence of Corps was printed in the Army List of September, 1930.

4

ORDER OF PRECEDENCE, 1881

General Order 41 of 1 May 1881, which gave effect to Cardwell's localization scheme, was accompanied by an Appendix showing 'the precedence, composition, and title' of the new Infantry Regiments of the Line (Cavalry of the Line remained as it was in 1861, *q.v.*). Comparison with the Order of Precedence of that year will show that the process of 'linking' produced some strange bedfellows. There were also several anomalies in this Appendix, and accordingly a number of changes and adjustments were made in the Army List two months later (for example, the precedence of the two Staffordshire regiments was reversed and the honour title transferred by General Order 70). These changes are shown in the tables below together with subsequent alterations and additions to titles. Note that the 26th/90th Foot and the 83rd/86th Foot were converted to Rifle Regiments in 1881, while The King's Royal Rifle Corps and Rifle Brigade each had four Regular battalions.

1881 *(General Order 41)*

1st Foot	The Lothian Regiment (Royal Scots)
2nd Foot	The Royal West Surrey Regiment (The Queen's)
3rd Foot	The Kentish Regiment (The Buffs)
4th Foot	The Royal Lancaster Regiment (The King's Own)
5th Foot	The Northumberland Fusiliers
6th Foot	The Royal Warwickshire Regiment
7th Foot	The City of London Regiment (Royal Fusiliers)
8th Foot	The Liverpool Regiment (The King's)
9th Foot	The Norfolk Regiment
10th Foot	The Lincolnshire Regiment
11th Foot	The Devonshire Regiment
12th Foot	The Suffolk Regiment
13th Foot	The Somersetshire Regiment (Prince Albert's Light Infantry)
14th Foot	The West Yorkshire Regiment (Prince of Wales's Own)
15th Foot	The East Yorkshire Regiment
16th Foot	The Bedfordshire Regiment
17th Foot	The Leicestershire Regiment
18th Foot	The Royal Irish Regiment
19th Foot	The North Yorkshire Regiment (Princess of Wales's Own)
20th Foot	The Lancashire Fusiliers
21st Foot	The Royal Scots Fusiliers
22nd Foot	The Cheshire Regiment

4

ORDER OF PRECEDENCE, 1881

1881 *(General Order 70)*

The Royal Scots (Lothian Regiment)
The Queen's (Royal West Surrey Regiment)
The Buffs (East Kent Regiment)
The King's Own (Royal Lancaster Regiment)
The Northumberland Fusiliers
The Royal Warwickshire Regiment
The Royal Fusiliers (City of London Regiment)
The King's (Liverpool Regiment)
The Norfolk Regiment
The Lincolnshire Regiment
The Devonshire Regiment
The Suffolk Regiment
Prince Albert's Light Infantry (Somersetshire Regiment)
The Prince of Wales's Own (West Yorkshire Regiment)
The East Yorkshire Regiment
The Bedfordshire Regiment ('Hertfordshire' added in *1919*)
The Leicestershire Regiment
The Royal Irish Regiment
The Princess of Wales's Own (Yorkshire Regiment)
The Lancashire Fusiliers
The Royal Scots Fusiliers
The Cheshire Regiment

1881 *(General Order 41)*

23rd Foot	The Royal Welsh Fusiliers
24th Foot	The South Wales Borderers
25th Foot	The York Regiment (King's Own Borderers)
26th/90th Foot	The Scotch Rifles (Cameronians)
27th/108th Foot	The Royal Inniskilling Fusiliers
28th/61st Foot	The Gloucestershire Regiment
29th/36th Foot	The Worcestershire Regiment
30th/59th Foot	The West Lancashire Regiment
31st/70th Foot	The East Surrey Regiment
32nd/46th Foot	The Duke of Cornwall's Light Infantry
33rd/76th Foot	The Halifax Regiment (Duke of Wellington's)
34th/55th Foot	The Cumberland Regiment
35th/107th Foot	The Royal Sussex Regiment
37th/67th Foot	The Hampshire Regiment
38th/80th Foot	The North Staffordshire Regiment
39th/54th Foot	The Dorsetshire Regiment
40th/82nd Foot	The South Lancashire Regiment (Prince of Wales's Volunteers)
41st/69th Foot	The Welsh Regiment
42nd/73rd Foot	The Royal Highlanders (Black Watch)
43rd/52nd Foot	The Oxfordshire Light Infantry
44th/56th Foot	The Essex Regiment
45th/95th Foot	The Derbyshire Regiment (Sherwood Foresters)
47th/81st Foot	The North Lancashire Regiment
48th/58th Foot	The Northamptonshire Regiment
49th/66th Foot	The Berkshire Regiment (Princess Charlotte of Wales's)
50th/97th Foot	The Royal West Kent Regiment (Queen's Own)
51st/105th Foot	The South Yorkshire Regiment (King's Own Light Infantry)
53rd/85th Foot	The Shropshire Regiment (King's Light Infantry)
57th/77th Foot	The Middlesex Regiment (Duke of Cambridge's Own)
60th Foot	The King's Royal Rifle Corps
62nd/99th Foot	The Wiltshire Regiment (Duke of Edinburgh's)
63rd/96th Foot	The Manchester Regiment
64th/98th Foot	The South Staffordshire Regiment (Prince of Wales's)
65th/84th Foot	The York and Lancaster Regiment
68th/106th Foot	The Durham Light Infantry
71st/74th Foot	The Highland Light Infantry
72nd/78th Foot	The Seaforth Highlanders
75th/92nd Foot	The Gordon Highlanders
79th Foot	The Queen's Own Cameron Highlanders
83rd/86th Foot	The Royal Irish Rifles
87th/89th Foot	The Royal Irish Fusiliers (Princess Victoria's)

1881 *(General Order 70)*

The Royal Welsh Fusiliers
The South Wales Borderers
The King's Own Borderers ('Scottish' added in *1887*)
The Cameronians (Scottish Rifles)
The Royal Inniskilling Fusiliers
The Gloucestershire Regiment
The Worcestershire Regiment
The East Lancashire Regiment
The East Surrey Regiment
The Duke of Cornwall's Light Infantry
The Duke of Wellington's (West Riding Regiment)
The Border Regiment
The Royal Sussex Regiment
The Hampshire Regiment
The South Staffordshire Regiment
The Dorsetshire Regiment
The Prince of Wales's Volunteers (South Lancashire Regiment)
The Welsh Regiment
The Black Watch (Royal Highlanders)
The Oxfordshire Light Infantry ('Buckinghamshire' added in *1908*)
The Essex Regiment
The Sherwood Foresters (Derbyshire Regiment) ('Nottinghamshire' added in *1902*)
The Loyal North Lancashire Regiment
The Northamptonshire Regiment
Princess Charlotte of Wales's (Berkshire Regiment) ('Royal' added in *1885*)
The Queen's Own (Royal West Kent Regiment)
The King's Own Light Infantry (South Yorkshire Regiment)
The King's Light Infantry (Shropshire Regiment)
The Duke of Cambridge's Own (Middlesex Regiment)
The King's Royal Rifle Corps
The Duke of Edinburgh's (Wiltshire Regiment)
The Manchester Regiment
The Prince of Wales's (North Staffordshire Regiment)
The York and Lancaster Regiment
The Durham Light Infantry
The Highland Light Infantry
The Seaforth Highlanders (Ross-shire Buffs, Duke of Albany's)
The Gordon Highlanders
The Queen's Own Cameron Highlanders
The Royal Irish Rifles
Princess Victoria's (The Royal Irish Fusiliers)

1881 *(General Order 41)*

88th/94th Foot	The Connaught Rangers
91st/93rd Foot	The Sutherland and Argyll Highlanders (Princess Louise's)
100th/109th Foot	The Prince of Wales's Royal Canadian Regiment
101st/104th Foot	The Royal Munster Fusiliers
102nd/103rd Foot	The Royal Dublin Fusiliers
	The Rifle Brigade (Prince Consort's Own)

NOTE

In 1920 infantry regiments were given the option of changing their titles and the great majority did so, reversing the pre-war order. Some adopted a new style and even a new name, e.g: The Royal Scots (The Royal Regiment); The Queen's Royal Regiment (West Surrey); The King's Own Royal Regiment (Lancaster); The Bedfordshire and Hertfordshire Regiment; The Green Howards (Alexandra, Princess of Wales's Own Yorkshire Regiment); The Royal Welch Fusiliers; The Welch Regiment; The Loyal Regiment (North Lancashire); The Royal Ulster Rifles.

1881 *(General Order 70)*

The Connaught Rangers
Princess Louise's (Argyll and Sutherland Highlanders) *(1882)*
The Prince of Wales's Leinster Regiment (Royal Canadians)
The Royal Munster Fusiliers
The Royal Dublin Fusiliers
The Prince Consort's Own (Rifle Brigade)

5

ORDER OF PRECEDENCE, 1983

The Life Guards and The Blues and Royals
Royal Horse Artillery
Royal Armoured Corps
  1st The Queen's Dragoon Guards
  The Royal Scots Dragoon Guards (Carabiniers and Greys)
  4th/7th Royal Dragoon Guards
  5th Royal Inniskilling Dragoon Guards
  The Queen's Own Hussars
  The Queen's Royal Irish Hussars
  9th/12th Royal Lancers (Prince of Wales's)
  The Royal Hussars (Prince of Wales's Own)
  13th/18th Royal Hussars (Queen Mary's Own)
  14th/20th King's Hussars
  15th/19th The King's Royal Hussars
  16th/5th The Queen's Royal Lancers
  17th/21st Lancers
  Royal Tank Regiment
Royal Regiment of Artillery
Corps of Royal Engineers
Royal Corps of Signals
Grenadier Guards
Coldstream Guards
Scots Guards
Irish Guards
Welsh Guards
The Royal Scots (The Royal Regiment)
The Queen's Regiment
The King's Own Royal Border Regiment

The Royal Regiment of Fusiliers
The King's Regiment
The Royal Anglian Regiment
The Devonshire and Dorset Regiment
The Light Infantry
The Prince of Wales's Own Regiment of Yorkshire
The Green Howards (Alexandra, Princess of Wales's Own Yorkshire Regiment)
The Royal Highland Fusiliers (Princess Margaret's Own Glasgow and Ayrshire Regiment)
The Cheshire Regiment
The Royal Welch Fusiliers
The Royal Regiment of Wales (24th/41st Foot)
The King's Own Scottish Borderers
(The Cameronians (Scottish Rifles))
The Royal Irish Rangers (27th (Inniskilling) 83rd and 87th)
The Gloucestershire Regiment
The Worcestershire and Sherwood Foresters Regiment (29th/45th Foot)
The Queen's Lancashire Regiment
The Duke of Wellington's Regiment (West Riding)
The Royal Hampshire Regiment
The Staffordshire Regiment (The Prince of Wales's)
The Black Watch (Royal Highland Regiment)
The Duke of Edinburgh's Royal Regiment (Berkshire and Wiltshire)
(The York and Lancaster Regiment)
Queen's Own Highlanders (Seaforth and Camerons)
The Gordon Highlanders
The Argyll and Sutherland Highlanders (Princess Louise's)
The Parachute Regiment
The Brigade of Gurkhas
The Royal Green Jackets
Special Air Service Regiment
Army Air Corps
Royal Army Chaplains' Department
Royal Corps of Transport
Royal Army Medical Corps
Royal Army Ordnance Corps
Corps of Royal Electrical and Mechanical Engineers
Corps of Royal Military Police
Royal Army Pay Corps
Royal Army Veterinary Corps
Military Provost Staff Corps
Royal Army Educational Corps
Royal Army Dental Corps
Royal Pioneer Corps

Intelligence Corps
Army Physical Training Corps
Army Catering Corps
Army Legal Corps
Queen Alexandra's Royal Army Nursing Corps
Women's Royal Army Corps

NOTES

1 Royal Horse Artillery. When on parade with their guns, to take the right and march at the head of the Household Cavalry.
2 The new Divisions take precedence according to their senior Regiment, viz: Guards, Scottish, Queen's, King's, Prince of Wales's, Light.
3 Royal Marines. When parading with the Army, to take precedence after The Duke of Edinburgh's Royal Regiment (Berkshire and Wiltshire) — viz: 49th/62nd.
4 The Territorial Army takes precedence in order of arms as for the Regular Army, except that the Royal Monmouthshire Royal Engineers (Militia), and the Honourable Artillery Company take the right of the Territorial line.
5 Regiments shown in parentheses were disbanded in 1968 but, according to precedent, remain in the Army List for 40 years from that date.

B

1
THE INFANTRY REGIMENTS BY NUMBER AND DESIGNATION

2
THE ROYAL REGIMENTS AND CORPS

3
THE PROCESS OF AMALGAMATION AND DISBANDMENT
1881 - 1971

The long march of the British Army has been reflected in a constantly shifting pattern and in periodic changes in the anatomy and designation of Regiments and Corps: in 1751 the introduction of consecutive numbering in the Infantry of the Line; in 1881 the ending of the numerical system and the introduction of the two-battalion regiment; in 1922 the disbanding of the old Irish regiments and the first Cavalry amalgamations; and since 1946 a complete restructuring of the whole Army.

The following Section presents three tables which illustrate this constantly shifting process:

1. The Infantry of the Line, showing the numerical sequence which continued until the end of June 1881 and the subsequent territorial and other designations which were introduced by General Order 41 of 1 July of that year. For further comparison and cross-references see Section C and the Orders of Precedence in Section A.

2. The Royal Regiments and Corps showing the dates on which the original distinction was conferred, and the result of the amalgamations of 1881, 1922 and of the post-1946 period.

3. The processes of amalgamation and disbandment of Regiments and Corps since 1881.

1

THE INFANTRY REGIMENTS BY NUMBER
AND DESIGNATION

**NUMBERED
UNTIL 1881**

NAMED AS AT 1947

By 1948 all regiments were reduced to a single battalion.

1st	The Royal Scots (The Royal Regiment)
2nd	The Queen's Royal Regiment (West Surrey)
3rd	The Buffs (Royal East Kent Regiment)
4th	The King's Own Royal Regiment (Lancaster)
5th	The Royal Northumberland Fusiliers
6th	The Royal Warwickshire Regiment (Fusiliers, 1963)
7th	The Royal Fusiliers (City of London Regiment)
8th	The King's Regiment (Liverpool)
9th	The Royal Norfolk Regiment
10th	The Royal Lincolnshire Regiment
11th	The Devonshire Regiment
12th	The Suffolk Regiment
13th	The Somerset Light Infantry (Prince Albert's)
14th	The West Yorkshire Regiment (The Prince of Wales's Own)
15th	The East Yorkshire Regiment (The Duke of York's Own)
16th	The Bedfordshire and Hertfordshire Regiment
17th	The Royal Leicestershire Regiment
18th	(The Royal Irish Regiment, *disbanded* 1922)
19th	The Green Howards
	(Alexandra, Princess of Wales's Own Yorkshire Regiment)
20th	The Lancashire Fusiliers
21st	The Royal Scots Fusiliers
22nd	The Cheshire Regiment
23rd	The Royal Welch Fusiliers
24th	The South Wales Borderers
25th	The King's Own Scottish Borderers

Two Battalions each (for 1st–25th)

26th	1st Bn, The Cameronians (Scottish Rifles)
27th	1st Bn, The Royal Inniskilling Fusiliers
28th	1st Bn, The Gloucestershire Regiment
29th	1st Bn, The Worcestershire Regiment
30th	1st Bn, The East Lancashire Regiment
31st	1st Bn, The East Surrey Regiment

NUMBERED UNTIL 1881	NAMED AS AT 1947
32nd	1st Bn, The Duke of Cornwall's Light Infantry
33rd	1st Bn, The Duke of Wellington's Regiment (West Riding)
34th	1st Bn, The Border Regiment
35th	1st Bn, The Royal Sussex Regiment
36th	2nd Bn, The Worcestershire Regiment
37th	1st Bn, The Royal Hampshire Regiment
38th	1st Bn, The South Staffordshire Regiment
39th	1st Bn, The Dorset Regiment
40th	1st Bn, The South Lancashire Regiment (The Prince of Wales's Volunteers)
41st	1st Bn, The Welch Regiment
42nd	1st Bn, The Black Watch (Royal Highland Regiment)
43rd	1st Bn, The Oxfordshire and Buckinghamshire Light Infantry
44th	1st Bn, The Essex Regiment
45th	1st Bn, The Sherwood Foresters (Nottinghamshire and Derbyshire Regiment)
46th	2nd Bn, The Duke of Cornwall's Light Infantry
47th	1st Bn, The Loyal Regiment (North Lancashire)
48th	1st Bn, The Northamptonshire Regiment
49th	1st Bn, The Royal Berkshire Regiment (Princess Charlotte of Wales's)
50th	1st Bn, The Queen's Own Royal West Kent Regiment
51st	1st Bn, The King's Own Yorkshire Light Infantry
52nd	2nd Bn, The Oxfordshire and Buckinghamshire Light Infantry
53rd	1st Bn, The King's Shropshire Light Infantry
54th	2nd Bn, The Dorset Regiment
55th	2nd Bn, The Border Regiment
56th	2nd Bn, The Essex Regiment
57th	1st Bn, The Middlesex Regiment (Duke of Cambridge's Own)
58th	2nd Bn, The Northamptonshire Regiment
59th	2nd Bn, The East Lancashire Regiment
60th	The King's Royal Rifle Corps (*two Battalions*)
61st	2nd Bn, The Gloucestershire Regiment
62nd	1st Bn, The Wiltshire Regiment (Duke of Edinburgh's)
63rd	1st Bn, The Manchester Regiment
64th	1st Bn, The North Staffordshire Regiment (The Prince of Wales's)
65th	1st Bn, The York and Lancaster Regiment
66th	2nd Bn, The Royal Berkshire Regiment (Princess Charlotte of Wales's)

NUMBERED UNTIL 1881	NAMED AS AT 1947
67th	2nd Bn, The Royal Hampshire Regiment
68th	1st Bn, The Durham Light Infantry
69th	2nd Bn, The Welch Regiment
70th	2nd Bn, The East Surrey Regiment
71st	1st Bn, The Highland Light Infantry (City of Glasgow Regiment)
72nd	1st Bn, Seaforth Highlanders (Ross-shire Buffs, The Duke of Albany's)
73rd	2nd Bn, The Black Watch (Royal Highland Regiment)
74th	2nd Bn, The Highland Light Infantry (City of Glasgow Regiment)
75th	1st Bn, The Gordon Highlanders
76th	2nd Bn, The Duke of Wellington's Regiment (West Riding)
77th	2nd Bn, The Middlesex Regiment (Duke of Cambridge's Own)
78th	2nd Bn, Seaforth Highlanders (Ross-shire Buffs, The Duke of Albany's)
79th	The Queen's Own Cameron Highlanders (*two Battalions*)
80th	2nd Bn, The South Staffordshire Regiment
81st	2nd Bn, The Loyal Regiment (North Lancashire)
82nd	2nd Bn, The South Lancashire Regiment (The Prince of Wales's Volunteers)
83rd	1st Bn, The Royal Ulster Rifles (*formerly* The Royal Irish Rifles)
84th	2nd Bn, The York and Lancaster Regiment
85th	2nd Bn, The King's Shropshire Light Infantry
86th	2nd Bn, The Royal Ulster Rifles (*formerly* The Royal Irish Rifles)
87th	1st Bn, The Royal Irish Fusiliers (Princess Victoria's)
88th	(1st Bn, The Connaught Rangers, *disbanded* 1922)
89th	2nd Bn, The Royal Irish Fusiliers (Princess Victoria's)
90th	2nd Bn, The Cameronians (Scottish Rifles)
91st	1st Bn, The Argyll and Sutherland Highlanders (Princess Louise's)
92nd	2nd Bn, The Gordon Highlanders
93rd	2nd Bn, The Argyll and Sutherland Highlanders (Princess Louise's)
94th	(2nd Bn, The Connaught Rangers, *disbanded* 1922)
95th	2nd Bn, The Sherwood Foresters (Nottinghamshire and Derbyshire Regiment)
96th	2nd Bn, The Manchester Regiment
97th	2nd Bn, The Queen's Own Royal West Kent Regiment
98th	2nd Bn, The North Staffordshire Regiment (The Prince of Wales's)

NUMBERED UNTIL 1881	NAMED AS AT 1947
99th	2nd Bn, The Wiltshire Regiment (Duke of Edinburgh's)
100th	(1st Bn, The Prince of Wales's Leinster Regiment (Royal Canadians), *disbanded* 1922)
101st	(1st Bn, The Royal Munster Fusiliers, *disbanded* 1922)
102nd	(1st Bn, The Royal Dublin Fusiliers, *disbanded* 1922)
103rd	(2nd Bn, The Royal Dublin Fusiliers, *disbanded* 1922)
104th	(2nd Bn, The Royal Munster Fusiliers, *disbanded* 1922)
105th	2nd Bn, The King's Own Yorkshire Light Infantry
106th	2nd Bn, The Durham Light Infantry
107th	2nd Bn, The Royal Sussex Regiment
108th	2nd Bn, The Royal Inniskilling Fusiliers
109th	(2nd Bn, The Prince of Wales's Leinster Regiment (Royal Canadians), *disbanded* 1922)
(previously 95th)	The Rifle Brigade (Prince Consort's Own) (*two Battalions*)

2

THE ROYAL REGIMENTS AND CORPS
(with dates of honour)

HOUSEHOLD CAVALRY

The Life Guards	1660
The Royal Horse Guards (The Blues)	1661

ROYAL HORSE ARTILLERY   1793

CAVALRY OF THE LINE

1st King's Dragoon Guards	1714
The Queen's Bays (2nd Dragoon Guards)	1727
4th Royal Irish Dragoon Guards	1788
1st (Royal Dragoons) — *retitled* The Royal Dragoons (1st Dragoons), 1961	1683
Royal Scots Greys (2nd Dragoons)	1692
3rd The King's Own Hussars	1714
4th Queen's Own Hussars	1788
5th Royal Irish Lancers (*disbanded* 1799, *re-formed* 1858)	1689
7th Queen's Own Hussars	1727
8th King's Royal Irish Hussars	1777
9th Queen's Royal Lancers	1830
10th Royal Hussars	1811
11th Hussars (Prince Albert's Own). *By special dispensation of Queen Victoria*	1840
12th Royal Lancers (Prince of Wales's)	1817
14th King's Hussars	1830
15th The King's Hussars	1766
16th The Queen's Lancers	1766
18th Royal Hussars (Queen Mary's Own)	1805 (*disbanded*); *then* 1919
19th Royal Hussars (Queen Alexandra's Own)	1908

(as a result of amalgamation, at dates shown)

1st The Queen's Dragoon Guards	1959
Royal Scots Dragoon Guards	1971
4th/7th Royal Dragoon Guards	1936
5th Royal Inniskilling Dragoon Guards	1935
The Queen's Own Hussars	1958
The Queen's Royal Irish Hussars	1958
9th/12th Royal Lancers (Prince of Wales's)	1960

The Royal Hussars (Prince of Wales's Own)	1969
13th/18th Royal Hussars (Queen Mary's Own)	1922
14th/20th King's Hussars	1922
15th/19th The King's Royal Hussars	1922
16th/5th The Queen's Royal Lancers	1922

ROYAL TANK REGIMENT (*on formation of* Royal Armoured Corps)   1939

ROYAL REGIMENT OF ARTILLERY   1716

FOOT GUARDS

Grenadier Guards	1660
Coldstream Guards	1661
Scots Guards	1660
Irish Guards	1900
Welsh Guards	1915

INFANTRY OF THE LINE

The Royal Scots (The Royal Regiment)	1684
The Queen's Royal Regiment (West Surrey)	1703
The King's Own Royal Regiment (Lancaster)	1715
The Royal Warwickshire Regiment – *retitled* Royal Warwickshire Fusiliers, 1963	1832
The Royal Fusiliers (City of London Regiment)	1685
The King's Regiment (Liverpool)	1716
The Somerset Light Infantry (Prince Albert's).	1842
By special dispensation of Queen Victoria	
The Royal Irish Regiment – *disbanded* 1922	1695
The Royal Scots Fusiliers	1712
The Royal Welch Fusiliers	1712
The King's Own Scottish Borderers	1805
The Royal Inniskilling Fusiliers	1881
The Royal Sussex Regiment	1832
The Black Watch (Royal Highland Regiment)	1758
The Royal Berkshire Regiment (Princess Charlotte of Wales's)	1885
The Queen's Own Royal West Kent Regiment	1831
The King's Own Yorkshire Light Infantry	1821
The King's Shropshire Light Infantry	1881
The King's Royal Rifle Corps	1755
The Queen's Own Cameron Highlanders	1873
The Royal Irish Rifles – *retitled* The Royal Ulster Rifles, 1921	1881
The Royal Irish Fusiliers	1827
The Leinster Regiment (Royal Canadians) – *disbanded* 1922	1881
The Royal Munster Fusiliers – *disbanded* 1922	1881
The Royal Dublin Fusiliers – *disbanded* 1922	1881

(added at dates shown)

The Buffs (Royal East Kent Regiment)	1935
The Royal Northumberland Fusiliers	1935
The Royal Norfolk Regiment	1935
The Royal Lincolnshire Regiment	1946
The Royal Leicestershire Regiment	1946
The Royal Hampshire Regiment	1946

(as a result of amalgamation, at dates shown):

The Queen's Regiment	1966
The King's Own Royal Border Regiment	1959
The King's Regiment	1958
The Royal Regiment of Fusiliers	1968
The Royal Anglian Regiment	1964
The Royal Highland Fusiliers	1959
The Royal Regiment of Wales (24th/41st Foot)	1969
The Royal Irish Rangers (27th Inniskilling, 83rd and 87th)	1968
The Queen's Lancashire Regiment	1958
The Duke of Edinburgh's Royal Regiment (Berkshire and Wiltshire)	1959
Queen's Own Highlanders (Seaforth and Camerons)	1961
The Royal Green Jackets	1966

CORPS

Corps of Royal Engineers	1787
Royal Flying Corps	1912
Royal Corps of Signals	1920
Royal Tank Corps	1923
Royal Army Chaplains' Department	1919
Royal Army Service Corps – *retitled* Royal Corps of Transport, 1965	1918
Royal Army Medical Corps	1898
Royal Army Ordnance Corps	1918
Royal Army Pay Corps	1920
Royal Army Veterinary Corps	1918

(added at dates shown):

Royal Armoured Corps	1939
Corps of Royal Electrical and Mechanical Engineers	1942
Corps of Royal Military Police	1946
Royal Army Educational Corps	1946
Royal Army Dental Corps	1946
Royal Pioneer Corps	1946
Queen Alexandra's Royal Army Nursing Corps	1949
Women's Royal Army Corps	1949

3

THE PROCESS OF AMALGAMATION AND DISBANDMENT 1881-1971

AMALGAMATIONS AND NEW TITLES
(in order of precedence of senior regiments)

CAVALRY

1st Life Guards
2nd Life Guards — **The Life Guards, 1922**

Royal Horse Guards
Royal Dragoons — **The Blues and Royals, 1969**

1st King's Dragoon Guards
2nd Dragoon Guards (The Bays) — **Queen's Dragoon Guards, 1959**

3rd Dragoon Guards
6th Dragoon Guards — 3rd/6th Dragoon Guards, **1922**   3rd Dragoon Guards

4th Dragoon Guards
7th Dragoon Guards — 4th/7th Dragoon Guards, **1922**

5th Dragoon Guards
6th (Inniskilling) Dragoons — 5th/6th Dragoons, **1922**

3rd Hussars
7th Hussars — **Queen's Own Hussars, 1958**

4th Hussars
8th Hussars — **Queen's Royal Irish Hussars, 1958**

5th Lancers
16th Lancers — **16th/5th Lancers, 1922**

9th Lancers
12th Lancers — **9th/12th Lancers, 1960**

3

THE PROCESS OF AMALGAMATION AND DISBANDMENT 1881-1971

(The Carabiniers), **1928**   Carabiniers
Royal Scots Greys ─┐ **Royal Scots Dragoon Guards, 1971**

4th/7th Royal Dragoon Guards, 1936

5th Inniskilling Dragoon Guards, **1927**   **5th Royal Inniskilling Dragoon Guards, 1935**

10th Hussars 11th Hussars	**Royal Hussars, 1969**
13th Hussars 18th Hussars	**13th/18th Hussars, 1922**
14th Hussars 20th Hussars	**14th/20th Hussars, 1922**
15th Hussars 19th Hussars	**15th/19th Hussars, 1922**
17th Lancers 21st Lancers	**17th/21st Lancers, 1922**

INFANTRY

2nd Foot 31st/70th Foot	Queen's Royal (West Surrey) East Surrey, **1881**	Queen's Royal Surrey, **1959**
3rd Foot 50th/97th Foot	Buffs Royal West Kent, **1881**	Queen's Own Buffs, **1961**
35th/107th Foot	Royal Sussex, **1881**	
57th/77th Foot	Middlesex, **1881**	
4th Foot 34th/55th Foot	King's Own Border, **1881**	**King's Own Royal Border, 1959**
5th Foot 6th Foot 7th Foot 20th Foot	Royal Northumberland Fusiliers Royal Warwickshire (Fusiliers, **1963**) Royal Fusiliers Lancashire Fusiliers	
8th Foot 63rd/96th Foot	King's (Liverpool) Manchester, **1881**	King's (Manchester and Liverpool), **1958**

*Queen's, 1966 (4th Battalion disbanded 1970)

*Royal Regiment of Fusiliers, 1968 (4th Battalion disbanded 1969)

King's, 1968

*A 'large' Regiment

9th Foot	Royal Norfolk	1st East Anglian (Royal Norfolk and Suffolk) **1959**
12th Foot	Suffolk	
10th Foot	Royal Lincolnshire	2nd East Anglian (Duchess of
48th/58th Foot	Northamptonshire, **1881**	
16th Foot	Bedfordshire (and Herts, **1919**)	3rd East Anglian (16th/44th) **1958**
44th/56th Foot	Essex, **1881**	
17th Foot	Royal Leicestershire	
11th Foot	Devonshire	**Devonshire and Dorset, 1958**
39th/54th Foot	Dorset, **1881**	
13th Foot	Somerset L. I.	Somerset and Cornwall L.I., **1959**
32nd/46th Foot	Duke of Cornwall's L.I., **1881**	
51st/105th Foot	King's Own Yorkshire L.I., **1881**	
53rd/85th Foot	King's Shropshire L.I., **1881**	
68th/106th Foot	Durham L.I., **1881**	
14th Foot	West Yorkshire	
15th Foot	East Yorkshire	
21st Foot	Royal Scots Fusiliers	**Royal Highland Fusiliers, 1959**
71st/74th Foot	Highland L.I., **1881**	
24th Foot	South Wales Borderers	
41st/69th Foot	Welch, **1881**	
27th/108th Foot	Royal Inniskilling Fusiliers, **1881**	***Royal Irish Rangers**
83rd/86th Foot	Royal Ulster Rifles, **1881, 1921**	
87th/89th Foot	Royal Irish Fusiliers, **1881**	
29th/36th Foot	Worcestershire, **1881**	
45th/95th Foot	Sherwood Foresters, **1881**	

*A 'large' Regiment

Gloucester's Own) **1960**   ***Royal Anglian, 1964 (4th Battalion disbanded 1970)**

*Light Infantry, 1968 (4th Battalion disbanded 1968)

Prince of Wales's Own Regiment of Yorkshire, 1958

Royal Regiment of Wales (24th/41st Foot), 1969

(27th (Inniskilling), 83rd and 87th), 1968 (3rd Battalion disbanded 1970)

Worcestershire and Sherwood Foresters (29th/45th Foot), 1970

*A 'large' Regiment

30th/59th Foot	East Lancashire, **1881**	⎤ **Lancashire, 1958**	⎤
40th/82nd Foot	South Lancashire, **1881**	⎦	
47th/81st Foot	Loyal North Lancashire, **1881**		⎦
38th/80th Foot	South Staffordshire, **1881**	⎤ **Staffordshire, 1959**	
64th/98th Foot	North Staffordshire, **1881**	⎦	
43rd/52nd Foot	Oxfordshire L.I., **1881** (and Bucks, **1908**)	⎤	
60th Foot	King's Royal Rifle Corps	⎦	
	Rifle Brigade		
49th/66th Foot	Royal Berkshire, **1881**	⎤ **Duke of Edinburgh's Royal, 1959**	
62nd/99th Foot	Wiltshire, **1881**	⎦	
72nd/78th Foot	Seaforth Highlanders, **1881**	⎤ **Queen's Own Highlanders, 1961**	
79th Foot	Cameron Highlanders, **1881**	⎦	

Queen's Lancashire, 1970

1st Green Jackets (43rd and 52nd), **1958**
2nd Green Jackets (K.R.R.C.), **1958**   ***Royal Green Jackets, 1966**
3rd Green Jackets (The Rifle Brigade), **1958**

*A 'large' Regiment

DISBANDMENTS

18th Foot	Royal Irish	**1922**
26th/90th Foot	Cameronians, **1881**	**1968**
65th/84th Foot	York and Lancaster, **1881**	**1968**
88th/94th Foot	Connaught Rangers, **1881**	**1922**
100th/109th Foot	Leinster, **1881**	**1922**
101st/104th Foot	Royal Munster Fusiliers, **1881**	**1922**
102nd/103rd Foot	Royal Dublin Fusiliers, **1881**	**1922**

NOTE

This following table shows the reduction (by Regiments, with Battalions in brackets) of the Regular Army as a result of amalgamation and disbandment between 1861 and 1971:

	1861		**1881**		**1939**		**1971**
Household Cavalry	3	to	3	to	2	to	2
Cavalry of the Line	28	to	28	to	20	to	13
Infantry of the Line*	110 (141)	to	69 (141)	to	64 (128)	to	33 (48)

NOTE

*(including Parachute Regiment and Brigade of Gurkhas)

(Regiments of Foot Guards increased from 3 to 5 during this period)

C

THE ANATOMY OF THE ARMY

The following Section presents the lineage of individual Regiments and Corps of the Regular Army from their date of raising until the present time. The entries are arranged in alphabetical order (for rank and seniority see Orders of Precedence in Section A), and are cross-referenced to the Spinal Column on pp. 61-5. Until 1751 the 'Marching Regiments of Foot' were known either by their Royal or distinctive title (e.g., The Highland Regiment) or by the name of their Colonel. In the individual entries only the names of original Colonels are shown, the regimental title subsequently changing with each change of command. A similar pattern was followed in the Cavalry of the Line. During the second half of the eighteenth century there was a constant and bewildering process by which regiments were raised, renumbered, disbanded, raised again and numbered again. In the individual entries this process has been simplified to avoid confusion, and to assist in identification.

Most of the modern service Corps have their origins in the period following the Crimean War and the abolition of the old Board of Ordnance in 1855. During the early formative years there was a curious policy which separated officers (under such group titles as 'Department' and 'Staff'), and other ranks (designated as 'Corps'). Under a Royal Warrant of 12 November 1869 a Control Department was introduced 'with a view to consolidating the Supply and Transport Services of Our Army, and of introducing a more effectual control over military expenditure, [so] that the various Departments now dealing with those services be consolidated into one Department to be entitled The Control Department.' It was organized into two executive sub-departments — viz., The Supply and Transport Sub-Department and The Pay Sub-Department — and acted as a kind of administrative sponge. It was not one of Cardwell's brightest inventions, and by Royal Warrant of 27 November 1875 it was abolished. The short-lived existence of this Control Department explains many of the changes of title in the individual entries of service Corps in the following Section.

THE ARGYLL AND SUTHERLAND HIGHLANDERS
(PRINCESS LOUISE'S*)
91st and 93rd

1794	98th (Argyllshire Highlanders) Foot	**1799**	93rd Highlanders
1796	*renumbered* 91st (Argyllshire Highlanders) Foot	**1861**	93rd (Sutherland Highlanders) Foot
1809	91st Foot		
1821	91st (Argyllshire) Foot		
1864	91st (Argyllshire) Highlanders		
1872	91st (Princess Louise's) Argyllshire Highlanders		

1881 (May)	The Princess Louise's (Sutherland and Argyll) Highlanders
1882 (July)	The Princess Louise's (Argyll and Sutherland) Highlanders
1920	The Argyll and Sutherland Highlanders (Princess Louise's)

*(1872) Princess Louise, Duchess of Argyll, fourth daughter of Queen Victoria

A regiment of the Scottish Division

ARMY AIR CORPS

1940 A Central Landing Establishment formed, consisting of No. 1 Parachute Training School and No. 1 Glider Training School

1941 Air Observation Post Squadron, Royal Artillery, formed

1942 Formation of The Army Air Corps (A.O.21) as an administrative centre for The Glider Pilot Regiment and The Parachute Regiment, both formed in this year

1944 The Special Air Service Regiment added as the third component of The Army Air Corps

1946 The Special Air Service Regiment disbanded

1947 The Special Air Service Regiment reconstituted

1949 The Parachute Regiment transferred from The Army Air Corps to Infantry of the Line (A.O.97)

1950 The Special Air Service Regiment constituted as a separate corps (A.O.66). Disbandment of The Army Air Corps

1957 Disbandment of The Glider Pilot Regiment. Re-formation of the present Army Air Corps (A.O.82) to include the Air Observation Post Squadrons, Royal Artillery. Corps organized into Divisional regiments of squadrons and independent 'support' squadrons and flights, serviced since 1973 by its own groundcrews

ARMY CATERING CORPS

Until the Second World War Army cooks were regimentally employed and carried on unit strengths, although an Army School of Cookery was established at Aldershot in **1920** (but *see also* footnote on p.45). In **1941**, however, all unit cooks were transferred to a single Corps which was set up by Army Order 35 and which controls their training, administration and deployment.

ARMY LEGAL CORPS

The Army Legal Service was renamed The Army Legal Corps on 1 November **1978**. Under the Directorate of Army Legal Services it fulfils two functions. Under *Service Law* it advises regimental officers and commanders on the rules of evidence and the preparation of cases for trial by court martial. It also edits the *Manual of Military Law*. Under *Civil Law* it provides a 'community' service to members of the Army in much the same way as solicitors in general practice, giving advice and assistance over a wide range of personal legal problems.

ARMY PHYSICAL TRAINING CORPS

Formed after the Crimean War as The Army Physical Training Staff, the title was changed to The Army Physical Training Corps by Army Order 165 of **1940**. The Corps provides instruction and assistance in every aspect of physical training and sporting recreation.

AUXILIARY TERRITORIAL SERVICE
See Women's Royal Army Corps

Formed under Royal Warrant on 9 September **1939**, the Service was disbanded in November **1954** (A.O.128) prior to the Regular establishment of the Women's Royal Army Corps (*q.v.*).

THE BEDFORDSHIRE AND HERTFORDSHIRE REGIMENT
16th

1688	Douglas's Regiment of Foot
1751	16th Foot
1782	16th (Buckinghamshire) Foot
1809	16th (Bedfordshire) Foot
1919	The Bedfordshire and Hertfordshire Regiment
1958	*amalgamated with* The Essex Regiment *to form* The 3rd East Anglian Regiment (16th/44th Foot)
1964	*redesignated* 3rd (16th/44th Foot) Battalion, The Royal Anglian Regiment
1968	*redesignated* 3rd Battalion, The Royal Anglian Regiment

THE BLACK WATCH (ROYAL HIGHLAND REGIMENT)
42nd and 73rd

1725	Independent Companies — The Black Watch	1758-62 1779-86	2nd Battalion 42nd (The Royal Highland) Foot
1739	The Highland Regiment of Foot	1786	73rd Highland Regiment of Foot
1751	The 42nd Foot	1809	73rd Foot
1758	42nd (The Royal Highland) Foot	1862	73rd (Perthshire) Foot
1861	42nd (The Royal Highland) Foot (The Black Watch)		

1881 The Black Watch (Royal Highlanders)
1934 The Black Watch (Royal Highland Regiment)

A regiment of the Scottish Division

THE BLUES AND ROYALS
(ROYAL HORSE GUARDS AND 1ST DRAGOONS)

Formed in 1969 by the amalgamation of The Royal Horse Guards (The Blues) and The Royal Dragoons (1st Dragoons).

THE BORDER REGIMENT
34th and 55th

1702	Lucas's Foot	1755	57th Foot
1751	34th Foot	1757	55th Foot
1782	34th (Cumberland) Foot	1782	55th (Westmoreland) Foot

1881 The Border Regiment
1959 *amalgamated with* The King's Own Royal Regiment (Lancaster) *to form* The King's Own Royal Border Regiment

THE BRIGADE OF GUARDS

Grenadier Guards
Coldstream Guards
Scots Guards
Irish Guards
Welsh Guards

Army Order 61, 1948

THE BRIGADE OF GURKHAS

(Formed by transfer from the Indian Army to the British establishment on 1 January **1948**)

2nd King Edward VII's Own Gurkha* Rifles (The Sirmoor Rifles) *(two battalions)*
6th Queen Elizabeth's Own Gurkha Rifles
7th Duke of Edinburgh's Own Gurkha Rifles *(two battalions)*
10th Princess Mary's Own Gurkha Rifles
The Queen's Gurkha Engineers *(affiliated to* The Corps of Royal Engineers, 1958)
The Queen's Gurkha Signals *(affiliated to* The Royal Corps of Signals, 1958)
The Gurkha Transport Regiment *(affiliated to* The Royal Corps of Transport, 1965)

* *Sometimes spelt* Goorkha

THE BUFFS (ROYAL EAST KENT REGIMENT)
3rd

1665	The Holland Regiment
1689	Prince George of Denmark's Regiment
1708	The Buffs
1751	3rd (*or* The Buffs) Foot
1782	3rd (East Kent - The Buffs) Foot
1881 (May)	The Kentish Regiment (The Buffs)
1881 (July)	The Buffs (East Kent Regiment)
1935	The Buffs (Royal East Kent Regiment)
1961	*amalgamated with* The Queen's Own Royal West Kent Regiment *to form* The Queen's Own Buffs, The Royal Kent Regiment
1966	*redesignated* 2nd Battalion, The Queen's Regiment

THE CAMERONIANS (SCOTTISH RIFLES)
26th and 90th

1689	The Earl of Angus's Regiment	**1794**	90th Perthshire Volunteers
1751	26th Foot ('The Cameronians')	**1815**	90th Perthshire Light Infantry
1786	26th Cameronian Regiment		

1881 (May)   The Scotch Rifles (Cameronians)
1881 (July)   The Cameronians (Scottish Rifles)
1968   *disbanded*

THE CHESHIRE REGIMENT
22nd

1689   Duke of Norfolk's Regiment of Foot
1751   22nd Foot
1782   22nd (The Cheshire) Foot
1881   The Cheshire Regiment

A regiment of the Prince of Wales's Division

COLDSTREAM GUARDS

1660   General Monk's Regiment of Foot (*also* 'The Coldstreamers')
1661   The Lord General's Regiment of Foot
1662   The Lord General's Regiment of Foot Guards
1670   The Coldstream Regiment of Footguards (*also* 2nd Foot Guards)
1817   The Coldstream Guards

A regiment of the Guards Division

THE CONNAUGHT RANGERS
88th and 94th

1760	88th (Royal Highland Volunteers) Foot		**1760**	94th (Royal Welsh Volunteers) Foot
1763	*disbanded*		**1763**	*disbanded*
1779	88th Foot		**1779**	94th Foot
1783	*disbanded*		**1783**	*disbanded*
1793	88th (Connaught Rangers) Foot		**1794**	94th (Irish) Foot
			1795	*disbanded*
			1803	94th (Scots Brigade) Foot
			1818	*disbanded*
			1823	94th Foot

1881 The Connaught Rangers
1922 *disbanded*

CORPS OF ROYAL ELECTRICAL AND MECHANICAL ENGINEERS

Formed under Army Order 70 of **1942** to provide specialist electrical and mechanical servicing and repairs which cannot be carried out within individual units. It also provides Light Aid Detachments (LADs) for units of The Royal Armoured Corps, and until **1973** serviced aircraft of The Army Air Corps. On its formation most of its personnel were transferred from its 'parent', The Royal Army Ordnance Corps, but included some specialists from RE and RASC (now RCT). The present title dates from Army Order 148 of **1949**.

CORPS OF ROYAL ENGINEERS

The Corps is one of the oldest in the British Army and can trace its origin to the formation of the Board of Ordnance in the fifteenth century. Its modern development is an interesting commentary on the process by which a military (officer) element was fused with a civilian (soldier) corps as exemplified in the 'departmentalism' of the nineteenth century.

1717 Constituted as a separate officer Corps of Engineers of the Board of Ordnance, taking precedence after the Royal Regiment of Artillery. 'Artificer Companies' remained civilian establishments.

1772 Formation of a Soldier Artificer Company at Gibraltar, the first permanent engineer soldiers of the Army.

1787 Corps of Royal Engineers given a Royal title. In the same year a Corps of Royal Military Artificers was formed. Officers were supplied by the Corps of Royal Engineers.

1797 The Gibraltar Company was absorbed into the new Corps.

1812 Title changed to Corps of Royal Sappers and Miners.

1855 On the abolition of the Board of Ordnance the officer Corps of Royal Engineers and the Corps of Royal Sappers and Miners were transferred to the control of the Commander-in-Chief.

1856 Corps of Royal Sappers and Miners absorbed into a single Corps of Royal Engineers.

1862 British officers and NCOs of the three Presidency Corps of the East India Company Engineer Corps transferred to the British establishment.

From this period until the end of the First World War the Royal Engineers were responsible for virtually every technical development and function of the Army, from communications, postal, and transportation (as opposed to transport) to military aviation. In **1912** the Royal Flying Corps (Military Wing) was formed (*q.v.*) and remained a Royal Engineer branch until the creation of The Royal Air Force in **1918**. In **1920** the Royal Corps of Signals was formed (*q.v.*) from the Royal Engineer Signal Service. And in **1965**, on the formation of The Royal Corps of Transport (*q.v.*), Royal Engineer Transportation and Movement Control Services were transferred to the new Corps. At the same period, responsibility for bomb disposal was shared with The Royal Army Ordnance Corps.

CORPS OF ROYAL MILITARY POLICE

The office of Provost-Marshal dates from the fifteenth century, which suggests that, if times change, soldiers do not. From the creation of the Standing Army, discipline, both ruthless and rigorous, was a matter for the Mutiny Act and regimental discretion. In **1885**, owing something, no doubt, to the Bow Street Horse Patrols which preceded the creation of the Metropolitan Police in **1829**, 15 cavalry NCOs were selected to act as Mounted Police. The experiment, especially in garrison towns, encouraged an increase in strength to nearly 150 within twenty years and to the formation of the Military Mounted Police. In **1885** the Military Foot Police was formed, and in **1926** the two elements were amalgamated to form the Corps of Military Police. The Royal title was granted under Army Order 167 of **1946**.

THE DEVONSHIRE REGIMENT
11th

1685	The Duke of Beaufort's Musketeers
1751	11th Foot
1782	11th (North Devonshire) Foot
1881	The Devonshire Regiment
1958	*amalgamated with* The Dorset Regiment *to form* The Devonshire and Dorset Regiment

THE DEVONSHIRE AND DORSET REGIMENT

Formed in 1958 by the amalgamation of The Devonshire Regiment and The Dorset Regiment

A regiment of the Prince of Wales's Division

THE DORSET REGIMENT
39th and 54th

1702	Coote's Regiment of Foot	**1755**	56th Foot
1751	39th Foot	**1757**	54th Foot
1782	39th (East Middlesex) Foot	**1782**	54th (West Norfolk) Foot
1807	39th (Dorsetshire) Foot		

1881	The Dorsetshire Regiment
1951	The Dorset Regiment
1958	*amalgamated with* The Devonshire Regiment *to form* The Devonshire and Dorset Regiment

THE ROYAL DRAGOONS
(1st DRAGOONS)

1661	The Tangier Horse
1683	The King's Own Royal Regiment of Dragoons
1690	The Royal Regiment of Dragoons
1751	The 1st (Royal) Dragoons
1961	The Royal Dragoons (1st Dragoons)
1969	*amalgamated with* The Royal Horse Guards (The Blues) *to form* The Blues and Royals (Royal Horse Guards and 1st Dragoons)

THE ROYAL SCOTS GREYS
(2nd DRAGOONS)

1681   A Regiment of Dragoons
1692   The Royal Regiment of Scots Dragoons (*unofficially* 'The Scots Greys')
1707   The Royal Regiment of North British Dragoons
1751   2nd Royal North British Dragoons
1786   2nd Royal North British Dragoons (Scots Greys)
1877   2nd Dragoons (Royal Scots Greys)
1921   The Royal Scots Greys (2nd Dragoons)
1971   *amalgamated with* 3rd Carabiniers (Prince of Wales's Dragoon Guards) *to form* The Royal Scots Dragoon Guards (Carabiniers and Greys)

THE INNISKILLINGS
(6th DRAGOONS)

1689   Cunningham's Regiment of Dragoons (*also known as* 'The Black Dragoons')
1751   6th (Inniskilling) Dragoons
1921   The Inniskillings (6th Dragoons)
1922   *amalgamated with* 5th Dragoon Guards *to form* 5th/6th Dragoons
1927   *redesignated* 5th Inniskilling Dragoon Guards
1935   *redesignated* 5th Royal Inniskilling Dragoon Guards

1st KING'S DRAGOON GUARDS

1685   The Queen's, or 2nd, Regiment of Horse
1714   The King's Own Regiment of Horse
1746   1st King's Dragoon Guards
1959   *amalgamated with* The Queen's Bays (2nd Dragoon Guards) *to form* 1st The Queen's Dragoon Guards

THE QUEEN'S* BAYS
(2nd DRAGOON GUARDS)

1685   Earl of Peterborough's Regiment of Horse
1688   The 3rd Regiment of Horse
1711   The Princess of Wales's Own Royal Regiment of Horse
1746   2nd Queen's Dragoon Guards
1872   2nd Dragoon Guards (Queen's Bays)
1921   The Queen's Bays (2nd Dragoon Guards)
1959   *amalgamated with* 1st King's Dragoon Guards *to form* 1st The Queen's Dragoon Guards

*(1727) Queen Caroline, wife of King George II

1st THE QUEEN'S DRAGOON GUARDS

Formed in 1959 by the amalgamation of 1st King's Dragoon Guards and The Queen's Bays (2nd Dragoon Guards)

3rd DRAGOON GUARDS
(PRINCE OF WALES'S*)

1685	The Earl of Plymouth's Regiment of Horse
1687	The 4th Regiment of Horse
1746	3rd Regiment of Dragoon Guards
1765	3rd (Prince of Wales's) Dragoon Guards
1922	*amalgamated with* The Carabiniers (6th Dragoon Guards) *to form* 3rd/6th Dragoon Guards
1928	*redesignated* 3rd Carabiniers (Prince of Wales's Dragoon Guards)
1971	*amalgamated with* The Royal Scots Greys (2nd Dragoons) *to form* The Royal Scots Dragoon Guards (Carabiniers and Greys)

(1765)   The future King George IV

3rd CARABINIERS
(PRINCE OF WALES'S DRAGOON GUARDS)

First formed in 1922 by the amalgamation of 3rd Dragoon Guards (Prince of Wales's) and The Carabiniers (6th Dragoon Guards) as 3rd/6th Dragoon Guards and redesignated in 1928 as 3rd Carabiniers (Prince of Wales's Dragoon Guards).

THE ROYAL SCOTS DRAGOON GUARDS
(CARABINIERS AND GREYS)

Formed in 1971, by the amalgation of 3rd Carabiniers (Prince of Wales's Dragoon Guards) and The Royal Scots Greys (2nd Dragoons).

4th ROYAL IRISH DRAGOON GUARDS

1685	The Earl of Arran's Cuirassiers
1690	The 5th Horse
1746	The 1st Irish Horse, or The Blue Horse
1788	4th (Royal Irish) Dragoon Guards
1921	4th Royal Irish Dragoon Guards
1922	*amalgamated with* 7th Dragoon Guards (Princess Royal's) *to form* 4th/7th Royal Dragoon Guards

4th/7th ROYAL DRAGOON GUARDS

Formed in 1922 by the amalgamation of 4th Royal Irish Dragoon Guards and 7th Dragoon Guards (Princess Royal's).

5th DRAGOON GUARDS
(PRINCESS CHARLOTTE OF WALES'S*)

1685	The Duke of Shrewsbury's Regiment of Horse
1687	The 6th Regiment of Horse
1717	The 2nd (*or* 'Green') Irish Horse
1784	5th Dragoon Guards
1804	5th (Princess Charlotte of Wales's) Dragoon Guards
1921	5th Dragoon Guards (Princess Charlotte of Wales's)
1922	*amalgamated with* The Inniskillings (6th Dragoons) *to form* 5th/6th Dragoons; *redesignated in* 1927 5th Inniskilling Dragoon Guards; *redesignated in* 1935 5th Royal Inniskilling Dragoon Guards

*(1804) Only daughter of the future King George IV

5th ROYAL INNISKILLING DRAGOON GUARDS

Formed in 1922 by amalgamation with The Inniskillings (6th Dragoons) as 5th/6th Dragoons; redesignated in 1927 5th Inniskilling Dragoon Guards; redesignated in 1935 5th Royal Inniskilling Dragoon Guards.

THE CARABINIERS
(6th DRAGOON GUARDS)

1685	The Queen Dowager's Regiment of Horse
1690	The 8th (*or* 9th) Regiment of Horse
1692	The First Regiment of Carabiniers
1745	The 3rd Irish Horse
1788	6th Regiment of Dragoon Guards
1826	6th Regiment of Dragoon Guards (Carabiniers)
1921	The Carabiniers (6th Dragoon Guards)
1922	*amalgamated with* 3rd Dragoon Guards (Prince of Wales's) *to form* 3rd/6th Dragoon Guards
1928	*redesignated* 3rd Carabiniers (Prince of Wales's) Dragoon Guards
1971	*amalgamated with* The Royal Scots Greys (2nd Dragoons) *to form* The Royal Scots Dragoon Guards (Carabiniers and Greys)

7th DRAGOON GUARDS
(PRINCESS ROYAL'S*)

1688	The Earl of Devonshire's Regiment of Horse, *or* The 10th Horse
1690	Schomberg's Horse, *also* The 8th Horse
1720	Ligonier's Horse
1746	The 4th (*or* 'Black') Irish Horse
1788	7th (The Princess Royal's) Dragoon Guards
1921	7th Dragoon Guards (Princess Royal's)
1922	*amalgamated with* 4th Royal Irish Dragoon Guards *to form* 4th/7th Royal Dragoon Guards

*Eldest daughter of King George III, later the Empress Frederick of Prussia

THE DUKE OF CORNWALL'S* LIGHT INFANTRY
32nd and 46th

1702	Fox's Regiment of Marines		**1741**	57th Foot
1704	Borr's Regiment of Marines		**1748**	*renumbered* 46th Foot
1715	32nd Foot		**1782**	46th (South Devonshire) Foot
1782	32nd (The Cornwall) Foot			
1858	32nd (Cornwall) Light Infantry			

1881	The Duke of Cornwall's Light Infantry
1959	*amalgamated with* The Somerset Light Infantry *to form* The Somerset and Cornwall Light Infantry
1968	*redesignated* 1st Battalion, The Light Infantry

(1881) Edward, Prince of Wales and Duke of Cornwall, the future King Edward VII

THE DUKE OF EDINBURGH'S ROYAL REGIMENT
(BERKSHIRE AND WILTSHIRE)

Formed in 1959 by the amalgamation of The Royal Berkshire Regiment (Princess Charlotte of Wales's) and The Wiltshire Regiment (Duke of Edinburgh's).

A regiment of the Prince of Wales's Division

THE DUKE OF WELLINGTON'S* REGIMENT
(WEST RIDING)
33rd and 76th

1702	The Earl of Huntingdon's Foot	**1756**	76th Foot
1751	33rd Foot	**1763**	*disbanded*
1782	33rd (1st York, West Riding) Foot	**1777**	76th (Macdonald's Highlanders) Foot
1853	33rd (Duke of Wellington's) Foot	**1784**	*disbanded*
		1787	76th (Hindoostan) Foot
		1812	76th Foot

1881 (May) The Halifax Regiment (Duke of Wellington's)
1881 (July) The Duke of Wellington's (West Riding Regiment)
1920 The Duke of Wellington's Regiment (West Riding)

A regiment of the King's Division

*(1853) The only regiment to bear the name of a commoner in its title

THE DURHAM LIGHT INFANTRY
68th and 106th

1756	2nd Bn, 23rd Royal Welsh Fusiliers	**1826**	2nd Bombay European Regiment
1758	68th Foot		(East India Company)
1782	68th (Durham) Foot	**1840**	2nd Bombay European Light Infantry
1812	68th (Durham - Light Infantry) Foot	**1858**	2nd Bombay Light Infantry
		1862	106th Bombay Light Infantry

1881 The Durham Light Infantry
1968 4th Battalion, The Light Infantry
1968 *disbanded* as 4th Battalion

THE EAST ANGLIAN BRIGADE

The Royal Norfolk Regiment
The Suffolk Regiment

amalgamated to form
1st East Anglian Regiment (Royal Norfolk and Suffolk), 1959

The Bedfordshire and Hertfordshire Regiment
The Essex Regiment

amalgamated to form
3rd East Anglian Regiment (16th/44th Foot), 1958

The Royal Lincolnshire Regiment
(*from* Midland Brigade)
The Northamptonshire Regiment

amalgamated to form
2nd East Anglian Regiment (Duchess of Gloucester's Own Royal Lincolnshire and Northamptonshire), 1960

Army Order 61, 1948

THE EAST ANGLIAN REGIMENT
See The East Anglian Brigade

THE EAST LANCASHIRE REGIMENT
30th and 59th

1689	Lord Castleton's Regiment of Foot	**1741**	59th Foot
1698	*disbanded*	**1748**	*renumbered* 48th Foot
1702	Sanderson's Regiment of Marines	**1756**	*renumbered* 61st Foot
1714	Willis's Regiment of Foot	**1757**	*renumbered* 59th Foot
1751	30th Foot	**1782**	59th (2nd Nottinghamshire) Foot
1782	30th (Cambridgeshire) Foot		

1881 (May) The West Lancashire Regiment
1881 (July) The East Lancashire Regiment
1958 *amalgamated with* The South Lancashire Regiment *to form* The Lancashire Regiment (Prince of Wales's Volunteers)
1970 *amalgamated with* The Loyal Regiment (North Lancashire) *to form* The Queen's Lancashire Regiment

THE EAST SURREY REGIMENT
31st and 70th

1702	Villier's Regiment of Marines	1756	2nd Bn, 31st Foot
1711	Goring's Marines	1758	70th Foot
1714	31st Foot	1782	70th (Surrey) Foot
1782	31st (Huntingdonshire) Foot	1812	70th (Glasgow Lowland) Regiment
		1825	70th (Surrey) Foot

1881	The East Surrey Regiment
1959	*amalgamated with* The Queen's Royal Regiment (West Surrey) *to form* The Queen's Royal Surrey Regiment
1966	*redesignated* 1st Battalion, The Queen's Regiment

THE EAST YORKSHIRE REGIMENT
(THE DUKE OF YORK'S* OWN)
15th

1685	Clifton's Regiment
1751	15th Foot
1782	15th (York, East Riding) Foot
1881	The East Yorkshire Regiment
1935	The East Yorkshire Regiment (The Duke of York's Own)
1958	*amalgamated with* The West Yorkshire Regiment (The Prince of Wales's Own) *to form* The Prince of Wales's Own Regiment of Yorkshire

(1935) Albert, Duke of York, second son of King George V, and later King George VI

THE ESSEX REGIMENT
44th and 56th

1741	55th Foot	1755	58th Foot
1748	*renumbered* 44th Foot	1756	*renumbered* 56th Foot
1782	44th (East Essex) Foot	1782	56th (West Essex) Foot

1881	The Essex Regiment
1958	*amalgamated with* The Bedfordshire and Hertfordshire Regiment *to form* The 3rd East Anglian Regiment (16th/44th Foot)
1968	*redesignated* 3rd Battalion, The Royal Anglian Regiment

THE FORESTER BRIGADE
(renamed from the previous Midland Brigade, 1962; *dispersed,* 1963)

The Royal Warwickshire Regiment (Fusiliers, 1963; *transferred to* Fusilier Brigade)
The Royal Lincolnshire Regiment (*to* East Anglian Brigade, 1957)
The Royal Leicestershire Regiment (*to* East Anglian Brigade, 1963)
The Sherwood Foresters (*to* Mercian Brigade, 1962)

Army Order 61, 1948

THE FUSILIER BRIGADE
(formed 1957)

The Royal Northumberland Fusiliers (*from* Yorkshire Brigade)
The Royal Fusiliers (City of London Regiment) (*from* Home Counties Brigade)
The Royal Warwickshire Fusiliers (*from* Forester Brigade, 1963)
The Lancashire Fusiliers (*from* Lancastrian Brigade)

GENERAL SERVICE CORPS

Formed under Army Order 19 of **1942** to provide a 'selection pool' for prospective officers before posting them to appropriate arms and services. Before the formation of the Intelligence Corps (*q.v.*), for example, candidates were placed either in the GSC or in the parallel 'General List'. The Corps remains as what may best be described as an 'active reserve'.

THE GLIDER PILOT REGIMENT
See Army Air Corps

THE GLOUCESTERSHIRE REGIMENT
28th and 61st

1694	Gibson's Regiment of Foot	**1756**	2nd Bn, 3rd Foot
1751	28th Foot	**1758**	61st Foot
1782	28th (North Gloucestershire) Foot	**1782**	61st (South Gloucestershire) Foot

1881   The Gloucestershire Regiment

A regiment of the Prince of Wales's Division

THE GORDON HIGHLANDERS
75th and 92nd

1758	75th Foot	**1794**	100th (Gordon Highlanders) Foot
1763	*disbanded*	**1798**	92nd (Highland) Regiment
1764	75th (Invalids) Foot	**1861**	92nd (Gordon Highlanders) Foot
1765	*disbanded*		
1778	75th (Prince of Wales's) Foot		
1783	*disbanded*		
1787	75th (Highland) Regiment		
1809	75th Foot		
1862	75th (Stirlingshire) Foot		

1881   The Gordon Highlanders

A regiment of the Scottish Division

THE GREEN HOWARDS
(ALEXANDRA, PRINCESS OF WALES'S* OWN YORKSHIRE REGIMENT)
19th

1688	Luttrell's Regiment
1751	19th Foot
1782	19th (1st Yorkshire, North Riding) Foot
1875	19th (1st Yorkshire, North Riding – Princess of Wales's Own) Foot
1881 (May)	The North Yorkshire Regiment (Princess of Wales's Own)
1881 (July)	The Princess of Wales's Own (Yorkshire) Regiment)
1921	The Green Howards (Alexandra, Princess of Wales's Own Yorkshire Regiment)

*(1875) *Alexandra, Princess of Denmark, wife of the future King Edward VII*

A regiment of the King's Division

THE GREEN JACKETS BRIGADE

The Oxfordshire and Buckinghamshire Light Infantry (*from* Light Infantry Brigade *as* 1st Green Jackets, 1958)
The King's Royal Rifle Corps (*redesignated* 2nd Green Jackets, 1958)
The Rifle Brigade (Prince Consort's Own) (*redesignated* 3rd Green Jackets, 1958)

Army Order 61, 1948

GRENADIER GUARDS

1660 The King's Royal Regiment of Guards
1685 The First Regiment of Foot Guards
1815 The 1st, *or* Grenadier Regiment of Foot Guards (*the title granted after defeating the Grenadiers of the Imperial Guard at Waterloo*)

A regiment of the Guards Division

THE GUARDS DIVISION
(*formerly* The Brigade of Guards)

Grenadier Guards
Coldstream Guards
Scots Guards
Irish Guards
Welsh Guards

Army Order 34, 1968

THE HIGHLAND BRIGADE

Seaforth Highlanders
The Queen's Own Cameron Highlanders

amalgamated as
Queen's Own Highlanders (Seaforth and Camerons), 1961

The Black Watch
The Highland Light Infantry (*to* Lowland Brigade, 1959)
The Gordon Highlanders
The Argyll and Sutherland Highlanders

Army Order 61, 1948

THE HIGHLAND LIGHT INFANTRY
(CITY OF GLASGOW REGIMENT)
71st and 74th

1777	1st Bn, 73rd (Highland) Foot	**1787**	74th (Highland) Foot
1786	71st (Highland) Foot		(*also* 'The Assaye Regiment', 1803)
1808	71st (Glasgow Highland) Foot	**1816**	74th Foot
1809	71st (Glasgow Highland Light Infantry) Regiment	**1845**	74th (Highlanders) Foot
1810	71st (Highland) Light Infantry		

1881 The Highland Light Infantry (City of Glasgow Regiment)
1959 *amalgamated with* The Royal Scots Fusiliers *to form* The Royal Highland Fusiliers (Princess Margaret's Own Glasgow and Ayrshire Regiment)

THE HOME COUNTIES BRIGADE

The Queen's Royal Regiment (West Surrey)
The East Surrey Regiment

amalgamated to form The Queen's Royal Surrey Regiment, 1959

The Buffs (Royal East Kent Regiment)
The Queen's Own Royal West Kent Regiment

amalgamated to form The Queen's Own Buffs, The Royal Kent Regiment, 1961

The Royal Fusiliers (City of London Regiment) *to* Fusilier Brigade, 1957

The Royal Sussex Regiment
The Middlesex Regiment (Duke of Cambridge's Own)

Army Order 61, 1948

3rd THE KING'S OWN HUSSARS

1685 The Queen Consort's Own Regiment of Dragoons
1714 The King's Own Regiment of Dragoons
1751 3rd (King's Own) Dragoons
1818 3rd (King's Own) Light Dragoons
1861 3rd (King's Own) Hussars
1921 3rd The King's Own Hussars
1958 *amalgamated with* 7th Queen's Own Hussars *to form* The Queen's Own Hussars

4th QUEEN'S* OWN HUSSARS

1685 Princess Anne of Denmark's Dragoons
1751 4th Dragoons
1788 4th, *or* Queen's Own Dragoons
1818 4th, *or* Queen's Own Light Dragoons
1861 4th (The Queen's Own) Hussars
1921 4th Queen's Own Hussars
1958 *amalgamated with* 8th King's Royal Irish Hussars *to form* The Queen's Royal Irish Hussars

*(1788) Queen Charlotte, wife of King George III

7th QUEEN'S* OWN HUSSARS

1690 Cunningham's Dragoons
1715 The Princess of Wales's Own Royal Dragoons
1727 The Queen's Own Dragoons
1751 7th, *or* Queen's Own Dragoons
1783 7th, *or* Queen's Own Light Dragoons
1805 7th (Queen's Own) Hussars
1921 7th Queen's Own Hussars
1958 *amalgamated with* 3rd King's Own Hussars *to form* The Queen's Own Hussars

*(1727) Queen Caroline, wife of King George II

8th KING'S ROYAL IRISH HUSSARS

1693 Cunningham's Regiment of Dragoons
1751 8th Dragoons
1775 8th Light Dragoons
1777 8th, *or* The King's Royal Irish Light Dragoons
1822 8th (The King's Royal Irish) Hussars
1921 8th King's Royal Irish Hussars
1958 *amalgamated with* 4th Queen's Own Hussars *to form* The Queen's Royal Irish Hussars

THE QUEEN'S OWN HUSSARS

Formed in 1958 by the amalgamation of 3rd The King's Own Hussars and 7th Queen's Own Hussars

THE QUEEN'S ROYAL IRISH HUSSARS

Formed in 1958 by the amalgamation of 4th Queen's Own Hussars and 8th King's Royal Irish Hussars

10th ROYAL HUSSARS
(PRINCE OF WALES'S* OWN)

1715	Gore's Regiment of Dragoons
1751	10th Dragoons
1783	10th, *or* Prince of Wales's Own Light Dragoons
1806	10th, *or* Prince of Wales's Own Hussars
1811	10th, The Prince of Wales's Own Royal Hussars
1921	10th Royal Hussars (Prince of Wales's Own)
1969	*amalgamated with* 11th Hussars (Prince Albert's Own) *to form* The Royal Hussars (Prince of Wales's Own)

(1783)   The future King George IV

11th HUSSARS
(PRINCE ALBERT'S OWN)

1715	Honywood's Regiment of Dragoons
1751	11th Dragoons
1783	11th Light Dragoons
1840	11th Prince Albert's Own Hussars
1921	11th Hussars (Prince Albert's Own)
1969	*amalgamated with* 10th Royal Hussars (Prince of Wales's Own) *to form* The Royal Hussars (Prince of Wales's Own)

THE ROYAL HUSSARS
(PRINCE OF WALES'S OWN)

Formed in 1969 by the amalgamation of 10th Royal Hussars (Prince of Wales's Own) and 11th Hussars (Prince Albert's Own)

13th HUSSARS

1715	Munden's Regiment of Dragoons
1751	13th Dragoons
1783	13th Light Dragoons
1861	13th Hussars
1922	*amalgamated with* 18th Royal Hussars (Queen Mary's Own) *to form* 13th/18th Royal Hussars (Queen Mary's Own)

13th/18th ROYAL HUSSARS (QUEEN MARY'S OWN)

Formed in 1922 by the amalgamation of 13th Hussars and 18th Royal Hussars (Queen Mary's Own)

14th KING'S HUSSARS

1715	Dormer's Regiment of Dragoons
1720	14th Dragoons
1776	14th Light Dragoons
1798	14th, *or* Duchess of York's Own Light Dragoons
1830	14th King's Light Dragoons
1861	14th (King's) Hussars
1921	14th King's Hussars
1922	*amalgamated with* 20th Hussars *to form* 14th/20th Hussars
1936	*redesignated* 14th/20th King's Hussars

14th/20th KING'S HUSSARS

Formed in 1922 by the amalgamation of 14th King's Hussars and 20th Hussars

15th THE KING'S HUSSARS

1759*	15th Light Dragoons
1766	1st, *or* King's Light Dragoons
1769	15th, *or* King's Light Dragoons
1806	15th, The King's Hussars
1861	15th (King's) Hussars
1921	15th The King's Hussars
1922	*amalgamated with* 19th Royal Hussars (Queen Alexandra's Own) *to form* 15th/19th The King's Royal Hussars

*Awarded the first official battle honour, EMSDORFF

15th/19th THE KING'S ROYAL HUSSARS

Formed in 1922 by the amalgamation of 15th The King's Hussars and 19th Royal Hussars (Queen Alexandra's Own)

18th ROYAL HUSSARS
(QUEEN MARY'S* OWN)

1759	19th Light Dragoons
1763	*renumbered* 18th Light Dragoons
1805	18th King's Irish Hussars
1822	*disbanded*
1858	18th Hussars
1910	18th (Queen Mary's Own) Hussars
1919	18th Royal Hussars (Queen Mary's Own)
1922	*amalgamated with* 13th Hussars *to form* 13th/18th Royal Hussars (Queen Mary's Own)

*(1910) Wife of King George V

19th ROYAL HUSSARS
(QUEEN ALEXANDRA'S* OWN)

1759	19th Light Dragoons
1761	*renumbered* 18th Light Dragoons
1763	*disbanded*
1779	19th Light Dragoons
1783	*disbanded*
1786	19th Light Dragoons
1817	19th Lancers
1821	*disbanded*
1858	1st Bengal European Cavalry (*East India Company*)
1861	19th Hussars
1902	19th (Alexandra, Princess of Wales's Own) Hussars
1908	19th (Queen Alexandra's Own Royal) Hussars
1921	19th Royal Hussars (Queen Alexandra's Own)
1922	*amalgamated with* 15th The King's Hussars *to form* 15th/19th The King's Royal Hussars

*(1908) Wife of King Edward VII

20th HUSSARS

1759   20th Inniskilling Light Dragoons
1763   *disbanded*
1778   20th Light Dragoons
1783   *disbanded*
1791   20th Jamaica Light Dragoons
1802   *redesignated* 20th Light Dragoons
1819   *disbanded*
1858   2nd Bengal European Light Cavalry (*East India Company*)
1861   20th Hussars
1922   *amalgamated with* 14th King's Hussars *to form* 14th/20th Hussars
1936   *redesignated* 14th/20th King's Hussars

INTELLIGENCE CORPS

Formed in July **1940** under Army Order 165.

IRISH GUARDS

Raised by Army Order 77, 1900 'to commemorate the bravery shown by the Irish regiments in the recent operations in South Africa'.

A regiment of the Guards Division

THE KING'S DIVISION

The King's Own Royal Border Regiment (1959)
The King's Regiment (1968)
The Prince of Wales's Own Regiment of Yorkshire (1958)
The Green Howards (Alexandra, Princess of Wales's Own Yorkshire Regiment)
The Royal Irish Rangers (27th (Inniskilling), 83rd and 87th) (1968)
The Queen's Lancashire Regiment (1970)
The Duke of Wellington's Regiment (West Riding)
The York and Lancaster Regiment (*disbanded*, 1968)

Army Order 34, 1968

THE KING'S REGIMENT

Formed in 1958 by the amalgamation of The King's Regiment (Liverpool) and The Manchester Regiment as The King's Regiment (Manchester and Liverpool). Redesignated The King's Regiment in 1969.

A regiment of the King's Division

THE KING'S REGIMENT
(LIVERPOOL)
8th

1685		The Princess Anne of Denmark's Regiment
1702		The Queen's Regiment
1716		The King's Regiment
1751		8th (The King's Regiment)
1881	(May)	The Liverpool Regiment (The King's)
1881	(July)	The King's (Liverpool Regiment)
1921		The King's Regiment (Liverpool)
1958		*amalgamated with* The Manchester Regiment *to form* The King's Regiment (Manchester and Liverpool)
1969		*redesignated* The King's Regiment

THE KING'S OWN ROYAL BORDER REGIMENT

Formed in 1959 by the amalgamation of The King's Own Royal Regiment (Lancaster) and The Border Regiment.

A regiment of the King's Division

THE KING'S OWN ROYAL REGIMENT
(LANCASTER)
4th

1680	The 2nd Tangier Regiment
1684	The Duchess of York and Albany's Regiment
1685	The Queen's Regiment
1688	The Queen Consort's Regiment
1702	The Queen's Marines
1715	The King's Own Regiment
1751	The 4th, or The King's Own Regiment
1867	The 4th (The King's Own Royal) Regiment
1881 (May)	The Royal Lancaster Regiment (King's Own)
1881 (July)	The King's Own Royal Regiment (Lancaster)
1959	*amalgamated with* The Border Regiment *to form* The King's Own Royal Border Regiment

THE KING'S OWN SCOTTISH BORDERERS
25th

1689	The Edinburgh Regiment of Foot
1751	25th (Edinburgh) Foot
1782	25th (Sussex) Foot
1805	25th (The King's Own Borderers) Foot
1881 (May)	The York Regiment (King's Own Borderers)
1881 (July)	The King's Own Borderers
1887	The King's Own Scottish Borderers

A regiment of the Scottish Division

THE KING'S OWN YORKSHIRE LIGHT INFANTRY
51st and 105th

1755	53rd Foot
1757	*renumbered* 51st Foot
1782	51st (2nd Yorkshire, West Riding) Foot
1809	51st (2nd Yorkshire, West Riding, Light Infantry) Regiment
1821	51st (2nd Yorkshire, West Riding, The King's Own Light Infantry) Regiment
1839	2nd Madras (European Light Infantry) Regiment (*East India Company*)
1858	2nd Madras (Light Infantry) Regiment
1861	105th (Madras Light Infantry) Regiment

1881 (May)	The South Yorkshire Regiment (King's Own Light Infantry)
1881 (July)	The King's Own Yorkshire Light Infantry
1968	2nd Battalion, The Light Infantry

THE KING'S ROYAL RIFLE CORPS
60th

1755	62nd (Royal American) Foot
1756	*renumbered* 60th (Royal American) Foot
1824	60th (Duke of York's Rifle Corps)
1830	60th, *or* The King's Royal Rifle Corps
1881	The King's Royal Rifle Corps *(four battalions)*
1958	*redesignated* 2nd Green Jackets (The King's Royal Rifle Corps)
1966	*redesignated* 2nd Battalion, The Royal Green Jackets (The King's Royal Rifle Corps)
1968	*redesignated* 2nd Battalion, The Royal Green Jackets

THE KING'S SHROPSHIRE LIGHT INFANTRY
53rd and 85th

1755	55th Foot		**1759**	85th Light Infantry, or Royal Volontiers
1757	*renumbered* 53rd Foot		**1778**	85th (Westminster Volontiers) Foot
1782	53rd (Shropshire) Foot		**1783**	*disbanded*
			1794	85th (Buck Volunteers) Foot
			1808	85th (Bucks Volunteers) (Light Infantry) Regiment
			1815	85th (Bucks Volunteers) (Duke of York's Own Light Infantry) Regiment
			1821	85th (Bucks Volunteers) (The King's Light Infantry) Regiment

1881 (May)	The Shropshire Regiment (King's Light Infantry)
1881 (July)	The King's Shropshire Light Infantry
1968	3rd Battalion, The Light Infantry

THE LANCASHIRE REGIMENT
(PRINCE OF WALES'S VOLUNTEERS)

Formed in 1958 by the amalgamation of The East Lancashire
Regiment and The South Lancashire Regiment (Prince of Wales's
Volunteers)

THE LANCASHIRE FUSILIERS
20th

1688	Peyton's Regiment of Foot
1751	20th Foot (*also* XXth Foot)
1782	20th (East Devonshire) Foot
1881	The Lancashire Fusiliers
1968	4th Battalion, The Royal Regiment of Fusiliers
1969	*disbanded as* 4th Battalion

THE LANCASTRIAN BRIGADE

The King's Own Royal Regiment (Lancaster)
The Border Regiment
⎤ *amalgamated as* The King's Own Royal Border Regiment, 1959

The King's Regiment (Liverpool)
The Manchester Regiment
⎤ *amalgamated as* The King's Regiment (Manchester and Liverpool), 1958

The Lancashire Fusiliers (*to* Fusilier Brigade, 1957)

The East Lancashire Regiment
The South Lancashire Regiment (PWV)
⎤ *amalgamated as* The Lancashire Regiment (PWV), 1958

The Loyal Regiment (North Lancashire)

Army Order 61, 1948

5th ROYAL IRISH LANCERS

1689	The Royal Irish Dragoons
1704	The Royal Dragoons of Ireland
1756	5th (Royal Irish) Dragoons
1799	*disbanded*
1858	*re-formed as* 5th (Royal Irish) Lancers
1921	5th Royal Irish Lancers
1922	*amalgamated with* 16th The Queen's Lancers *to form* 16th/5th The Queen's Royal Lancers

9th QUEEN'S* ROYAL LANCERS

1715 Wynne's Regiment of Dragoons
1751 9th Dragoons
1783 9th Light Dragoons
1816 9th Lancers
1830 9th (Queen's Royal) Lancers
1921 9th Queen's Royal Lancers
1960 *amalgamated with* 12th Royal Lancers (Prince of Wales's) *to form* 9th/12th Royal Lancers (Prince of Wales's)

*(1830) Queen Adelaide, wife of King William IV

12th ROYAL LANCERS
(PRINCE OF WALES'S*)

1715 Bowles's Regiment of Dragoons
1751 12th Dragoons
1768 12th (The Prince of Wales's) Light Dragoons
1816 12th (The Prince of Wales's) Lancers
1817 12th (The Prince of Wales's Royal) Lancers
1921 12th Royal Lancers (Prince of Wales's)
1960 *amalgamated with* 9th Queen's Royal Lancers *to form* 9th/12th Royal Lancers (Prince of Wales's)

*(1768) The future King George IV

9th/12th ROYAL LANCERS
(PRINCE OF WALES'S)

Formed in 1960 by the amalgamation of 9th Queen's Royal Lancers and 12th Royal Lancers (Prince of Wales's).

16th THE QUEEN'S* LANCERS

1759 16th Light Dragoons
1769 16th, *or* Queen's Light Dragoons
1815 16th (The Queen's) Lancers
1921 16th The Queen's Lancers
1922 *amalgamated with* 5th Royal Irish Lancers *to form* 16th/5th The Queen's Royal Lancers

*(1766) Queen Charlotte, wife of King George III

16th/5th THE QUEEN'S ROYAL LANCERS

Formed in 1922 by the amalgamation of 16th The Queen's Lancers and 5th Royal Irish Lancers.

17th LANCERS
(DUKE OF CAMBRIDGE'S* OWN)

1759   18th Light Dragoons
1763   *renumbered* 17th Light Dragoons
1822   17th Lancers
1876   17th Lancers (Duke of Cambridge's Own)
1922   *amalgamated with* 21st Lancers (Empress of India's) *to form* 17th/21st Lancers

*(1876) George, Duke of Cambridge, cousin of Queen Victoria

21st LANCERS
(EMPRESS OF INDIA'S*)

1759   21st Light Dragoons
1763   *disbanded*
1779   21st Light Dragoons
1783   *disbanded*
1794   21st Light Dragoons
1819   *disbanded*
1858   3rd Bengal European Cavalry *(East India Company)*
1861   21st Hussars
1897   21st Lancers
1899   21st (Empress of India's) Lancers
1921   21st Lancers (Empress of India's)
1922   *amalgamated with* 17th Lancers (Duke of Cambridge's Own) *to form* 17th/21st Lancers

*(1899) Queen Victoria

17th/21st LANCERS

Formed in 1922 by the amalgamation of 17th Lancers (Duke of Cambridge's Own) and 21st Lancers (Empress of India's).

THE LIFE GUARDS

1661 'His Majesties own Troope of Guards, His Highness Royall the Duke of Yorke his Troope of Guards, and his Grace the Duke of Albermarle his Troope of Guards.' *(On Monk's death* the Duke of Albemarle's Troop *redesignated* The Queen's Troop)
1661 The Life Guards
1788 The 1st and 2nd Life Guards
1922 The Life Guards

THE LIGHT INFANTRY

Formed in 1968 by the amalgamation of The Somerset and Cornwall Light Infantry, The King's Own Yorkshire Light Infantry, The King's Shropshire Light Infantry, and The Durham Light Infantry. Reduced to three battalions in 1970.

A regiment of the Light Division

THE LIGHT DIVISION

The Light Infantry (1968)
The Royal Green Jackets (1966)

Army Order 34, 1968

THE LIGHT INFANTRY BRIGADE

The Somerset Light Infantry ⎤ *amalgamated as* The Somerset and Cornwall
The Duke of Cornwall's Light Infantry ⎦ Light Infantry, 1959

The Oxfordshire and Buckinghamshire Light Infantry (*to* Green Jackets Brigade, 1958)

The King's Own Yorkshire Light Infantry
The King's Shropshire Light Infantry
The Durham Light Infantry

Army Order 61, 1948

THE LOWLAND BRIGADE

The Royal Scots (The Royal Regiment)

The Royal Scots Fusiliers
The Highland Light Infantry
(*from* Highland Brigade, 1959)
    amalgamated as The Royal Highland Fusiliers (Princess Margaret's Own Glasgow and Ayrshire Regiment), 1959

The King's Own Scottish Borderers

The Cameronians (Scottish Rifles) *disbanded* 1968

Army Order 61, 1948

THE LOYAL* REGIMENT
(NORTH LANCASHIRE)
47th and 81st

1741	Mordaunt's Regiment of Foot	**1759**	81st (Invalids) Regiment
1751	47th Foot	**1763**	*disbanded*
1782	47th (Lancashire) Foot	**1778**	81st (Aberdeen Highlanders) Foot
		1783	*disbanded*
		1793	81st (Loyal Lincoln Volunteers) Regiment
		1794	81st Foot
		1833	81st (Loyal Lincoln Volunteers) Foot

1881 (May)   The North Lancashire Regiment
1881 (July)   The Loyal North Lancashire Regiment
1921   The Loyal Regiment (North Lancashire)
1970   *amalgamated with* The Lancashire Regiment (Prince of Wales's Volunteers) *to form* The Queen's Lancashire Regiment

*(1793) 'Loyal' from the motto of the first Colonel of the 81st Foot

---

THE MACHINE GUN CORPS

When the Expeditionary Force went to France in 1914 the war establishment of cavalry regiments and infantry battalions included a section of two machine-guns. As a result of the serious lack of these weapons, underlined in the early fighting, a 'Motor Machine Gun Service' was formed in November and provided one 'battery' for each Division. Volunteers for the new arm were transferred to The Royal Artillery. Under Army Order 414 of 22 October 1915, the Service was reconstituted as The Machine Gun Corps divided into three branches: Cavalry of the Line, Infantry of the Line, and Motor Machine Gun Service. In July 1916 a 'Heavy Branch' was formed. This was a cover-name for the new tank arm, and with the creation of The Tank Corps on 27 July 1917 the Heavy Branch ceased to exist. Finally, on 8 May 1918, a separate Guards Machine Gun Regiment was formed. The Corps was disbanded in 1922.

THE MANCHESTER REGIMENT
63rd and 96th

1744	63rd (American) Foot	**1760**	96th Foot
1748	*renumbered* 49th Foot	**1763**	*disbanded*
1757	2nd Bn, The 8th (King's) Regiment	**1780**	96th (British Musketeers) Regiment
1758	63rd Foot	**1783**	*disbanded*
1782	63rd (West Suffolk) Foot	**1793**	96th (The Queen's Royal Irish) Regiment
		1798	*disbanded*
		1803	*raised, renumbered and*
		1818	*disbanded three times*
		1824	96th Foot

1881 The Manchester Regiment
1958 *amalgamated with* The King's Regiment *as* The King's Regiment (Manchester and Liverpool)
1969 *redesignated* The King's Regiment

THE MERCIAN BRIGADE

The Cheshire Regiment

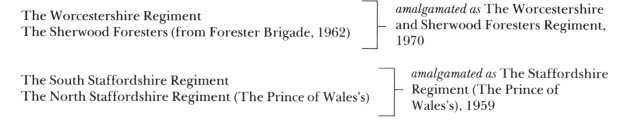

The Worcestershire Regiment
The Sherwood Foresters (from Forester Brigade, 1962) — *amalgamated as* The Worcestershire and Sherwood Foresters Regiment, 1970

The South Staffordshire Regiment
The North Staffordshire Regiment (The Prince of Wales's) — *amalgamated as* The Staffordshire Regiment (The Prince of Wales's), 1959

Army Order 61, 1948

THE MIDDLESEX REGIMENT
(DUKE OF CAMBRIDGE'S* OWN)
57th and 77th

1741	57th Foot
1748	*renumbered* 46th Foot
1755	59th Foot
1757	57th Foot
1782	57th (West Middlesex) Foot

1756	77th (Montgomery Highlanders) Regiment
1763	*disbanded*
1775	77th (Atholl Highlanders) Regiment
1783	*disbanded*
1787	77th Foot
1807	77th (East Middlesex) Foot
1876	77th (East Middlesex) (Duke of Cambridge's Own) Foot

1881	The Middlesex Regiment (Duke of Cambridge's Own)
1900	3rd and 4th Regular Battalions *raised. Disbanded* 1922
1966	*redesignated* 4th Battalion, The Queen's Regiment (Middlesex)
1968	*redesignated* 4th Battalion, The Queen's Regiment
1970	*disbanded* as 4th Battalion

(1881) George, Duke of Cambridge, cousin of Queen Victoria

THE MIDLAND BRIGADE
(*renamed* The Forester Brigade, 1962)

The Royal Warwickshire Regiment (*to* Fusilier Brigade, 1963)

The Royal Lincolnshire Regiment (*to* East Anglian Brigade, 1957)

The Royal Leicestershire Regiment (*to* East Anglian Brigade, 1963)

The Sherwood Foresters (*to* Mercian Brigade, 1962)

Army Order 61, 1948

MILITARY PROVOST STAFF CORPS

Formed in **1901** as the Military Prison Staff Corps and redesignated by its present title in **1906**. It consists of officers, warrant officers and non-commissioned officers only, and provides the supervisory staffs of military prisons and detention centres.

THE NORTHAMPTONSHIRE REGIMENT
48th and 58th

1740	Cholmondeley's Regiment of Foot	**1740**	58th Foot
1751	48th Foot	**1748**	*renumbered* 47th Foot
1782	48th (Northamptonshire) Foot	**1755**	*renumbered* 60th Foot
		1757	*renumbered* 58th Foot
		1782	58th (Rutlandshire) Foot

1881   The Northamptonshire Regt

1960   *amalgamated with* The Royal Lincolnshire Regiment *to form*
       The 2nd East Anglian Regiment (Duchess of Gloucester's
       Own Royal Lincolnshire and Northamptonshire)

1964   *redesignated* 2nd (Duchess of Gloucester's Own Royal
       Lincolnshire and Northamptonshire) Battalion, The Royal
       Anglian Regiment

1968   *redesignated* 2nd Battalion, The Royal Anglian Regiment

---

THE NORTH IRISH BRIGADE

The Royal Inniskilling Fusiliers
The Royal Ulster Rifles
The Royal Irish Fusiliers (Princess Victoria's)

Army Order 61, 1948

THE NORTH STAFFORDSHIRE REGIMENT
(THE PRINCE OF WALES'S*)
64th and 98th

1756	2nd Bn, 11th Foot	**1760**	98th Foot
1758	64th Foot	**1763**	*disbanded*
1782	64th (2nd Staffordshire) Foot	**1779**	98th Foot
		1784	*disbanded*
		1793	98th (Highland) Regiment
		1802	*renumbered* 91st Foot
		1803-	*renumbered and*
		1818	*disbanded three times*
		1824	98th Foot
		1876	98th (The Prince of Wales's) Foot

1881 (May)   The South Staffordshire Regiment (The Prince of Wales's)
1881 (July)   The North Staffordshire Regiment (The Prince of Wales's)
1959   *amalgamated with* The South Staffordshire Regiment *to form*
       The Staffordshire Regiment (The Prince of Wales's)

*(1876) The future King Edward VII

THE OXFORDSHIRE AND BUCKINGHAMSHIRE LIGHT INFANTRY
43rd and 52nd

1741	54th Foot	**1755**	54th Foot
1748	*renumbered* 43rd Foot	**1757**	52nd Foot
1782	43rd (Monmouthshire) Foot	**1782**	52nd (Oxfordshire) Foot
1803	43rd (Monmouthshire Light Infantry) Regiment	**1803**	52nd (Oxfordshire Light Infantry) Regiment

1881 The Oxfordshire Light Infantry
1908 The Oxfordshire and Buckinghamshire Light Infantry
1958 *redesignated* 1st Green Jackets (43rd and 52nd)
1966 *redesignated* 1st Battalion, The Royal Green Jackets (43rd and 52nd)
1968 *redesignated* 1st Battalion, The Royal Green Jackets

THE PARACHUTE REGIMENT
See Army Air Corps

Formed under Army Order 128 on 1 August **1942**. Transferred in **1949** to the Infantry of the Line, and consisting **(1983)** of three battalions with supporting arms and services.

THE PRINCE OF WALES'S* LEINSTER REGIMENT
(ROYAL CANADIANS)
100th and 109th

1761	100th (Highland) Regiment	**1761**	109th Foot
1763	*disbanded*	**1763**	*disbanded*
1794	100th (Gordon Highlanders) Foot	**1794**	100th (Aberdeenshire) Foot
1805	100th (Prince Regent's County of Dublin) Foot	**1795**	*disbanded*
1858	100th (Prince of Wales's Royal Canadian) Foot	**1854**	3rd (Bombay European) Regiment *(East India Company)*
		1861	109th (Bombay Infantry) Regiment

1881 (May) The Prince of Wales's Royal Canadian Regiment
1881 (July) The Prince of Wales's Leinster Regiment (Royal Canadians)
1922 *disbanded*

*(1858) The future King Edward VII

THE PRINCE OF WALES'S OWN REGIMENT OF YORKSHIRE

Formed in 1958 by the amalgamation of The West Yorkshire Regiment (The Prince of Wales's Own) and The East Yorkshire Regiment (The Duke of York's Own).

A regiment of the King's Division

THE PRINCE OF WALES'S DIVISION

The Devonshire and Dorset Regiment (1958)
The Cheshire Regiment
The Royal Welch Fusiliers
The Royal Regiment of Wales (24th/41st Foot) (1969)
The Gloucestershire Regiment
The Worcestershire and Sherwood Foresters Regiment (29th/45th Foot) (1970)
The Royal Hampshire Regiment
The Staffordshire Regiment (The Prince of Wales's) (1959)
The Duke of Edinburgh's Royal Regiment (Berkshire and Wiltshire) (1959)

Army Order 34, 1968

QUEEN ALEXANDRA'S IMPERIAL MILITARY NURSING SERVICE
See Queen Alexandra's Royal Army Nursing Corps

QUEEN ALEXANDRA'S ROYAL ARMY NURSING CORPS

Parallel with the reassessment of Army medical organization after the sombre lessons of the Crimean War, an Army Nursing Service was formed in **1881**; and in keeping with the object of the main Cardwell reform, a Nursing Reserve was established in **1897**. Both the Service and the Reserve were reorganized after the South African War and named Queen Alexandra's Imperial Military Nursing Service. This remained on an auxiliary basis until it was redesignated Queen Alexandra's Royal Army Nursing Corps by Army Order 5 of **1949** and taken onto the Regular establishment.

THE QUEEN'S DIVISION

The Queen's Regiment (1966)
The Royal Regiment of Fusiliers (1968)
The Royal Anglian Regiment (1964)

Army Order 34, 1968

THE QUEEN'S REGIMENT

Formed in 1966 by the amalgamation of The Queen's Royal Surrey Regiment; The Queen's Own Buffs, The Royal Kent Regiment; The Royal Sussex Regiment; The Middlesex Regiment (Duke of Cambridge's Own). Reduced to three battalions in 1970.

A regiment of the Queen's Division

THE QUEEN'S LANCASHIRE REGIMENT

Formed in 1970 by the amalgamation of The Lancashire Regiment (Prince of Wales's Volunteers) and The Loyal Regiment (North Lancashire).

A regiment of the King's Division

THE QUEEN'S OWN BUFFS, THE ROYAL KENT REGIMENT

Formed in 1961 by the amalgamation of The Buffs (Royal East Kent Regiment) and The Queen's Own Royal West Kent Regiment.

THE QUEEN'S* OWN CAMERON HIGHLANDERS
79th

1793	79th Foot (Cameronian Volunteers)
1804	79th Foot (Cameronian Highlanders)
1806	79th Foot, or Cameron Highlanders
1873	79th Regiment, The Queen's Own Cameron Highlanders
1881	The Queen's Own Cameron Highlanders
1897	2nd Battalion *formed*
1961	*amalgamated with* Seaforth Highlanders (Ross-shire Buffs, The Duke of Albany's) *to form* Queen's Own Highlanders (Seaforth and Camerons)

*(1873) Queen Victoria

QUEEN'S OWN HIGHLANDERS
(SEAFORTH AND CAMERONS)

Formed in 1961 by the amalgamation of The Queen's Own Cameron Highlanders and Seaforth Highlanders (Ross-shire Buffs, The Duke of Albany's).

A regiment of the Scottish Division

THE QUEEN'S* OWN ROYAL WEST KENT REGIMENT
50th and 97th

1757	50th Foot	**1759**	97th Foot
1782	50th (West Kent) Foot	**1763**	*disbanded*
1827	50th (Duke of Clarence's) Foot	**1779**	97th Foot
1831	50th (The Queen's Own) Regiment of Foot	**1783**	*disbanded*
		1794	97th (Strathspey Highlanders) Regiment
		1795	*disbanded*
		1798	97th (Queen's Germans)
		1804	*renumbered* 98th Foot
		1818	*disbanded as* 97th Foot
		1824	97th (The Earl of Ulster's) Foot

1881	(May)	The Royal West Kent Regiment (The Queen's Own)
1881	(July)	The Queen's Own (Royal West Kent Regiment)
1961		*amalgamated with* The Buffs (Royal East Kent Regiment) *to form* The Queen's Own Buffs, The Royal Kent Regiment
1966		*redesignated* 2nd Battalion, The Queen's Regiment

*(1831) Queen Adelaide, wife of King William IV

THE QUEEN'S ROYAL SURREY REGIMENT

Formed in 1959 by the amalgamation of The Queen's Royal Regiment (West Surrey) and The East Surrey Regiment.

THE QUEEN'S* ROYAL REGIMENT
(WEST SURREY)
2nd

1661		The Tangier Regiment
1684		The Queen's Regiment
1686		The Queen Dowager's Regiment
1703		The Queen's Royal Regiment
1715		The Princess of Wales's Own Regiment of Foot
1727		The Queen's Own Royal Regiment of Foot
1881	(May)	The Royal West Surrey Regiment (The Queen's)
1881	(July)	The Queen's (Royal West Surrey Regiment)
1921		The Queen's Royal Regiment (West Surrey)
1959		*amalgamated with* The East Surrey Regiment *to form* The Queen's Royal Surrey Regiment
1966		*redesignated* 1st Battalion, The Queen's Regiment

*(1684) Queen Catherine of Braganza, wife of King Charles II

THE RIFLE BRIGADE
(PRINCE CONSORT'S OWN)

1800	An Experimental Corps of Riflemen; *also* The Rifle Corps
1802	95th (Rifle) Regiment
1816	*On Wellington's recommendation taken out of the numbered regiments of the Line and named* Rifle Brigade *(four battalions)*
1862	The Prince Consort's Own Rifle Brigade
1881 (May)	Rifle Brigade (The Prince Consort's Own)
1881 (July)	The Prince Consort's Own (Rifle Brigade)
1920	The Rifle Brigade (Prince Consort's Own)
1958	*redesignated* The 3rd Green Jackets, The Rifle Brigade
1966	*redesignated* 3rd Battalion, The Royal Green Jackets (The Rifle Brigade)
1968	*redesignated* 3rd Battalion, The Royal Green Jackets

THE ROYAL ANGLIAN REGIMENT

Formed in 1964 by the amalgamation of the 1st, 2nd and 3rd East Anglian Regiment and The Royal Leicestershire Regiment. In 1968 county affiliations were dropped and the Regiment redesignated 1st, 2nd, 3rd and 4th Battalions, The Royal Anglian Regiment. Reduced to three battalions in 1970*.

A regiment of the Queen's Division

*On 16 January 1980 territorial suffixes were reintroduced as follows:
1st Battalion (Norfolk, Suffolk and Cambridgeshire);
2nd Battalion (Lincolnshire, Leicestershire and Northamptonshire);
3rd Battalion (Bedfordshire, Hertfordshire and Essex)

ROYAL ARMOURED CORPS

Formed in April **1939** (A.O.58) as a parent Corps to The Royal Tank Corps (redesignated The Royal Tank Regiment on joining) and to those Cavalry Regiments of the Line which had been mechanized by that date. In due course the remaining Regular Cavalry* and certain Yeomanry Regiments were added to the Corps, together with six Cavalry Regiments and The Reconnaissance Corps which were raised during the Second World War and subsequently disbanded. During the War 33 battalions of infantry were temporarily converted to mechanized regiments of the Corps. Since **1946** Cavalry Regiments of the Line have reassumed their individual identities and The Royal Armoured Corps has reverted to its pre-War parent status.

*The mechanized squadrons of the Household Cavalry do not belong to the Corps

ROYAL ARMY CHAPLAINS' DEPARTMENT

Until the end of the eighteenth century chaplains were employed on a regimental basis. But a Royal Warrant of 23 September **1796** laid down 'that whenever an army is formed, or a body of troops ordered to be assembled for service abroad, and in all Garrisons and Stations where several Regiments are near together, Chaplains shall be appointed according to the number of the Corps, in the proportion of one to each Brigade, or to every three or four Regiments.' Until **1827** only Church of England Chaplains were authorized, but in that year Presbyterians were recognized; in **1836**, Roman Catholics; in **1881**, Wesleyans; and in **1892**, Jewish Chaplains. Thus The Department (still so called since it does not include other ranks) has the longest unbroken existence of any Administrative Department and Corps in the Army and accordingly ranks above all such others. The Royal title was conferred in February **1919**.

ROYAL ARMY DENTAL CORPS

Until the end of the First World War dental officers had served on the establishment of all medical units. The Corps was given its separate identity under Army Order 4 of **1921**. The Royal title was conferred in **1946.**

ROYAL ARMY EDUCATIONAL CORPS

Not until the middle of the nineteenth century was any serious attempt made to improve standards of education in the Army, even if the Peninsular War revealed a surprising amount of literary talent in the ranks. On 2 July **1846**, however, a Corps of Army Schoolmasters was created by Royal Warrant and in **1868** a Council of Military Education could report that the startling rate of illiteracy among the rank and file had been more than halved (a superior education, it may be added, was not at that date among the obvious qualifications for a commission). In **1870** a Director-General of Military Education was appointed and, despite much diehard opposition, there was added to the old verity that 'a clean soldier makes a good soldier' the greater truth that 'an educated soldier makes a better soldier'. Promotion was made dependent on a system of certificates of education. The Corps of Army Schoolmasters was disbanded by Army Order 231 of **1920** and redesignated The Army Educational Corps. The Royal title was conferred in **1946**.

ROYAL ARMY MEDICAL CORPS

During the first two hundred years of the Standing Army medical services in the Army were 'organized' on a private and strictly regimental basis although, predictably, both Marlborough and Wellington paid much attention to the problem of the treatment and evacuation of sick and wounded soldiers. Like so much else in the development of administrative services in the Army, the catalyst was provided by the Crimean War. The first step was the establishment by Royal Warrant of June **1855** of the Medical Staff Corps (other ranks) which in turn was replaced in August **1857** by the Army Hospital Corps, which title it retained until **1884**, when it reverted to its previous designation. Meanwhile a Royal Warrant of 1 March **1873** had established the Army Medical Department (officers). In September **1884** Department and Staff Corps were linked together, and finally under Army Order 93 of **1898** the present Royal Army Medical Corps came into existence.

ROYAL ARMY ORDNANCE CORPS
See also Royal Army Service Corps *and* Corps of Royal
Electrical and Mechanical Engineers

As its title implies, the Corps has its origin in the old Board of Ordnance. Its modern development dates from the post-Crimea period.

1858	Corps of Armourer-Sergeants
1861	Military Stores Department (officers)
1865	Military Store Staff Corps (other ranks)

With the formation of the Control Department in **1870** the officers were absorbed into that Department and the other ranks into the new Army Service Corps. With the abolition of the Control Department in **1875** and the formation of the Supply and Transport Sub-Department, the Corps developed thus:

1875	Ordnance Store Department
1877	Ordnance Store Branch
1881	Ordnance Store Corps
1882	Corps of Ordnance Artificers
1896	Army Ordnance Department
	Army Ordnance Corps
1918	Royal Army Ordnance Corps

ROYAL ARMY PAY CORPS

Until the latter half of the nineteenth century paymasters were employed on a regimental basis. However, with the establishment of the Control Department in **1870**, a Pay Sub-Department was formed and this developed as follows:

1877	Army Pay Department (officers), by Royal Warrant of 22 October
1893	Army Pay Corps (other ranks) (A.O.134)
1905	APD redesignated the Army Accounts Department
1909	AAD abolished and reconstructed again as the Army Pay Department
1920	By Army Order 146 a Royal title was conferred on both the Army Pay Department and the Army Pay Corps; and by Army Order 498 Department and Corps were amalgamated to form the present Royal Army Pay Corps.

NOTE
A Corps of Military Accountants was formed in **1919** (A.O.405), but was disbanded in **1927** (A.O. 137)

ROYAL ARMY SERVICE CORPS
See also Royal Corps of Transport

The Corps originated in the commissariat branch of the Board of Ordnance and its history illustrates the haphazard attitude towards the administrative services of the Army until the present century.

1794	Corps of Waggoners
1796	Royal Wagon Train
1853	Purveyors' Department (officers)
1855	Land Transport Corps
1856	Military Train
1858	Commissariat Department (officers)
1859	Commissariat Staff Corps (other ranks)
1870	Army Service Corps (other ranks)

With the establishment of the Control Department in **1870** the Army Service Corps absorbed the other ranks of: the Military Train, the Commissariat Staff Corps, the Military Store Staff Corps (forerunner of RAOC) and the Barrack Department. The Control Department absorbed the officers of: the Military Train, the Commissariat Department, the Military Store Department (to become RAOC), and the Barrack Department. On the abolition of the Control Department in **1875**, the two functions of the Supply and Transport Sub-Department were separated, the transport element taking the following road:

1875	Commissariat and Transport Department
1877	Commissariat and Transport Branch
1880	Commissariat and Transport Staff
1881	Commissariat and Transport Corps
1889	Army Service Corps (formed by the amalgamation of C & T Staff and C & T Corps under Army Order 3)
1918	Royal Army Service Corps (A.O.362)
1965	Royal Corps of Transport (*q.v.*)

ROYAL ARMY VETERINARY CORPS

Until the nineteenth century the care of horses in all arms and services was entrusted to farriers, but by Royal Warrant of 1 July **1859** veterinary surgeons of military rank were appointed and the Veterinary Medical Department and all regimental appointments (other than those in the Household Cavalry) were abolished. In **1903** an Army Veterinary Corps (other ranks) was formed, and by Army Order 180 of that year, Department and Corps were amalgamated as the Army Veterinary Corps. The Royal title was conferred in **1918** (A.O.362).

THE ROYAL BERKSHIRE REGIMENT
(PRINCESS CHARLOTTE OF WALES'S*)
49th and 66th

1742	49th, *or* Cotterell's Marines	**1755**	2nd Bn, 19th Foot
1743	*disbanded*	**1758**	66th Foot
1744	63rd *or* Trelawney's Foot	**1782**	66th (Berkshire) Foot
1748	49th Foot		
1782	49th (Hertfordshire) Foot		
1816	49th (Princess of Wales's) Hertfordshire Foot		

1881 (May)	The Berkshire Regiment (Princess Charlotte of Wales's)
1881 (July)	Princess Charlotte of Wales's (Berkshire Regiment)
1885	Princess Charlotte of Wales's (Royal Berkshire Regiment)
1921	The Royal Berkshire Regiment (Princess Charlotte of Wales's
1959	*amalgamated with* The Wiltshire Regiment (Duke of Edinburgh's) *to form* The Duke of Edinburgh's Royal Regiment (Berkshire and Wiltshire)

*(1816) Only daughter of the future King George IV

ROYAL CORPS OF SIGNALS
See also Corps of Royal Engineers

Originating in **1908** as the Royal Engineer Signal Service, the present Corps was formed as a separate entity in **1920**, taking precedence immediately after the Royal Engineers. It is responsible for all forms of communication in the Army above unit level.

ROYAL CORPS OF TRANSPORT
See also Royal Army Service Corps

Designated as such in **1965**. On its establishment it took over not only the transport functions of the Royal Army Service Corps but also the transportation and movement control duties of the Corps of Royal Engineers. At the same time it transferred its responsibility for the supply of stores and equipment to the Royal Army Ordnance Corps. The RCT also operates through its Fleet branch a variety of sea-going craft, and also its own light aircraft and helicopters.

THE ROYAL DUBLIN FUSILIERS
102nd and 103rd

1648	Madras European Regiment		**1661**	The Bombay Regiment
1702	East India Company's European Regiment		**1668**	East India Company's Bombay (European) Regiment
1830	East India Company's Madras (European) Regiment		**1839**	East India Company's 1st Bombay (European) Regiment
1839	1st Madras (European) Regiment		**1844**	East India Company's 1st Bombay (European) Fusiliers
1843	1st Madras (European) Fusiliers			
1858	1st Madras Fusiliers		**1858**	1st Bombay Fusiliers
1861	102nd Royal Madras Fusiliers		**1861**	103rd Royal Bombay Fusiliers

1881   The Royal Dublin Fusiliers
1922   *disbanded*

ROYAL FLYING CORPS
(MILITARY WING)

1878   First military experiments with balloons conducted at Woolwich
1884-5   Balloon detachments employed during operations in Africa
1890   Balloon Section formed as a unit of the Royal Engineers
1907   First Army airship introduced
1911   Air Battalion, Royal Engineers formed. Formation of a Royal Flying Corps recommended by Committee of Imperial Defence
1912   Royal Flying Corps formed by Royal Warrant of 13 April
1913   Military Wing consisted of eight squadrons, each of 24 aircraft
1914   First reconnaissance flight made over Belgium on 19 August
1916   32 RFC squadrons in action on Western Front
1917   In November establishment raised to 86 squadrons. Air Council created in December
1918   Royal Air Force created on 1 April

THE ROYAL FUSILIERS
(CITY OF LONDON REGIMENT)
7th

1685   Our Royal Regiment of Fuziliers; *also* Our Ordnance Regiment
1689   7th (Royal Fusiliers)
1881 (May)   The City of London Regiment (Royal Fusiliers)
1881 (July)   The Royal Fusiliers (City of London Regiment)
1898   3rd Battalion *raised*; *disbanded* 1922
1900   4th Battalion *raised*; *disbanded* 1922
1968   *amalgamated with* The Royal Northumberland Fusiliers, The Royal Warwickshire Fusiliers, *and* The Lancashire Fusiliers *to form* The Royal Regiment of Fusiliers

THE ROYAL GREEN JACKETS

Formed in 1966 by the amalgamation of 1st Green Jackets (43rd and 52nd); 2nd Green Jackets (The King's Royal Rifle Corps); and 3rd Green Jackets (The Rifle Brigade)

A regiment of the Light Division

THE ROYAL HAMPSHIRE REGIMENT
37th and 67th

1702	Meredith's Regiment of Foot	**1758**	67th Foot
1751	37th Foot	**1782**	67th (South Hampshire) Foot
1782	37th (North Hampshire) Foot		

1881   The Hampshire Regiment
1946   The Royal Hampshire Regiment

A regiment of the Prince of Wales's Division

THE ROYAL HIGHLAND FUSILIERS
(PRINCESS MARGARET'S* OWN GLASGOW AND AYRSHIRE REGIMENT)

Formed in 1959 by the amalgamation of The Royal Scots Fusiliers and The Highland Light Infantry (City of Glasgow Regiment)

A regiment of the Scottish Division

*(1959) Second daughter of King George VI

ROYAL HORSE ARTILLERY
See also Royal Regiment of Artillery

Raised in January **1793** as the first branch of the Royal Regiment in which all ranks were mounted military personnel and equipped with a light 6-pdr gun as mobile support for the cavalry arm. In **1947** The Riding Troop, formed for ceremonial duties, was named 'The King's Troop', a title which it has retained under the present Sovereign. Since **1946** the RHA has been reduced from five Regiments to three.

NOTE

In **1857**, on the recommendation of the Duke of Cambridge, the RHA was given precedence over all other Regiments and Corps of the British Army. This was subsequently amended so that to-day the RHA 'on parade, *with their guns*, take the right and march at the head of the Household Cavalry'.

THE ROYAL HORSE GUARDS
(THE BLUES)

1661 The Earl of Oxford's Regiment of Horse
then variously
The King's Regiment of Horse Guards
The Royal Regiment of Horse Guards
The Oxford Blues
1750 The Royal Horse Guards (Blue)
1819 The Royal Horse Guards (The Blues)
1969 The Blues and Royals (Royal Horse Guards and 1st Dragoons)

THE ROYAL INNISKILLING FUSILIERS
27th and 108th

1689 Tiffin's Regiment of Foot
1751 27th (Inniskilling) Foot

1854 East India Company's 3rd (Madras Infantry) Regiment
1858 3rd (Madras) Regiment
1861 108th (Madras Infantry) Regiment

1881 The Royal Inniskilling Fusiliers
1968 *amalgamated with* The Royal Ulster Rifles *and* The Royal Irish Fusiliers *to form* The Royal Irish Rangers (27th (Inniskilling) 83rd and 87th)

THE ROYAL IRISH REGIMENT
18th

1684 The Earl of Granard's Regiment of Foot
1695 The Royal Regiment of Ireland
1751 18th (The Royal Irish) Foot
1881 The Royal Irish Regiment
1922 *disbanded*

THE ROYAL IRISH FUSILIERS
(PRINCESS VICTORIA'S*)
87th and 89th

1793	87th (The Prince of Wales's Irish) Foot	**1793**	89th Foot
1811	87th (The Prince of Wales's Own Irish) Foot	**1866**	89th (Princess Victoria's) Foot
1827	87th (The Royal Irish Fusiliers)		

1881 (May)	The Royal Irish Fusiliers (Princess Victoria's)
1881 (July)	Princess Victoria's (The Royal Irish Fusiliers)
1920	The Royal Irish Fusiliers (Princess Victoria's)
1968	*amalgamated with* The Royal Inniskilling Fusiliers *and* The Royal Ulster Rifles *to form* The Royal Irish Rangers
1970	*disbanded* as 3rd Battalion, Royal Irish Rangers

(1866) To commemorate the presentation of Colours in 1833 by Princess Victoria, the future Queen

---

THE ROYAL IRISH RANGERS
(27th (INNISKILLING) 83rd and 87th)

Formed in 1968 by the amalgamation of The Royal Inniskilling Fusiliers; The Royal Ulster Rifles; and The Royal Irish Fusiliers. Reduced to two battalions in 1970.

A regiment of the King's Division

THE ROYAL IRISH RIFLES
83rd and 86th

1793	Fitch's Corps	**1793**	Cuyler's Shropshire Volunteers
1794	83rd Foot	**1794**	86th Foot
1859	83rd (County of Dublin) Foot	**1809**	86th (The Leinster) Foot
		1812	86th (Royal County Down) Foot

1881	The Royal Irish Rifles
1921	*redesignated* The Royal Ulster Rifles
1968	*amalgamated with* The Royal Inniskilling Fusiliers *and* The Royal Irish Fusiliers *to form* The Royal Irish Rangers

THE ROYAL LEICESTERSHIRE REGIMENT
17th

1688	Richard's Regiment of Foot
1751	17th Foot
1782	17th (Leicestershire) Foot
1881	The Leicestershire Regiment
1946	The Royal Leicestershire Regiment
1964	4th (Leicestershire) Battalion, The Royal Anglian Regiment
1968	*redesignated* 4th Battalion, The Royal Anglian Regiment
1970	*disbanded* as 4th Battalion

THE ROYAL LINCOLNSHIRE REGIMENT
10th

1685	Granville's Regiment of Foot
1751	10th Foot
1782	10th (North Lincolnshire) Foot
1881	The Lincolnshire Regiment
1946	The Royal Lincolnshire Regiment
1960	*amalgamated with* The Northamptonshire Regiment *to form* The 2nd East Anglian Regiment (Duchess of Gloucester's Own Royal Lincolnshire and Northamptonshire)
1964	*redesignated* The 2nd (Duchess of Gloucester's* Own Royal Lincolnshire and Northamptonshire) Battalion, The Royal Anglian Regiment
1968	*redesignated* 2nd Battalion, The Royal Anglian Regiment

*(1960) Princess Alice, wife of Prince Henry, Duke of Gloucester

THE ROYAL MARINES

1664	The Duke of York and Albany's Maritime Regiment of Foot, *or* The Admiral's Regiment	**1755**	The Marines (raised by the Board of Admiralty)
1685	Prince George of Denmark's Regiment of Foot	**1802**	The Royal Marines
		1804-62	Marine Artillery Companies
1690-98	Two Marine Regiments of Foot	**1855-62**	The Royal Marines (Light Infantry)
1698-99	Four Regiments of Marines		
1702-13	Six Regiments of Marines	**1862**	Royal Marine Artillery and Royal Marine Light Infantry
1714-39	Four Invalid Companies of Marines	**1923**	The Royal Marines
1739-48	Ten Regiments of Marines (and Three Colonial Regiments of Marines, 1739-43)		

During the Second World War, among many other specialist units, The Royal Marines raised nine Commandos as assault and raiding troops. Presently established as 3 Commando Brigade (40 Commando RM; 42 Commando RM; 45 Commando Group; with air, ancillary, and support services).

It is a measure of British dependence on maritime power that 32 infantry regiments of the Line have at some stage in their history served as marines (5 hold a 'naval' distinction on their colours and appointments). The Royal Marines bear a single battle honour — 'Gibraltar' — on their colours. When parading with the Army, the Corps takes precedence after The Duke of Edinburgh's Royal Regiment (*Queen's Regulations*, Ch.8)

THE ROYAL MUNSTER FUSILIERS
101st and 104th

1759	East India Company's Bengal (European) Regiment	**1839**	East India Company's 2nd Bengal (European) Regiment
1840	East India Company's 1st Bengal (European) Regiment	**1850**	East India Company's 2nd (Bengal European) Fusiliers
1841	East India Company's 1st (Bengal European) Light Infantry	**1858**	2nd Bengal Fusiliers
		1861	104th Bengal Fusiliers
1846	East India Company's 1st (Bengal European) Fusiliers		
1858	1st Bengal Fusiliers		
1861	101st (Royal Bengal Fusiliers)		

1881	The Royal Munster Fusiliers
1922	*disbanded*

THE ROYAL NORFOLK REGIMENT
9th

1685	Cornwell's Regiment of Foot
1751	9th Foot
1782	9th (East Norfolk) Foot
1881	The Norfolk Regiment
1935	The Royal Norfolk Regiment
1959	*amalgamated with* The Suffolk Regiment *to form* The 1st East Anglian Regiment (Royal Norfolk and Suffolk)
1964	*redesignated* 1st (Royal Norfolk and Suffolk) Battalion, The Royal Anglian Regiment
1968	*redesignated* 1st Battalion, The Royal Anglian Regiment

THE ROYAL NORTHUMBERLAND FUSILIERS
5th

1674	The Irish Regiment (*also a* 'Holland Regiment')
1751	5th Foot
1782	5th, *or* Northumberland Foot
1836	5th, *or* Northumberland Fusiliers
1881	The Northumberland Fusiliers
1935	The Royal Northumberland Fusiliers
1968	*amalgamated with* The Royal Warwickshire Fusiliers, The Royal Fusiliers (City of London Regiment) *and* The Lancashire Fusiliers *to form* The Royal Regiment of Fusiliers

ROYAL PIONEER CORPS

First formed in **1762** but disbanded in the following year. In **1917** a non-combatant Labour Corps, including more than 100,000 Chinese, was raised in France to relieve the shortage of manpower for active duty. The Corps was disbanded in **1919**. In October **1939** (A.O.200) an Auxiliary Military Pioneer Corps was formed (redesignated the following year as the Pioneer Corps). It was fully combatant, and by the end of the Second World War its strength, apart from civilian and prisoner-of-war elements, was in excess of 400,000. The Royal title was conferred in **1946** (A.O.167). The Corps remained an auxiliary organization until **1950** when it was taken onto the Regular establishment.

ROYAL REGIMENT OF ARTILLERY

Until the eighteenth century 'traynes' of artillery were raised and manned on an *ad hoc* basis for a particular campaign. With the end of hostilities they were disbanded.

1716	The first two permanent companies (by modern designation 'batteries') raised by Royal Warrant of George I
1722	These companies grouped with those at Gibraltar and Minorca to form The Royal Regiment of Artillery
1757	24 companies formed into two battalions (later 'brigades') and the Regiment given precedence of all Foot Guards and 'marching regiments' *(but see p.71)*
1771	Strength had increased to four battalions
1794	Corps of Captains Commissaries and Drivers formed
1801	Renamed Corps of Gunner Drivers
1806	Renamed again Royal Artillery Drivers
1855	Board of Ordnance abolished and Royal Artillery transferred to War Office control
1859	Battalions 'brigaded'
1861	Horse and foot artillery of the East India Company transferred to the British establishment
1899	Regiment divided into Royal Garrison Artillery (Coast Defence, Mountain, and Heavy batteries), Royal Horse (*q.v.*), and Field Artillery
1914-18	Anti Aircraft batteries formed
1924	RGA and RFA united as a single corps of Royal Artillery. Royal Horse Artillery retained its separate identity
1938	Mechanization introduced. 'Brigades' renamed 'Regiments'
1939	Anti Tank batteries formed
post-1945	Anti Tank role discontinued. Anti Aircraft Command abolished (1955). Surface to Air Guided Weapons, Surface to Surface Guided Weapons, and Free Flight Rocket systems introduced

---

THE ROYAL REGIMENT OF FUSILIERS

Formed in 1968 by the amalgamation of The Royal Northumberland Fusiliers; The Royal Warwickshire Fusiliers; The Royal Fusiliers (City of London Regiment); and The Lancashire Fusiliers. Reduced to three battalions in 1970.

A regiment of the Queen's Division

THE ROYAL REGIMENT OF WALES
(24th/41st Foot)

Formed in 1969 by the amalgamation of The South Wales Borderers and The Welch Regiment.

A regiment of the Prince of Wales's Division

THE ROYAL SCOTS
(THE ROYAL REGIMENT)
1st

1633-78	In French service as Le Régiment d'Hébron and Le Régiment Douglas except for two brief periods at home between 1661 and 1667
*1678	Earl of Dumbarton's Regiment of Foot
1684	The Royal Regiment of Foot
1751	1st, *or* Royal Regiment of Foot
1812	1st Regiment of Foot, *or* Royal Scots
1821	1st, *or* The Royal Regiment of Foot
1871	1st, *or* The Royal Scots Regiment
1881 (May)	The Lothian Regiment (Royal Scots)
1881 (July)	The Royal Scots (The Lothian Regiment)
1920	The Royal Scots (The Royal Regiment)

*A regiment of the Scottish Division with precedence from 1661 as the senior infantry regiment of the Line

THE ROYAL SCOTS FUSILIERS
21st

1678	Earl of Mar's Regiment of Foot
1686	The Scots Fusiliers Regiment of Foot
1712	The Royal North British Fusiliers
1751	21st (Royal North British) Fusiliers
1877	21st (Royal Scots Fusiliers)
1881	The Royal Scots Fusiliers
1959	*amalgamated with* The Highland Light Infantry (City of Glasgow Regiment) *to form* The Royal Highland Fusiliers (Princess Margaret's Own Glasgow and Ayrshire Regiment)

THE ROYAL SUSSEX REGIMENT
35th and 107th

1701	Earl of Donegall's Regiment of Foot	**1854**	East India Company's 3rd (Bengal European Light Infantry) Regiment
1751	35th Foot		
1782	35th (Dorsetshire) Foot		
1805	35th (Sussex) Foot	**1858**	3rd (Bengal Light Infantry) Regiment
1832	35th (Royal Sussex) Foot	**1861**	107th Bengal Infantry Regiment

1881	The Royal Sussex Regiment
1966	*redesignated* 3rd Battalion, The Queen's Regiment (Royal Sussex)
1968	*redesignated* 3rd Battalion, The Queen's Regiment

ROYAL TANK CORPS
See also Royal Tank Regiment

1916	6 companies of tanks formed called variously the Armoured Car Section of the Motor Machine Gun Corps; Heavy Section, the Machine Gun Corps; and in November Heavy Branch, Machine Gun Corps
1917	Named by Royal Warrant of 27 July The Tank Corps. By the date of the Armistice twenty-five battalions had been formed
1923	The Royal title was conferred on 18 October
1939	*Redesignated* The Royal Tank Regiment (*q.v.*) on formation of The Royal Armoured Corps

ROYAL TANK REGIMENT
See also Royal Tank Corps

1939	So designated on 4 April on formation of The Royal Armoured Corps and promoted in the Order of Precedence of the Regular Army to rank after Cavalry of the Line. On the outbreak of the Second World War there were eight Regular battalions, increased by the end of 1940 to twelve
1939-45	Strength of RTR increased by the addition of six battalions and, indirectly, by the conversion of 33 infantry battalions to mechanized units of the then 'active' formation, The Royal Armoured Corps (*q.v.*) During the post-**1945** period, The Royal Tank Regiment has undergone a continuous process of reorganization and reduction, the former Battalions now redesignated as Regiments

THE ROYAL ULSTER RIFLES
83rd and 86th
See The Royal Irish Rifles

THE ROYAL WARWICKSHIRE REGIMENT (FUSILIERS)
6th

1675	Vane's Regiment (*in Dutch service*)
1685	*Taken on the English establishment*
1751	6th Foot
1782	6th (1st Warwickshire) Foot
1832	6th (Royal Warwickshire) Foot
1881	The Royal Warwickshire Regiment
1963	The Royal Warwickshire Fusiliers
1968	*amalgamated with* The Royal Northumberland Fusiliers; The Royal Fusiliers (City of London Regiment); *and* The Lancashire Fusiliers *to form* The Royal Regiment of Fusiliers

THE ROYAL WELCH FUSILIERS
23rd

1688	Lord Herbert's Regiment of Foot
1712	The Royal Regiment of Welch Fuzileers
1714	The Prince of Wales's Own Royal Regiment of Welch Fusiliers
1727	The Royal Welch Fusiliers
1751	23rd (Royal Welch Fusiliers)
1881	The Royal Welsh Fusiliers
1920	The Royal Welch Fusiliers

A regiment of the Prince of Wales's Division

SCOTS GUARDS

1660	The Scots Regiment of Guards
1712	3rd Foot Guards
1831	The Scots Fusilier Guards
1877	The Scots Guards

A regiment of the Guards Division

THE SCOTTISH DIVISION

The Royal Scots (The Royal Regiment)
The Royal Highland Fusiliers (Princess Margaret's Own Glasgow and Ayrshire Regiment) (1959)
The King's Own Scottish Borderers
The Cameronians (Scottish Rifles) (*disbanded,* 1968)
The Black Watch (Royal Highland Regiment)
Queen's Own Highlanders (Seaforth and Camerons) (1961)
The Gordon Highlanders
The Argyll and Sutherland Highlanders (Princess Louise's)

Army Order 34, 1968

SEAFORTH HIGHLANDERS
(ROSS-SHIRE BUFFS, THE DUKE OF ALBANY'S*)
72nd and 78th

1778 78th Highland Regiment (Seaforth's Highlanders)

1786 72nd (Highland) Regiment

1823 72nd, *or* The Duke of Albany's Own Highlanders

1793 78th (Highland) Regiment, *or* The Ross-shire Buffs

1881 The Seaforth Highlanders (Ross-shire Buffs, The Duke of Albany's)

1961 *amalgamated with* The Queen's Own Cameron Highlanders *to form* Queen's Own Highlanders (Seaforth and Camerons)

*(1823) Frederick, Duke of York and Albany, second son of King George III, and Commander-in-Chief

---

THE SHERWOOD FORESTERS
(NOTTINGHAMSHIRE AND DERBYSHIRE REGIMENT)
45th and 95th

1741 Houghton's Regiment of Foot (56th)

1748 Warburton's Regiment of Foot (45th)

1751 45th Foot

1782 45th (1st Nottinghamshire) Foot

1866 45th (Nottinghamshire Regiment) Sherwood Foresters

1823 95th Foot

1825 95th, *or* Derbyshire Foot

1881 (May) The Derbyshire Regiment (Sherwood Foresters)

1881 (July) The Sherwood Foresters (Derbyshire Regiment)

1902 *redesignated* The Sherwood Foresters (Nottinghamshire and Derbyshire Regiment)

1970 *amalgamated with* The Worcestershire Regiment *to form* The Worcestershire and Sherwood Foresters Regiment (29th/45th Foot)

THE SOMERSET LIGHT INFANTRY
(PRINCE ALBERT'S)
13th

1685	Earl of Huntingdon's Regiment of Foot
1751	13th Foot
1782	13th (1st Somersetshire) Foot
1822	13th (1st Somersetshire Light Infantry)
1842	13th (1st Somersetshire) (Prince Albert's Light Infantry)
1881 (May)	The Somersetshire Regiment (Prince Albert's Light Infantry)
1881 (July)	Prince Albert's Light Infantry (Somersetshire Regiment) *later redesignated* The Somerset Light Infantry (Prince Albert's)
1959	*amalgamated with* The Duke of Cornwall's Light Infantry *to form* The Somerset and Cornwall Light Infantry
1968	*redesignated* 1st Battalion, The Light Infantry

THE SOMERSET AND CORNWALL LIGHT INFANTRY

Formed in 1959 by the amalgamation of The Somerset Light Infantry and The Duke of Cornwall's Light Infantry. Redesignated in 1968 as 1st Battalion, The Light Infantry.

THE SOUTH LANCASHIRE REGIMENT
(THE PRINCE OF WALES'S* VOLUNTEERS)
40th and 82nd

1717	Philip's Regiment of Foot	**1793**	82nd (The Prince of Wales's Volunteers) Foot
1751	40th Foot		
1782	40th (2nd Somersetshire) Foot		

1881	The South Lancashire Regiment (The Prince of Wales's Volunteers)
1958	*amalgamated with* The East Lancashire Regiment *to form* The Lancashire Regiment (Prince of Wales's Volunteers)
1970	*amalgamated* with The Loyal Regiment (North Lancashire) *to form* The Queen's Lancashire Regiment

*(1793) The future King George IV

THE SOUTH STAFFORDSHIRE REGIMENT
38th and 80th

1705	Lillingstone's Regiment of Foot	**1758**	80th (Light-armed) Foot
1751	38th Foot	**1764**	*disbanded*
1782	38th (1st Staffordshire) Foot	**1778**	80th (Royal Edinburgh Volunteers) Foot
		1784	*disbanded*
		1793	80th (Staffordshire Volunteers) Foot

1881 (May)   The North Staffordshire (The Prince of Wales's) Regiment

1881 (July)   The South Staffordshire Regiment

1959   *amalgamated with* The North Staffordshire Regiment (The Prince of Wales's) *to form* The Staffordshire Regiment (The Prince of Wales's)

THE SOUTH WALES BORDERERS
24th

1689   Dering's Regiment of Foot

1751   24th Foot

1782   24th (2nd Warwickshire) Foot

1881   The South Wales Borderers

1969   *amalgamated with* The Welch Regiment *to form* The Royal Regiment of Wales (24th/41st Foot)

THE SPECIAL AIR SERVICE REGIMENT
See also Army Air Corps

Formed from specialist groups in North Africa in **1940** and **1941**, the Regiment was added as a third component to The Army Air Corps in **1944**. Disbanded in **1946**, it was reconstituted as the 22nd S.A.S in **1947** and given a separate and independent identity under Army Order 66 of **1950**, ranking in precedence after the Infantry of the Line

THE STAFFORDSHIRE REGIMENT
(THE PRINCE OF WALES'S)

Formed in 1959 by the amalgamation of The South Staffordshire Regiment and The North Staffordshire Regiment (The Prince of Wales's).

A regiment of the Prince of Wales's Division

THE SUFFOLK REGIMENT
12th

1685	Duke of Norfolk's Regiment of Foot
1686	Earl of Lichfield's Regiment of Foot
1751	12th Foot
1782	12th (East Suffolk) Foot
1881	The Suffolk Regiment
1959	*amalgamated with* The Royal Norfolk Regiment *to form* The 1st East Anglian Regiment (Royal Norfolk and Suffolk)
1964	*redesignated* 1st (Royal Norfolk and Suffolk) Battalion, The Royal Anglian Regiment
1968	*redesignated* 1st Battalion, The Royal Anglian Regiment

THE WELCH REGIMENT
41st and 69th

1719	Independent Companies of Invalids, *subsequently* The 41st (Royal Invalids) Regiment	**1756**	2nd Battalion, 24th Foot
		1758	69th Foot
		1782	69th (South Lincolnshire) Foot
1787	41st Foot		
1822	41st (The Welsh) Foot		

1881	The Welsh Regiment
1920	*redesignated* The Welch Regiment
1969	*amalgamated with* The South Wales Borderers *to form* The Royal Regiment of Wales (24th/41st Foot)

THE WELSH BRIGADE

The South Wales Borderers
The Welch Regiment
⎱ *amalgamated as* The Royal Regiment of Wales (24th/41st Foot), **1969**

The Royal Welch Fusiliers

Army Order 61, 1948

WELSH GUARDS

Raised by Royal Warrant in 1915

A regiment of the Guards Division

THE WESSEX BRIGADE

The Devonshire Regiment
The Dorset Regiment   *amalgamated as* The Devonshire and Dorset Regiment, 1958

The Gloucestershire Regiment

The Royal Hampshire Regiment

The Royal Berkshire Regiment
(Princess Charlotte of Wales's)
The Wiltshire Regiment   *amalgamated as* The Duke of Edinburgh's Royal Regiment
(Duke of Edinburgh's)   (Berkshire and Wiltshire), 1959

Army Order 61, 1948

THE WEST YORKSHIRE REGIMENT
(THE PRINCE OF WALES'S* OWN)
14th

1685	Hales's Regiment of Foot
1751	14th Foot
1782	14th (Bedfordshire) Foot
1809	14th (Buckinghamshire) Foot
1876	14th (Buckinghamshire — The Prince of Wales's Own) Foot
1881 (May)	The West Yorkshire Regiment (Prince of Wales's Own)
1881 (July)	The Prince of Wales's Own (West Yorkshire Regiment)
1920	The West Yorkshire Regiment (The Prince of Wales's Own)
1958	*amalgamated with* The East Yorkshire Regiment (The Duke of York's Own) *to form* The Prince of Wales's Own Regiment of Yorkshire

*(1876) The future King Edward VII

THE WILTSHIRE REGIMENT
(DUKE OF EDINBURGH'S*)
62nd and 99th

1743	62nd Foot	**1760**	99th Foot
1748	*disbanded*	**1763**	*disbanded*
1755	62nd (Royal American) Foot	**1780**	99th (Jamaica) Foot
1756	2nd Battalion, 4th King's Own Regiment	**1783**	*disbanded*
		1794	99th Foot
1758	62nd Foot	**1798**	*disbanded*
1782	62nd (Wiltshire) Foot	**1804-18**	*three times renumbered and disbanded*
		1824	99th (Lanarkshire) Foot
		1874	99th (The Duke of Edinburgh's) Foot

1881 The Wiltshire Regiment (Duke of Edinburgh's)

1959 *amalgamated with* The Royal Berkshire Regiment (Princess Charlotte of Wales's) *to form* The Duke of Edinburgh's Royal Regiment (Berkshire and Wiltshire)

(1874) Prince Alfred, Duke of Edinburgh, second son of Queen Victoria

WOMEN'S ROYAL ARMY CORPS

The Corps has its origin in the Women's Auxiliary Corps, formed in **1917**, redesignated Queen Mary's Auxiliary Army Corps in **1918**, and disbanded the following year. In **1939** the Auxiliary Territorial Service (ATS) was formed (*q.v.*). The present Corps was formed by Royal Warrant in **1949** (A.O.6) and was taken onto the Regular establishment in that year, ranking after Queen Alexandra's Royal Army Nursing Corps.

THE WORCESTERSHIRE REGIMENT
29th and 36th

1694	Farington's Regiment of Foot	**1701**	Viscount Charlemont's Regiment of Foot
1751	29th Foot	**1751**	36th Foot
1782	29th (Worcestershire) Foot	**1782**	36th (Herefordshire) Foot

1881 The Worcestershire Regiment

1900 3rd and 4th Battalions *raised*; *disbanded* 1922

1970 *amalgamated with* The Sherwood Foresters (Nottinghamshire and Derbyshire Regiment) *to form* The Worcestershire and Sherwood Foresters Regiment (29th/45th Foot)

THE WORCESTERSHIRE AND SHERWOOD FORESTERS REGIMENT
(29th/45th FOOT)

Formed in 1970 by the amalgamation of The Worcestershire Regiment and The Sherwood Foresters (Nottinghamshire and Derbyshire Regiment) to form The Worcestershire and Sherwood Foresters Regiment (29th/45th Foot).

A regiment of the Prince of Wales's Division

THE YORK AND LANCASTER REGIMENT
65th and 84th

1756	2nd Battalion, 12th Foot	**1783**	84th Foot
1758	65th Foot	**1809**	84th (York and Lancaster) Foot
1782	65th (2nd Yorkshire, North Riding) Foot		

1881	The York and Lancaster Regiment
1968	*disbanded*

THE YORKSHIRE AND NORTHUMBERLAND BRIGADE
(*renamed* The Yorkshire Brigade, 1957)

The Royal Northumberland Fusiliers (*to* Fusilier Brigade, 1957)

The West Yorkshire Regiment ⎤ *amalgamated as* The Prince of Wales's Own Regiment of
The East Yorkshire Regiment ⎦ Yorkshire, 1958

The Green Howards

The Duke of Wellington's Regiment (West Riding)

The York and Lancaster Regiment (*disbanded*, 1968)

Army Order 61, 1948

THE YORKSHIRE REGIMENT
19th
See The Green Howards

D

BATTLE HONOURS
1662 - 1902
1914 - 1953
1982

'A Battle Honour is a public commemoration of a battle, action or engagement, of which not only past and present, but also future generations of the Regiment can be proud.' Thus Army Council Instruction No. 48 of 28 January 1956. It was not always so.

By the year 1800 the British Army had been engaged in more than two hundred actions on four continents; yet only three had been marked by an award for victories won or for distinguished conduct in the field. The reason for this excessive self-effacement is simply explained. It is yet another example — perhaps the most shabby — of that pathological contempt for the Army which disfigured both public and political attitudes. If (so ran the received wisdom of the age) the soldier's trade was one of little virtue and less pride, what purpose then to dignify it with tunes of glory or trophies of victory? If the Sovereign saw fit to authorize the bearing of 'royal and ancient badges' on the Regimental Colour, that was an eccentricity reserved for kings and queens. The public had no part of it, and cared not at all. In 1759 Canada was no less a far-off country of which it knew little than Czechoslovakia would be two centuries later. The name Quebec was a distant echo[1] and James Wolfe a soldiers' idol, but not yet a popular hero. He was only thirty-two when he died.

The three distinctions which found their way into the military pantheon during this bleak period illustrate most vividly the curious chemistry of the British Army, a synthesis of anomaly, anachronism and sometimes plain absurdity.

William III's Flanders campaign produced a single victory at the siege of Namur in 1695. To mark the occasion the King — probably as a political gesture — singled out the Earl of Granard's Irish Regiment of Foot (18th), redesignated it The Royal Regiment of Ireland, and awarded it the badge of the Lion of Nassau and the motto *Virtutis Namurcensis Praemium*. Not till 215 years later were the thirteen other regiments present at the siege granted the honour NAMUR 1695.

In 1760 the 15th Light Dragoons [*15th Hussars*], raised only in the previous year, distinguished itself as the sole British regiment present at the battle of EMSDORFF. On the recommendation of Prince Ferdinand of Brunswick, who 'could not enough commend the bravery, good conduct, and good countenance with which that Regt. fought', it was permitted by Royal Warrant of 1768 to bear the honour on its Guidon.[2]

The last of these three original distinctions is of an altogether different order, for it shows the entirely arbitrary way in which battle honours were, and would long be, selected and awarded. On 14 April 1784 the commanding officers of the 12th, 39th, 56th and 58th Foot[3] were informed by the Adjutant-General that

> in commemoration of the Glorious Defence ... of Gibraltar during the late memorable siege ... His Majesty has been graciously pleased to permit you to have the word GIBRALTAR put upon your Grenadier and Light Infantry Caps, as also upon your Accoutrements .... and like wise upon the second Colour of the Regiment underneath the number of it.

Accordingly this became the first instance of the emblazoning of a battle

[1] It was not to be gazetted as a battle honour for another 123 years.
[2] The honour was not in fact emblazoned until 1822.
[3] For modern designations see table on pp. 95-8.

honour on the Regimental Colour, as the following contemporary illustration shows:

However, the matter did not end there. On 9 December *1836* the same four regiments were advised that they were permitted to add to their Regimental Colour 'THE CASTLE AND KEY, being part of the Armorial Bearings of that Fortress together with the motto *Montis Insignia Calpe* [The Arms of the Rock of Gibraltar].'

This raised a problem. Gibraltar was first captured in 1704. The occasion was marked at the time by the issue of a medal to all senior officers, but not to the rank and file. No battle honour was awarded, since the practice had not yet been adopted. In *1909*, however, the Ewart Committee (see p.179), in its detailed review of honours and awards since the raising of the Standing Army, awarded GIBRALTAR 1704-5 to the eight regiments engaged in that action. And to avoid confusion it added the dates 1779-1783 to the distinction already awarded to the four regiments which had taken part in the subsequent siege.[4] It was by no means the first, or last, such piece of improvisation.

The new century marked a radical change of both attitudes and policy. Why it should have happened at this particular time it is difficult to be sure, but the most likely explanation is the influential presence at the Horse Guards of Frederick, Duke of York, Captain-General of the Army and a man with a sense of history and a rare understanding of regimental tradition. From now on battle honours came thick and fast — and so did the anomalies, the omissions and the inclusion of engagements which were little more than minor incidents. The first award is an interesting example.

On 1 January 1801 the battle honour MINDEN was granted to the 9th, 20th, 23rd, 25th, 37th and 51st Foot. Why Minden in particular? Certainly it had been

[4]In *1908* (Army Order 73) the former 71st Foot (Highland Light Infantry) was awarded the same distinction, but with the dates 1780-83. Inexplicably, no honour was granted to any regiment involved in the siege of 1727. Twelve would have qualified.

a famous victory (1759), but there had been greater feats of arms before, and equal successes since. It may be presumed that a small but effective regimental lobby was at work, and this theory is supported by yet another anomaly.

In 1760, the year after Minden and fifteen days after Emsdorff, the Marquis of Granby had charged 'bald-headed' to victory at Warburg. Yet WARBURG was not gazetted as a battle honour until *1909* (Army Order 180), and was granted only to the twelve cavalry regiments present. The twelve infantry corps also engaged were ignored. This eclectic pattern was to be repeated many times.

There quickly followed the first 'campaign' award. On 6 July 1802, to mark Abercromby's successful operations of the previous year, the King awarded to the thirty-one regiments present the distinction of a Sphinx superscribed EGYPT to be borne on Guidons and Regimental Colours (it was also to find its way into the headdress badge of eight infantry corps). The *London Gazette* ran as follows:

> ...as a distinguished mark of His Majesty's royal approbation, and as a lasting memorial of the glory acquired to His Majesty's arms [*the closest approximation yet to the idea of a 'Royal Army'*] by the zeal, discipline, and intrepidity of his troops in that arduous and important campaign.

There surely speaks the Duke of York, champion of the common soldier.

Once again the award was followed by two 'afterthoughts'. On 18 December *1841* an exclusive variation of the distinction — the Sphinx superscribed MARABOUT — was granted to the 54th Foot [*2nd Dorset*], while 'five-and-forty years later, after much discussion and not a little opposition, the grant of the Peninsular [*sic*] medal was extended to the survivors of the campaign'.[5]

It is not possible to list in detail here the large number of awards — some of very curious provenance — which were made up to the radical reform of the infantry in 1881 (all are recorded in the accompanying table), but a few will suffice to illustrate some of the curiosities and inconsistencies:

MAIDA (1806). Awarded in 1807 and 1808 to the seven regiments of General Stuart's force operating in Italy. A special clasp to the *Peninsula* medal was granted to survivors of the battle in *1847*.

COPENHAGEN (1801). Awarded in 1819 and 1821 to The Royal Berkshire Regiment and The Rifle Brigade for service with the Fleet. Not until *1951*, however, were these two corps permitted to add to their appointments 'a Naval Crown superscribed 2nd April, 1801'.

PENINSULA. One campaign and twenty-three battle honours were awarded between 1812 and 1842, although four of them with modest justification.[6]

PLASSEY (1757). Awarded to the 39th Foot [*1st Dorset*] on 17 November *1835*, together with the motto *Primus in Indis* to commemorate the first honour granted to a 'Crown' regiment serving in India.

CRIMEA (1854-55). Four battle honours awarded, but no campaign honour.

---

[5]Norman, *Battle Honours of the British Army.*
[6] Regiments were added to the original lists of honours in 1890, 1910 and *1951* (in the latter year SALAMANCA was awarded to 12th Lancers, Coldstream Guards, Scots Guards and The Black Watch).

It is also proper to mention here a small triumph for persistence. Throughout this early period (and indeed long after it) repeated efforts were made to obtain the award of an honour for BELLEISLE (1761). This largely unknown and long-forgotten combined operation became something of an obsession to the units concerned, and their patience was partly rewarded when in *1951* (Army Order 136), 190 years after the action, the honour was granted; partly, that is, because of the fifteen entitled regiments only eight received the award. If there is an explanation, it is that the remaining seven had long since been granted the honours MARTINIQUE 1762 and HAVANNAH, which actions followed in quick succession after the reduction of Belleisle.

In 1881, largely to clarify the situation arising out of the infantry amalgamations of that year, a committee was convened under General Alison to review the whole question of battle honours. Its report, published eight months later, came to the following conclusion: 'The names of such victories only should be retained as either in themselves or by their results have left a mark in history which render their names familiar, not only to the British Army, but also to every educated gentleman.' It was an admirable Victorian sentiment, although it would have been an exceptionally educated gentleman who was familiar with SURINAM (1804), ARABIA (1809), BANDA (1810), BENI BOO ALI (1823), RESHIRE and BUSHIRE (1856), to name but a few. And it threw up some glaring omissions. Thus on 13 March 1882 there were added BLENHEIM, RAMILLIES, OUDENARDE, MALPLAQUET, LOUISBURG and QUEBEC; and on 13 September DETTINGEN.

In more general terms the committee recommended the principles that only victories should be commemorated (always a difficult and contentious issue), and that in order to qualify the Headquarters and at least half the regiment must have been present (a rule not always strictly observed).

In 1909 another committee was convened under General Ewart to examine further claims for honours, and to confirm the awards for the South African War, 1899-1902. This committee ranged considerably more widely than its predecessor. As a result it added the oldest of all battle honours, TANGIER 1662-1680, although in doing so it created another anomaly; for it omitted the old 2nd Tangier Regiment (the 4th Foot, or King's Own Royal Regiment (Lancaster)), which took part in the final actions against the Moors before the evacuation of the town in 1684. It also added, as we have seen, NAMUR 1695 and WARBURG, as well as a number of eighteenth-century battles, and several forgotten West Indies campaigns. It considered, but rejected, claims for Marlborough's victory at Schellenburg and for four of his most celebrated sieges. It confirmed the general rules of eligibility laid down by the Alison Committee, but wisely did not disqualify any past awards which, either in spirit or letter, transgressed those guidelines.[7]

Inevitably the anomalies and apparent inequities remained. The award of battle honours was, and remains, an inexact science, for it is not possible to

---

[7]It refused once more to sanction the still persistent claims for BELLEISLE.

devise, so to speak, a points-table by which to compare the quality of one military achievement with another, or to quantify victory in war. Neither the size of the force involved nor the number of casualties sustained are relevant yardsticks. Wilhelmstahl and Waterloo? Blenheim and Balaklava? The Defence of Ladysmith and the Relief of Ladysmith? In the record of battle honours covered by the period 1662-1902 there are some manifest injustices and as many manifest absurdities. Neither detract from the splendour of the British Army's achievement across those years in which the soldiers and sailors of this island race, from land to land and from coast to coast, built a great Empire. Their reward is not to be measured by committees.

If ever it were impossible to quantify battle honours, that was now to be terribly demonstrated. Where men had been counted in thousands, now they were numbered in millions. The following bare statistics tell their own story. During the First World War the four regiments which comprise the present Royal Regiment of Fusiliers[8] raised between them 15 more battalions than the entire pre-war infantry strength of the Regular Army: that is to say, 163 against 148. Their casualties in killed alone totalled 63,150. They won in all 116 honours.

Throughout that war 163 battles, or series of battles, were selected as honours; or, more strikingly, 5920 separate awards were made to 205 individual regiments. Many have become familiar not only to 'educated gentlemen' but, since the war reached out to every family in the land, have become part of a universal litany of public pride: MONS, YPRES, HILL 60, GALLIPOLI, SOMME, PASSCHENDAELE; but there are also less-remembered fields: BAKU, DOIRAN, NONNE BOSSCHEN, NYANGAO, SCIMITAR HILL. For no war had ranged so widely within so narrow a compass of years.

The magnitude of the task which faced the Army Council after the end of hostilities was of a quite different order to that for which the Alison and Ewart committees had been convened, and its first conclusions were published in Army Order 338 of 4 September 1922, of which the following is an extract:

> His Majesty the King has been graciously pleased to approve of the award of battle honours to regiments and corps under the following conditions:
>
> Regiments and corps will have awarded to them honours due for taking part in the battles enumerated in... the tabulated list of engagements given in the report of the Battles Nomenclature Committee.
>
> There will be only one Honours List for a regiment or corps [viz: *inclusive of all Yeomanry, Special Reserve, Territorial, and Service units*]
>
> Regiments ... will have emblazoned on their Standards, Guidons, and Colours not more than 24 honours of which not more than 10 will be "Great War" honours....
>
> The guiding principle in the selection and allotment of battle honours will be that Headquarters and at least 50 per cent of the effective strength of a unit in a theatre of war must have been present....
>
> Regimental Committees under the chairmanship of their regimental colonels ..... will be set up to select the particular honours for Regimental Colours.

[8]The Royal Northumberland Fusiliers (5th), The Royal Warwickshire Fusiliers (6th), The Royal Fusiliers (7th) and The Lancashire Fusiliers (20th).

When these Committees went to work it soon became clear that many regiments would have difficulty in accommodating even 10 new honours on their existing Regimental Colours, and accordingly a second Army Order (470) was issued on 16 December 1922:

> To obviate the necessity of removing honours at present emblazoned on the colours of regiments and corps, His Majesty the King has been graciously pleased to approve that...
>
> Regiments of cavalry... will have emblazoned on their standards and guidons Battle Honours earned.... up to a maximum of 10, in addition to those already carried....
>
> Battalions of infantry... will have emblazoned on their King's Colour Battle Honours up to a maximum of 10 to commemorate their services in the Great War .... [These] will be shown in the Army List in thicker type.

Accordingly, regiments submitted their claims, and between February 1924 (AO. 49) and November 1924 (AO. 421) ten official lists were published. Between the latter date and August 1939 (AO 150) three additional awards and nine lists of corrections were issued, partly as a result of the cavalry amalgamations of 1922. It was, in almost every respect, a model exercise.

There were 633 separate battle honours awarded to British regiments in the Second World War, almost twice the number granted up to 1939. The reason for this seemingly extravagant proliferation lies not only in the truly global character of the conflict but more particularly in the fundamental change in the nature of war itself. At no stage throughout the six years of its duration was there a static 'front line' in the 1914-18 sense of the Western Front. Instead of massive battles of attrition and the paralysis of trench warfare, it was largely a conflict of movement and of fluid battle, of combined operations and buccaneer raids. There were great set-pieces, but much of the land fighting may be likened to a series of chain-reactions linked together in greater or lesser concentrations of force. Above all, it was dominated by the two great innovations of the First World War, the aeroplane and the tank. This element of fragmentation is reflected in the relative scale of honours as defined by the first report of the post-war Battles Nomenclature Committee: theatre operations, operations, battles, actions, subsidiary actions, engagements.

The Committee's recommendations were published in Army Orders 1 and 2 of 28 January 1956. Army Order No. 1 opens thus:

> Her Majesty the Queen has been graciously pleased to approve the award of Battle Honours to Regiments as outlined below.
>
> Regiments will have awarded to them ... the honours due to them for taking part in the operations enumerated in the tabulated lists of battles, actions and engagements given in the Report of the Battles Nomenclature Committee. Theatre Honours will also be awarded.

Army Council Instruction No. 58, published on the same date, dealt with the submission of claims and set down the official definition of 'units' and 'sub-units'; and the complexity of the subject, even by comparison with the First World War, is underlined by the fact that the ACI ran to 37 paragraphs.

Nevertheless, the rules laid down were almost identical to those which followed the First World War. All battalions of a Regiment, whether Regular, Territorial or Service, were entitled to claim honours, although 'there will only be one Honours List for a Regiment'. With minor and necessary variations, the rule that the Headquarters and at least 50 per cent of a 'unit' had been engaged remained the qualification for an award. Regiments were permitted to select 10 honours to be emblazoned on Standards, Guidons and Queen's Colours, 'the new Honours to be additional to those already carried'.

There remained a matter which had been the subject of some controversy for many years. The Alison Committee of 1881 had ruled that 'only victories' should be commemorated by honours, although this was no more than confirmation of an existing precedent. No honours had been granted for any engagement of the American War of Independence or, more arguably, for Fontenoy, and subsequently no awards were given for actions such as Colenso and Spion Kop. The precedent covered a period when 'battles' could be tidily identified as such, and when they rarely exceeded the compass of a single day. All such precedents, however, had been swept away early in the First World War when, for example, the honour YPRES 1914 covered four separate but overlapping 'battles': La Bassée, Armentières, Messines and Ypres itself (the latter broken down in the official nomenclature into 'Langemarck', 'Gheluvelt' and 'Nonne Bosschen'). War had become a monstrous confusion.

In a conflict of this dimension it was no longer possible to define with eighteenth-century nicety the terms 'victory' and 'defeat', for each was often the consequence of the other. A case in point is GALLIPOLI 1915-16, an honour awarded, together with six associated actions, by the 1922 Committee. Historians account the venture as a whole to have been a defeat, but it is no less arguable that in the context of a four-year war it contributed significantly to ultimate victory.

It is entirely proper that the Committee's view prevailed. 'A Battle Honour is a public commemoration of a battle, action or engagement of which not only past and present, but also future generations of the Regiment can be proud.' And not only the Regiment. There is equal cause for national pride in celebrating gallantry and distinguished conduct in action whatever the immediate outcome may have been. Thus it is very meet and right that DUNKIRK, DIEPPE, CRETE and ARNHEM should have taken their place in the register of honours alongside ALAMEIN, ANZIO, KOHIMA and NORMANDY LANDING.

There remained one further duty for the Battles Nomenclature Committee. Eighteen regiments were engaged in the Korean War, 1950-53, two cavalry, fifteen infantry and The Royal Tank Regiment. Army Order 58 of 1958 published a list of sixteen battle honours. It also gave formal authority for two selected honours to be emblazoned on the Standards, Guidon and Colours of all qualified regiments. (But *see also* p.262)

There is an apparent anomaly in the attribution of battle honours, for since an Army is the sum of its parts it might properly be thought that they are awarded to all Regiments and Corps, irrespective of their role or station; that gunners and sappers, craftsmen and transport drivers, medical orderlies and pioneers should rank equally with the other arms of the service in this 'public commemoration of a battle, action or engagement'. But it is not so — and the reason is a quirk of history.

During the period when the practice of awarding battle honours was slowly finding acceptance the Royal Artillery and the Royal Engineers were still partly civilian organizations, administered and controlled by a separate Board of Ordnance, while the modern service Corps either did not exist at all or where they did consisted largely of civilian personnel outside the competence of the Commander-in-Chief. As the modern Army took shape and shed its civilian tail a curiously unconvincing logic — still exemplified in the phrase 'custom and tradition' — arose; namely, that since the Royal Artillery, the Royal Engineers and the service Corps are present in greater or lesser strength at every engagement, their devotion to duty needs no public acknowledgment.[9] So it is that battle honours are still awarded only to the cavalry and infantry arms and to The Royal Tank Regiment. The British Army is indeed a very singular institution.

The same logic applies to Standards, Guidons and Colours, which are carried only by the cavalry, The Royal Tank Regiment and (with one exception) the infantry. The exception is the Rifle Regiments, which by reason of their original role as skirmishers fighting in extended order did not seek to advertise their presence, and so did not — and do not — carry Colours. The Royal Regiment of Artillery needs no visible symbol. Its Colours are its guns. Standards are carried by the Household Cavalry, Dragoon Guards and The Royal Tank Regiment; Guidons, by Hussars and Lancers; Colours by Foot Guards and Infantry of the Line.

The practice of 'emblazoning' honours dates from the award of GIBRALTAR in 1784, and became common practice from the early years of the nineteenth century. Until 1914 all gazetted honours were emblazoned, in the case of the infantry on the Second, or Regimental, Colour.

However, with the proliferation of awards after the First World War many infantry regiments found it difficult to accommodate any further honours on their Regimental Colours, and accordingly they were authorized by Army Order 170 of 1922 to emblazon 10 selected awards on their First, or King's, Colour. For the same reason the practice was extended after the Second World War, and infantry regiments were authorized to add a further 10 selected honours on their Queen's Colour.

The problem, however, was accentuated after the wholesale amalgamation of infantry regiments after 1958. For example, The Queen's Regiment, formed in 1966 from ten pre-Cardwell regiments (2nd, 3rd, 31st, 35th, 50th, 57th, 70th, 77th, 97th and 107th), found itself with the following 'accumulation' of honours: 65, pre-1914; 107, First World War; 155, Second World War; and 7, Korean War. The same, in greater or lesser degree, applied to most of the other new infantry corps, and accordingly regiments were authorized to emblazon up to 40 honours on each of the Regimental and the Queen's Colours. It was not the least of the problems brought about by amalgamation, for it went to the very root of regimental tradition and pride. The solution, as so often in the long history of the Army, was a not always easy compromise — first the honours common to all the old original regiments, and thereafter a process of free collective bargaining. Unlike many compromises, it was struck without an excess of dust and heat.

Illustrated below, with explanatory captions, are examples of a Standard, a Guidon and infantry Colours, showing different stages of the process of emblazoning:

[9]This disability did not deter Norman Ramsay from his famous exploit at Fuentes d'Oñor, or 'L' Battery, Royal Horse Artillery, from winning three Victoria Crosses at Néry on 1 September 1914.

A

B

C

D

E

F

The following tables are divided into two sections. The first lists every battle honour from 1662 to 1902 in alphabetical order, showing — by modern designation — the regiments entitled to each, with dates of the respective campaigns and actions. It is, however, manifestly impossible within a book of this compass to apply the same method to the honours of the two World Wars. Accordingly in the second section awards covering the period 1914 to 1953 are shown by regiments in order of precedence, giving the honours as authorized in the Army List, with those selected for emblazoning on Standards, Guidons and Colours printed in bold type. Appended on p.262 are the honours awarded for the Falkland Islands campaign of 1982.

A *Standard* of 5th Royal Inniskilling Dragoon Guards (post-1958) In the centre the Castle of Enniskillen above the monogram VDG. In the first and fourth corners the White Horse of Hanover. Note the two Korean battle honours.

B *Guidon* of 13th/18th Royal Hussars (Queen Mary's Own) (post-1954). In the centre the interlaced Cypher QMO. In the first and fourth corners the White Horse of Hanover.

C *Regimental Colour* of The Royal Inniskilling Fusiliers (1954), bearing the pre-1914 honours. In the centre the Castle of Enniskillen. In the four corners the White Horse of Hanover.

D *King's Colour* of 2nd Battalion, The Royal Inniskilling Fusiliers (post-1925), bearing 10 selected First World War honours.

E *Queen's Colour* of The Royal Inniskilling Fusiliers (post-1956), bearing 10 selected honours from the First and Second World Wars.

F *Regimental Colour* of The King's Own Royal Border Regiment (post-amalgamation, 1959) bearing 28 pre-1914 honours. In the centre the Royal Cypher within the Garter. In the four corners the Lion of England (King's Own Royal Regiment (Lancaster)) and below, the China Dragon (The Border Regiment).

BATTLE HONOURS
1662 - 1902

The dates, other than those within brackets, appear on Regimental Colours.
Awards shown in inverted commas are campaign honours.

ABU KLEA   (1885)
  Sudan/Sudanese

19th Hussars
Royal Sussex

'ABYSSINIA'   (1867-1868)
  Abyssinia/Abyssinians

3rd Dragoon Guards
King's Own
Cameronians
Duke of Wellington's
Sherwood Foresters

ADEN   (1839)
  Arabia/Arabs

Royal Dublin Fusiliers
  (then 1st Bombay Europeans)

'AFGHANISTAN, 1839'
  First Afghan War
  Afghanistan/Afghans

4th Hussars
16th Lancers
Queen's
Somerset L.I.
Royal Leicestershire
Royal Munster Fusiliers
  (then 1st Bengal Europeans)

'AFGHANISTAN, 1878-1879'
  Second Afghan War
  Afghanistan/Afghans

10th Hussars
Royal Leicestershire
East Surrey
Loyal North Lancashire
Rifle Brigade

'AFGHANISTAN, 1878-1880'
  Second Afghan War
  Afghanistan/Afghans

9th Lancers
15th Hussars
Royal Northumberland Fusiliers
King's
Suffolk
King's Own Scottish Borderers
East Lancashire
Royal Hampshire
King's Own Yorkshire L.I.
King's Royal Rifle Corps
Seaforth Highlanders
Gordon Highlanders
2nd Gurkha Rifles

Abu Klea. 28 January 1885

'AFGHANISTAN, 1879-1880'
Second Afghan War
Afghanistan/Afghans

6th Dragoon Guards
8th Hussars
Royal Fusiliers
Royal Norfolk
Devonshire
West Yorkshire
East Yorkshire
Royal Irish
King's Own Shropshire L.I.
Manchester
Royal Berkshire
Seaforth Highlanders

AHMAD KHEL (1880)
Afghanistan/Afghans

East Lancashire
King's Royal Rifle Corps

ALBUHERA (1811)
Peninsular War
Spain/French

3rd Dragoon Guards
4th Hussars
13th Hussars
Buffs
Royal Fusiliers
Royal Welch Fusiliers
Gloucestershire
Worcestershire
East Surrey
Border
Dorset
Northamptonshire
Royal Berkshire
Middlesex
King's Royal Rifle Corps

ALI MASJID (1878)
Afghanistan/Afghans

10th Hussars
Royal Leicestershire
Loyal North Lancashire
King's Own Yorkshire L.I.
Rifle Brigade

ALIWAL (1846)
Conquest of The Punjab
(First Sikh War)
India/Sikhs

16th Lancers
East Surrey
Royal West Kent
King's Shropshire L.I.
2nd Gurkha Rifles

ALLY GHUR (1803)
First Mahratta War
India/Indians

Duke of Wellington's

ALMA (1854)
Crimean War
Crimea/Russians

4th Hussars
8th Hussars
11th Hussars
13th Hussars
17th Lancers
Grenadier Guards
Coldstream Guards
Scots Guards
Royal Scots
King's Own
Royal Fusiliers
Green Howards

59th Foot (East Lancashire) at *Ahmad Khel*

57th Foot (Middlesex -'Diehards') at *Albuhera*

16th Lancers at *Aliwal*

Scots Fusilier Guards at *The Alma*

Lancashire Fusiliers
Royal Scots Fusiliers
Royal Welch Fusiliers
Gloucestershire
East Lancashire
Duke of Wellington's
Border
South Staffordshire
Welch
Black Watch
Essex
Sherwood Foresters
Loyal North Lancashire
Royal Berkshire
Royal West Kent
Middlesex
Manchester
Durham L.I.
Cameron Highlanders
Connaught Rangers
Argyll and Sutherland Highlanders
Rifle Brigade

ALMARAZ (1812)
Peninsular War
Spain/French

Royal West Kent
Highland L.I.
Gordon Highlanders

AMBOOR (1767)
Carnatic
India/Indians

Royal Dublin Fusiliers
(then 1st Madras Europeans)

AMBOYNA (1796, 1810)
East Indies/Dutch

Royal Dublin Fusiliers
(then 1st Madras Europeans)

'ARABIA' (1809)
Arabia/Pirates

York and Lancaster

ARCOT (1751)
  India/French

Royal Dublin Fusiliers
  (then 1st Madras Europeans)

ARROYO DOS MOLINOS (1811)
  Peninsular War
  Spain/French

Border

'ASHANTEE' (1873-1874)
  West Africa/Ashantis

Royal Welch Fusiliers
Black Watch
Rifle Brigade

ASSAYE (1803)
  First Mahratta War
  India/Indians

19th Hussars
Highland L.I.
Seaforth Highlanders

A distinction, with the Elephant, borne on Guidon and
Regimental Colours

ATBARA (1898)
  Sudan/Sudanese

Royal Warwickshire
Royal Lincolnshire
Seaforth Highlanders
Cameron Highlanders

'AVA' (1824-1826)
  First Burmese War
  Burma/Burmese

Royal Scots
Somerset L.I.
South Staffordshire
Dorset
Welch
Essex
Sherwood Foresters
Loyal North Lancashire
Royal Irish Fusiliers
Royal Dublin Fusiliers
  (then 1st Madras Europeans)

BADAJOS (1812)
  Peninsular War
  Spain/French

King's Own
Royal Northumberland Fusiliers
Royal Fusiliers
Royal Welch Fusiliers
Royal Inniskilling Fusiliers
East Lancashire
South Staffordshire
South Lancashire
Oxford and Bucks L.I.
Essex
Sherwood Foresters
Northamptonshire
Middlesex
King's Royal Rifle Corps
Highland L.I.
Royal Irish Rifles
  (Royal Ulster Rifles)
Connaught Rangers
Rifle Brigade

Assaye. 28 September 1803

Queen's Own Cameron Highlanders at *Atbara*

BADARA (1759)
  India/Dutch

Royal Munster Fusiliers
  (then 1st Bengal Europeans)

BALAKLAVA (1854)
  Crimean War
  Crimea/Russians

4th Dragoon Guards
5th Dragoon Guards
Royal Dragoons
Royal Scots Greys
4th Hussars
Inniskilling Dragoons
8th Hussars
11th Hussars
13th Hussars
17th Lancers
Argyll and Sutherland Highlanders

BANDA (1796, 1810)
  East Indies/Dutch

Royal Dublin Fusiliers
  (then 1st Madras Europeans)

BARROSA (1811)
  Peninsular War
  Spain/French

Grenadier Guards
Coldstream Guards
Scots Guards
Gloucestershire
Royal Hampshire
Royal Irish Fusiliers
Rifle Brigade

BEAUMONT (1794)
  Flanders/French

Royal Horse Guards
King's Dragoon Guards
3rd Dragoon Guards
5th Dragoon Guards
Royal Dragoons
7th Hussars
11th Hussars
16th Lancers

BELLEISLE (1761)
  (Not awarded until *1951*)
  Atlantic/French

Buffs

Balaklava. Charge of the Heavy Brigade

87th Foot (Royal Irish Fusiliers) at *Barrosa*

Belleisle. 1761

Royal Norfolk
Green Howards
Royal Scots Fusiliers
Worcestershire
East Lancashire
Royal Hampshire
Welch

BENI BOO ALLI (1821)
Persian Gulf/Pirates

Royal Dublin Fusiliers
   (then 1st Bombay Europeans)

BHURTPORE (1826)
India/Indians

11th Hussars
16th Lancers
West Yorkshire
East Lancashire
Royal Munster Fusiliers
   (then 1st Bengal Europeans)
2nd Gurkha Rifles

BLADENSBURG (1814)
War of 1812-1814
America/Americans

King's Own
Royal Scots Fusiliers
Essex
King's Shropshire L.I.

BLENHEIM (1704)
War of the Spanish Succession
Germany/French

King's Dragoon Guards
3rd Dragoon Guards
5th Dragoon Guards
6th Dragoon Guards
7th Dragoon Guards
Royal Scots Greys
5th Lancers
Grenadier Guards
Royal Scots
Buffs
King's
Royal Lincolnshire
East Yorkshire
Bedfordshire and Hertfordshire
Royal Irish
Royal Scots Fusiliers
Royal Welch Fusiliers
South Wales Borderers
Cameronians
Royal Hampshire

BOURBON (1810)
(Now known as *'Réunion'*)
Indian Ocean/French

Welch
Royal Irish Rifles
   (Royal Ulster Rifles)

'BURMAH,1885-1887'
Third Burmese War
Burma/Burmese

Queen's
King's

Bhurtpore. January 1826

Blenheim. 13 August 1704

Somerset L.I.
Royal Scots Fusiliers
Royal Welch Fusiliers
South Wales Borderers
Royal Hampshire
King's Own Yorkshire L.I.
Royal Munster Fusiliers
Rifle Brigade
6th Gurkha Rifles

BUSACO (1810)
Peninsular War
Portugal/French

Royal Scots
Royal Northumberland Fusiliers
Royal Fusiliers
Royal Norfolk
South Wales Borderers
Gloucestershire
South Staffordshire
Black Watch
Oxford and Bucks L.I.
Sherwood Foresters
King's Royal Rifle Corps
Highland L.I.
Cameron Highlanders
Royal Irish Rifles
   (Royal Ulster Rifles)
Connaught Rangers
Rifle Brigade

BUSHIRE (1856)
Persia/Persians

North Staffordshire
Durham L.I.

BUXAR (1764)
India/French

Royal Munster Fusiliers
   (then 1st Bengal Europeans)
Royal Dublin Fusiliers
   (then 1st Bombay Europeans)

A distinction, with the Royal Tiger, borne on the Regimental Colour of the Royal Dublin Fusiliers

CABOOL, 1842
First Afghan War
Afghanistan/Afghans

South Lancashire
Welch

CANDAHAR, 1842
First Afghan War
Afghanistan/Afghans

3rd Hussars
Royal Norfolk
Somerset L.I.

East Surrey
South Lancashire
Welch

CANTON (1857)
Second Chinese War
China/Chinese

East Lancashire

'CAPE OF GOOD HOPE, 1806'
South Africa/Dutch

South Wales Borderers
East Lancashire
Highland L.I.
Seaforth Highlanders
Royal Irish Rifles
   (Royal Ulster Rifles)
Argyll and Sutherland Highlanders

'CARNATIC' (1778-1791)
India/Indians

Highland L.I.
Seaforth Highlanders
Royal Munster Fusiliers
   (then 2nd Bengal Europeans)
Royal Dublin Fusiliers
(then 1st Bombay Europeans)

A distinction, with the Elephant, borne on the Regimental Colour of The Royal Dublin Fusiliers

'CENTRAL INDIA' (1857-1858)
Indian Mutiny
India/Indians

8th Hussars
12th Lancers
14th Hussars
17th Lancers
Royal Inniskilling Fusiliers
South Staffordshire
Sherwood Foresters
Highland L.I.
Seaforth Highlanders
Royal Irish Rifles
   (Royal Ulster Rifles)
Connaught Rangers
Leinster

CHARASIAH (1879)
Second Afghan War
Afghanistan/Afghans

9th Lancers
Royal Hampshire
Seaforth Highlanders
Gordon Highlanders

9th Lancers at *Charasiah*

CHILLIANWALLAH (1849)
Conquest of the Punjab (Second Sikh War)
India/Sikhs

3rd Hussars
9th Lancers
14th Hussars
South Wales Borderers
Gloucestershire
Worcestershire
Royal Munster Fusiliers
   (then 2nd Bengal Europeans)

CHINA (WITH THE DRAGON)
(1840-1842)
China/Chinese

Royal Irish
Cameronians
Border
Royal Berkshire
North Staffordshire

A distinction borne on Regimental Colours

CHITRAL (1895)
North West Frontier/Indians

Buffs
Bedfordshire and Hertfordshire
King's Own Scottish Borderers
East Lancashire
King's Royal Rifle Corps
Seaforth Highlanders
Gordon Highlanders

CIUDAD RODRIGO (1812)
Peninsular War
Spain/French

Royal Northumberland Fusiliers
Oxford and Bucks L.I.
Sherwood Foresters
Middlesex
King's Royal Rifle Corps
Highland L.I.
Royal Irish Rifles
   (Royal Ulster Rifles)
Connaught Rangers
Rifle Brigade

CONDORE (1758)
India/French

Royal Munster Fusiliers
   (then 1st Bengal Europeans)
Royal Dublin Fusiliers
   (then 1st Madras Europeans)

COPENHAGEN (1801)
Naval Engagement
Denmark/Danes

Royal Berkshire

Chillianwallah. 13 January 1849

Rifle Brigade

A Naval Crown superscribed 2nd April, 1801 was awarded in 1951

CORUNNA (1809)
Peninsular War
Spain/French

Grenadier Guards
Royal Scots
Queen's
King's Own
Royal Northumberland Fusiliers
Royal Warwickshire
Royal Norfolk
West Yorkshire
Lancashire Fusiliers
Royal Welch Fusiliers
Cameronians
Gloucestershire
Worcestershire
East Lancashire
Duke of Cornwall's L.I.
Duke of Wellington's
South Staffordshire
South Lancashire
Black Watch
Oxford and Bucks L.I.
Loyal North Lancashire
Royal West Kent
King's Own Yorkshire L.I.
Highland L.I.
Gordon Highlanders
Cameron Highlanders
Argyll and Sutherland Highlanders
Rifle Brigade

DEIG (1804)
First Mahratta War
India/Indians

Duke of Wellington's
Royal Munster Fusiliers
(then 1st Bengal Europeans)

DELHI, 1803
First Mahratta War
India/Indians

Duke of Wellington's

DELHI, 1857
Indian Mutiny
India/Indians

6th Dragoon Guards
9th Lancers
King's
Gloucestershire
Oxford and Bucks L.I.
King's Royal Rifle Corps
Gordon Highlanders
Royal Munster Fusiliers
(then 1st and 2nd Bengal European Fusiliers)
2nd Gurkha Rifles

DETROIT (1812)
War of 1812-1814
America/Americans

Welch

DETTINGEN (1743)
War of the Austrian Succession
Germany/French

Life Guards
Royal Horse Guards

23rd Foot (Royal Welch Fusiliers) and 42nd Foot (Black Watch) at *Corunna*

75th Foot (Gordon Highlanders) and 1st Bengal European Fusiliers (Royal Munster Fusiliers) at *Delhi*

Dettingen. 27 June 1743

King's Dragoon Guards
7th Dragoon Guards
Royal Dragoons
Royal Scots Greys
3rd Hussars
4th Hussars
Inniskilling Dragoons
7th Hussars
Grenadier Guards
Coldstream Guards
Scots Guards
Buffs
King's
Devonshire
Suffolk
Somerset L.I.
Lancashire Fusiliers
Royal Scots Fusiliers
Royal Welch Fusiliers
East Surrey
Duke of Cornwall's L.I.
Duke of Wellington's
Royal Hampshire

DOMINICA (1805)
West Indies/French

Duke of Cornwall's L.I.

DOURO (1809)
Peninsular War
Portugal/French

14th Hussars
Buffs
Northamptonshire
Royal Berkshire

EGMONT-OP-ZEE (1799)
Holland/French

15th Hussars
Grenadier Guards
Royal Scots
Lancashire Fusiliers
King's Own Scottish Borderers
Royal Berkshire
Manchester
Gordon Highlanders
Cameron Highlanders

Passage of the Douro. 12 May 1809

'EGYPT (WITH THE SPHINX)' (1801)
Egypt/French

11th Hussars
12th Lancers
Coldstream Guards
Scots Guards
Royal Scots
Queen's
King's
Royal Lincolnshire
Somerset L.I.
Royal Irish
Lancashire Fusiliers
Royal Welch Fusiliers
South Wales Borderers
King's Own Scottish Borderers
Cameronians
Royal Inniskilling Fusiliers
Gloucestershire
East Lancashire
South Staffordshire
Dorset
South Lancashire
Black Watch
Essex
Northamptonshire
Royal West Kent
Manchester
Gordon Highlanders
Cameron Highlanders
Royal Irish Rifles

(Royal Ulster Rifles)
Royal Irish Fusiliers
Connaught Rangers

A distinction borne on Regimental Guidons and Colours. Awarded in July, 1802.

'EGYPT, 1882-84'
Egypt/Egyptians

Life Guards
Royal Horse Guards
4th Dragoon Guards
7th Dragoon Guards
19th Hussars
Grenadier Guards
Coldstream Guards
Scots Guards
Royal Irish
Duke of Cornwall's L.I.
Royal Sussex
South Staffordshire
Black Watch
Sherwood Foresters
Royal Berkshire
Royal West Kent
King's Shropshire L.I.
King's Royal Rifle Corps
Manchester
York and Lancaster
Highland L.I.
Seaforth Highlanders
Gordon Highlanders
Cameron Highlanders
Royal Irish Fusiliers

61st Foot (Gloucestershire) at *Alexandria, 1801.* The origin of the Regiment's 'back-badge'

Emsdorff. 15th Light Dragoons

'EGYPT, 1884'
 Egypt/Egyptians

10th Hussars

EMSDORFF (1760)
 Seven Years' War
  (The first recorded battle honour)
 Germany/French

15th Hussars

FEROZESHAH (1845)
 Conquest of the Punjab (First Sikh War)
 India/Sikhs

3rd Hussars
Royal Norfolk
Worcestershire
East Surrey
South Staffordshire
Royal West Kent
Wiltshire
Royal Munster Fusiliers
  (then 1st Bengal European L.I.)

FISHGUARD (1797)
  (A *Militia* honour)
 Wales/French

Pembrokeshire Yeomanry

An honour borne on the Regiment's cap badge

9th Foot (Royal Norfolk), 29th Foot (Worcestershire), and
31st Foot (East Surrey) at *Ferozeshah*

FUENTES D'OÑOR (1811)
 Peninsular War
 Spain/French

Royal Dragoons
14th Hussars
16th Lancers
Coldstream Guards
Scots Guards
South Wales Borderers
Black Watch
Oxford and Bucks L.I.
Sherwood Foresters
King's Own Yorkshire L.I.
King's Shropshire L.I.
King's Royal Rifle Corps
Durham L.I.
Gordon Highlanders
Cameron Highlanders
Royal Irish Rifles
  (Royal Ulster Rifles)
Connaught Rangers
Rifle Brigade

GHUZNEE, 1839
 First Afghan War
 Afghanistan/Afghans

4th Hussars
16th Lancers
Queen's
Somerset L.I.
Royal Leicestershire
Royal Munster Fusiliers
  (then 1st Bengal Europeans)

Royal Horse Artillery. Captain Ramsay's Troop at *Fuentes d'Oñor*

GHUZNEE, 1842
First Afghan War
Afghanistan/Afghans

South Lancashire
Welch

GIBRALTAR, 1704-5
Gibraltar/Spanish & French

Grenadier Guards
Coldstream Guards
King's Own
Somerset L.I.
East Lancashire
East Surrey
Duke of Cornwall's L.I.
Royal Sussex

GIBRALTAR, 1779-1783
(With Castle and Key, and motto 'Montis Insignia Calpe')
Gibraltar/French

Suffolk
Dorset
Essex
Northamptonshire
Highland L.I. (1780-83)

GOOJERAT (1849)
Conquest of the Punjab (Second Sikh War)
India/Sikhs

3rd Hussars

9th Lancers
14th Hussars
Royal Lincolnshire
South Wales Borderers
Gloucestershire
Worcestershire
Duke of Cornwall's L.I.
King's Shropshire L.I.
King's Royal Rifle Corps
Royal Munster Fusiliers
    (then 2nd Bengal Europeans)
Royal Dublin Fusiliers
    (then 1st Bombay European Fusiliers)

GUADELOUPE, 1759
West Indies/French

Buffs
King's Own
Gloucestershire
South Staffordshire
Welch
Manchester
North Staffordshire
York and Lancaster

GUADELOUPE, 1810
West Indies/French

East Yorkshire
Cameronians
East Surrey
Manchester

Ghuznee. August 1842

Siege and relief of Gibraltar, 1779-83

Guadeloupe, 1810

'GUZERAT' (1776-1782)
   Carnatic
   India/Indians

Royal Munster Fusiliers
   (then 1st Bengal Europeans)
Royal Dublin Fusiliers
   (then 1st Bombay Europeans)

HAFIR (1896)
   Sudan/Sudanese

North Staffordshire

HAVANNAH (1762)
   Cuba/Spanish

Royal Scots
Royal Norfolk
East Yorkshire
Royal Leicestershire
Cheshire
Royal Inniskilling Fusiliers
Gloucestershire
Border
Royal Sussex

South Lancashire
Black Watch
Oxford and Bucks L.I.
Essex
Northamptonshire
King's Royal Rifle Corps

'HINDOOSTAN' (1790-1823)
   India/Indians

8th Hussars
Royal Leicestershire*
Worcestershire
Duke of Wellington's**
Oxford and Bucks L.I.
Highland L.I.
Seaforth Highlanders

A distinction, with the Royal Tiger or the Elephant**,
borne on Regimental Colours. Awarded variously between
1807 and 1837*

HYDERABAD (1843)
   Conquest of Scinde
   India/Indians

Cheshire

'INDIA' (1796-1826)
India/Indians

Suffolk
West Yorkshire
Royal Hampshire
Welch
York and Lancaster
Gordon Highlanders
Royal Irish Rifles
  (Royal Ulster Rifles)

A distinction, with the Royal Tiger borne on the Regimental Colours of West Yorkshire, Royal Hampshire, York and Lancaster, and Gordon Highlanders

INKERMAN (1854)
Crimean War
Crimea/Russians

4th Hussars
8th Hussars
11th Hussars
13th Hussars
17th Lancers
Grenadier Guards
Coldstream Guards
Scots Guards
Royal Scots
King's Own
Royal Fusiliers
Green Howards
Lancashire Fusiliers
Royal Scots Fusiliers
Royal Welch Fusiliers
Gloucestershire
East Lancashire
Duke of Wellington's
Border
South Staffordshire
Welch
Essex
Sherwood Foresters
Loyal North Lancashire
Royal Berkshire
Royal West Kent
Middlesex
Manchester
Durham L.I.
Connaught Rangers
Rifle Brigade

JAVA (1811)
East Indies/French

West Yorkshire
East Lancashire
Welch
Seaforth Highlanders
Royal Irish Fusiliers

JELLALABAD (1842)
First Afghan War
Afghanistan/Afghans

Somerset L.I.

An honour, with Mural Crown, borne on the Regimental Colour and appointments

JERSEY, 1781
(A *Militia* honour)
Channel Islands/French

Royal Jersey Light Infantry

KABUL, 1879
Second Afghan War
Afghanistan/Afghans

9th Lancers
Royal Norfolk
Royal Hampshire
Seaforth Highlanders
Gordon Highlanders
2nd Gurkha Rifles

KANDAHAR, 1880
Second Afghan War
Afghanistan/Afghans

9th Lancers
Royal Fusiliers
Royal Berkshire
King's Royal Rifle Corps
Seaforth Highlanders
Gordon Highlanders
2nd Gurkha Rifles

'KHARTOUM' (1898)
Sudan/Sudanese

21st Lancers
Grenadier Guards
Royal Northumberland Fusiliers
Royal Warwickshire
Royal Lincolnshire
Lancashire Fusiliers
Seaforth Highlanders
Cameron Highlanders
Rifle Brigade

KHELAT (1839)
First Afghan War
Afghanistan/Afghans

Queen's
Royal Leicestershire

KIMBERLEY, DEFENCE OF (1899-1900)
Second Boer War
South Africa/Boers

Loyal North Lancashire

Jersey, 1781

Charge of 9th Lancers at *Kandahar*

KIMBERLEY, RELIEF OF (1900)
Second Boer War
South Africa/Boers

Life Guards
Royal Horse Guards
6th Dragoon Guards
Royal Scots Greys
9th Lancers
10th Hussars
12th Lancers
16th Lancers
Buffs
Green Howards
Gloucestershire
Duke of Wellington's
Welch
Oxford and Bucks L.I.
Essex

KIRBEKAN (1885)
Sudan/Sudanese

South Staffordshire
Black Watch

KIRKEE (1817)
Second Mahratta War
India/Indians

Royal Dublin Fusiliers
(then 1st Bombay Europeans)

KOOSH-AB (1857)
Persia/Persians

North Staffordshire
Durham L.I.
Seaforth Highlanders

LADYSMITH, DEFENCE OF (1899-1900)
Second Boer War
South Africa/Boers

5th Dragoon Guards
5th Lancers
18th Hussars
19th Hussars
King's
Devonshire
Royal Leicestershire
Gloucestershire
King's Royal Rifle Corps
Manchester
Gordon Highlanders
Rifle Brigade

LADYSMITH, RELIEF OF (1900)
Second Boer War
South Africa/Boers

Royal Dragoons
13th Hussars
14th Hussars
Queen's
King's Own
Royal Fusiliers
Devonshire

Charge of 21st Lancers at *Omdurman*

Somerset L.I.
West Yorkshire
Lancashire Fusiliers
Royal Scots Fusiliers
Royal Welch Fusiliers
Cameronians
Royal Inniskilling Fusiliers
East Surrey
Border
Dorset
South Lancashire
Northamptonshire
King's Royal Rifle Corps
York and Lancaster
Durham L.I.
Royal Irish Fusiliers
Connaught Rangers
Royal Dublin Fusiliers
Rifle Brigade

LESWARREE (1803)
First Mahratta War
India/Indians

8th Hussars
Duke of Wellington's

LINCELLES (1793)
France/French

Grenadier Guards
Coldstream Guards
Scots Guards

Kirkee. 5 November 1817

LOUISBURG (1758)
Canada/French

Royal Scots
East Yorkshire
Royal Leicestershire
Cheshire
Gloucestershire
Royal Sussex
South Lancashire
Sherwood Foresters
Loyal North Lancashire
Northamptonshire
King's Royal Rifle Corps
Wiltshire

LUCKNOW (1857-1858)
Indian Mutiny
India/Indians

Queen's Bays
7th Hussars
9th Lancers
Royal Northumberland Fusiliers
King's
Royal Lincolnshire
Lancashire Fusiliers
Cameronians
Duke of Cornwall's L.I.
Border
South Staffordshire
South Lancashire
Black Watch
Royal West Kent

Koosh-ab. 8 February 1857

8th Light Dragoons at *Leswarree*

Queen's Bays at *Lucknow*

King's Shropshire L.I.
North Staffordshire
York and Lancaster
Seaforth Highlanders
Gordon Highlanders
Cameron Highlanders
Argyll and Sutherland Highlanders
Royal Munster Fusiliers
   (then 1st Bengal European Fusiliers)
Royal Dublin Fusiliers
   (then 1st Bombay European Fusiliers)

MAHARAJPORE (1843)
   Gwalior Campaign
   India/Indians

16th Lancers
Dorset
South Lancashire

MAHEIDPORE (1817)
   Second Mahratta War
   India/Indians

Royal Scots
Royal Dublin Fusiliers
   (then 1st Madras Europeans)

MAIDA (1806)
   Italy/French

Lancashire Fusiliers
Royal Inniskilling Fusiliers
Gloucestershire
Royal Sussex

Loyal North Lancashire
Northamptonshire
Seaforth Highlanders

MALPLAQUET (1709)
   War of the Spanish Succession
   Flanders/French

King's Dragoon Guards
3rd Dragoon Guards
5th Dragoon Guards
6th Dragoon Guards
7th Dragoon Guards
Royal Scots Greys
5th Lancers
Grenadier Guards
Coldstream Guards
Royal Scots
Buffs
King's
Royal Lincolnshire
East Yorkshire
Bedfordshire and Hertfordshire
Royal Irish
Green Howards
Royal Scots Fusiliers
Royal Welch Fusiliers
South Wales Borderers
Cameronians
Royal Hampshire

MANDORA (1801)
   Egypt/French

Cameronians
Gordon Highlanders

Maida. 4 July 1806

MANGALORE (1783)
Carnatic
India/Indians

Black Watch

MARABOUT (1802)
Egypt/French

Dorset

A distinction, with the Sphinx, borne on the Regimental Colour and appointments

MARTINIQUE, 1762
West Indies/French

East Yorkshire
Royal Leicestershire
Cheshire
Royal Inniskilling Fusiliers
Gloucestershire
Royal Sussex
South Staffordshire
South Lancashire
Welch
Black Watch
Oxford and Bucks L.I.
Northamptonshire
King's Royal Rifle Corps

MARTINIQUE, 1794
West Indies/French

Royal Warwickshire
Royal Norfolk
East Yorkshire
Royal Scots Fusiliers
East Surrey
Dorset
Oxford and Bucks L.I.
Northamptonshire
North Staffordshire
York and Lancaster

MARTINIQUE, 1809
West Indies/French

Royal Fusiliers
King's
Somerset L.I.
East Yorkshire
Royal Welch Fusiliers
King's Own Scottish Borderers
Cameronians
King's Royal Rifle Corps
Manchester

MASULIPATAM (1759)
India/French

Royal Munster Fusiliers
 (then 1st Bengal Europeans)

MEDITERRANEAN

Awarded to ten *Militia* Battalions for services during the Crimean War, but withdrawn on creation of the Special Reserve.

MEDITERRANEAN, 1900-02

Awarded to eight *Militia* Battalions for services during the Second Boer War, but withdrawn on creation of the Special Reserve.

MEEANEE (1843)
Conquest of Scinde
India/Indians

Cheshire

Malplaquet. 11 September 1709

Storming of *Fort Royal, Martinique, 24 March 1794*

Meeanee. 17 February 1843

MIAMI (1813)
War of 1812-1814
America/Americans

Welch

MINDEN (1759)
Seven Years' War
Germany/French

Suffolk
Lancashire Fusiliers
Royal Welch Fusiliers
King's Own Scottish Borderers
Royal Hampshire
King's Own Yorkshire L.I.

MODDER RIVER (1899)
Second Boer War
South Africa/Boers

9th Lancers
Grenadier Guards
Coldstream Guards
Scots Guards
Royal Northumberland Fusiliers
Northamptonshire
King's Own Yorkshire L.I.
Highland L.I.
Argyll and Sutherland Highlanders

MONTE VIDEO (1807)
South America/Spanish

South Staffordshire
South Lancashire
Royal Irish Fusiliers
Rifle Brigade

MOODKEE (1845)
Conquest of the Punjab (First Sikh War)
India/Sikhs

3rd Hussars
Royal Norfolk
East Surrey
South Staffordshire
Royal West Kent

MOOLTAN (1849)
Conquest of the Punjab (Second Sikh War)
India/Sikhs

Royal Lincolnshire
Duke of Cornwall's L.I.
King's Royal Rifle Corps
Royal Dublin Fusiliers
   (then 1st Bombay European Fusiliers)

MORO (1762)
Cuba/Spanish

Essex

'MYSORE' (1789-91)
India/Indians

19th Hussars

Minden. 1 August 1759

Monte Video, 1807

31st Foot (East Surrey) at *Moodkee*

Worcestershire
Duke of Wellington's
Black Watch
Oxford and Bucks L.I.
Middlesex
Highland L.I.
Seaforth Highlanders
Gordon Highlanders
Royal Dublin Fusiliers
 (then 1st Madras Europeans)

A distinction, with the Elephant, borne on the Regimental Colour of the Royal Dublin Fusiliers

NAGPORE (1817)
**Second Mahratta War
India/Indians**

Royal Scots

NAMUR, 1695
Awarded in *1910*
Flanders/French

Grenadier Guards
Coldstream Guards
Scots Guards
Royal Scots
Queen's
King's Own
Royal Warwickshire
Royal Fusiliers
West Yorkshire
Bedfordshire and Hertfordshire
Royal Leicestershire

Royal Irish
Royal Welch Fusiliers
King's Own Scottish Borderers

The motto 'Virtutis Namurcensis Praemium' borne on the Regimental Colour of the Royal Irish alone

NAVAL CROWN, 12th APRIL, 1782
**Naval engagement
West Indies/French**

Welch

A distinction borne on the Regimental Colour

NAVAL CROWN, 1st JUNE, 1794
**Naval engagement
Atlantic/French**

Queen's
Worcestershire

A distinction borne on the Regimental Colours

NEW ZEALAND (1846-1847)
**Maori Wars
New Zealand/Maoris**

Northamptonshire
Wiltshire
Manchester

NEW ZEALAND (1860-1861)
**Maori Wars
New Zealand/Maoris**

Suffolk
West Yorkshire

Namur, July 1695

South Lancashire
Middlesex
York and Lancaster

NEW ZEALAND (1863-1866)
Maori Wars
New Zealand/Maoris

Suffolk
West Yorkshire
Royal Irish
East Surrey
Oxford and Bucks L.I.
Royal West Kent
Durham L.I.

NIAGARA (1813)
War of 1812-1814
America/Americans

19th Hussars
Royal Scots

Royal Warwickshire
King's
South Lancashire
Welch
Royal Irish Fusiliers
Leinster

NIEUPORT (1793)
Flanders/French

King's Shropshire L.I.

'NILE, 1884-85'
Sudan/Sudanese

19th Hussars
Royal Irish
Duke of Cornwall's L.I.
Royal Sussex
South Staffordshire
Black Watch
Essex
Royal West Kent
Gordon Highlanders
Cameron Highlanders

14th Foot (West Yorkshire) in *New Zealand, 1861*

Argyll and Sutherland Highlanders
Rifle Brigade

NIVE (1813)
Peninsular War
Spain/French

16th Lancers
Grenadier Guards
Coldstream Guards
Scots Guards
Royal Scots
Buffs
King's Own
Royal Norfolk
Devonshire
Gloucestershire
Worcestershire
East Lancashire
East Surrey
Duke of Cornwall's L.I.
Duke of Wellington's
Border
South Staffordshire
Dorset
Black Watch
Oxford and Bucks L.I.
Loyal North Lancashire
Royal Berkshire
Royal West Kent
King's Shropshire L.I.
Middlesex
King's Royal Rifle Corps
Wiltshire
York and Lancaster
Highland L.I.
Gordon Highlanders
Cameron Highlanders

NIVELLE (1813)
Peninsular War
Spain/French

Queen's
Buffs
Royal Northumberland Fusiliers
Devonshire
Royal Welch Fusiliers
South Wales Borderers
Royal Inniskilling Fusiliers
Gloucestershire
Worcestershire
East Surrey
Duke of Cornwall's L.I.
Border
Dorset
South Lancashire
Black Watch
Oxford and Bucks L.I.
Sherwood Foresters
Northamptonshire
Royal Berkshire
King's Own Yorkshire L.I.
King's Shropshire L.I.
Middlesex
King's Royal Rifle Corps
Durham L.I.
Highland L.I.
Cameron Highlanders
Royal Irish Rifles
    (Royal Ulster Rifles)
Royal Irish Fusiliers
Connaught Rangers

Argyll and Sutherland Highlanders
Rifle Brigade

'NORTH AMERICA, 1763-64'
America/Indians

Black Watch
King's Royal Rifle Corps

NUNDY DROOG   (1791)
Conquest of Mysore
India/Indians

Royal Dublin Fusiliers
  (then 1st Madras Europeans)

ORTHES   (1814)
Peninsular War
Spain/French

7th Hussars
13th Hussars
14th Hussars
Buffs
Royal Northumberland Fusiliers
Royal Warwickshire
Royal Fusiliers

Devonshire
Lancashire Fusiliers
Royal Welch Fusiliers
South Wales Borderers
Royal Inniskilling Fusiliers
Gloucestershire
Worcestershire
East Surrey
Duke of Cornwall's L.I.
Border
Dorset
South Lancashire
Black Watch
Oxford and Bucks L.I.
Sherwood Foresters
Northamptonshire
Royal Berkshire
Royal West Kent
King's Own Yorkshire L.I.
King's Royal Rifle Corps
Durham L.I.
Highland L.I.
Gordon Highlanders
Royal Irish Fusiliers
Royal Irish Rifles
  (Royal Ulster Rifles)
Connaught Rangers

Nundy Droog. 19 October 1791

Argyll and Sutherland Highlanders
Rifle Brigade

OUDENARDE (1708)
War of the Spanish Succession
Flanders/French

King's Dragoon Guards
3rd Dragoon Guards
5th Dragoon Guards
6th Dragoon Guards
7th Dragoon Guards
Royal Scots Greys
5th Lancers
Grenadier Guards
Coldstream Guards
Royal Scots
Buffs
King's
Royal Lincolnshire
East Yorkshire
Bedfordshire and Hertfordshire
Royal Irish
Royal Scots Fusiliers
Royal Welch Fusiliers
South Wales Borderers
Cameronians
Royal Hampshire

PAARDEBERG (1900)
Second Boer War
South Africa/Boers

Life Guards

Royal Horse Guards
6th Dragoon Guards
Royal Scots Greys
9th Lancers
10th Hussars
12th Lancers
16th Lancers
Buffs
Royal Norfolk
Royal Lincolnshire
Green Howards
King's Own Scottish Borderers
Gloucestershire
Duke of Cornwall's L.I.
Duke of Wellington's
Royal Hampshire
Welch
Black Watch
Oxford and Bucks L.I.
Essex
King's Shropshire L.I.
Seaforth Highlanders
Gordon Highlanders
Argyll and Sutherland Highlanders

'PEGU' (1852-1853)
Second Burmese War
Burma/Burmese

Royal Irish
South Staffordshire
King's Own Yorkshire L.I.
Royal Munster Fusiliers
   (then 2nd Bengal European Fusiliers)

Oudenarde. 30 June 1708

Paardeberg. February 1900

Royal Dublin Fusiliers
  (then 1st Bombay European Fusiliers)

PEIWAR KOTAL   **(1878)**
  Second Afghan War
  Afghanistan/Afghans

King's
Seaforth Highlanders

PEKIN, 1860
  Second Chinese War
  China/Chinese

King's Dragoon Guards
Royal Scots
Queen's
Royal Hampshire
King's Royal Rifle Corps
Wiltshire

PEKIN, 1900
  Boxer Rebellion
  China/Chinese

Royal Welch Fusiliers

'PENINSULA'   **(1808-1814)**
  Iberia/French

Life Guards
Royal Horse Guards
3rd Dragoon Guards
4th Dragoon Guards
5th Dragoon Guards
Royal Dragoons
3rd Hussars
4th Hussars
7th Hussars
9th Lancers

10th Hussars
11th Hussars
12th Lancers
13th Hussars
14th Hussars
15th Hussars
16th Lancers
18th Hussars
20th Hussars
Grenadier Guards
Coldstream Guards
Scots Guards
Royal Scots
Queen's
Buffs
King's Own
Royal Northumberland Fusiliers
Royal Warwickshire
Royal Fusiliers
Royal Norfolk
Royal Lincolnshire
Devonshire
Lancashire Fusiliers
Royal Welch Fusiliers
South Wales Borderers
Royal Inniskilling Fusiliers
Gloucestershire
Worcestershire
East Lancashire
East Surrey
Duke of Cornwall's L.I.
Duke of Wellington's
Border
Royal Hampshire
South Staffordshire
Dorset
South Lancashire
Black Watch
Oxford and Bucks L.I.
Essex
Sherwood Foresters

Peninsula. 95th (Rifle) Regiment (The Rifle Brigade)

Loyal North Lancashire
Northamptonshire
Royal Berkshire
Royal West Kent
King's Own Yorkshire L.I.
King's Shropshire L.I.
Middlesex
King's Royal Rifle Corps
Wiltshire
Manchester
York and Lancaster
Durham L.I.
Highland L.I.
Gordon Highlanders
Cameron Highlanders
Royal Irish Rifles
   (Royal Ulster Rifles)
Royal Irish Fusiliers
Connaught Rangers
Argyll and Sutherland Highlanders
Rifle Brigade

'PERSIA' (1856-1857)
Persia/Persians

14th Hussars
North Staffordshire
Durham L.I.
Seaforth Highlanders

PLASSEY (1757)
First 'Crown' battle honour in India
India/French

Dorset
   (with motto 'Primus in Indis')
Royal Munster Fusiliers
   (then 1st Bengal Europeans)
Royal Dublin Fusiliers
   (then 1st Madras Europeans)

A distinction, with the Royal Tiger, borne on the Regimental Colours of the two latter regiments

PONDICHERRY (1761, 1778, 1793)
India/French

Royal Dublin Fusiliers
   (then 1st Madras Europeans)

'PUNJAUB' (1848-1849)
Second Sikh War
India/Sikhs

3rd Hussars
9th Lancers
14th Hussars
Royal Lincolnshire
South Wales Borderers
Gloucestershire
Worcestershire
Duke of Cornwall's L.I.
King's Shropshire L.I.
King's Royal Rifle Corps
North Staffordshire

Royal Munster Fusiliers
(then 1st Bengal Europeans)
Royal Dublin Fusiliers
(then 1st Bombay Europeans)

PUNNIAR (1843)
Gwalior Campaign
India/Indians

9th Lancers
Buffs
Royal West Kent

PYRENEES (1813)
Peninsular War
Spain/French

14th Hussars
Queen's
Buffs
Royal Warwickshire
Royal Fusiliers
Devonshire
Lancashire Fusiliers
Royal Welch Fusiliers
South Wales Borderers
Royal Inniskilling Fusiliers
Gloucestershire
Worcestershire
East Surrey
Duke of Cornwall's L.I.
Border
South Lancashire
Black Watch

Oxford and Bucks L.I.
Sherwood Foresters
Northamptonshire
Royal Berkshire
Royal West Kent
King's Own Yorkshire L.I.
King's Shropshire L.I.
Middlesex
King's Royal Rifle Corps
Durham L.I.
Highland L.I.
Gordon Highlanders
Cameron Highlanders
Connaught Rangers
Argyll and Sutherland Highlanders
Rifle Brigade

QUEBEC (1759)
Canada/French

East Yorkshire
Gloucestershire
Royal Sussex
Oxford and Bucks L.I.
Loyal North Lancashire
Northamptonshire
King's Royal Rifle Corps

QUEENSTOWN (1812)
War of 1812-1814
America/Americans

Welch
Royal Berkshire

Quebec. 13 September 1759

Ramillies. 12 May 1706

RAMILLIES (1706)
War of the Spanish Succession
Flanders/French

King's Dragoon Guards
3rd Dragoon Guards
5th Dragoon Guards
6th Dragoon Guards
7th Dragoon Guards
Royal Scots Greys
5th Lancers
Grenadier Guards
Royal Scots
Buffs
King's
Royal Lincolnshire
East Yorkshire
Bedfordshire and Hertfordshire
Royal Irish
Royal Scots Fusiliers
Royal Welch Fusiliers
South Wales Borderers
Cameronians
Gloucestershire
Worcestershire
Royal Hampshire

RESHIRE (1856)
Persia/Persians

North Staffordshire
Durham L.I.

ROHILCUND, 1774
India/Indians

Royal Munster Fusiliers
(then 2nd Bengal Europeans)

ROHILCUND, 1794
Conquest of Mysore
India/Indians

Royal Munster Fusiliers
(then 2nd Bengal Europeans)

ROLICA (1808)
Peninsular War
Portugal/French

Royal Northumberland Fusiliers
Royal Warwickshire
Royal Norfolk
Worcestershire
Duke of Cornwall's L.I.
South Staffordshire
South Lancashire
Sherwood Foresters
King's Royal Rifle Corps

Highland L.I.
Argyll and Sutherland Highlanders
Rifle Brigade

SAHAGUN (1808)
Peninsular War
Spain/French

15th Hussars

ST HELENA (1900-1902)
Second Boer War
A *Militia* curiosity

ST. LUCIA, 1778
West Indies/French

King's Own
Royal Northumberland Fusiliers
East Yorkshire
Royal Inniskilling Fusiliers
Gloucestershire
Duke of Cornwall's L.I.
Border
Royal Sussex
South Lancashire
Royal Berkshire

ST. LUCIA, 1796
West Indies/French

Royal Inniskilling Fusiliers
King's Shropshire L.I.

ST. LUCIA, 1803
West Indies/French

Royal Scots
North Staffordshire

ST. VINCENT (1795)
Naval engagement
West Indies/French

Welch

SALAMANCA (1812)
Peninsular War
Spain/French

5th Dragoon Guards
3rd Hussars
4th Hussars
11th Hussars
12th Lancers
14th Hussars
16th Lancers
Coldstream Guards
Scots Guards
Royal Scots
Queen's
King's Own
Royal Northumberland Fusiliers

Royal Fusiliers
Royal Norfolk
Devonshire
Royal Welch Fusiliers
South Wales Borderers
Royal Inniskilling Fusiliers
Gloucestershire
Worcestershire
East Lancashire
Duke of Cornwall's L.I.
South Staffordshire
South Lancashire
Black Watch
Oxford and Bucks L.I.
Essex
Sherwood Foresters
Northamptonshire
King's Own Yorkshire L.I.
King's Shropshire L.I.
King's Royal Rifle Corps
Durham L.I.
Highland L.I.
Cameron Highlanders
Royal Irish Rifles
   (Royal Ulster Rifles)
Connaught Rangers
Rifle Brigade

SAN SEBASTIAN (1813)
Peninsular War
Spain/French

Royal Scots
King's Own
Royal Norfolk
East Lancashire
South Staffordshire
Loyal North Lancashire

'SCINDE' (1843)
India/Indians

Cheshire

SERINGAPATAM (1799)
Conquest of Mysore
India/Indians

19th Hussars
Suffolk
Duke of Wellington's
Black Watch
Middlesex
Highland L.I.
Gordon Highlanders
Connaught Rangers
Royal Dublin Fusiliers
   (then 1st Bombay Europeans)

76th Foot (Duke of Wellington's) at *Seringapatam*

'SEVASTAPOL' (1854-1855)
Crimean War
Crimea/Russians

King's Dragoon Guards
4th Dragoon Guards
5th Dragoon Guards
6th Dragoon Guards
Royal Dragoons
Royal Scots Greys
4th Hussars
Inniskilling Dragoons
8th Hussars
10th Hussars
11th Hussars
12th Hussars
13th Hussars
17th Lancers
Grenadier Guards
Coldstream Guards
Scots Guards
Royal Scots
Buffs
King's Own
Royal Fusiliers
Royal Norfolk
Somerset L.I.

West Yorkshire
Royal Leicestershire
Royal Irish
Green Howards
Lancashire Fusiliers
Royal Scots Fusiliers
Royal Welch Fusiliers
Cameronians
Gloucestershire
East Lancashire
East Surrey
Duke of Cornwall's L.I.
Duke of Wellington's
Border
South Staffordshire
Dorset
South Lancashire
Welch
Black Watch
Essex
Sherwood Foresters
Loyal North Lancashire
Northamptonshire
Royal Berkshire
Royal West Kent
Middlesex
Wiltshire
Manchester
Durham L.I.
Highland L.I.

Seaforth Highlanders
Cameron Highlanders
Royal Irish Fusiliers
Connaught Rangers
Argyll and Sutherland Highlanders
Rifle Brigade

SHOLINGHUR (1781)
Carnatic
India/Indians

Highland L.I.
Royal Munster Fusiliers
  (then 1st Bengal Europeans)
Royal Dublin Fusiliers
  (then 1st Madras Europeans)

SOBRAON (1846)
Conquest of Punjab (First Sikh War)
India/Sikhs

3rd Hussars
9th Lancers
16th Lancers
Royal Norfolk
Royal Lincolnshire
Worcestershire
East Surrey
South Staffordshire
Royal West Kent
King's Shropshire L.I.
Wiltshire
Royal Munster Fusiliers
2nd Gurkha Rifles

'SOUTH AFRICA, 1835'
South Africa/Kaffirs

Royal Inniskilling Fusiliers
Seaforth Highlanders
Gordon Highlanders

'SOUTH AFRICA, 1846-47'
South Africa/Gaikas

7th Dragoon Guards
Royal Warwickshire
Cameronians
Royal Inniskilling Fusiliers
Black Watch
Sherwood Foresters
Argyll and Sutherland Highlanders
Rifle Brigade

'SOUTH AFRICA, 1851-53'
South Africa/Gaikas

12th Lancers
Queen's
Royal Warwickshire
Suffolk
Black Watch
Oxford and Bucks L.I.
King's Royal Rifle Corps
Highland L.I.
Argyll and Sutherland Highlanders
Rifle Brigade

'SOUTH AFRICA, 1877-79'
Zula War
South Africa/Zulus

South Wales Borderers
Cameronians
Connaught Rangers

Sobraon. 10 February 1846

South Africa, 1846

South Africa, 1851

'SOUTH AFRICA, 1878-79'
Zulu War
South Africa/Zulus

Somerset L.I.
South Staffordshire

'SOUTH AFRICA, 1879'
Zulu War
South Africa/Zulus

King's Dragoon Guards
17th Lancers
Buffs
King's Own
Royal Scots Fusiliers
Northamptonshire
Middlesex
King's Royal Rifle Corps

Wiltshire
Argyll and Sutherland Highlanders

'SOUTH AFRICA, 1899-1902'
Second Boer War
South Africa/Boers

Life Guards, 1899-1900
Royal Horse Guards, 1899-1900
King's Dragoon Guards, 1901-02
Queen's Bays, 1901-02
3rd Dragoon Guards, 1901-02
5th Dragoon Guards
6th Dragoon Guards
7th Dragoon Guards, 1900-02
Royal Dragoons
Royal Scots Greys
3rd Hussars, 1902

5th Lancers
Inniskilling Dragoons
7th Hussars, 1901-02
8th Hussars, 1900-02
9th Lancers
10th Hussars
12th Lancers
13th Hussars
14th Hussars 1900-02
16th Lancers 1900-02
17th Lancers 1900-02
18th Hussars
19th Hussars
20th Hussars, 1901-02
Grenadier Guards
Coldstream Guards
Scots Guards
Royal Scots
Queen's
Buffs, 1900-02
King's Own
Royal Northumberland Fusiliers
Royal Warwickshire
Royal Fusiliers
King's
Royal Norfolk, 1900-02
Royal Lincolnshire, 1900-02
Devonshire
Suffolk
Somerset L.I.

West Yorkshire
East Yorkshire, 1900-02
Bedfordshire and Hertfordshire, 1900-02
Royal Leicestershire
Royal Irish, 1900-02
Green Howards
Lancashire Fusiliers
Royal Scots Fusiliers
Cheshire, 1900-02
Royal Welch Fusiliers
South Wales Borderers, 1900-02
King's Own Scottish Borderers
Cameronians
Royal Inniskilling Fusiliers
Gloucestershire
Worcestershire, 1900-02
East Lancashire, 1900-02
East Surrey
Duke of Cornwall's L.I.
Duke of Wellington's, 1900-02
Border
Royal Sussex, 1900-02
Royal Hampshire, 1900-02
South Staffordshire, 1900-02
Dorset
South Lancashire
Welch
Black Watch
Oxford and Bucks L.I., 1900-02
Essex
Sherwood Foresters
Loyal North Lancashire

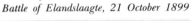

Battle of Elandslaagte, 21 October 1899

Northamptonshire
Royal Berkshire
Royal West Kent, 1900-02
King's Own Yorkshire L.I.
King's Shropshire L.I.
Middlesex, 1900-02
King's Royal Rifle Corps
Manchester
Wiltshire, 1900-02
North Staffordshire, 1900-02
York and Lancaster
Durham L.I.
Highland L.I.
Seaforth Highlanders
Gordon Highlanders
Cameron Highlanders, 1900-02
Royal Irish Rifles
    (Royal Ulster Rifles)
Royal Irish Fusiliers
Connaught Rangers
Argyll and Sutherland Highlanders
Leinster, 1900-02
Royal Munster Fusiliers
Royal Dublin Fusiliers
Rifle Brigade

Varying dates of the honour as shown

SUAKIN, 1885
Sudan/Sudanese

5th Lancers
20th Hussars
Grenadier Guards
Coldstream Guards
Scots Guards
East Surrey
Royal Berkshire
King's Shropshire L.I.

SURINAM (1804)
South America/Dutch

Bedfordshire and Hertfordshire
North Staffordshire

Talavera, 27 July 1809

TAKU FORTS (1860)
Second Chinese War
China/Chinese

King's Dragoon Guards
Royal Scots
Queen's
Buffs
East Surrey
Royal Hampshire
Essex
King's Royal Rifle Corps

TALAVERA (1809)
Peninsular War
Spain/French

3rd Dragoon Guards
4th Hussars
14th Hussars
16th Lancers
Coldstream Guards
Scots Guards
Buffs
Royal Fusiliers
South Wales Borderers
Gloucestershire
Worcestershire
East Surrey
South Lancashire
Sherwood Foresters
Northamptonshire
Royal Berkshire
King's Shropshire L.I.
King's Royal Rifle Corps
Royal Irish Rifles
    (Royal Ulster Rifles)
Royal Irish Fusiliers
Connaught Rangers

'TANGIER, 1662-1680'
(Awarded *1910*)
North Africa/Moors

Royal Dragoons
Queen's
Grenadier Guards ('1680' only)
Coldstream Guards ('1680' only)

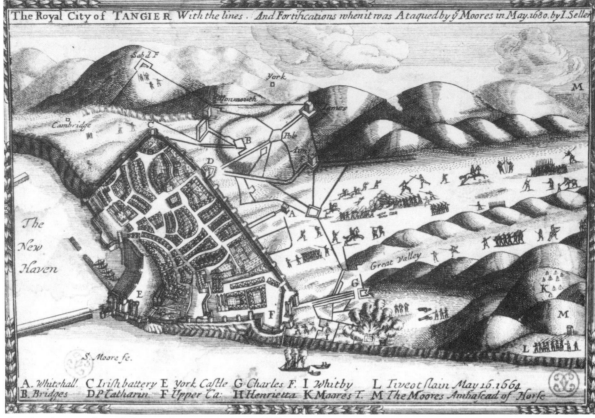

The Royal City of TANGIER With the lines. And Fortifications when it was Ataqued by ye Moores in May.1680. by I. Seller

A. Whitehall. C Irish battery E York Castle G Charles F. I Whitby L Two of slain May 16.1664
B. Bridges D P Catharin F Upper Ca: H Henrietta K Moores T. M The Moores Ambassad of Horse

S. Moore fe.

Tangier. A rare plan of the garrison town, dated 1680

Royal Scots ('1680' only)

The King's Own were also present in 1680 but did not receive the award

TARIFA (1811)
Peninsular War
Spain/French

Loyal North Lancashire
Royal Irish Fusiliers

TEL-EL-KEBIR (1882)
Egypt/Egyptians

Life Guards
Royal Horse Guards
4th Dragoon Guards
7th Dragoon Guards
19th Hussars
Grenadier Guards
Coldstream Guards
Scots Guards
Royal Irish
Duke of Cornwall's L.I.
Black Watch
King's Royal Rifle Corps
York and Lancaster
Highland L.I.
Seaforth Highlanders
Gordon Highlanders
Cameron Highlanders
Royal Irish Fusiliers

TERNATE (1801, 1810)
East Indies/Dutch

Royal Dublin Fusiliers
(then 1st Madras Europeans)

TIRAH (1897-1898)
N. W. Frontier/Afridis

Queen's
Devonshire
Green Howards
Royal Scots Fusiliers
King's Own Scottish Borderers
Dorset
Sherwood Foresters
Northamptonshire
Gordon Highlanders
2nd Gurkha Rifles

TOFREK (1885)
Sudan/Sudanese

Royal Berkshire

Tel-el-Kebir. 12 September 1882

TOULOUSE (1814)
Peninsular War
France/French

5th Dragoon Guards
3rd Hussars
4th Hussars
13th Hussars
Queen's
Buffs
Royal Northumberland Fusiliers
Royal Fusiliers
Devonshire
Lancashire Fusiliers
Royal Welch Fusiliers
Royal Inniskilling Fusiliers
Gloucestershire
Worcestershire
South Lancashire
Black Watch
Oxford and Bucks L.I.
Sherwood Foresters
Northamptonshire
King's Shropshire L.I.
King's Royal Rifle Corps
Highland L.I.
Cameron Highlanders
Royal Irish Rifles
   (Royal Ulster Rifles)
Royal Irish Fusiliers
Connaught Rangers
Argyll and Sutherland Highlanders
Rifle Brigade

TOURNAY (1794)
Flanders/French

West Yorkshire
Royal Hampshire
King's Shropshire L.I.

VILLERS-EN-CAUCHIES (1794)
France/French

15th Hussars

VIMIERA (1808)
Peninsular War
Portugal/French

20th Hussars
Queen's
Royal Northumberland Fusiliers
Royal Warwickshire
Royal Norfolk
Lancashire Fusiliers
Worcestershire
Duke of Cornwall's L.I.
South Staffordshire
South Lancashire
Oxford and Bucks L.I.
Sherwood Foresters
Royal West Kent
King's Royal Rifle Corps
Highland L.I.
Argyll and Sutherland Highlanders
Rifle Brigade

VITTORIA (1813)
Peninsular War
Spain/French

3rd Dragoon Guards
5th Dragoon Guards
3rd Hussars
4th Hussars
10th Hussars
13th Hussars
14th Hussars
15th Hussars
16th Lancers
Royal Scots
Queen's

15th Light Dragoons at *Villers-en-Cauchies*

Buffs
King's Own
Royal Northumberland Fusiliers
Royal Warwickshire
Royal Fusiliers
Royal Norfolk
Lancashire Fusiliers
Royal Welch Fusiliers
South Wales Borderers
Royal Inniskilling Fusiliers
Gloucestershire
East Lancashire
East Surrey
Border
South Staffordshire
Dorset
South Lancashire
Oxford and Bucks L.I.
Sherwood Foresters
Loyal North Lancashire
Northamptonshire
Royal Berkshire
Royal West Kent
King's Own Yorkshire L.I.
King's Shropshire L.I.
Middlesex
King's Royal Rifle Corps
Durham L.I.
Highland L.I.

Gordon Highlanders
Royal Irish Rifles
  (Royal Ulster Rifles)
Royal Irish Fusiliers
Connaught Rangers
Rifle Brigade

WANDEWASH   (1760)
India/French

Royal Dublin Fusiliers
  (then 1st Madras Europeans)

WARBURG   (1760)
Seven Years' War
Germany/French

Royal Horse Guards
King's Dragoon Guards
Queen's Bays
3rd Dragoon Guards
6th Dragoon Guards
7th Dragoon Guards
Royal Dragoons
Royal Scots Greys
Inniskilling Dragoons
7th Hussars
10th Hussars
11th Hussars

The honour was awarded in 1909, but not to the 12 infantry regiments present

52nd Light Infantry (Oxfordshire and Buckinghamshire) at *Waterloo*

WATERLOO (1815)
Flanders/French

Life Guards
Royal Horse Guards
King's Dragoon Guards
Royal Dragoons
Royal Scots Greys
Inniskilling Dragoons
7th Hussars
10th Hussars
11th Hussars
12th Lancers
13th Hussars
15th Hussars
16th Lancers
18th Hussars
Grenadier Guards
Coldstream Guards
Scots Guards
Royal Scots
King's Own
West Yorkshire
Royal Welch Fusiliers
Royal Inniskilling Fusiliers
Gloucestershire
East Lancashire
Duke of Cornwall's L.I.
Duke of Wellington's

South Lancashire
Welch
Black Watch
Oxford and Bucks L.I.
Essex
King's Own Yorkshire L.I.
Highland L.I.
Gordon Highlanders
Cameron Highlanders
Rifle Brigade

WILHELMSTAHL (1762)
Seven Years' War
Germany/French

Royal Northumberland Fusiliers

WILLEMS (1794)
Flanders/French

Royal Horse Guards
Queen's Bays
3rd Dragoon Guards
6th Dragoon Guards
Royal Dragoons
Royal Scots Greys
Inniskilling Dragoons
7th Hussars
11th Hussars
15th Hussars
16th Lancers

BATTLE HONOURS
1914 - 1953

THE LIFE GUARDS

First World War
Mons, Le Cateau, Retreat from Mons, **Marne 1914, Aisne 1914, Messines 1914,** Armentières 1914, **Ypres 1914, 15, 17,** Langemarck 1914, Gheluvelt, Nonne Bosschen, St. Julien, Frezenberg, **Somme 1916, 18,** Albert 1916, **Arras 1917, 18,** Scarpe 1917, 18, Broodseinde, Poelcapelle, Passchendaele, Bapaume 1918, **Hindenburg Line,** Épéhy, St. Quentin Canal, Beaurevoir, Cambrai 1918, Selle, **France and Flanders 1914-18**

Second World War
Mont Pincon, **Souleuvre,** Noireau Crossing, Amiens 1944, **Brussels,** Neerpelt, **Nederrijn,** Nijmegen, Lingen, Bentheim, **North-West Europe 1944-45,** Baghdad 1941, **Iraq 1941, Palmyra, Syria 1941, El Alamein, North Africa 1942-43,** Arezzo, Advance to Florence, Gothic Line, **Italy 1944**

THE ROYAL HORSE GUARDS
(THE BLUES)

First World War
Mons, **Le Cateau,** Retreat from Mons, **Marne 1914,** Aisne 1914, **Messines 1914,** Armentières 1914, **Ypres 1914, 15, 17,** Langemarck 1914, **Gheluvelt,** Nonne Bosschen, St. Julien, **Frezenberg, Loos, Arras 1917,** Scarpe 1917, Broodseinde, Poelcapelle, Passchendaele, Hindenburg Line, Cambrai 1918, **Sambre, France and Flanders 1914-18**

Second World War
Mont Pincon, **Souleuvre,** Noireau Crossing, Amiens 1944, **Brussels,** Neerpelt, **Nederrijn,** Nijmegen, Lingen, Bentheim, **North-West Europe 1944-45,** Baghdad 1941, **Iraq 1941, Palmyra, Syria 1941, El Alamein, North Africa 1942-43,** Arezzo, Advance to Florence, Gothic Line, **Italy 1944**

1st KING'S DRAGOON GUARDS

First World War
Somme 1916, Morval, France and Flanders 1914-17

Afghanistan 1919

Second World War
Beda Fomm, Defence of Tobruk, Tobruk 1941, Tobruk Sortie, Relief of Tobruk, Gazala, Bir Hacheim, **Defence of Alamein Line,** Alam el Halfa, El Agheila, **Advance on Tripoli, Tebaga Gap,** Point 201 (Roman Wall), El Hamma, Akarit, **Tunis, North Africa 1941-43,** Capture of Naples, Scafati Bridge, **Monte Camino,** Garigliano Crossing, Capture of Perugia, Arezzo, **Gothic Line, Italy 1943-44,** Athens, Greece 1944-45

THE QUEEN'S BAYS
(2nd DRAGOON GUARDS)

First World War
Mons, Le Cateau, Retreat from Mons, **Marne 1914,** Aisne 1914, **Messines 1914,** Armentières 1914, **Ypres 1914, 15,** Frezenberg, Bellewaarde, **Somme 1916, 18,** Flers-Courcelette, Arras 1917, **Scarpe 1917, Cambrai 1917, 18,** St Quentin, Bapaume 1918, Rosières, **Amiens,** Albert 1918, Hindenburg Line, St. Quentin Canal, Beaurevoir, **Pursuit to Mons,** France and Flanders 1914-18

Second World War
Somme 1940, Withdrawal to Seine, North-West Europe 1940, Msus, **Gazala,** Bir el Aslagh, Cauldron, Knightsbridge, Via Balbia, Mersa Matruh, **El Alamein,** Tebaga Gap, **El Hamma,** El Kourzia, Djebel Kournine, **Tunis,** Creteville Pass, **North Africa 1941-43, Coriano,** Carpineta, **Lamone Crossing,** Lamone Bridgehead, **Rimini Line,** Ceriano Ridge, Cesena, **Argenta Gap,** Italy 1944-45

3rd DRAGOON GUARDS
(PRINCE OF WALES'S)

First World War
Ypres 1914, 15, Nonne Bosschen, Frezenberg, **Loos, Arras 1917, Scarpe 1917,** Somme 1918, **St. Quentin,** Avre, Amiens, **Hindenburg Line,** Beaurevoir, Cambrai 1918, **Pursuit to Mons, France and Flanders 1914-18**

THE CARABINIERS
(6th DRAGOON GUARDS)

First World War
Mons, Le Cateau, **Retreat from Mons, Marne 1914, Aisne 1914, Messines 1914,** Armentières 1914, **Ypres 1915,** St. Julien, Bellewaarde, Arras 1917, Scarpe 1917, **Cambrai 1917, 18, Somme 1918,** St. Quentin, Lys, Hazebrouck, **Amiens,** Bapaume 1918, Hindenburg Line, Canal du Nord, Selle, **Sambre, France and Flanders 1914-18**

4th ROYAL IRISH DRAGOON GUARDS

First World War

Mons, Le Cateau, Retreat from Mons, Marne 1914, Aisne 1914, La Bassée 1914, **Messines 1914,** Armentières 1914, **Ypres 1914, 15,** St. Julien, Frezenberg, Bellewaarde, **Somme 1916,** 18, Flers-Courcelette, Arras 1917, Scarpe 1917, **Cambrai 1917, 18,** St. Quentin, Rosières, Amiens, Albert 1918, Hindenburg Line, **Pursuit to Mons,** France and Flanders 1914-18

7th DRAGOON GUARDS (PRINCESS ROYAL'S)

First World War

La Bassée 1914, Givenchy 1914, Somme 1916, 18, Bazentin, Flers-Courcelette, **Cambrai 1917, 18, St. Quentin, Avre,** Lys, Hazebrouck, **Amiens, Hindenburg Line,** St. Quentin Canal, Beaurevoir, **Pursuit to Mons,** France and Flanders 1914-18

4th/7th ROYAL DRAGOON GUARDS

Second World War

Dyle, **Dunkirk 1940, Normandy Landing, Odon, Mont Pincon,** Seine 1944, **Nederrijn, Geilenkirchen,** Roer, **Rhineland,** Cleve, **Rhine,** Bremen, North-West Europe 1940, 44-45

5th DRAGOON GUARDS (PRINCESS CHARLOTTE OF WALES'S)

First World War

Mons, Le Cateau, Retreat from Mons, **Marne 1914,** Aisne 1914, La Bassée 1914, **Messines 1914,** Armentières 1914, **Ypres 1914, 15,** Frezenberg, **Bellewaarde, Somme 1916, 18,** Flers-Courcelette, Arras 1917, Scarpe 1917, **Cambrai 1917, 18,** St. Quentin, Rosières, **Amiens,** Albert 1918, Hindenburg Line, St. Quentin Canal, Beaurevoir, **Pursuit to Mons,** France and Flanders 1914-18

THE INNISKILLINGS (6th DRAGOONS)

First World War

Somme 1916, 18, Morval, Cambrai 1917, 18, St. Quentin, Avre, Lys, Hazebrouck, **Amiens, Hindenburg Line, St. Quentin Canal,** Beaurevoir, **Pursuit to Mons, France and Flanders 1914-18**

5th ROYAL INNISKILLING DRAGOON GUARDS

Second World War

Withdrawal to Escaut, St. Omer-La Bassée, Dunkirk 1940, Mont Pincon, St. Pierre La Vielle, Lisieux, Risle Crossing, **Lower Maas,** Roer, Ibbenburen, North-West Europe 1940, 44-45

Korean War

The Hook 1952, Korea 1951-52

THE ROYAL DRAGOONS (1st DRAGOONS)

First World War

Ypres 1914, 15, Langemarck 1914, Gheluvelt, Nonne Bosschen, **Frezenberg, Loos, Arras 1917,** Scarpe 1917, **Somme 1918,** St. Quentin, Avre, **Amiens, Hindenburg Line,** Beaurevoir, **Cambrai 1918, Pursuit to Mons, France and Flanders 1914-18**

Second World War

Nederrijn, Veghel, **Rhine, North-West Europe 1944-45, Syria 1941,** Msus, Gazala, **Knightsbridge,** Defence of Alamein Line, **El Alamein,** El Agheila, **Advance on Tripoli, North Africa 1941-43, Sicily 1943, Italy 1943**

THE ROYAL SCOTS GREYS (2nd DRAGOONS)

First World War

Mons, **Retreat from Mons, Marne 1914, Aisne 1914,** Messines 1914, **Ypres 1914, 15,** Gheluvelt, Neuve Chapelle, St. Julien, Bellewaarde, **Arras 1917,** Scarpe 1917, Cambrai 1917, 18, Lys, Hazebrouck, **Amiens, Somme 1918,** Albert 1918, Bapaume 1918, **Hindenburg Line,** St. Quentin Canal, Beaurevoir, **Pursuit to Mons, France and Flanders 1914-18**

Second World War

Caen, **Hill 112, Falaise,** Venlo Pocket, **Hochwald, Aller, Bremen,** North-West Europe 1944-45, **Merjayun,** Syria 1941, **Alam El Halfa, El Alamein,** El Agheila, **Nofilia,** Advance on Tripoli, North Africa 1942-43, **Salerno,** Battipaglia, Volturno Crossing, **Italy 1943**

3rd THE KING'S OWN HUSSARS

First World War

Mons, Le Cateau, **Retreat from Mons, Marne 1914, Aisne 1914, Messines 1914,** Armentières 1914, **Ypres 1914, 15,** Gheluvelt, St. Julien, Bellewaarde, **Arras 1917,** Scarpe 1917, **Cambrai 1917, 18, Somme 1918,** St. Quentin, Lys, Hazebrouck, **Amiens,**

1918, St. Quentin, Lys, Hazebrouck, **Amiens,** Bapaume 1918, Hindenburg Line, Canal du Nord, Selle, Sambre, **France and Flanders 1914-18**

Second World War
Sidi Barrani, Buq Buq, Beda Fomm, Sidi Suleiman, El Alamein, North Africa 1940-42, Citta del Pieve, Citta di Castello, Italy 1944, Crete

4th QUEEN'S OWN HUSSARS

First World War
Mons, Le Cateau, Retreat from Mons, **Marne 1914, Aisne 1914,** Messines 1914, Armentières 1914, **Ypres 1914, 15,** Langemarck 1914, Gheluvelt, **St. Julien,** Bellewaarde, **Arras 1917,** Scarpe 1917, **Cambrai 1917, Somme 1918, Amiens,** Hindenburg Line, Canal du Nord, Pursuit to Mons, France and Flanders 1914-18

Second World War
Gazala, Defence of Alamein Line, **Ruweisat, Alam el Halfa, El Alamein,** North Africa 1942, **Coriano,** San Clemente, **Senio Pocket, Rimini Line,** Conventello-Comacchio, Senio, Santerno Crossing, **Argenta Gap,** Italy 1944-45, **Proasteion, Corinth Canal, Greece 1941**

5th ROYAL IRISH LANCERS

First World War
Mons, Le Cateau, Retreat from Mons, Marne 1914, Aisne 1914, Messines 1914, Ypres 1914, 15, Gheluvelt, St. Julien, Bellewaarde, Arras 1917, Scarpe 1917, **Cambrai 1917,** Somme 1918, **St. Quentin,** Amiens, Hindenburg Line, Canal du Nord, **Pursuit to Mons,** France and Flanders 1914-18

16th THE QUEEN'S LANCERS

First World War
Mons, Le Cateau, Retreat from Mons, **Marne 1914, Aisne 1914, Messines 1914,** Armentières 1914, **Ypres 1914, 15,** Gheluvelt, St. Julien, **Bellewaarde, Arras 1917,** Scarpe 1917, **Cambrai 1917, Somme 1918,** Amiens, Hindenburg Line, Canal du Nord, Pursuit to Mons, France and Flanders 1914-18

16th/5th THE QUEEN'S ROYAL LANCERS

Second World War
Kasserine, **Fondouk,** Kairouan, **Bordj, Djebel Kournine, Tunis,** Gromballa, Bou Ficha, **North Africa 1942-43, Cassino II, Liri Valley,** Monte Piccolo, Capture of Perugia, Arezzo, **Advance to Florence, Argenta Gap,** Traghetto, **Italy 1944-45**

7th QUEEN'S OWN HUSSARS

First World War
Khan Baghdadi, Sharqat, Mesopotamia 1917-18

Second World War
Egyptian Frontier 1940, Beda Fomm, Sidi Rezegh 1941, North Africa 1940-41, Ancona, Rimini Line, Italy 1944-45, Pegu, Paungde, Burma 1942

8th KING'S ROYAL IRISH HUSSARS

First World War
Givenchy 1914, Somme 1916, 18, Bazentin, Flers-Courcelette, **Cambrai 1917, 18,** St. Quentin, **Bapaume 1918, Rosières, Amiens, Albert 1918,** Hindenburg Line, St. Quentin Canal, **Beaurevoir, Pursuit to Mons, France and Flanders 1914-18**

Second World War
Villers Bocage, Mont Pincon, Dives Crossing, Nederrijn, Best, **Lower Maas, Roer, Rhine, North-West Europe 1944-45,** Egyptian Frontier 1940, Sidi Barrani, **Buq Buq, Sidi Rezegh 1941,** Relief of Tobruk, **Gazala,** Bir el Igela, Mersa Matruh, Alam el Halfa, **El Alamein, North Africa 1940-42**

Korean War
Seoul, Hill 327, **Imjin,** Kowang-San, **Korea 1950-51**

9th QUEEN'S ROYAL LANCERS

First World War
Mons, Le Cateau, **Retreat from Mons, Marne 1914, Aisne 1914,** La Bassée 1914, **Messines 1914,** Armentières 1914, **Ypres 1914, 15,** Gravenstafel, St. Julien, Frezenburg, Bellewaarde, **Somme 1916, 18,** Pozières, Flers-Courcelette, **Arras 1917,** Scarpe 1917, **Cambrai 1917, 18,** St. Quentin, **Rosières,** Avre, Amiens, Albert 1918, Hindenburg Line, **Pursuit to Mons,** France and Flanders 1914-18

Second World War
Somme 1940, Withdrawal to Seine, **North-West Europe 1940,** Saunnu, **Gazala,** Bir el Aslagh, Sidi Rezegh 1942, Defence of Alamein Line, **Ruweisat,** Ruweisat Ridge, **El Alamein,** Tebaga Gap, **El Hamma,** El Kourzia, Tunis, Creteville Pass, **North Africa 1942-43,** Coriano, Capture of Forli, Lamone Crossing, Pideura, **Lamone Bridgehead, Argenta Gap, Italy 1944-45**

10th ROYAL HUSSARS (PRINCE OF WALES'S OWN)

First World War
Ypres 1914, 15 Langemarck 1914, Gheluvelt, Nonne Bosschen, **Rezenberg, Loos, Arras 1917, 18,** Scarpe

1917, **Somme 1918,** St. Quentin, **Avre, Amiens, Drocourt-Quéant,** Hindenburg Line, Beaurevoir, Cambrai 1918, **Pursuit to Mons, France and Flanders 1914-18**

Second World War
Somme 1940, North-West Europe 1940, **Saunnu, Gazala,** Bir el Aslagh, Alam el Halfa, **El Alamein, El Hamma,** El Kourzia, Djebel Kournine, **Tunis,** North Africa 1942-43, **Coriano, Santarcangelo,** Cosina Canal Crossing, Senio Pocket, Cesena, **Valli di Comacchio, Argenta Gap,** Italy 1944-45

11th HUSSARS
(PRINCE ALBERT'S OWN)

First World War
Mons, **Le Cateau, Retreat from Mons, Marne 1914, Aisne 1914, Messines 1914,** Armentières 1914, **Ypres 1914, 15,** Frezenberg, Bellewaarde, **Somme 1916, 18,** Flers-Courcelette, Arras 1917, Scarpe 1917, **Cambrai 1917, 18,** St. Quentin, Rosières, **Amiens,** Albert 1918, Hindenburg Line, St. Quentin Canal, Beaurevoir, Selle, **France and Flanders 1914-18**

Second World War
Villers Bocage, Bourguebus Ridge, Mont Pincon, Jurques, Dives Crossing, La Vie Crossing, Lisieux, Le Touques Crossing, Risle Crossing, **Roer, Rhine,** Ibbenburen, Aller, North-West Europe 1944 45, **Egyptian Frontier 1940,** Withdrawal to Matruh, Bir Enba, **Sidi Barrani,** Buq Buq, Bardia 1941, Capture of Tobruk, **Beda Fomm,** Halfaya 1941, Sidi Suleiman, Tobruk 1941, Gubi I, II, Gabr Saleh, **Sidi Rezegh 1941,** Taieb el Essom, Relief of Tobruk, Saunnu, Msus, Defence of Alamein Line, Alam el Halfa, **El Alamein,** Advance on Tripoli, Enfidaville, **Tunis,** North Africa 1940-43, Capture of Naples, Volturno Crossing, **Italy 1943**

12th ROYAL LANCERS
(PRINCE OF WALES'S)

First World War
Mons, Retreat from Mons, Marne 1914, Aisne 1914, Messines 1914, Ypres 1914, 15, Neuve Chapelle, St. Julien, Bellewaarde, **Arras 1917,** Scarpe 1917, **Cambrai 1917, 18, Somme 1918,** St. Quentin, Lys, Hazebrouck, Amiens, Albert 1918, Hindenburg Line, St. Quentin Canal, Beaurevoir, **Sambre,** France and Flanders 1914-18

Second World War
Dyle, Defence of Arras, Arras counter attack, **Dunkirk 1940, North-West Europe 1940, Chor es Sufan, Gazala,** Alam el Halfa, **El Alamein,** Advance on Tripoli, Tebaga Gap, El Hamma, Akarit, El Kourzia, Djebel Kournine, **Tunis,** Creteville Pass,

North Africa 1941-43, Citerna, Gothic Line, Capture of Forli, Conventello-Comacchio, **Bologna,** Sillaro Crossing, Idice Bridgehead, **Italy 1944-45**

13th HUSSARS

First World War
France and Flanders 1914-16, Kut al Amara 1917, Baghdad, Sharqat, Mesopotamia 1916-18

18th ROYAL HUSSARS
(QUEEN MARY'S OWN)

First World War
Mons, Le Cateau, Retreat from Mons, **Marne 1914, Aisne 1914,** La Bassée 1914, **Messines 1914,** Armentières 1914, **Ypres 1914, 15,** Gravenstafel, St. Julien, Frezenberg, Bellewaarde, **Somme 1916, 18,** Flers-Courcelette, Arras 1917, Scarpe 1917, **Cambrai 1917, 18,** St Quentin, Rosières, **Amiens,** Albert 1918, **Hindenburg Line,** Pursuit to Mons, **France and Flanders 1914-18**

13th/18th ROYAL HUSSARS
(QUEEN MARY'S OWN)

Second World War
Dyle, Withdrawal to Escaut, **Ypres-Comines Canal, Normandy Landing,** Bretteville, **Caen,** Bourguebus Ridge, **Mont Pincon,** St. Pierre la Vielle, **Geilenkirchen, Roer, Rhineland,** Waal Flats, **Goch,** Rhine, Bremen, **North-West Europe 1940, 44-45**

14th KING'S HUSSARS

First World War
Tigris 1916, Kut al Amara 1917, Baghdad, Mesopotamia 1915-18, Persia 1918

20th HUSSARS

First World War
Mons, Retreat from Mons, Marne 1914, Aisne 1914, Messines 1914, Ypres 1914, 15, Neuve Chapelle, St. Julien, Bellewaarde, Arras 1917, Scarpe 1917, **Cambrai 1917, 18, Somme 1918,** St. Quentin, Lys, Hazebrouck, **Amiens,** Albert 1918, Bapaume 1918, Hindenburg Line, St. Quentin Canal, Beaurevoir, **Sambre,** France and Flanders 1914-18

14th/20th KING'S HUSSARS

Second World War
Bologna, Medicina, Italy 1945

15th THE KING'S HUSSARS

First World War

Mons, **Retreat from Mons, Marne 1914, Aisne 1914, Ypres 1914, 15,** Langemarck 1914, Gheluvelt, Nonne Bosschen, Frezenberg, **Bellewaarde, Somme 1916, 18,** Flers-Courcelette, **Cambrai 1917, 18,** St. Quentin, **Rosières,** Amiens, Albert 1918, Bapaume 1918, Hindenburg Line, St. Quentin Canal, Beaurevoir, **Pursuit to Mons, France and Flanders 1914-18**

19th ROYAL HUSSARS (QUEEN ALEXANDRA'S OWN)

First World War

Le Cateau, Retreat from Mons, Marne 1914, Aisne 1914, Armentières 1914, Ypres 1915, Frezenberg, Bellewaarde, **Somme 1916, 18,** Flers-Courcelette, **Cambrai 1917, 18,** St. Quentin, Rosières, **Amiens,** Albert 1918, Bapaume 1918, Hindenburg Line, St. Quentin Canal, Beaurevoir, **Pursuit to Mons,** France and Flanders 1914-18

15th/19th THE KING'S ROYAL HUSSARS

Second World War

Withdrawal to Escaut, Seine 1944, Hechtel, **Nederrijn,** Venraij, **Rhineland, Hochwald, Rhine, Ibbenburen, Aller, North-West Europe 1940, 44-45**

17th LANCERS (DUKE OF CAMBRIDGE'S OWN)

First World War

Festubert 1914, Somme 1916, 18, Morval, Cambrai 1917, 18, St. Quentin, Avre, Lys, **Hazebrouck, Amiens,** Hindenburg Line, St. Quentin Canal, Beaurevoir, **Pursuit to Mons, France and Flanders 1914-18**

21st LANCERS (EMPRESS OF INDIA'S)

First World War

N. W. Frontier India 1915, 16

17th/21st LANCERS

Second World War

Tebourba Gap, Bou Arada, **Kasserine,** Thala, **Fondouk, El Kourzia, Tunis,** Hammam Lif, **North Africa 1942-43, Cassino II,** Monte Piccolo, **Capture of Perugia,** Advance to Florence, Argenta Gap, Fossa Cembalina, **Italy 1944-45**

ROYAL TANK REGIMENT

First World War

Somme 1916, 18, Arras 1917, 18, Messines 1917, Ypres 1917, Cambrai 1917, St. Quentin 1918, **Villers Bretonneux, Amiens, Bapaume 1918, Hindenburg Line,** Épéhy, Selle, **France and Flanders 1916-18,** Gaza

Second World War

Arras counter attack, Calais 1940, St. Omer-La Bassée, Somme 1940, Odon, Caen, Bourguebus Ridge, Mont Pincon, Falaise, Nederrijn, Scheldt, Venlo Pocket, Rhineland, **Rhine,** Bremen, **North-West Europe 1940, 44-45, Abyssinia 1940,** Sidi Barrani, Beda Fomm, Sidi Suleiman, **Tobruk 1941,** Sidi Rezegh 1941, Belhamed, Gazala, Cauldron, Knightsbridge, Defence of Alamein Line, Alam el Halfa, **El Alamein,** Mareth, Akarit, Fondouk, El Kourzia, Medjez Plain, Tunis, **North Africa 1940-43,** Primosole Bridge, Gerbini, Adrano, **Sicily 1943,** Sangro, Salerno, Volturno Crossing, Garigliano Crossing, Anzio, Advance to Florence, Gothic Line, Coriano, Lamone Crossing, Rimini Line, Argenta Gap, **Italy 1943-45, Greece 1941, Burma 1942**

Korean War
Korea 1951-53

GRENADIER GUARDS

First World War

Mons, Retreat from Mons, **Marne 1914, Aisne 1914, Ypres 1914, 17,** Langemarck 1914, Gheluvelt, Nonne Bosschen, Neuve Chapelle, Aubers, Festubert 1915, **Loos, Somme 1916, 18,** Ginchy, Flers-Courcelette, Morval, Pilckem, Menin Road, Poelcapelle, Passchendaele, **Cambrai 1917, 18,** St. Quentin, Bapaume 1918, **Arras 1918,** Lys, **Hazebrouck,** Albert 1918, Scarpe 1918, **Hindenburg Line,** Havrincourt, Canal du Nord, Selle, Sambre, **France and Flanders 1914-18**

Second World War

Dyle, **Dunkirk 1940,** Cagny, **Mont Pincon, Nijmegen,** Reichswald, **Rhine,** North-West Europe 1940, 44-45, **Mareth, Medjez Plain,** North Africa 1942-43, **Salerno,** Volturno Crossing, **Monte Camino, Anzio, Gothic Line,** Battaglia, Italy 1943-45

COLDSTREAM GUARDS

First World War

Mons, **Retreat from Mons, Marne 1914, Aisne 1914, Ypres 1914, 17,** Langemarck 1914, Gheluvelt, Nonne Bosschen, Givenchy 1914, Neuve Chapelle, Aubers, Festubert 1915, **Loos,** Mount Sorrel, **Somme 1916, 18,** Flers-Courcelette, Morval, Pilckem, Menin Road,

Poelcapelle, Passchendaele, **Cambrai 1917, 18,** St. Quentin, Bapaume 1918, **Arras 1918,** Lys, **Hazebrouck,** Albert 1918, Scarpe 1918, Drocourt-Quéant, **Hindenburg Line,** Havrincourt, Canal du Nord, Selle, Sambre, France and Flanders 1914-18

Second World War
Dyle, Defence of Escaut, **Dunkirk 1940,** Cagny, **Mont Pincon,** Quarry Hill, Estry, Heppen, Nederrijn, Venraij, Meijel, Roer, **Rhineland,** Reichswald, Cleve, Goch, Moyland, Hochwald, Rhine, Lingen, Uelzen, **North-West Europe 1940, 44-45,** Egyptian Frontier 1940, **Sidi Barrani,** Halfaya 1941, **Tobruk 1941, 1942,** Msus, Knightsbridge, Defence of Alamein Line, Medenine, Mareth, Longstop Hill 1942, Sbiba, Steamroller Farm, **Tunis,** Hammam Lif, North Africa 1940-43, **Salerno,** Battipaglia, Cappezano, Volturno Crossing, Monte Camino, Calabritto, Garigliano Crossing, **Monte Ornito,** Monte Piccolo, Capture of Perugia, Arezzo, Advance to Florence, Monte Domini, Catarelto Ridge, Argenta Gap, **Italy 1943-45**

SCOTS GUARDS

First World War
Retreat from Mons, Marne 1914, Aisne 1914, Ypres 1914, 17, Langemarck 1914, Gheluvelt, Nonne Bosschen, Givenchy 1914, Neuve Chapelle, Aubers, **Festubert 1915, Loos, Somme 1916, 18,** Flers-Courcelette, Morval, Pilckem, Poelcapelle, Passchendaele, **Cambrai 1917, 18,** St. Quentin, Albert 1918, Bapaume 1918, Arras 1918, Drocourt-Quéant, **Hindenburg Line,** Havrincourt, Canal du Nord, Selle, Sambre, **France and Flanders 1914-18**

Second World War
Stien, Norway 1940, Mont Pincon, **Quarry Hill,** Estry, Venlo Pocket, **Rhineland,** Reichswald, Cleve, Moyland, Hochwald, Rhine, Lingen, Uelzen, **North-West Europe 1944-45,** Halfaya 1941, Sidi Suleiman, Tobruk 1941, **Gazala,** Knightsbridge, Defence of Alamein Line, **Medenine,** Tadjera Khir, Medjez Plain, Grich el Oued, **Djebel Bou Aoukaz 1943,** I, **North Africa 1941-43,** Salerno, Battipaglia, Volturno Crossing, Rochetta e Croce, **Monte Camino, Anzio,** Campoleone, Carroceto, Trasimene Line, Advance to Florence, Monte San Michele, Catarelto Ridge, Argenta Gap, **Italy 1943-45**

IRISH GUARDS

First World War
Mons, **Retreat from Mons, Marne 1914, Aisne 1914, Ypres 1914, 17,** Langemarck 1914, Gheluvelt, Nonne Bosschen, **Festubert 1915, Loos, Somme 1916, 18,** Flers-Courcelette, Morval, Pilckem, Poelcapelle, Passchendaele, **Cambrai 1917, 18,** St. Quentin, Lys,

Hazebrouck, Albert 1918, Bapaume 1918, Arras 1918, Scarpe 1918, Drocourt-Quéant, **Hindenburg Line,** Canal du Nord, Selle, Sambre, France and Flanders 1914-18

Second World War
Pothus, **Norway 1940, Boulogne 1940,** Cagny, **Mont Pincon, Neerpelt, Nijmegen,** Aam, **Rhineland,** Hochwald, Rhine, Bentheim, **North-West Europe 1944-45,** Medjez Plain, **Djebel Bou Aoukaz 1943, North Africa 1943, Anzio,** Aprilia, Carroceto, Italy 1943-44

WELSH GUARDS

First World War
Loos, Somme 1916, 18, **Ginchy, Flers-Courcelette, Morval,** Ypres 1917, **Pilckem, Poelcapelle,** Passchendaele, **Cambrai 1917, 18, Bapaume 1918,** Arras 1918, Albert 1918, Drocourt-Quéant, Hindenburg Line, Havrincourt, **Canal du Nord,** Selle, **Sambre,** France and Flanders 1915-18

Second World War
Defence of Arras, Boulogne 1940, St. Omer-La Bassée, Bourguebus Ridge, Cagny, **Mont Pincon, Brussels, Hechtel,** Nederrijn, Rhineland, Lingen, North-West Europe 1940, 44-45, **Fondouk,** Djebel el Rhorab, Tunis, **Hammam Lif,** North Africa 1943, **Monte Ornito,** Liri Valley, **Monte Piccolo,** Capture of Perugia, Arezzo, Advance to Florence, Gothic Line, **Battaglia,** Italy 1944-45

THE ROYAL SCOTS
(THE ROYAL REGIMENT)

First World War
Mons, **Le Cateau,** Retreat from Mons, **Marne 1914, 18,** Aisne 1914, La Bassée 1914, Neuve Chapelle, **Ypres 1915, 17, 18,** Gravenstafel, St. Julien, Frezenberg, Bellewaarde, Aubers, Festubert 1915, **Loos, Somme 1916, 18,** Albert 1916, 18, Bazentin, Pozières, Flers-Courcelette, Le Transloy, Ancre Heights, Ancre 1916, 18, **Arras 1917, 18,** Scarpe 1917, 18, Arleux, Pilckem, Langemarck 1917, Menin Road, Polygon Wood, Poelcapelle, Passchendaele, Cambrai 1917, St. Quentin, Rosières, **Lys,** Estaires, Messines 1918, Hazebrouck, Bailleul, Kemmel, Béthune, Soissonnais-Ourcq, Tardenois, Amiens, Bapaume 1918, Drocourt-Quéant, Hindenburg Line, Canal du Nord, St. Quentin Canal, Beaurevoir, Courtrai, Selle, Sambre, France and Flanders 1914-18, **Struma,** Macedonia 1915-18, Helles, Landing at Helles, Krithia, Suvla, Scimitar Hill, **Gallipoli 1915-16,** Rumani, Egypt 1915-16, Gaza, El Mughar, Nebi Samwil, Jaffa, **Palestine 1917-18,** Archangel 1918-19

Second World War
Dyle, **Defence of Escaut,** St. Omer-La Bassée, **Odon,** Cheux, Defence of Rauray, Caen, Esquay, Mont Pincon, **Aart,** Nederrijn, Best, Scheldt, **Flushing,** Meijel, Venlo Pocket, Roer, Rhineland, Reichswald, Cleve, Goch, **Rhine,** Uelzen, Bremen, Artlenberg, **North-West Europe 1940, 44-45, Gothic Line,** Marradi, Monte Gamberaldi, **Italy 1944-45,** South East Asia 1941, Donbaik, **Kohima,** Relief of Kohima, Aradura, Shwebo, Mandalay, **Burma 1943-45**

THE QUEEN'S ROYAL REGIMENT
(WEST SURREY)

First World War
Mons, **Retreat from Mons,** Marne 1914, 18, Aisne 1914, **Ypres 1914, 17, 18,** Langemarck 1914, Gheluvelt, Aubers, Festubert 1915, Loos, **Somme 1916, 18,** Albert 1916, 18, Bazentin, Delville Wood, Pozières, Guillemont, Flers-Courcelette, Morval, Thiepval, Le Transloy, Ancre Heights, Ancre 1916, 18, Arras 1917, 18, Scarpe 1917, Bullecourt, **Messines 1917,** Pilckem, Menin Road, Polygon Wood, Broodseinde, Passchendaele, Cambrai 1917, 18, St. Quentin, Bapaume 1918, Rosières, Avre, Villers Bretonneux, Lys, Hazebrouck, Bailleul, Kemmel, Soissonnais-Ourcq, Amiens, **Hindenburg Line,** Épéhy, St. Quentin Canal, Courtrai, Selle, Sambre, France and Flanders 1914-18, Piave, **Vittorio Veneto,** Italy 1917, 18, Suvla, Landing at Suvla, Scimitar Hill, **Gallipoli 1915,** Rumani, Egypt 1915, 16, Gaza, El Mughar, Jerusalem, Jericho, Tell Asur, **Palestine 1917-18,** Khan Baghdadi, **Mesopotamia 1915-18, N. W. Frontier India 1916-17**

Afghanistan 1919

Second World War
Defence of Escaut, **Villers Bocage,** Mont Pincon, Lower Maas, Roer, North-West Europe 1940, 44-45, Syria 1941, Sidi Barrani, **Tobruk 1941,** Tobruk Sortie, Deir el Munasib, **El Alamein,** Advance on Tripoli, **Medenine,** Tunis, North Africa 1940-43, **Salerno,** Monte Stella, Scafati Bridge, Volturno Crossing, **Monte Camino,** Garigliano Crossing, Damiano, **Anzio,** Gothic Line, **Gemmano Ridge,** Senio Pocket, Senio Floodbank, Casa Fabbri Ridge, Menate, Filo, Argenta Gap, Italy 1943-45, **North Arakan, Kohima,** Yenangyaung 1945, Sittang 1945, Chindits 1944, Burma 1943-45

THE BUFFS
(ROYAL EAST KENT REGIMENT)

First World War
Asine 1914, **Armentières 1914, Ypres 1915, 17,** Gravenstafel, St. Julien, Frezenberg, Bellewaarde, Hooge 1915, **Loos, Somme 1916, 18,** Albert 1916, 18,

Bazentin, Delville Wood, Pozières, Flers-Courcelette, Morval, Thiepval, Le Transloy, Ancre Heights, Ancre 1916, 18, **Arras 1917,** Scarpe 1917, Messines 1917, Pilckem, Passchendaele, Cambrai 1917, 18, St. Quentin, Avre, **Amiens,** Bapaume 1918, **Hindenburg Line,** Épéhy, St. Quentin Canal, Selle, Sambre, France and Flanders 1914-18, **Struma,** Doiran 1918, Macedonia 1915-18, Gaza, **Jerusalem,** Tell Asur, Palestine 1917-18, Aden, Tigris 1916, Kut al Amara 1917, **Baghdad,** Mesopotamia 1915-18

Second World War
Defence of Escaut, St. Omer-La Bassée, Withdrawal to Seine, **North-West Europe 1940,** Sidi Suleiman, **Alem Hamza,** Alam el Halfa, **El Alamein,** El Agheila, Advance on Tripoli, Tebaga Gap, El Hamma, Akarit, Djebel Azzag 1943, **Robaa Valley,** Djebel Bech, Heidows, Medjez Plain, Longstop Hill 1943, North Africa 1941-43, Centuripe, Monte Rivoglia, **Sicily 1943,** Termoli, **Trigno,** Sangro, **Anzio,** Cassino I, Liri Valley, Aquino, Rome, Trasimene Line, Coriano, Monte Spaduro, Senio, **Argenta Gap,** Italy 1943-45, Leros, Middle East 1943, Malta 1940-42, **Shwell,** Myitson, Burma 1945

THE KING'S OWN ROYAL REGIMENT
(LANCASTER)

First World War
Le Cateau, Retreat from Mons, **Marne 1914,** Aisne 1914, Armentières 1914, **Ypres 1915, 17,** Gravenstafel, St. Julien, Frezenberg, Bellewaarde, Festubert 1915, Loos, **Somme 1916, 18,** Albert 1916, 18, Bazentin, Delville Wood, Pozières, Guillemont, Ginchy, Flers-Courcelette, Morval, Le Transloy, Ancre Heights, Ancre 1916, **Arras 1917, 18,** Scarpe 1917, 18, Arleux, **Messines 1917,** Pilckem, Menin Road, Polygon Wood, Broodseinde, Poelcapelle, Passchendaele, Cambrai 1917, 18, St. Quentin, **Lys,** Estaires, Hazebrouck, Béthune, Bapaume 1918, Drocourt-Quéant, Hindenburg Line, Canal du Nord, Selle, Valenciennes, Sambre, **France and Flanders 1914-18,** Struma, Doiran 1917, 18, **Macedonia 1915, 18,** Suvla, Sari Bair, **Gallipoli 1915,** Egypt 1916, Tigris 1916, Kut al Amara 1917, Baghdad, **Mesopotamia 1916, 18**

Second World War
St. Omer-La Bassée, **Dunkirk 1940, North-West Europe 1940, Defence of Habbaniya,** Falluja, Iraq 1941, **Merjayun,** Jebel Mazar, Syria 1941, Tobruk 1941, **Tobruk Sortie, North Africa 1940-42, Montone,** Citta di Castello, San Martino Sogliano, **Lamone Bridgehead,** Italy 1944-45, **Malta 1941-42, Chindits 1944,** Burma 1944

THE ROYAL NORTHUMBERLAND FUSILIERS

First World War
Mons, Le Cateau, Retreat from Mons, **Marne 1914,** Aisne 1914, 18, La Bassée 1914, Messines 1914, 17, 18, Armentières 1914, **Ypres 1914, 15, 17, 18,** Nonne Bosschen, Gravenstafel, **St. Julien,** Frezenberg, Bellewaarde, Loos, **Somme 1916, 18,** Albert 1916, 18, Bazentin, Delville Wood, Pozières, Flers-Courcelette, Morval, Thiepval, Le Transloy, Ancre Heights, Ancre 1916, Arras 1917, 18, **Scarpe 1917, 18,** Arleux, Pilckem, Langemarck 1917, Menin Road, Polygon Wood, Broodseinde, Passchendaele, Cambrai 1917, 18, St. Quentin, Bapaume 1918, Rosières, Lys, Estaires, Hazebrouck, Bailleul, Kemmel, Béthune, Scherpenberg, Drocourt-Quéant, Hindenburg Line, Épéhy, Canal du Nord, St. Quentin Canal, Beaurevoir, Courtrai, **Selle,** Valenciennes, Sambre, France and Flanders 1914-18, **Piave,** Vittorio Veneto, Italy 1917, 18, **Struma,** Macedonia 1915-18, **Suvla,** Landing at Suvla, Scimitar Hill, Gallipoli 1915, Egypt 1916-17

Second World War
Defence of Escaut, Arras counter attack, St. Omer-La Bassée, **Dunkirk 1940,** Odon, **Caen,** Cagny, Falaise, Nederrijn, **Rhineland,** North-West Europe 1940, 44-45, **Sidi Barrani, Defence of Tobruk, Tobruk 1941,** Belhamed, **Cauldron,** Ruweisat Ridge, **El Alamein,** Advance on Tripoli, Medenine, North Africa 1940-43, **Salerno,** Volturno Crossing, Monte Camino, Garigliano Crossing, **Cassino II,** Italy 1943-45, Singapore Island

Korean War
Seoul, **Imjin,** Kowang-San, **Korea 1950-51**

THE ROYAL WARWICKSHIRE REGIMENT

First World War
Le Cateau, Retreat from Mons, **Marne 1914,** Aisne 1914, 18, Armentières 1914, **Ypres 1914, 15, 17,** Langemarck 1914, 17, Gheluvelt, Neuve Chapelle, St. Julien, Frezenberg, Bellewaarde, Aubers, Festubert 1915, Loos, **Somme 1916, 18,** Albert 1916, 18, Bazentin, Delville Wood, Pozières, Guillemont, Flers-Courcelette, Morval, Le Transloy, Ancre Heights, Ancre 1916, **Arras 1917, 18,** Vimy 1917, Scarpe 1917, 18, Arleux, Oppy, Bullecourt, Messines 1917, 18, Pilckem, Menin Road, Polygon Wood, Broodseinde, Poelcapelle, Passchendaele, Cambrai 1917, 18, St. Quentin, Bapaume 1918, Rosières, **Lys,** Estaires, Hazebrouck, Bailleul, Kemmel, Béthune, Drocourt-Quéant, **Hindenburg Line,** Épéhy, Canal du Nord, Beaurevoir, Selle, Valenciennes, Sambre, France and Flanders 1914-18, **Piave,** Vittorio Veneto, Italy 1917-18, Suvla, **Sari Bair,** Gallipoli 1915-16,

Tigris 1916, Kut al Amara 1917, **Baghdad,** Mesopotamia 1916-18, Baku, Persia 1918

Second World War
Defence of Escaut, Wormhoudt, Ypres - Comines Canal, Normandy Landing, Caen, Bourguebus Ridge, **Mont Pincon,** Falaise, **Venrail,** Rhineland, Lingen, Brinkum, **Bremen, North-West Europe 1940, 44-45, Burma 1945**

THE ROYAL FUSILIERS (CITY OF LONDON REGIMENT)

First World War
Mons, Le Cateau, Retreat from Mons, **Marne 1914,** Aisne 1914, La Bassée 1914, Messines 1914, 17, Armentières 1914, **Ypres 1914, 15, 17, 18,** Nonne Bosschen, Gravenstafel, St. Julien, Frezenberg, Bellewaarde, Hooge 1915, Loos, **Somme 1916, 18,** Albert 1916, 18, Bazentin, Delville Wood, Pozières, Flers-Courcelette, Thiepval, Le Transloy, Ancre Heights, Ancre 1916, 18, **Arras 1917, 18,** Vimy 1917, Scarpe 1917, Arleux, Pilckem, Langemarck 1917, Menin Road, Polygon Wood, Broodseinde, Poelcapelle, Passchendaele, **Cambrai 1917, 18,** St. Quentin, Bapaume 1918, Rosières, Avre, Villers Bretonneux, Lys, Estaires, Hazebrouck, Béthune, Amiens, Drocourt-Quéant, **Hindenburg Line,** Havrincourt, Épéhy, Canal du Nord, St. Quentin Canal, Beaurevoir, Courtrai, Selle, Sambre, France and Flanders 1914-18, Italy 1917-18, **Struma,** Macedonia 1915-18, Helles, **Landing at Helles,** Krithia, Suvla, Scimitar Hill, Gallipoli 1915-16, Egypt 1916, Megiddo, Nablus, **Palestine 1918,** Troitsa, Archangel 1919, Kilimanjaro, Behobeho, Nyangao, E. Africa 1915-17

Second World War
Dunkirk 1940, North-West Europe 1940, Agordat, **Keren,** Syria 1941, Sidi Barrani, Djebel Tebaga, Peters Corner, **North Africa 1940, 43,** Sangro, **Mozzagrogna,** Caldari, **Salerno,** St. Lucia, Battipaglia, Teano, Monte Camino, **Garigliano Crossing,** Damiano, **Anzio, Cassino II,** Ripa Ridge, Gabbiano, Advance to Florence, Monte Scalari, **Gothic Line, Coriano,** Croce, Casa Fortis, Savio Bridgehead, Valli di Comacchio, Senio, Argenta Gap, Italy 1943-45, Athens, Greece 1944-45

Korean War
Korea 1952-53

THE KING'S REGIMENT (LIVERPOOL)

First World War
Mons, **Retreat from Mons, Marne 1914, Aisne 1914, Ypres 1914, 15, 17,** Langemarck 1914, 17, Gheluvelt,

Nonne Bosschen, Neuve Chapelle, Gravenstafel, St. Julien, Frezenberg, Bellewaarde, Aubers, **Festubert 1915, Loos, Somme 1916, 18,** Albert 1916, 18, Bazentin, Delville Wood, Guillemont, Ginchy, Flers-Courcelette, Morval, Le Transloy, Ancre 1916, Bapaume 1917, 18, **Arras 1917, 18, Scarpe 1917, 18,** Arleux, Pilckem, Menin Road, Polygon Wood, Poelcapelle, Passchendaele, **Cambrai 1917, 18,** St. Quentin, Rosières, Avre, Lys, Estaires, Messines 1918, Bailleul, Kemmel, Béthune, Scherpenberg, Drocourt-Quéant, Hindenburg Line, Épéhy, Canal du Nord, St. Quentin Canal, Selle, Sambre, France and Flanders 1914-18, Doiran 1917, Macedonia 1915-18, N. W. Frontier India 1915, Archangel 1918-19

Afghanistan 1919

Second World War
Normandy Landing, North-West Europe 1944, **Cassino II, Trasimene Line, Tuori, Capture of Forli, Rimini Line,** Italy 1944-45, **Athens,** Greece 1944-45, **Chindits 1943, Chindits 1944,** Burma 1943-44

Korean War
The Hook 1953, Korea 1952-53

THE ROYAL NORFOLK REGIMENT

First World War
Mons, Le Cateau, Retreat from Mons, **Marne 1914,** Aisne 1914, La Bassée 1914, **Ypres 1914, 15, 17, 18,** Gravenstafel, St. Julien, Frezenberg, Bellewaarde, Loos, **Somme 1916, 18,** Albert 1916, 18, Delville Wood, Pozières, Guillemont, Flers-Courcelette, Morval, Thiepval, Le Transloy, Ancre Heights, Ancre 1916, 18, Arras 1917, Vimy 1917, Scarpe 1917, Arleux, Oppy, Pilckem, Langemarck 1917, Polygon Wood, Broodseinde, Poelcapelle, Passchendaele, Cambrai 1917, 18, St. Quentin, Bapaume 1918, Lys, Bailleul, Kemmel, Scherpenberg, Amiens, **Hindenburg Line,** Épéhy, Canal du Nord, St. Quentin Canal, Beaurevoir, Selle, Sambre, France and Flanders 1914-18, Italy 1917-18, Suvla, **Landing at Suvla,** Scimitar Hill, Gallipoli 1915, Egypt 1915-17, **Gaza,** El Mughar, Nebi Samwil, Jerusalem, Jaffa, Tell Asur, Megiddo, Sharon, Palestine 1917-18, **Shaiba, Kut al Amara 1915, 17,** Ctesiphon, Defence of Kut al Amara, Mesopotamia 1914-18

Second World War

Defence of Escaut, **St. Omer-La Bassée,** St. Valéry-en-Caux, **Normandy Landing,** Caen, Le Perier Ridge, **Brieux Bridgehead, Venraij, Rhineland,** Hochwald, Lingen, Brinkum, **North-West Europe 1940, 44-45,** Johore, Muar, Batu Pahat, **Singapore Island,** Malaya 1942, **Kohima, Aradura,** Mandalay, **Burma 1944-45**

Korean War
Korea 1951-52

THE ROYAL LINCOLNSHIRE REGIMENT

First World War
Mons, Le Cateau, Retreat from Mons, **Marne 1914,** Aisne 1914, 18, La Bassée 1914, **Messines 1914, 17, 18,** Armentières 1914, **Ypres 1914, 15, 17,** Nonne Bosschen, **Neuve Chapelle,** Gravenstafel, St. Julien, Frezenberg, Bellewaarde, Aubers, **Loos, Somme 1916, 18,** Albert 1916, 18, Bazentin, Delville Wood, Pozières, Flers-Courcelette, Morval, Thiepval, Ancre 1916, 18, Arras 1917, 18, Scarpe 1917, 18, Arleux, Pilckem, Langemarck 1917, Menin Road, Polygon Wood, Broodseinde, Poelcapelle, Passchendaele, Cambrai 1917, 18, St. Quentin, Bapaume 1918, **Lys,** Estaires, Bailleul, Kemmel, Amiens, Drocourt-Quéant, **Hindenburg Line,** Épéhy, Canal du Nord, St. Quentin Canal, Beaurevoir, Selle, Sambre, France and Flanders 1914-18, **Suvla,** Landing at Suvla, Scimitar Hill, Gallipoli 1915, Egypt 1916

Second World War
Vist, Norway 1940, **Dunkirk 1940, Normandy Landing,** Cambes, **Fontenay le Pesnil,** Defence of Rauray, Caen, Orne, Bourguebus Ridge, Troarn, Nederrijn, Le Havre, **Antwerp-Turnhout Canal,** Venraij, Venlo Pocket, **Rhineland,** Hochwald, Lingen, Bremen, Arnhem 1945, North-West Europe 1940, 44-45, Sedjenane I, Mine de Sedjenane, Argoub Sellah, **North Africa 1943, Salerno,** Vietri Pass, Capture of Naples, Cava di Tirreni, Volturno Crossing, Garigliano Crossing, Monte Tuga, **Gothic Line,** Monte Gridolfo, Gemmano Ridge, Lamone Crossing, San Marino, Italy 1943-45, Donbaik, Point 201 (Arakan), North Arakan, Buthidaung, **Ngakyedauk Pass,** Ramree, **Burma 1943-45**

THE DEVONSHIRE REGIMENT

First World War
Aisne 1914, 18, **La Bassée 1914,** Armentières 1914, Neuve Chapelle, Hill 60, **Ypres 1915, 17,** Gravenstafel, St. Julien, Frezenberg, Aubers, **Loos, Somme 1916, 18,** Albert 1916, Bazentin, Delville Wood, Guillemont, Flers-Courcelette, Morval, Arras 1917, Vimy 1917, Scarpe 1917, Bullecourt, Pilckem, Langemarck 1917, Polygon Wood, Broodseinde, Poelcapelle, Passchendaele, Rosières, Villers Bretonneux, Lys, Hazebrouck, **Bois des Buttes,** Marne 1918, Tardenois, Bapaume 1918, **Hindenburg Line,** Havrincourt, Épéhy, Canal du Nord, Beaurevoir, Cambrai 1918, Selle, Sambre, France and Flanders 1914-18, Piave, **Vittorio Veneto,** Italy 1917-18, **Doiran 1917, 18,** Macedonia 1915-18, Egypt 1916-17, Gaza, Nebi Samwil, Jerusalem, Tell

Asur, **Palestine 1917-18**, Tigris 1916, Kut al Amara 1917, **Mesopotamia 1916-18**

Second World War
Normandy Landing, Port en Bessin, Tilly sur Seulles, **Caen,** St. Pierre la Vielle, Nederrijn, Roer, **Rhine, Ibbenburen, North-West Europe 1944-45, Landing in Sicily, Regalbuto,** Sicily 1943, Landing at Porto San Venere, Italy 1943, **Malta 1940-42, Imphal,** Shenam Pass, Tamu Road, Ukhrul, **Myinmu Bridgehead,** Kyaukse 1945, **Burma 1943-45**

THE SUFFOLK REGIMENT

First World War
Mons, **Le Cateau,** Retreat from Mons, Marne 1914, Aisne 1914, La Bassée 1914, Givenchy 1914, **Neuve Chapelle, Ypres 1915, 17, 18,** Gravenstafel, St. Julien, Frezenberg, Bellewaarde, Aubers, Hooge 1915, Loos, **Somme 1916, 18,** Albert 1916, 18, Bazentin, Delville Wood, Pozières, Flers-Courcelette, Morval, Thiepval, Le Transloy, Ancre Heights, Ancre 1916, 18, **Arras 1917, 18,** Scarpe 1917, 18, Arleux, Pilckem, Langemarck 1917, Menin Road, Polygon Wood, Poelcapelle, Passchendaele, **Cambrai 1917, 18,** St. Quentin, Bapaume 1918, Lys, Estaires, Messines 1918, Hazebrouck, Bailleul, Kemmel, Béthune, Scherpenberg, Amiens, **Hindenburg Line,** Épéhy, Canal du Nord, Courtrai, Selle, Valenciennes, Sambre, France and Flanders 1914-18, Struma, Doiran 1918, **Macedonia 1915-18,** Suvla, **Landing at Suvla,** Scimitar Hill, Gallipoli 1915, Egypt 1915-17, **Gaza,** El Mughar, Nebi Samwil, Jerusalem, Jaffa, Tell Asur, Megiddo, Sharon, Palestine 1917-18

Second World War
Dunkirk 1940, Normandy Landing, Odon, Falaise, Venraij, Brinkum, North-West Europe 1940, 44-45, **Singapore Island,** Malaya 1942, **North Arakan, Imphal, Burma 1943-45**

THE SOMERSET LIGHT INFANTRY (PRINCE ALBERT'S)

First World War
Le Cateau, Retreat from Mons, **Marne 1914, 18, Aisne 1914,** Armentières 1914, **Ypres 1915, 17, 18,** St. Julien, Frezenberg, Bellewaarde, Hooge 1915, Loos, Mount Sorrel, **Somme 1916, 18, Albert 1916, 18,** Delville Wood, Guillemont, Flers-Courcelette, Morval, Le Transloy, Ancre 1916, 18, **Arras 1917, 18,** Vimy 1917, Scarpe 1917, 18, Arleux, Langemarck 1917, Menin Road, Polygon Wood, Broodseinde, Poelcapelle, Passchendaele, **Cambrai 1917, 18,** St. Quentin, Bapaume 1918, Rosières, Avre, Lys, Hazebrouck, Béthune, Soissonnais-Ourcq, Drocourt-Quéant, **Hindenburg Line,** Havrincourt, Épéhy, Canal du Nord, Courtrai, Selle, Valenciennes,

Sambre, France and Flanders 1914-18, Gaza, El Mughar, Nebi Samwil, Jerusalem, Megiddo, Sharon, **Palestine 1917-18, Tigris 1916,** Sharqat, Mesopotamia 1916-18, N. W. Frontier India 1915

Afghanistan 1919

Second World War
Odon, Caen, **Hill 112, Mont Pincon,** Noireau Crossing, Seine 1944, Nederrijn, Geilenkirchen, Roer, **Rhineland,** Cleve, Goch, Hochwald, Xanten, **Rhine,** Bremen, **North-West Europe 1944-45, Cassino II,** Trasimene Line, Arezzo, Advance to Florence, Capture of Forli, **Cosina Canal Crossing, Italy 1944-45,** Athens, Greece 1944-45, **North Arakan,** Buthidaung, **Ngakyedauk Pass,** Burma 1943-44

THE WEST YORKSHIRE REGIMENT (THE PRINCE OF WALES'S OWN)

First World War
Aisne 1914, 18, **Armentières 1914, Neuve Chapelle,** Aubers, Hooge 1915, Loos, **Somme 1916, 18,** Albert 1916, 18, Bazentin, Pozières, Flers-Courcelette, Morval, Thiepval, Le Transloy, Ancre Heights, Ancre 1916, Arras 1917, 18, Scarpe 1917, 18, Bullecourt, Hill 70, Messines 1917, 18, **Ypres 1917, 18,** Pilckem, Langemarck 1917, Menin Road, Polygon Wood, Poelcapelle, Passchendaele, **Cambrai 1917, 18,** St. Quentin, Rosières, **Villers Bretonneux, Lys,** Hazebrouck, Bailleul, Kemmel, Marne 1918, **Tardenois,** Amiens, Bapaume 1918, Drocourt-Quéant, Hindenburg Line, Havrincourt, Épéhy, Canal du Nord, Selle, Valenciennes, Sambre, France and Flanders 1914-18, **Piave,** Vittorio Veneto, Italy 1917-18, **Suvla,** Landing at Suvla, Scimitar Hill, Gallipoli 1915, Egypt 1915-16

Second World War
North-West Europe 1940, Jebel Dafeis, **Keren,** Ad Teclesan, Abyssinia 1940-41, Cauldron, **Defence of Alamein Line,** North Africa 1940-42, **Pegu 1942, Yenangyaung 1942,** North Arakan, **Maungdaw, Defence of Sinzweya, Imphal, Bishenpur,** Kanglatongbi, **Meiktila,** Capture of Meiktila, Defence of Meiktila, Rangoon Road, Pyawbwe, **Sittang 1945,** Burma 1942-45

THE EAST YORKSHIRE REGIMENT (THE DUKE OF YORK'S OWN)

First World War
Aisne 1914, 18, Armentières 1914, Ypres 1915, 17, 18, Gravenstafel, St. Julien, Frezenberg, Bellewaarde, Hooge 1915, **Loos, Somme 1916, 18,** Albert 1916, 18, Bazentin, Delville Wood, Pozières, Flers-Courcelette, Morval, Thiepval, Ancre Heights, Ancre 1916, **Arras**

1917, 18, Scarpe 1917, 18, Arleux, Oppy, Messines 1917, 18, Pilckem, Langemarck 1917, Menin Road, Polygon Wood, Broodseinde, Poelcapelle, Passchendaele, **Cambrai 1917, 18,** St. Quentin, Bapaume 1918, Rosières, Lys, Estaires, Hazebrouck, Kemmel, Scherpenberg, Amiens, Hindenburg Line, Épéhy, Canal du Nord, St. Quentin Canal, **Selle,** Sambre, France and Flanders 1914-18, Struma, **Doiran 1917,** Macedonia 1915-18, Suvla, Landing at Suvla, Scimitar Hill, **Gallipoli 1915,** Egypt 1915-16

Second World War
Withdrawal to Escaut, Defence of Escaut, Defence of Arras, French Frontier 1940, Ypres-Comines Canal, **Dunkirk 1940, Normandy Landing,** Tilly sur Seulles, **Odon,** Caen, Bourguebus Ridge, Troarn, Mont Pincon, St. Pierre la Vielle, Gheel, Nederrijn, Aam, Venraij, Rhineland, **Schaddenhof,** Brinkum, Bremen, **North-West Europe 1940, 44-45, Gazala,** Mersa Matruh, Defence of Alamein Line, **El Alamein, Mareth,** Wadi Zigzaou, Akarit, North Africa 1942-43, Primosole Bridge, **Sicily 1943,** Sittang 1945, **Burma 1945**

THE BEDFORDSHIRE AND HERTFORDSHIRE REGIMENT

First World War
Mons, Le Cateau, Retreat from Mons, **Marne 1914,** Aisne 1914, La Bassée 1914, **Ypres 1914, 15, 17,** Langemarck 1914, 17, Gheluvelt, Nonne Bosschen, Neuve Chapelle, Hill 60, St. Julien, Frezenberg, Bellewaarde, Aubers, Festubert 1915, **Loos, Somme 1916, 18,** Albert 1916, 18, Bazentin, Delville Wood, Pozières, Guillemont, Flers-Courcelette, Morval, Thiepval, Le Transloy, Ancre Heights, Ancre 1916, 18, **Arras 1917, 18,** Vimy 1917, Scarpe 1917, Arleux, Oppy, Messines 1917, Pilckem, Polygon Wood, Broodseinde, Poelcapelle, Passchendaele, **Cambrai 1917, 18,** St. Quentin, Bapaume 1918, Rosières, Avre, Villers Bretonneux, Lys, Hazebrouck, Scherpenberg, Amiens, Drocourt-Quéant, Hindenburg Line, Épéhy, Canal du Nord, St. Quentin Canal, Selle, **Sambre,** France and Flanders 1914-18, Italy 1917-18, **Suvla,** Landing at Suvla, Scimitar Hill, Gallipoli 1915, Egypt 1915-17, **Gaza,** El Mughar, Nebi Samwil, Jerusalem, Jaffa, Tell Asur, Megiddo, Sharon, Palestine 1917-18

Second World War
Dunkirk 1940, North-West Europe 1940, Tobruk 1941, **Tobruk Sortie, Belhamed, Tunis, North Africa 1941, 43, Cassino II, Trasimene Line, Italy 1944-45,** Athens, Greece 1944-45, Singapore Island, Malaya 1942, **Chindits 1944,** Burma 1944

THE ROYAL LEICESTERSHIRE REGIMENT

First World War
Aisne 1914, 18, La Bassée 1914, Armentières 1914, Festubert 1914, 15, **Neuve Chapelle,** Aubers, Hooge 1915, **Somme 1916, 18,** Bazentin, Flers-Courcelette, Morval, Le Transloy, **Ypres 1917,** Polygon Wood, **Cambrai 1917, 18,** St. Quentin, **Lys,** Bailleul, Kemmel, Scherpenberg, Albert 1918, Bapaume 1918, Hindenburg Line, Épéhy, **St. Quentin Canal,** Beaurevoir, Selle, Sambre, **France and Flanders 1914-18,** Megiddo, Sharon, Damascus, **Palestine 1918,** Tigris 1916, Kut al Amara 1917, Baghdad, **Mesopotamia 1915-18**

Second World War
Norway 1940, Antwerp-Turnhout Canal, **Scheldt,** Zetten, **North-West Europe 1944-45,** Jebel Mazar, Syria 1941, **Sidi Barrani,** Tobruk 1941, Montagne Farm, **North Africa 1940-41, 43, Salerno,** Calabritto, **Gothic Line,** Monte Gridolfo, Monte Colombo, **Italy 1943-45, Crete,** Heraklion, Kampar, **Malaya 1941-42, Chindits 1944**

Korean War
Maryang-San, **Korea 1951-52**

THE ROYAL IRISH REGIMENT

First World War
Mons, Le Cateau, Retreat from Mons, **Marne 1914,** Aisne 1914, La Bassée 1914, **Ypres 1915, 17, 18,** Gravenstafel, St. Julien, Frezenberg, Bellewaarde, **Somme 1916, 18,** Albert 1916, 18, Bazentin, Delville Wood, Guillemont, Ginchy, **Messines 1917,** Pilckem, Langemarck 1917, St. Quentin, Rosières, Arras 1918, Drocourt-Quéant, **Hindenburg Line,** Canal du Nord, St. Quentin Canal, Beaurevoir, Cambrai 1918, Courtrai, France and Flanders 1914-18, **Struma,** Macedonia 1915-17, **Suvla,** Landing at Suvla, Gallipoli 1915, **Gaza,** Jerusalem, Tell Asur, Megiddo, Nablus, Palestine 1917-18

THE GREEN HOWARDS (ALEXANDRA, PRINCESS OF WALES'S OWN YORKSHIRE REGIMENT)

First World War
Ypres 1914, 15, 17, Langemarck 1914, 17, Gheluvelt, Neuve Chapelle, St. Julien, Frezenberg, Bellewaarde, Aubers, Festubert 1915, **Loos, Somme 1916, 18,** Albert 1916, Bazentin, Pozières, Flers-Courcelette, Morval, Thiepval, Le Transloy, Ancre Heights, Ancre 1916, **Arras 1917, 18,** Scarpe 1917, 18, **Messines 1817, 18,** Pilckem, Menin Road, Polygon Wood, Broodseinde, Poelcapelle, Passchendaele, Cambrai 1917, 18, St. Quentin, Bapaume 1918,

Rosières, Lys, Estaires, Hazebrouck, Kemmel, Scherpenberg, Aisne 1918, Drocourt-Quéant, Hindenburg Line, Canal du Nord, Beaurevoir, Selle, **Valenciennes, Sambre, France and Flanders 1914-18,** Piave, **Vittorio Veneto,** Italy 1917-18, **Suvla,** Landing at Suvla, Scimitar Hill, Gallipoli 1915, Egypt 1916, Archangel 1918

Afghanistan 1919

Second World War
Otta, **Norway 1940,** Defence of Arras, Dunkirk 1940, **Normandy Landing,** Tilly sur Seulles, St. Pierre la Vielle, Gheel, Nederrijn, **North-West Europe 1940, 44-45, Gazala,** Defence of Alamein Line, **El Alamein, Mareth, Akarit,** North Africa 1942-43, Landing in Sicily, Lentini, **Sicily 1943, Minturno, Anzio,** Italy 1943-44, Arakan Beaches, Burma 1945

THE LANCASHIRE FUSILIERS

First World War
Le Cateau, **Retreat from Mons,** Marne 1914, **Aisne 1914, 18,** Armentières 1914, **Ypres 1915, 17, 18,** St. Julien, Bellewaarde, **Somme 1916, 18,** Albert 1916, 18, Bazentin, Delville Wood, Pozières, Ginchy, Flers-Courcelette, Morval, Thiepval, Le Transloy, Ancre Heights, Ancre 1916, 18, **Arras 1917, 18,** Scarpe 1917, 18, Arleux, Messines 1917, Pilckem, Langemarck 1917, Menin Road, Polygon Wood, Broodseinde, Poelcapelle, **Passchendaele, Cambrai 1917, 18,** St. Quentin, Bapaume 1918, Rosières, Lys, Estaires, Hazebrouck, Bailleul, Kemmel, Béthune, Scherpenberg, Amiens, Drocourt-Quéant, **Hindenburg Line,** Épéhy, Canal du Nord, St. Quentin Canal, Courtrai, Selle, Sambre, France and Flanders 1914-18, Doiran 1917, **Macedonia 1915-18,** Helles, **Landing at Helles,** Krithia, Suvla, Landing at Suvla, Scimitar Hill, Gallipoli 1915, Rumani, Egypt 1915-17

Second World War
Defence of Escaut, St. Omer-La Bassée, **Caen,** North-West Europe 1940, 44, **Medjez el Bab,** Oued Zarga, North Africa 1942-43, Adrano, Sicily 1943, Termoli, Trigno, **Sangro, Cassino II,** Trasimene Line, Monte Ceco, Monte Spaduro, Senio, **Argenta Gap,** Italy 1943-45, **Malta 1941-42,** Rathedaung, Htizwe, **Kohima,** Naga Village, **Chindits 1944, Burma 1943-45**

THE CHESHIRE REGIMENT

First World War
Mons, Le Cateau, Retreat from Mons, Marne 1914, 18, Aisne 1914, 18, La Bassée 1914, Armentières 1914, **Ypres 1914, 15, 17, 18,** Nonne Bosschen, Gravenstafel, St. Julien, Frezenburg, Bellewaarde,

Loos, **Somme 1916, 18,** Albert 1916, 18, Bazentin, Delville Wood, Pozières, Guillemont, Flers-Courcelette, Morval, Thiepval, Le Transloy, Ancre Heights, Ancre 1916, **Arras 1917, 18,** Vimy 1917, Scarpe 1917, 18, Oppy, **Messines 1917, 18,** Pilckem, Langemarck 1917, Menin Road, Polygon Wood, Broodseinde, Poelcapelle, Passchendaele, Cambrai 1917, 18, St. Quentin, **Bapaume 1918,** Rosières, Lys, Estaires, Hazebrouck, Bailleul, Kemmel, Scherpenberg, Soissonnais-Ourcq, Hindenburg Line, Canal du Nord, Courtrai, Selle, Valenciennes, Sambre, France and Flanders 1914-18, Italy 1917-18, Struma, **Doiran 1917, 18,** Macedonia 1915-18, **Suvla,** Sari Bair, Landing at Suvla, Scimitar Hill, Gallipoli 1915, Egypt 1915-17, **Gaza,** El Mughar, Jerusalem, Jericho, Tell Asur, Palestine 1917-18, Tigris 1916, **Kut al Amara 1917,** Baghdad, Mesopotamia 1916-18

Second World War
Dyle, Withdrawal to Escaut, **St. Omer-La Bassée,** Wormhoudt, Cassel, Dunkirk 1940, **Normandy Landing,** Mont Pincon, St. Pierre La Vielle, Gheel, Nederrijn, Aam, Aller, North-West Europe 1940, 44-45, Sidi Barrani, **Capture of Tobruk,** Gazala, Mersa Matruh, Defence of Alamein Line, Deir el Shein, **El Alamein, Mareth,** Wadi Zeuss East, Wadi Zigzaou, Akarit, Wadi Akarit East, Enfidaville, North Africa 1940-43, Landing in Sicily, Primosole Bridge, Simeto Bridgehead, **Sicily 1943,** Sangro, **Salerno,** Santa Lucia, Battipaglia, Volturno Crossing, Monte Maro, Teano, Monte Camino, Garigliano Crossing, Minturno, Damiano, Anzio, **Rome, Gothic Line,** Coriano, Gemmano Ridge, Savignano, Scnio Floodbank, Rimini Line, Ceriano Ridge, Valli di Comacchio, Italy 1943-45, **Malta 1941-42**

THE ROYAL SCOTS FUSILIERS

First World War
Mons, Le Cateau, Retreat from Mons, **Marne 1914,** Aisne 1914, La Bassée 1914, **Ypres 1914, 17, 18,** Langemarck 1914, Gheluvelt, Nonne Bosschen, Neuve Chapelle, Aubers, Festubert 1915, Loos, **Somme 1916, 18,** Albert 1916, 18, Bazentin, Delville Wood, Pozières, Flers-Courcelette, Le Transloy, Ancre Heights, Ancre 1916, **Arras 1917, 18,** Scarpe 1917, 18, Arleux, Messines 1917, Pilckem, Menin Road, Polygon Wood, St. Quentin, Bapaume 1918, Rosières, **Lys,** Estaires, Hazebrouck, Bailleul, Béthune, Scherpenberg, Drocourt-Quéant, **Hindenburg Line,** Canal du Nord, Courtrai, Selle, France and Flanders 1914-18, **Doiran 1917, 18,** Macedonia 1916-18, Helles, **Gallipoli 1915-18,** Rumani, Egypt 1916-17, Gaza, El Mughar, Nebi Samwil, Jerusalem, Jaffa, Tell Asur, **Palestine 1917-18**

Second World War
Defence of Arras, **Ypres-Comines Canal,** Somme

1940, Withdrawal to Seine, **Odon,** Fontenay le Pesnil, Cheux, Defence of Rauray, Mont Pincon, Estry, **Falaise,** La Vie Crossing, La Touques Crossing, Aart, Nederrijn, Best, Le Havre, Antwerp-Turnhout Canal, **Scheldt,** South Beveland, Lower Maas, Meijel, Venlo Pocket, Roer, Rhineland, Reichswald, Cleve, Goch, **Rhine,** Dreirwalde, Uelzen, **Bremen,** Artlenberg, North-West Europe 1940, 44-45, **Landing in Sicily,** Sicily 1943, Sangro, **Garigliano Crossing,** Minturno, Anzio, Advance to Tiber, Italy 1943-44, Madagascar, Middle East 1942, **North Arakan,** Razabil, **Pinwe,** Schweli, Mandalay, Burma 1944-45

THE ROYAL WELCH FUSILIERS

First World War
Mons, Le Cateau, Retreat from Mons, **Marne 1914, Aisne 1914, 18, La Bassée 1914, Messines 1914, 17, 18, Armentières 1914, Ypres 1914, 17, 18,** Langemarck 1914, 17, Gheluvelt, Givenchy 1914, Neuve Chapelle, Aubers, Festubert 1915, Loos, **Somme 1916, 18,** Albert 1916, 18, Bazentin, Delville Wood, Pozières, Guillemont, Flers-Courcelette, Morval, Le Transloy, Ancre Heights, Ancre 1916, 18, Arras 1917, Scarpe 1917, Arleux, Bullecourt, Pilckem, Menin Road, Polygon Wood, Broodseinde, Poelcapelle, Passchendale, Cambrai 1917, 18, St. Quentin, Bapaume 1918, Lys, Bailleul, Kemmel, Scherpenberg, **Hindenburg Line,** Havrincourt, Épéhy, St. Quentin Canal, Beaurevoir, Selle, Valenciennes, Sambre, France and Flanders 1914-18, Piave, **Vittorio Veneto,** Italy 1917-18, **Doiran 1917, 18,** Macedonia 1915-18, Suvla, Sari Bair, Landing at Suvla, Scimitar Hill, **Gallipoli 1915-16,** Rumani, **Egypt 1915-17, Gaza,** El Mughar, Jerusalem, Jericho, Tell Asur, Megiddo, Nablus, Palestine 1917-18, Tigris 1916, Kut al Amara 1917, **Baghdad,** Mesopotamia 1916-18

Second World War
Dyle, Defence of Escaut, **St. Omer-La Bassée, Caen,** Esquay, Falaise, Nederrijn, **Lower Maas,** Venlo Pocket, Ourthe, Rhineland, **Reichswald,** Goch, **Weeze, Rhine,** Ibbenburen, Aller, North-West Europe 1940, 44-45, **Madagascar,** Middle East 1942, **Donbaik, North Arakan, Kohima,** Mandalay, Ava, Burma 1943-45

THE SOUTH WALES BORDERERS

First World War
Mons, Retreat from Mons, **Marne 1914,** Aisne 1914, 18, **Ypres 1914, 17, 18,** Langemarck 1914, 17, **Gheluvelt,** Nonne Bosschen, Givenchy 1914, Aubers, Loos, **Somme 1916, 18,** Albert 1916, 18, Bazentin,

Pozières, Flers-Courcelette, Morval, Ancre Heights, Ancre 1916, Arras 1917, 18, Scarpe 1917, Messines 1917, 18, Pilckem, Menin Road, Polygon Wood, Broodseinde, Poelcapelle, Passchendaele, **Cambrai 1917, 18,** St. Quentin, Bapaume 1918, Lys, Estaires, Hazebrouck, Bailleul, Kemmel, Béthune, Scherpenberg, Drocourt-Quéant, Hindenberg Line, Havrincourt, Épéhy, St. Quentin Canal, Beaurevoir, Courtrai, Selle, Valenciennes, Sambre, France and Flanders 1914-18, **Doiran 1917, 18,** Macedonia 1915-18, Helles, **Landing at Helles,** Krithia, Suvla, Sari Bair, Scimitar Hill, Gallipoli 1915-16, Egypt 1916, Tigris 1916, Kut al Amara 1917, **Baghdad,** Mesopotamia 1916-18, **Tsingtao**

Second World War
Norway 1940, Normandy Landing, Sully, Caen, Falaise, Risle Crossing, **Le Havre,** Antwerp-Turnhout Canal, Scheldt, Zetten, Arnhem 1945, **North-West Europe 1944-45,** Gazala, **North Africa 1942,** North Arakan, **Mayu Tunnels, Pinwe,** Schweli, Myitson, **Burma 1944-45**

THE KING'S OWN SCOTTISH BORDERERS

First World War
Mons, Le Cateau, Retreat from Mons, Marne 1914, 18, **Aisne 1914,** La Bassée 1914, Messines 1914, **Ypres 1914, 15, 17, 18,** Nonne Bosschen, Hill 60, Gravenstafel, St. Julien, Frezenberg, Bellewaarde, **Loos, Somme 1916, 18,** Albert 1916, 18, Bazentin, Delville Wood, Pozières, Guillemont, Flers-Courcelette, Morval, Le Transloy, Ancre Heights, **Arras 1917, 18,** Vimy 1917, Scarpe 1917, 18, Arleux, Pilckem, Langemarck 1917, Menin Road, Polygon Wood, Broodseinde, Poelcapelle, Passchendaele, Cambrai 1917, 18, St. Quentin, Lys, Estaires, Hazebrouck, Kemmel, **Soissonnais-Ourcq,** Bapaume 1918, Drocourt-Quéant, **Hindenburg Line,** Épéhy, Canal du Nord, Courtrai, Selle, Sambre, France and Flanders 1914-18, Italy 1917-18, Helles, Landing at Helles, Krithia, Suvla, Scimitar Hill, **Gallipoli 1915-16,** Rumani, Egypt 1916, **Gaza,** El Mughar, Nebi Samwil, Jaffa, Palestine 1917-18

Second World War
Dunkirk 1940, Cambes, **Odon,** Cheux, Defence of Rauray, **Caen,** Esquay, Troarn, Mont Pincon, Estry, Aart, Nederrijn, **Arnhem 1944,** Best, Scheldt, **Flushing,** Venraij, Meijel, Venlo Pocket, Roer, Rhineland, Reichswald, Cleve, Goch, **Rhine,** Ibbenburen, Lingen, Dreirwalde, Uelzen, **Bremen,** Artlenberg, North-West Europe 1940, 44-45, North Arakan, Buthidaung, **Ngakyedauk Pass, Imphal,** Kanglatongbi, Ukhrul, Meiktila, **Irrawaddy,** Kama, Burma 1943, 45

Korean War
Kowang-San, Maryang-San, **Korea 1951-52**

THE CAMERONIANS (SCOTTISH RIFLES)

First World War
Mons, Le Cateau, Retreat from Mons, **Marne 1914, 18,** Aisne 1914, La Bassée 1914, Messines 1914, Armentières 1914, **Neuve Chapelle,** Aubers, **Loos, Somme 1916, 18,** Albert 1916, Bazentin, Pozières, Flers-Courcelette, Le Transloy, Ancre Heights, Arras 1917, 18, Scarpe 1917, 18, Arleux, **Ypres 1917, 18,** Pilckem, Langemarck 1917, Menin Road, Polygon Wood, Passchendaele, St. Quentin, Rosières, Avre, Lys, Hazebrouck, Bailleul, Kemmel, Scherpenberg, Soissonnais-Ourcq, Drocourt-Quéant, **Hindenburg Line,** Épéhy, Canal du Nord, St. Quentin Canal, Cambrai 1918, Courtrai, Selle, Sambre, France and Flanders 1914-18, Doiran 1917, 18, **Macedonia 1915-18, Gallipoli 1915,** Rumani, Egypt 1916-17, Gaza, El Mughar, Nebi Samwil, Jaffa, **Palestine 1917-18**

Second World War
Ypres-Comines Canal, **Odon,** Cheux, Caen, Mont Pincon, Estry, Nederrijn, Best, **Scheldt,** South Beveland, Walcheron Causeway, Asten, Roer, **Rhineland,** Reichswald, Moyland, **Rhine,** Dreirwalde, Bremen, Artenburg, **North-West Europe 1940, 44-45,** Landing in Sicily, Simeto Bridgehead, **Sicily 1943,** Garigliano Crossing, **Anzio,** Advance to Tiber, **Italy 1943-44,** Pegu 1942, Paungde, Yenangyaung 1942, **Chindits 1944, Burma 1942, 44**

THE ROYAL INNISKILLING FUSILIERS

First World War
Le Cateau, Retreat from Mons, Marne 1914, 18, Aisne 1914, Messines 1914, 17, Armentières 1914, Aubers, Festubert 1915, **Somme 1916, 18,** Albert 1916, Bazentin, Guillemont, Ginchy, Ancre 1916, Arras 1917, Scarpe 1917, **Ypres 1917, 18,** Pilckem, Langemarck 1917, Polygon Wood, Broodseinde, Poelcapelle, Cambrai 1917, 18, **St. Quentin,** Rosières, **Hindenburg Line,** Beaurevoir, Courtrai, Selle, Sambre, **France and Flanders 1914-18,** Kosturino, Struma, **Macedonia 1915-18,** Helles, **Landing at Helles,** Krithia, Suvla, Landing at Suvla, Scimitar Hill, **Gallipoli 1915-16,** Egypt 1916, Gaza, Jerusalem, Tell Asur, **Palestine 1917-18**

Second World War
Defence of Arras, Ypres-Comines Canal, **North-West Europe 1940,** Two Tree Hill, Bou Arada, Oued Zarga, Djebel Bel Mahdi, **Djebel Tanngoucha, North Africa 1942-43,** Landing in Sicily, Solarino, Simeto Bridgehead, Adrano, **Centuripe,** Simeto Crossing, Pursuit to Messina, **Sicily 1943,** Termoli, Trigno, San Salvo, Sangro, **Garigliano Crossing,** Minturno, Anzio, **Cassino II,** Massa Tambourini, Liri Valley,

Rome, Advance to Tiber, Trasimene Line, Monte Spaduro, Argenta Gap, **Italy 1943-45,** Middle East 1942, **Yenangyaung 1942,** Donbaik, **Burma 1942-43**

THE GLOUCESTERSHIRE REGIMENT

First World War
Mons, Retreat from Mons, Marne 1914, 18, Aisne 1914, 18, **Ypres 1914, 15, 17,** Langemarck 1914, 17, Gheluvelt, Nonne Bosschen, Givenchy 1914, Gravenstafel, St. Julien, Frezenberg, Bellewaarde, Aubers, **Loos, Somme 1916, 18,** Albert 1916, 18, Bazentin, Delville Wood, Pozières, Guillemont, Flers-Courcelette, Morval, Ancre Heights, Ancre 1916, Arras 1917, 18, Vimy 1917, Scarpe 1917, Messines 1917, 18, Pilckem, Menin Road, Polygon Wood, Broodseinde, Poelcapelle, Passchendaele, Cambrai 1917, 18, St. Quentin, Bapaume 1918, Rosières, Avre, **Lys,** Estaires, Hazebrouck, Bailleul, Kemmel, Béthune, Drocourt-Quéant, Hindenburg Line, Épéhy, Canal du Nord, St. Quentin Canal, Beaurevoir, **Selle,** Valenciennes, Sambre, France and Flanders 1914-18, Piave, **Vittorio Veneto,** Italy 1917-18, Struma, **Doiran 1917,** Macedonia 1915-18, Suvla, **Sari Bair,** Scimitar Hill, Gallipoli 1915-16, Egypt 1916, Tigris 1916, Kut al Amara 1917, **Baghdad,** Mesopotamia 1916-18, Persia 1918

Second World War
Defence of Escaut, St. Omer-La Bassée, Wormhoudt, **Cassel,** Villers Bocage, **Mont Pincon, Falaise,** Risle Crossing, Le Havre, Zetten, **North-West Europe 1940, 44-45, Taukyan, Paungde,** Monywa 1942, North Arakan, Mayu Tunnels, **Pinwe,** Shweli, **Myitson, Burma 1942, 44-45**

Korean War
Hill 327, **Imjin, Korea 1950-51**

THE WORCESTERSHIRE REGIMENT

First World War
Mons, Le Cateau, Retreat from Mons, Marne 1914, Aisne 1914, 18, La Bassée 1914, Armentières 1914, **Ypres 1914, 15, 17, 18,** Langemarck 1914, 17, **Gheluvelt,** Nonne Bosschen, **Neuve Chapelle,** Aubers, Festubert 1915, Loos, **Somme 1916, 18,** Albert 1916, Bazentin, Delville Wood, Pozières, Le Transloy, Ancre Heights, Ancre 1916, Arras 1917, Scarpe 1917, Arleux, Messines 1917, 18, Pilckem, Menin Road, Polygon Wood, Broodseinde, Poelcapelle, **Cambrai 1917, 18,** St. Quentin, Bapaume 1918, Rosières, Villers Bretonneux, **Lys,** Estaires, Hazebrouck, Bailleul, Kemmel, Scherpenberg, Hindenburg Line, Canal du Nord, St. Quentin Canal, Beaurevoir, Courtrai, Selle, Valenciennes, Sambre, France and Flanders 1914-18, Piave, Vittorio Veneto, **Italy 1917-18,** Doiran 1917,

18, Macedonia 1915-18, Helles, Landing at Helles, Krithia, Suvla, Sari Bair, Scimitar Hill, **Gallipoli 1915-16,** Egypt 1916, Tigris 1916, Kut al Amara 1917, **Baghdad,** Mesopotamia 1916-18, Baku, Persia 1918

Second World War
Defence of Escaut, St. Omer-La Bassée, Wormhoudt, Odon, Bourguebus Ridge, Maltot, **Mont Pincon,** Jurques, La Varinière, Noireau Crossing, **Seine 1944,** Nederrijn, **Geilenkirchen,** Rhineland, **Goch,** Rhine, **North-West Europe 1940, 44-45,** Gogni, Barentu, **Keren,** Amba Alagi, Abyssinia 1940-41, **Gazala,** Via Balbia, North Africa 1941-42, **Kohima,** Naga Village, Mao Songsang, Shwebo, **Mandalay,** Irrawaddy, Mt. Popa, **Burma 1944-45**

THE EAST LANCASHIRE REGIMENT

First World War
Le Cateau, **Retreat from Mons, Marne 1914, Aisne 1914, 18,** Armentières 1914, **Neuve Chapelle, Ypres 1915, 17, 18,** St. Julien, Frezenberg, Bellewaarde, Aubers, **Somme 1916, 18,** Albert 1916, 18, Bazentin, Pozières, Le Transloy, Ancre Heights, Ancre 1916, 18, **Arras 1917, 18,** Vimy 1917, Scarpe 1917, 18, Arleux, Oppy, Messines 1917, Pilckem, Langemarck 1917, Menin Road, Polygon Wood, Broodseinde, Poelcapelle, Passchendaele, St. Quentin, Bapaume 1918, Rosières, Villers Bretonneux, Lys, Estaires, Hazebrouck, Bailleul, Kemmel, Hindenburg Line, Canal du Nord, Cambrai 1918, Selle, Valenciennes, Sambre, France and Flanders 1914-18, Kosturino, **Doiran 1917, 18,** Macedonia 1915-18, **Helles,** Krithia, Suvla, Sari Bair, Gallipoli 1915, Rumani, Egypt 1915-17, Tigris 1916, **Kut al Amara 1917,** Baghdad, Mesopotamia 1916-17

Second World War
Defence of Escaut, **Dunkirk 1940,** Caen, **Falaise,** Nederrijn, **Lower Maas, Ourthe,** Rhineland, **Reichswald, Weeze,** Rhine, Ibbenburen, **Aller,** North-West Europe 1940, 44-45, **Madagascar,** North Arakan, **Pinwe, Burma 1944-45**

THE EAST SURREY REGIMENT

First World War
Mons, Le Cateau, Retreat from Mons, **Marne 1914,** Aisne 1914, **La Bassée 1914,** Armentières 1914, Hill 60, **Ypres 1915, 17, 18,** Gravenstafel, St. Julien, Frezenberg, Bellewaarde, **Loos, Somme 1916, 18, Albert 1916, 18,** Bazentin, Delville Wood, Pozières, Guillemont, Flers-Courcelette, Morval, Thiepval, Le Transloy, Ancre Heights, Ancre 1916, Arras 1917, 18, Vimy 1917, Scarpe 1917, Messines 1917, Pilckem, Langemarck 1917, Menin Road, Polygon Wood, Broodseinde, Poelcapelle, Passchendaele, **Cambrai**

1917, 18, St. Quentin, Bapaume 1918, Rosières, Avre, Lys, Estaires, Hazebrouck, Amiens, Hindenburg Line, Épéhy, Canal du Nord, St. Quentin Canal, Courtrai, **Selle,** Sambre, France and Flanders 1914-18, Italy 1917-18, Struma, **Doiran 1918,** Macedonia 1915-18, Egypt 1915, Aden, Mesopotamia 1917-18, Murman 1919

Second World War
Defence of Escaut, **Dunkirk 1940, North-West Europe 1940,** Tebourba, Fort McGregor, **Oued Zarga,** Djebel Ang, Djebel Djaffa Pass, Medjez Plain, **Longstop Hill 1943,** Tunis, Montarnaud, **North Africa 1942-43,** Adrano, Centuripe, **Sicily 1943,** Trigno, **Sangro, Cassino,** Capture of Forli, Argenta Gap, **Italy 1943-45,** Greece 1944-45, Kampar, **Malaya 1941-42**

THE DUKE OF CORNWALL'S LIGHT INFANTRY

First World War
Mons, Le Cateau, Retreat from Mons, **Marne 1914,** Aisne 1914, La Bassée 1914, Armentières 1914, **Ypres 1915, 17,** Gravenstafel, St. Julien, Frezenberg, Bellewaarde, Hooge 1915, Mount Sorrel, **Somme 1916, 18,** Delville Wood, Guillemont, Flers-Courcelette, Morval, Le Transloy, Ancre 1916, Bapaume 1917, 18, **Arras 1917,** Vimy 1917, Scarpe 1917, Arleux, Langemarck 1917, Menin Road, Polygon Wood, Broodseinde, Poelcapelle, **Passchendaele, Cambrai 1917, 18,** St. Quentin, Rosières, Lys, Estaires, Hazebrouck, Albert 1918, Hindenburg Line, Havrincourt, Canal du Nord, Selle, **Sambre,** France and Flanders 1914-18, Italy 1917-18, Struma, **Doiran 1917, 18,** Macedonia 1915-18, **Gaza,** Nebi Samwil, Jerusalem, Tell Asur, Megiddo, Sharon, Palestine 1917-18, Aden

Second World War
Defence of Escaut, Cheux, **Hill 112, Mont Pincon,** Noireau Crossing, **Nederrijn,** Opheusden, **Geilenkirchen, Rhineland,** Goch, Rhine, **North-West Europe 1940, 44-45, Gazala, Medjez Plain,** Si Abdallah, North Africa 1942-43, **Cassino II,** Trasimene Line, Advance to Florence, **Incontro,** Rimini Line, Italy 1944-45

THE DUKE OF WELLINGTON'S REGIMENT (WEST RIDING)

First World War
Mons, Le Cateau, Retreat from Mons, **Marne 1914, 18,** Aisne 1914, La Bassée 1914, **Ypres 1914, 15, 17,** Nonne Bosschen, **Hill 60,** Gravenstafel, St. Julien, Aubers, **Somme 1916, 18,** Albert 1916, 18, Bazentin, Delville Wood, Pozières, Flers-Courcelette, Morval,

Thiepval, Le Transloy, Ancre Heights, **Arras 1917, 18,** Scarpe 1917, 18, Arleux, Bullecourt, Messines 1917, 18, Langemarck 1917, Menin Road, Polygon Wood, Broodseinde, Poelcapelle, Passchendaele, **Cambrai 1917, 18,** St. Quentin, Ancre 1918, **Lys,** Estaires, Hazebrouck, Bailleul, Kemmel, Béthune, Scherpenberg, Tardenois, Amiens, Bapaume 1918, Drocourt-Quéant, Hindenburg Line, Havrincourt, Épéhy, Canal du Nord, Selle, Valenciennes, Sambre, France and Flanders 1914-18, **Piave,** Vittorio Veneto, Italy 1917-18, Suvla, **Landing at Suvla,** Scimitar Hill, Gallipoli 1915, Egypt 1916

Afghanistan 1919

Second World War
Dunkirk 1940, St. Valéry-en-Caux, Tilly sur Seulles, Odon, **Fontenay Le Pesnil, North-West Europe 1940, 44-45,** Banana Ridge, Medjez Plain, Gueriat el Atach Ridge, Tunis, **Djebel Bou Aoukaz 1943,** North Africa 1943, **Anzio,** Campoleone, Rome, **Monte Ceco,** Italy 1943-45, **Sittang 1942,** Paungde, Kohima, **Chindits 1944, Burma 1942-44**

Korean War
The Hook 1953, Korea 1952-53

THE BORDER REGIMENT

First World War
Ypres 1914, 15, 17, 18, Langemarck 1914, 17, Gheluvelt, Neuve Chapelle, Frezenberg, Bellewaarde, Aubers, Festubert 1915, Loos, **Somme 1916, 18,** Albert 1916, 18, Bazentin, Delville Wood, Pozières, Guillemont, Flers-Courcelette, Morval, Thiepval, Le Transloy, Ancre Heights, Ancre 1916, **Arras 1917, 18,** Scarpe 1917, Bullecourt, Messines 1917, 18, Pilckem, Polygon Wood, Broodseinde, Poelcapelle, Passchendaele, **Cambrai 1917, 18,** St. Quentin, Rosières, **Lys,** Estaires, Hazebrouck, Bailleul, Kemmel, Scherpenberg, Aisne 1918, Amiens, Bapaume 1918, Hindenburg Line, Épéhy, St. Quentin Canal, Beaurevoir, Courtrai, Selle, Sambre, **France and Flanders 1914-18,** Piave, **Vittorio Veneto,** Italy 1917-18, Doiran 1917, 18, **Macedonia 1915-18,** Helles, Landing at Helles, Krithia, Suvla, Landing at Suvla, Scimitar Hill, **Gallipoli 1915-16,** Egypt 1916, N. W. Frontier India 1916-17

Afghanistan 1919

Second World War
Defence of Escaut, **Dunkirk 1940,** Somme 1940, **Arnhem 1944, North-West Europe 1940, 44, Tobruk 1941, Landing in Sicily, Imphal,** Sakawng, Tamu Road, Shenam Pass, Kohima, Ukhrul, Mandalay, **Myinmu Bridgehead, Meiktila,** Rangoon Road, Pyawbwe, Sittang 1945. **Chindits 1944, Burma 1943-45**

THE ROYAL SUSSEX REGIMENT

First World War
Mons, **Retreat from Mons, Marne 1914, 18,** Aisne 1914, **Ypres 1914, 17, 18,** Gheluvelt, Nonne Bosschen, Givenchy 1914, Aubers, Loos, **Somme 1916, 18,** Albert 1916, 18, Bazentin, Delville Wood, Pozières, Flers-Courcelette, Morval, Thiepval, Le Transloy, Ancre Heights, Ancre 1916, 18, Arras 1917, 18, Vimy 1917, Scarpe 1917, Arleux, Messines 1917, **Pilckem,** Langemarck 1917, Menin Road, Polygon Wood, Broodseinde, Poelcapelle, Passchendaele, Cambrai 1917, 18, St. Quentin, Bapaume 1918, Rosières, Avre, Lys, Kemmel, Scherpenberg, Soissonnais-Ourcq, Amiens, Drocourt-Quéant, **Hindenburg Line,** Épéhy, St. Quentin Canal, Beaurevoir, Courtrai, Selle, Sambre, France and Flanders 1914-18, Piave, Vittorio Veneto, **Italy 1917-18,** Suvla, Landing at Suvla, Scimitar Hill, **Gallipoli 1915,** Rumani, Egypt 1915-17, Gaza, El Mughar, Jerusalem, Jericho, Tell Asur, **Palestine 1917-18, N. W. Frontier India 1915, 1916-17,** Murman 1918-19

Afghanistan 1919

Second World War
Defence of Escaut, Amiens 1940, St. Omer-La Bassée, Foret de Nieppe, **North-West Europe 1940,** Karora-Marsa Taclai, Cub cub, Mescelit Pass, Keren, Mt. Engiahat, Massawa, **Abyssinia 1941, Omars,** Benghazi, **Alam el Halfa, El Alamein, Akarit,** Djebel el Meida, Tunis, **North Africa 1940-43, Cassino II,** Monastery Hill, Gothic Line, Pian di Castello, Monte Reggiano, **Italy 1944-45,** North Arakan, Pinwe, Shweli, **Burma 1943-45**

THE ROYAL HAMPSHIRE REGIMENT

First World War
Le Cateau, **Retreat from Mons,** Marne 1914, 18, Aisne 1914, Armentières 1914, **Ypres 1915, 17, 18,** St. Julien, Frezenberg, Bellewaarde, **Somme 1916, 18,** Albert 1916, Guillemont, Ginchy, Flers-Courcelette, Thiepval, Le Transloy, Ancre Heights, Ancre 1916, **Arras 1917, 18,** Vimy 1917, Scarpe 1917, 18, Messines 1917, Pilckem, Langemarck 1917, Menin Road, Polygon Wood, Broodseinde, Poelcapelle, Passchendaele, **Cambrai 1917, 18,** St. Quentin, Bapaume 1918, Rosières, Lys, Estaires, Hazebrouck, Bailleul, Kemmel, Béthune, Tardenois, Drocourt-Quéant, Hindenburg Line, Havrincourt, Canal du Nord, Courtrai, Selle, Valenciennes, Sambre, France and Flanders 1914-18, Italy 1917-18, Kosturino, Struma, **Doiran 1917, 18,** Macedonia 1915-18, Helles, **Landing at Helles,** Krithia, **Suvla,** Sari Bair, Landing at Suvla, Scimitar Hill, Gallipoli 1915-16, Egypt 1915-17, **Gaza,** El Mughar, Nebi Samwil, Jerusalem, Jaffa, Tell Asur, Megiddo,

Sharon, Palestine 1917-18, Aden, Shaiba, **Kut al Amara 1915, 17,** Tigris 1916, Baghdad, Sharqat, Mesopotamia 1915-18, Persia 1918-19, Archangel 1919, Siberia 1918-19

Second World War
Dunkirk 1940, Normandy Landing, Tilly sur Seulles, **Caen,** Hill 112, Mont Pincon, Jurques, St. Pierre La Vielle, Nederrijn, Roer, Rhineland, Goch, **Rhine,** North-West Europe 1940, 44-45, **Tebourba Gap,** Sidi Nsir, **Hunt's Gap,** Montagne Farm, Fondouk, Pichon, El Kourzia, Ber Rabai, North Africa 1940-43, Landing in Sicily, Regalbuto, Sicily 1943, Landing at Porto San Venere, **Salerno,** Salerno Hills, Battipaglia, Cava di Tirreni, Volturno Crossing, Garigliano Crossing, Damiano, Monte Ornito, Cerasola, **Cassino II,** Massa Vertecchi, Trasimene Line, Advance to Florence, **Gothic Line,** Monte Gridolfo, Montegaudio, Coriano, Montilgallo, Capture of Forli, Cosina Canal Crossing, Lamone Crossing, Pideura, Rimini Line, Montescudo, Frisoni, Italy 1943-45, Athens, Greece 1944-45, **Malta 1941-42**

THE SOUTH STAFFORDSHIRE REGIMENT

First World War
Mons, Retreat from Mons, **Marne 1914, Aisne 1914, 18, Ypres 1914, 17,** Langemarck 1914, 17, Gheluvelt, Nonne Bosschen, Neuve Chapelle, Aubers, Festubert 1915, **Loos, Somme 1916, 18,** Albert 1916, 18, Bazentin, Delville Wood, Pozières, Flers-Courcelette, Morval, Thiepval, Ancre 1916, Bapaume 1917, 18, Arras 1917, 18, Scarpe 1917, 18, Arleux, Bullecourt, Hill 70, Messines 1917, 18, Menin Road, Polygon Wood, Broodseinde, Poelcapelle, Passchendaele, **Cambrai 1917, 18,** St. Quentin, Lys, Bailleul, Kemmel Scherpenberg, Drocourt-Quéant, Hindenburg Line, Havrincourt, Canal du Nord, **St. Quentin Canal,** Beaurevoir, Selle, Sambre, France and Flanders 1914-18, Piave, **Vittorio Veneto,** Italy 1917-18, **Suvla,** Landing at Suvla, Scimitar Hill, Gallipoli 1915, Egypt 1916

Second World War
Caen, Noyers, Falaise, Arnhem 1944, North-West Europe 1940, 44, Sidi Barrani, **North Africa 1940, Landing in Sicily, Sicily 1943,** Italy 1943, **Chindits 1944, Burma 1944**

THE DORSET REGIMENT

First World War
Mons, Le Cateau, Retreat from Mons, **Marne 1914,** Aisne 1914, La Bassée 1914, Armentières 1914, **Ypres 1915, 17,** Gravenstafel, St. Julien, Bellewaarde, **Somme 1916, 18,** Albert 1916, 18, Flers-Courcelette, Thiepval, Ancre 1916, 18, Arras 1917, Scarpe 1917,

Messines 1917, Langemarck 1917, Polygon Wood, Broodseinde, Poelcapelle, Passchendaele, St. Quentin, Amiens, Bapaume 1918, **Hindenburg Line,** Épéhy, Canal du Nord, St. Quentin Canal, Beaurevoir, Cambrai 1918, Selle, **Sambre,** France and Flanders 1914-18, **Suvla,** Landing at Suvla, Scimitar Hill, Gallipoli 1915, Egypt 1916, **Gaza,** El Mughar, Nebi Samwil, Jerusalem, Tell Asur, Megiddo, Sharon, Palestine 1917-18, Basra, **Shaiba,** Kut al Amara 1915, 17, **Ctesiphon,** Defence of Kut al Amara, Baghdad, Mesopotamia 1914-18

Second World War
St. Omer-La Bassée, Normandy Landing, Villers Bocage, Tilly sur Seulles, **Caen,** Mont Pincon, St. Pierre La Vielle, **Arnhem 1944, Aam, Geilenkirchen,** Goch, Rhine, Twente Canal, North-West Europe 1940, 44-45, **Landing in Sicily,** Agira, Regalbuto, Sicily 1943, Landing at Porto San Venere, Italy 1943, **Malta 1940-42, Kohima, Mandalay,** Mt. Popa, Burma 1944-45

THE SOUTH LANCASHIRE REGIMENT (PRINCE OF WALES'S VOLUNTEERS)

First World War
Mons, Le Cateau, Retreat from Mons, Marne 1914, **Aisne 1914, 18,** La Bassée 1914, **Messines 1914, 17, 18,** Armentières 1914, **Ypres 1914, 15, 17, 18,** Nonne Bosschen, St. Julien, Frezenberg, Bellewaarde, **Somme 1916, 18,** Albert 1916, Bazentin, Pozières, Guillemont, Ginchy, Flers-Courcelette, Morval, Le Transloy, Ancre Heights, Ancre 1916, Arras 1917, 18, Scarpe 1917, 18, Pilckem, Langemarck 1917, Menin Road, Polygon Wood, Passchendaele, Cambrai 1917, 18, St. Quentin, Bapaume 1918, Posières, **Lys,** Estaires, Hazebrouck, Bailleul, Kemmel, Scherpenberg, Drocourt-Quéant, Hindenburg Line, Canal du Nord, Courtrai, Selle, Sambre, France and Flanders 1914-18, **Doiran 1917, 18,** Macedonia 1915-18, Suvla, **Sari Bair,** Gallipoli 1915, Egypt 1916, Tigris 1916, Kut al Amara 1917, **Baghdad,** Mesopotamia 1916-18, **Baluchistan 1918**

Afghanistan 1919

Second World War
Dunkirk 1940, Normandy Landing, Odon, **Bourguebus Ridge,** Troarn, **Falaise,** Venraij, **Rhineland,** Hochwald, Bremen, **North-West Europe 1940, 44-45, Madagascar,** Middle East 1942, **North Arakan,** Mayu Tunnels, **Kohima,** Meiktila, **Nyaungu Bridgehead,** Letse, Irrawaddy, Burma 1943-45

THE WELCH REGIMENT

First World War
Mons, Retreat from Mons, Marne 1914, **Aisne 1914,**

18, **Ypres 1914, 15, 17,** Langemarck 1914, 17, **Gheluvelt,** Nonne Bosschen, Givenchy 1914, Gravenstafel, St. Julien, Frezenberg, Bellewaarde, Aubers, Loos, **Somme 1916, 18,** Albert 1916, 18, Bazentin, Pozières, Flers-Courcelette, Morval, Ancre Heights, Ancre 1916, 18, Messines 1917, 18, **Pilckem,** Menin Road, Polygon Wood, Broodseinde, Poelcapelle, Passchendaele, **Cambrai 1917, 18,** St. Quentin, Bapaume 1918, Lys, Estaires, Hazebrouck, Bailleul, Kemmel, Béthune, Scherpenberg, Arras 1918, Drocourt-Quéant, Hindenburg Line, Épéhy, St. Quentin Canal, Beaurevoir, Selle, Valenciennes, Sambre, France and Flanders 1914-18, Struma, Doiran 1917, 18, **Macedonia 1915-18,** Suvla, Sari Bair, Landing at Suvla, Scimitar Hill, **Gallipoli 1915,** Egypt 1915-17, Gaza, El Mughar, Jerusalem, Tell Asur, Megiddo, Nablus, **Palestine 1917-18,** Tigris 1916, Kut al Amara 1917, Baghdad, **Mesopotamia 1916-18**

Second World War
Falaise, Lower Maas, Reichswald, North-West Europe 1944-45, Benghazi, North Africa 1940-42, Sicily 1943, Coriano, **Croce,** Rimini Line, Ceriano Ridge, Argenta Gap, **Italy 1943-45,** Crete, **Canea,** Withdrawal to Sphakia, Middle East 1941, **Kyaukmyaung Bridgehead,** Maymyo, Rangoon Road, **Sittang 1945, Burma 1944-45**

Korean War
Korea 1951-52

THE BLACK WATCH
(ROYAL HIGHLAND REGIMENT)

First World War
Retreat from Mons, **Marne 1914, 18,** Aisne 1914, La Bassée 1914, **Ypres 1914, 17, 18,** Langemarck 1914, Gheluvelt, Nonne Bosschen, Givenchy 1914, Neuve Chapelle, Aubers, Festubert 1915, **Loos, Somme 1916, 18,** Albert 1916, Bazentin, Delville Wood, Pozières, Flers-Courcelette, Morval, Thiepval, Le Transloy, Ancre Heights, Ancre 1916, **Arras 1917, 18,** Vimy 1917, Scarpe 1917, 18, Arleux, Pilckem, Menin Road, Polygon Wood, Poelcapelle, Passchendaele, Cambrai 1917, 18, St. Quentin, Bapaume 1918, Rosières, **Lys,** Estaires, Messines 1918, Hazebrouck, Kemmel, Béthune, Scherpenberg, Soissonnais-Ourcq, Tardenois, Drocourt-Quéant, **Hindenburg Line,** Épéhy, St. Quentin Canal, Beaurevoir, Courtrai, Selle, Sambre, France and Flanders 1914-18, **Doiran 1917,** Macedonia 1915-18, Egypt 1916, Gaza, Jerusalem, Tell Asur, **Megiddo,** Sharon, Damascus, Palestine 1917-18, Tigris 1916, **Kut al Amara, 1917,** Baghdad, Mesopotamia 1915-17

Second World War
Defence of Arras, Ypres-Comines Canal, Dunkirk

1940, St. Valéry-en-Caux, Saar, Breville, Odon, Fontenay le Pesnil, Defence of Rauray, Caen, Falaise, **Falaise Road,** La Vie Crossing, Le Havre, Lower Maas, Venlo Pocket, Ourthe, Rhineland, Reichswald, Goch, **Rhine,** North-West Europe 1940, 44-45, Barkasan, British Somaliland 1940, **Tobruk 1941,** Tobruk Sortie, **El Alamein,** Advance on Tripoli, Medenine, Zemlet el Lebene, Mareth, **Akarit,** Wadi Akarit East, Djebel Roumana, Medjez Plain, Si Mediene, **Tunis,** North Africa 1941-43, Landing in Sicily, Vizzini, Sferro, Gerbini, Adrano, Sferro Hills, **Sicily 1943, Cassino II,** Liri Valley, Advance to Florence, Monte Scalari, Casa Fortis, Rimini Line, Casa Fabbri Ridge, Savio Bridgehead, Italy 1944-45, Athens, Greece 1944-45, **Crete,** Heraklion, Middle East 1941, Chindits 1944, **Burma 1944**

Korean War
The Hook 1952, Korea 1952-53

THE OXFORDSHIRE AND
BUCKINGHAMSHIRE LIGHT INFANTRY

First World War
Mons, Retreat from Mons, Marne 1914, **Ypres 1914, 17, Langemarck 1914, 17,** Gheluvelt, **Nonne Bosschen,** Aubers, Festubert 1915, Hooge 1915, Loos, Mount Sorrel, **Somme 1916, 18,** Albert 1916, 18, Bazentin, Delville Wood, Pozières, Guillemont, Flers-Courcelette, Morval, Le Transloy, Ancre Heights, Ancre 1916, Bapaume 1917, 18, Arras 1917, Vimy 1917, Scarpe 1917, Arleux, Menin Road, Polygon Wood, Broodseinde, Poelcapelle, Passchendaele, **Cambrai 1917, 18,** St. Quentin, Rosières, Avre, Lys, Hazebrouck, Béthune, Hindenburg Line, Havrincourt, Canal du Nord, Selle, Valenciennes, France and Flanders 1914-18, **Piave,** Vittorio Veneto, Italy 1917-18, **Doiran 1917, 18,** Macedonia 1915-18, Kut al Amara 1915, **Ctesiphon, Defence of Kut al Amara,** Khan Baghdadi, Mesopotamia 1914-18, Archangel 1919

Second World War
Defence of Escaut, **Cassel, Ypres-Comines Canal, Normandy Landing, Pegasus Bridge,** Caen, Esquay, Lower Maas, Ourthe, Rhineland, **Reichswald, Rhine,** Ibbenburen, North-West Europe 1940, 44-45, **Enfidaville,** North Africa 1943, **Salerno,** St. Lucia, Salerno Hills, Teano, Monte Camino, Garigliano Crossing, Damiano, **Anzio,** Coriano, **Gemmano Ridge,** Italy 1943-45, Arakan Beaches, Tamandu, Burma 1943-45

THE ESSEX REGIMENT

First World War
Le Cateau, Retreat from Mons, **Marne 1914,** Aisne 1914, Messines 1914, Armentières 1914, **Ypres 1915,**

17, St. Julien, Frezenberg, Bellewaarde, **Loos, Somme 1916, 18,** Albert 1916, 18, Bazentin, Delville Wood, Pozières, Flers-Courcelette, Morval, Thiepval, Le Transloy, Ancre Heights, Ancre 1916, 18, Bapaume 1917, 18, **Arras 1917, 18,** Scarpe 1917, 18, Arleux, Pilckem, Langemarck 1917, Menin Road, Broodseinde, Poelcapelle, Passchendaele, **Cambrai 1917, 18,** St. Quentin, Avre, Villers Bretonneux, Lys, Hazebrouck, Béthune, Amiens, Drocourt-Quéant, Hindenburg Line, Havrincourt, Épéhy, St. Quentin Canal, **Selle,** Sambre, France and Flanders 1914-18, Helles, Landing at Helles, Krithia, Suvla, Landing at Suvla, Scimitar Hill, **Gallipoli 1915-16,** Rumani, Egypt 1915-17, **Gaza,** Jaffa, Megiddo, Sharon, Palestine 1917-18

Second World War
St. Omer-La Bassée, Tilly sur Seulles, Le Havre, Antwerp-Turnhout Canal, Scheldt, **Zetten,** Arnhem 1945, **North-West Europe 1940, 44-45,** Abyssinia 1940, Falluja, Baghdad 1941, Iraq 1941, **Palmyra,** Syria 1941, **Tobruk 1941,** Belhamed, Mersa Matruh, **Defence of Alamein Line,** Deir el Shein, Ruweisat, Ruweisat Ridge, El Alamein, Matmata Hills, Akarit, **Enfidaville,** Djebel Garci, Tunis, Ragoubet Souissi, North Africa 1941-43, Trigno, **Sangro, Villa Grande, Cassino I,** Castle Hill, Hangman's Hill, Italy 1943-44, Athens, Greece 1944-45, Kohima, **Chindits 1944,** Burma 1943-45

THE SHERWOOD FORESTERS (NOTTINGHAMSHIRE AND DERBYSHIRE REGIMENT)

First World War
Aisne 1914, 18, Armentières 1914, **Neuve Chapelle,** Aubers, Hooge 1915, **Loos, Somme 1916, 18,** Albert 1916, 18, Bazentin, Delville Wood, Pozières, Ginchy, Flers-Courcelette, Morval, Thiepval, Le Transloy, Ancre Heights, Ancre 1916, Arras 1917, 18, Vimy 1917, Scarpe 1917, 18, Messines 1917, **Ypres 1917, 18,** Pilckem, Langemarck 1917, Menin Road, Polygon Wood, Broodseinde, Poelcapelle, Passchendaele, **Cambrai 1917, 18,** St. Quentin, Bapaume 1918, Rosières, Villers Bretonneux, Lys, Bailleul, Kemmel, Scherpenberg, Amiens, Drocourt-Quéant, Hindenburg Line, Épéhy, Canal du Nord, **St. Quentin Canal,** Beaurevoir, Courtrai, Selle, Sambre, **France and Flanders 1914-18,** Piave, **Italy 1917-18,** Suvla, Landing at Suvla, Scimitar Hill, **Gallipoli 1915,** Egypt 1916

Second World War
Norway 1940, St. Omer-La Bassée, Ypres-Comines Canal, Dunkirk 1940, North-West Europe 1940, **Gazala, El Alamein,** Djebel Guerba, Tamera, Medjez Plain, **Tunis,** North Africa 1942-43, **Salerno,** Volturno Crossing, Monte Camino, **Anzio, Campoleone,** Advance to Tiber, **Gothic Line,**

Coriano, Cosina Canal Crossing, Monte Ceco, Italy 1943-45, **Singapore Island,** Malaya 1942

THE LOYAL REGIMENT (NORTH LANCASHIRE)

First World War
Mons, Retreat from Mons, Marne 1914, 18, **Aisne 1914, 18, Ypres 1914, 17, 18,** Langemarck 1914, Gheluvelt, Nonne Bosschen, Givenchy 1914, Aubers, Festubert 1915, Loos, **Somme 1916, 18,** Albert 1916, Bazentin, Pozières, Guillemont, Ginchy, Flers-Courcelette, Morval, Ancre Heights, Ancre 1916, Arras 1917, 18, Scarpe 1917, Arleux, Messines 1917, Pilckem, Menin Road, Polygon Wood, Poelcapelle, Passchendaele, Cambrai 1917, 18, St. Quentin, Bapaume 1918, **Lys,** Estaires, Bailleul, Kemmel, Béthune, Scherpenberg, Soissannais-Ourcq, Drocourt-Quéant, **Hindenburg Line,** Épéhy, Canal du Nord, St. Quentin Canal, Courtrai, Selle, Sambre, France and Flanders 1914-18, Doiran 1917, Macedonia 1917, **Suvla,** Sari Bair, Gallipoli 1915, Egypt 1916, **Gaza,** Nebi Samwil, Jerusalem, Jaffa, Tell Asur, Palestine 1917-18, Tigris 1916, Kut al Amara 1917, **Baghdad,** Mesopotamia 1916-18, **Kilimanjaro,** E. Africa 1914-16

Second World War
Dunkirk 1940, North-West Europe 1940, Banana Ridge, **Djebel Kesskiss,** Mediez Plain, **Gueriat el Atach Ridge,** Djebel Bou Aoukaz 1943, I, Gab Gab Gap, **North Africa 1943, Anzio,** Rome, **Fiesole,** Gothic Line, Monte Gamberaldi, Monte Ceco, **Monte Grande, Italy 1944-45, Johore,** Batu Pahat, **Singapore Island,** Malaya 1941-42

THE NORTHAMPTONSHIRE REGIMENT

First World War
Mons, Retreat from Mons, **Marne 1914, Aisne 1914, 18, Ypres 1914, 17,** Langemarck 1914, 17, Gheluvelt, Nonne Bosschen, Givenchy 1914, **Neuve Chapelle,** Aubers, **Loos, Somme 1916, 18,** Albert 1916, 18, Bazentin, Delville Wood, Pozières, Flers-Courcelette, Morval, Thiepval, Le Transloy, Ancre Heights, Ancre 1916, 18, Bapaume 1917, 18, **Arras 1917, 18,** Vimy 1917, Scarpe 1917, 18, Arleux, Messines 1917, Pilckem, Passchendaele, Cambrai 1917, 18, St. Quentin, Rosières, Avre, Villers Bretonneux, Amiens, Drocourt-Quéant, Hindenburg Line, **Épéhy,** St. Quentin Canal, Selle, Sambre, France and Flanders 1914-18, Suvla, Landing at Suvla, Scimitar Hill, Gallipoli 1915, Egypt 1915-17, **Gaza,** El Mughar, Nebi Samwil, Jerusalem, Jaffa, Tell Asur, Megiddo, Sharon, Palestine 1917-18

Second World War
Defence of Escaut, Defence of Arras, Ypres-Comines

Canal, **North-West Europe 1940, 45,** Djedeida, Djebel Djaffa, Oued Zarga, Djebel Tanngoucha, Sidi Ahmed, **North Africa 1942-43,** Landing in Sicily, Adrano, Sicily 1943, Sangro, **Garigliano Crossing, Anzio, Cassino II,** Monte Gabbione, Trasimene Line, Monte La Pieve, Argenta Gap, **Italy 1943-45,** Madagascar, **Yu, Imphal,** Tamu Road, Bishenpur, Monywa 1945, **Myinmu Bridgehead,** Irrawaddy, **Burma 1943-45**

THE ROYAL BERKSHIRE REGIMENT (PRINCESS CHARLOTTE OF WALES'S)

First World War

Mons, Retreat from Mons, Marne 1914, Aisne 1914, 18, **Ypres 1914, 1918,** Langemarck 1914, 17, Gheluvelt, Nonne Bosschen, **Neuve Chapelle,** Aubers, Festubert 1915, **Loos, Somme 1916, 18,** Albert 1916, 18, Bazentin, Delville Wood, Pozières, Flers-Courcelette, Morval, Thiepval, Le Transloy, Ancre Heights, Ancre 1916, 18, **Arras 1917, 18,** Scarpe 1917, 18, Arleux, Pilckem, Polygon Wood, Broodseinde, Poelcapelle, Passchendaele, **Cambrai 1917, 18,** St. Quentin, Bapaume 1918, Rosières, Avre, Villers Bretonneux, Lys, Hazebrouck, Béthune, Amiens, Hindenburg Line, Havrincourt, Épéhy, Canal du Nord, St. Quentin Canal, **Selle,** Valenciennes, Sambre, France and Flanders 1914-18, Piave, **Vittorio Veneto,** Italy 1917-18, **Doiran 1917, 18,** Macedonia 1915-18

Second World War

Dyle, St. Omer-La Bassée, **Dunkirk 1940, Normandy Landing, Rhine,** North-West Europe 1940, 44-45, Pursuit to Messina, **Sicily 1943,** Monte Camino, Calabritto, Garigliano Crossing, **Damiano, Anzio,** Carroceto, Italy 1943-45, Donbaik, **Kohima,** Mao Songsang, Shwebo, Kyaukmyaung Bridgehead, **Mandalay,** Fort Dufferin, Rangoon Road, Toungoo, **Burma 1942-45**

THE QUEEN'S OWN ROYAL WEST KENT REGIMENT

First World War

Mons, Le Cateau, Retreat from Mons, Marne 1914, Aisne 1914, La Bassée 1914, Messines 1914, 17, **Ypres 1914, 15, 17, 18, Hill 60,** Gravenstafel, St. Julien, Frezenberg, Loos, **Somme 1916, 18,** Albert 1916, 18, Bazentin, Delville Wood, Pozières, Guillemont, Flers-Courcelette, Morval, Thiepval, Le Transloy, Ancre Heights, Ancre 1916, 18, Arras 1917, 18, **Vimy 1917,** Scarpe 1917, Oppy, Pilckem, Langemarck 1917, Menin Road, Polygon Wood, Broodseinde, Passchendaele, Cambrai 1917, 18, St. Quentin, Rosières, Avre, Villers Bretonneux, Lys,

Hazebrouck, Kemmel, Amiens, Bapaume 1918, Hindenburg Line, Épéhy, Canal du Nord, St. Quentin Canal, Courtrai, Selle, Sambre, France and Flanders 1914-18, **Italy 1917-18,** Suvla, Landing at Suvla, Scimitar Hill, **Gallipoli 1915,** Rumani, Egypt 1915-16, **Gaza,** El Mughar, Jerusalem, Jericho, Tell Asur, Palestine 1917-18, **Defence of Kut al Amara, Sharqat,** Mesopotamia 1915-18

Afghanistan 1919

Second World War

Defence of Escaut, Forêt de Nieppe, **North-West Europe 1940,** Alam el Halfa, **El Alamein,** Djebel Abiod, Djebel Azzag 1942, Oued Zarga, Djebel Ang, **Medjez Plain,** Longstop Hill 1943, Si Abdallah, North Africa 1942-43, **Centuripe,** Monte Rivoglia, Sicily 1943, Termoli, San Salvo, **Sangro,** Romagnoli, Impossible Bridge, Villa Grande, **Cassino,** Castle Hill, Liri Valley, Piedimonte Hill, **Trasimene Line,** Arezzo, Advance to Florence, Monte Scalari, Casa Fortis, Rimini Line, Savio Bridgehead, Monte Pianoereno, Monte Spaduro, Senio, **Argenta Gap,** Italy 1943-45, Greece 1944-45, Leros, **Malta 1940-42,** North Arakan, Razabil, Mayu Tunnels, **Defence of Kohima,** Taungtha, Sittang 1945, Burma 1943-45

THE KING'S OWN YORKSHIRE LIGHT INFANTRY

First World War

Mons, **Le Cateau,** Retreat from Mons, **Marne 1914,** 18, Aisne 1914, 18, La Bassée 1914, **Messines 1914, 17, 18, Ypres 1914, 15, 17, 18,** Hill 60, Gravenstafel, St. Julien, Frezenberg, Bellewaarde, Hooge 1915, Loos, **Somme 1916, 18,** Albert 1916, 18, Bazentin, Delville Wood, Pozières, Guillemont, Flers-Courcelette, Morval, Le Transloy, Ancre 1916, Arras 1917, 18, Scarpe 1917, Langemarck 1917, Menin Road, Polygon Wood, Broodseinde, Poelcapelle, Passchendaele, **Cambrai 1917, 18,** St. Quentin, Bapaume 1918, Lys, Hazebrouck, Bailleul, Kemmel, Scherpenberg, Tardenois, Amiens, Hindenburg Line, **Havrincourt,** Épéhy, Canal du Nord, St. Quentin Canal, Beaurevoir, Selle, Valenciennes, **Sambre,** France and Flanders 1914-18, Piave, Vittorio Veneto, **Italy 1917-18,** Struma, **Macedonia 1915-17,** Egypt 1915-16

Second World War

Kvam, **Norway 1940, Fontenay le Pesnil,** Le Havre, Antwerp-Turnhout Canal, Lower Maas, **North-West Europe 1944-45,** Mine de Sedjenane, **Argoub Sellah,** North Africa 1943, **Sicily 1943, Salerno,** Salerno Hills, Cava di Tirreni, Volturno Crossing, Garigliano Crossing, **Minturno,** Monte Tuga, **Anzio, Gemmano Ridge,** Carpineta, Lamone Bridgehead, Italy 1943-45, Sittang 1942, **Burma 1942**

THE KING'S SHROPSHIRE LIGHT INFANTRY

First World War
Aisne 1914, 18, **Armentières 1914, Ypres 1915, 17,**
Gravenstafel, St. Julien, **Frezenberg,** Bellewaarde,
Hooge 1915, Mount Sorrel, **Somme 1916, 18,** Albert
1916, 18, Bazentin, Delville Wood, Guillemont, Flers-
Courcelette, Morval, Le Transloy, Ancre 1916, **Arras
1917, 18,** Scarpe 1917, Arleux, Hill 70, Langemarck
1917, Menin Road, Polygon Wood, Passchendaele,
Cambrai 1917, 18, St. Quentin, Bapaume 1918,
Rosières, Lys, Estaires, Messines 1918, Hazebrouck,
Bailleul, Kemmel, Béthune, **Bligny,** Hindenburg
Line, **Épéhy,** Canal du Nord, Selle, Valenciennes,
Sambre, France and Flanders 1914-18, **Doiran 1917,
18,** Macedonia 1915-18, Gaza, **Jerusalem,** Jericho,
Tell Asur, Palestine 1917-18

Second World War
Defence of Escaut, **Dunkirk 1940, Normandy
Landing,** Odon, Caen, Bourguebus Ridge, Troarn,
Mont Pincon, Souleuvre, Le Perier Ridge, Falaise,
Antwerp, Nederrijn, **Venraij,** Rhineland, **Hochwald,**
Ibbenburen, Lingen, Aller, **Bremen, North-West
Europe 1940, 44-45,** Gueriat el Atach Ridge, **Tunis,**
Djebel Bou Aoukaz 1943, II, North Africa 1943,
Anzio, Campoleone, Carroceto, Gothic Line, Monte
Ceco, Monte Grande, **Italy 1943-45**

Korean War
Hill 227 I, **Kowang-San, Korea 1951-52**

THE MIDDLESEX REGIMENT (DUKE OF CAMBRIDGE'S OWN)

First World War
Mons, Le Cateau, Retreat from Mons, **Marne 1914,**
Aisne 1914, 18, La Bassée 1914, Messines 1914, 17,
18, Armentières 1914, Neuve Chapelle, **Ypres 1915,
17, 18,** Gravenstafel, St. Julien, Frezenberg,
Bellewaarde, Aubers, Hooge 1915, Loos, Somme
1916, 18, **Albert 1916, 18, Bazentin,** Delville Wood,
Pozières, Ginchy, Flers-Courcelette, Morval,
Thiepval, Le Transloy, Ancre Heights, Ancre 1916,
18, Bapaume 1917, 18, Arras 1917, 18, Vimy 1917,
Scarpe 1917, 18, Arleux, Pilckem, Langemarck 1917,
Menin Road, Polygon Wood, Broodseinde,
Poelcapelle, Passchendaele, **Cambrai 1917, 18,** St.
Quentin, Rosières, Avre, Villers Bretonneux, Lys,
Estaires, Hazebrouck, Bailleul, Kemmel,
Scherpenberg, **Hindenburg Line,** Canal du Nord, St.
Quentin Canal, Courtrai, Selle, Valenciennes,
Sambre, France and Flanders 1914-18, Italy 1917-18,
Struma, Doiran 1918, Macedonia 1915-18, **Suvla,**
Landing at Suvla, Scimitar Hill, Gallipoli 1915,

Rumani, Egypt 1915-17, Gaza, El Mughar,
Jerusalem, Jericho, Jordan, Tell Asur, Palestine
1917-18, **Mesopotamia 1917-18,** Murman 1919,
Dukhovskaya, Siberia 1918-19

Second World War
Dyle, Defence of Escaut, Ypres-Comines Canal,
Dunkirk 1940, Normandy Landing, Cambes,
Breville, Odon, **Caen,** Orne, Hill 112, Bourguebus
Ridge, Troarn, **Mont Pincon,** Falaise, Seine 1944,
Nederrijn, Le Havre, Lower Maas, Venraij, Meijel,
Geilenkirchen, Venlo Pocket, Rhineland, Reichswald,
Goch, **Rhine,** Lingen, Brinkum, Bremen, North-
West Europe 1940, 44-45, **El Alamein,** Advance on
Tripoli, Mareth, **Akarit,** Djebel Roumana, North
Africa 1942-43, Francofonte, Sferro, Sferro Hills,
Sicily 1943, Anzio, Carroceto, Gothic Line, Monte
Grande, Italy 1944-45, **Hong Kong,** South-East Asia
1941

Korean War
Naktong Bridgehead, Chongju, Chongchon II,
Chaum-ni, Kapyong-chon, Kapyong, **Korea 1950-51**

THE KING'S ROYAL RIFLE CORPS

First World War
Mons, Retreat from Mons, **Marne 1914,** Aisne 1914,
Ypres 1914, 15, 17, 18, Langemarck 1914, 17,
Gheluvelt, Nonne Bosschen, Givenchy 1914,
Gravenstafel, St. Julien, Frezenberg, Bellewaarde,
Aubers, Festubert 1915, Hooge 1915, Loos, **Somme
1916, 18,** Albert 1916, 18, Bazentin, Delville Wood,
Pozières, Guillemont, Flers-Courcelette, Morval, Le
Transloy, Ancre Heights, Ancre 1916, 18, **Arras
1917, 18,** Scarpe 1917, Arleux, **Messines 1917, 18,**
Pilckem, Menin Road, Polygon Wood, Broodseinde,
Poelcapelle, Passchendaele, Cambrai 1917, 18, St.
Quentin, Rosières, Avre, Lys, Bailleul, Kemmel,
Béthune, Bapaume 1918, Drocourt-Quéant,
Hindenburg Line, Havrincourt, **Épéhy, Canal du
Nord,** St. Quentin Canal, Beaurevoir, Courtrai, **Selle,
Sambre,** France and Flanders 1914-18, Italy 1917-18,
Macedonia 1916-18

Second World War
Calais 1940, Mont Pincon, Falaise, Roer, **Rhineland,**
Cleve, Goch, Hochwald, Rhine, Dreirwalde, Aller,
**North-West Europe 1940, 44-45, Egyptian Frontier
1940,** Sidi Barrani, Derna Aerodrome, Tobruk 1941,
Sidi Rezegh 1941, Gazala, Bir Hacheim,
Knightsbridge, Defence of Alamein Line, Ruweisat,
Fuka Airfield, **Alam el Halfa, El Alamein,** Capture of
Halfaya Pass, Nofilia, Tebaga Gap, Argoub el Megas,
Tunis, **North Africa 1940-43,** Sangro, Arezzo,
Coriano, Lamone Crossing, Argenta Gap, **Italy 1943-
45,** Veve, **Greece 1941, 44-45,** Crete, Middle East
1941

THE WILTSHIRE REGIMENT (DUKE OF EDINBURGH'S)

First World War
Mons, Le Cateau, Retreat from Mons, Marne 1914, Aisne 1914, 18, La Bassée 1914, **Messines 1914, 17, 18,** Armentières 1914, **Ypres 1914, 17,** Langemarck 1914, Nonne Bosschen, Neuve Chapelle, Aubers, Festubert 1915, Loos, **Somme 1916, 18,** Albert 1916, 18, Bazentin, Pozières, Le Transloy, Ancre Heights, Ancre 1916, **Arras 1917,** Scarpe 1917, Pilckem, Menin Road, Polygon Wood, Broodseinde, Poelcapelle, Passchendaele, St. Quentin, Lys, Bailleul, Kemmel, Scherpenberg, **Bapaume 1918,** Hindenburg Line, Épéhy, Canal du Nord, St. Quentin Canal, Beaurevoir, Cambrai 1918, Selle, Sambre, France and Flanders 1914-18, Doiran 1917, **Macedonia 1915-18,** Suvla, Sari Bair, **Gallipoli 1915-16,** Gaza, Nebi Samwil, Jerusalem, Megiddo, Sharon, **Palestine 1917-18,** Tigris 1916, Kut al Amara 1917, **Baghdad,** Mesopotamia 1916-18

Second World War
Defence of Arras, Ypres-Comines Canal, Odon, Caen, **Hill 112,** Bourgucbus Ridge, **Maltot, Mont Pincon,** La Varinièrc, **Seine 1944,** Nederrijn, Roer, Rhineland, **Cleve,** Goch, Xanten, Rhine, Bremen, North-West Europe 1940, 44-45, Solarino, Simeto Bridgehead, Sicily 1943, **Garigliano Crossing,** Minturno, **Anzio, Rome,** Advance to Tiber, Italy 1943-44, Middle East 1942, **North Arakan,** Point 551, Mayu Tunnels, Ngakyedauk Pass, Burma 1943-44

THE MANCHESTER REGIMENT

First World War
Mons, Le Cateau, Retreat from Mons, Marne 1914, Aisne 1914, La Bassée 1914, Armentières 1914, **Givenchy 1914,** Neuve Chapelle, **Ypres 1915, 17, 18,** Gravenstafel, St. Julien, Frezenberg, Bellewaarde, Aubers, **Somme 1916, 18,** Albert 1916, 18, Bazentin, Delville Wood, Guillemont, Flers-Courcelette, Thiepval, Le Transloy, Ancre Heights, Ancre 1916, 18, Arras 1917, 18, Scarpe 1917, Bullecourt, Messines 1917, Pilckem, Langemarck 1917, Menin Road, Polygon Wood, Broodseinde, Poelcapelle, Passchendaele, St. Quentin, Bapaume 1918, Rosières, Lys, Kemmel, Amiens, **Hindenburg Line,** Épéhy, Canal du Nord, St. Quentin Canal, Beaurevoir, Cambrai 1918, Courtrai, Selle, Sambre, France and Flanders 1914-18, **Piave,** Vittorio Veneto, Italy 1917-18, Doiran 1917, **Macedonia 1915-18,** Helles, Krithia, Suvla, Landing at Suvla, Scimitar Hill, **Gallipoli 1915,** Rumani, Egypt 1915-17, **Megiddo,** Sharon, Palestine 1918, Tigris 1916, Kut al Amara 1917, **Baghdad,** Mesopotamia 1916-18

Second World War
Dyle, Withdrawal to Escaut, Defence of Escaut,

Defence of Arras, St. Omer-La Bassée, Ypres-Comines Canal, **Caen,** Esquay, Falaise, Nederrijn, **Scheldt,** Walcheren Causeway, Flushing, **Lower Maas,** Venlo Pocket, **Roer,** Ourthe, Rhineland, **Reichswald,** Goch, Weeze, Rhine, Ibbenburen, Dreirwalde, Aller, Bremen, North-West Europe 1940, 44-45, **Gothic Line,** Monte Gridolfo, Coriano, San Clemente, Gemmano Ridge, Montilgallo, Capture of Forli, Lamone Crossing, Lamone Bridgehead, Rimini Line, Montescudo, Cesena, Italy 1944, **Malta 1940,** Singapore Island, Malaya 1941-42, North Arakan, **Kohima,** Pinwe, Shwebo, Myinmu Bridgehead, Irrawaddy, Burma 1944-45

THE NORTH STAFFORDSHIRE REGIMENT (THE PRINCE OF WALES'S)

First World War
Aisne 1914, 18, **Armentières 1914,** Loos, **Somme 1916, 18,** Albert 1916, 18, Bazentin, Delville Wood, Pozières, Guillemont, Ancre Heights, Ancre 1916, **Arras 1917,** Scarpe 1917, Arleux, **Messines 1917, 18, Ypres 1917, 18,** Pilckem, Langemarck 1917, Menin Road, Polygon Wood, Broodseinde, Poelcapelle, Passchendaele, Cambrai 1917, 18, St. Quentin, Bapaume 1918, Rosières, Avre, Lys, Bailleul, Kemmel, Hindenburg Line, Havrincourt, Canal du Nord, **St. Quentin Canal,** Beaurevoir, Courtrai, **Selle,** Valenciennes, Sambre, France and Flanders 1914-18, Suvla, **Sari Bair,** Gallipoli 1915-16, Egypt 1916, Tigris 1916, **Kut al Amara 1917,** Baghdad, Mesopotamia 1916-18, Baku, Persia 1918,, **N. W. Frontier India 1915**

Afghanistan 1919

Second World War
Dyle, Defence of Escaut, **Ypres-Comines Canal, Caen,** Orne, Noyers, Mont Pincon, **Brieux Bridgehead,** North-West Europe 1940, 44, Djebel Kesskiss, **Medjez Plain,** Gueriat el Atach Ridge, Gab Gab Gap, **North Africa 1943, Anzio,** Carroceto, **Rome,** Advance to Tiber, Gothic Line, **Marradi,** Italy 1944-45, **Burma 1943**

THE YORK AND LANCASTER REGIMENT

First World War
Aisne 1914, Armentières 1914, **Ypres 1915, 17, 18,** Gravenstafel, St. Julien, Frezenberg, Bellewaarde, Hooge 1915, Loos, **Somme 1916, 18,** Albert 1916, Pozières, Flers-Courcelette, Morval, Thiepval, Le Transloy, Ancre Heights, Ancre 1916, Arras 1917, 18, Scarpe 1917, 18, Arleux, Oppy, **Messines 1917, 18,** Langemarck 1917, Menin Road, Polygon Wood, Broodseinde, Poelcapelle, **Passchendaele, Cambrai 1917, 18,** St. Quentin, Bapaume 1918, **Lys,**

Hazebrouck, Bailleul, Kemmel, Scherpenberg, Marne 1918, Tardenois, Drocourt-Quéant, Hindenburg Line, Havrincourt, Épéhy, Canal du Nord, **Selle,** Valenciennes, Sambre, France and Flanders 1914-18, **Piave,** Vittorio Veneto, Italy 1917-18, Struma, Doiran 1917, **Macedonia 1915-18,** Suvla, Landing at Suvla, Scimitar Hill, **Gallipoli 1915,** Egypt 1916

Second World War
Norway 1940, Odon, **Fontenay Le Pesnil,** Caen, La Vie Crossing, La Touques Crossing, Foret de Bretonne, Le Havre, **Antwerp-Turnhout Canal,** Scheldt, Lower Maas, Arnhem 1945, North-West Europe 1940, 44-45, **Tobruk 1941,** Tobruk Sortie 1941, **Mine de Sedjenane,** Djebel Kournine, North Africa 1941, 43, Landing in Sicily, Simeto Bridgehead, Pursuit to Messina, **Sicily 1943, Salerno,** Vietri Pass, Capture of Naples, Cava di Terreni, Volturno Crossing, Monte Camino, Calabritto, Colle Cedro, Garigliano Crossing, **Minturno,** Monte Tuga, Anzio, Advance to Tiber, Gothic Line, Coriano, San Clemente, Gemmano Ridge, Carpineta, Lamone Crossing, Defence of Lamone Bridgehead, Rimini Line, San Marino, Italy 1943-45, **Crete,** Heraklion, Middle East 1941, **North Arakan,** Maungdaw, Rangoon Road, Toungoo, Arakan Beaches, **Chindits 1944,** Burma 1943-45

THE DURHAM LIGHT INFANTRY

First World War
Aisne 1914, 18, Armentières 1914, **Ypres 1915, 17, 18,** Gravenstafel, St. Julien, Frezenberg, Bellewaarde, **Hooge 1915, Loos, Somme 1916, 18,** Albert 1916, 18, Bazentin, Delville Wood, Pozières, Guillemont, Flers-Courcelette, Morval, Le Transloy, Ancre Heights, **Arras 1917, 18,** Scarpe 1917, Arleux, Hill 70, **Messines 1917,** Pilckem, Langemarck 1917, Menin Road, Polygon Wood, Broodseinde, Passchendaele, Cambrai 1917, 18, St. Quentin, Rosières, **Lys,** Estaires, Hazebrouck, Bailleul, Kemmel, Scherpenberg, Marne 1918, Tardenois, Bapaume 1918, **Hindenburg Line,** Havrincourt, Épéhy, Canal du Nord, St. Quentin Canal, Beaurevoir, Courtrai, Selle, **Sambre,** France and Flanders 1914-18, Piave, Vittorio Veneto, Italy 1917-18, Macedonia 1916-18, Egypt 1915-16, N. W. Frontier India 1915, 1916-17, Archangel 1918-19

Afghanistan 1919

Second World War
Dyle, Arras counter attack, St. Omer-La Bassée, **Dunkirk 1940,** Villers Bocage, **Tilly sur Seulles, Defence of Rauray,** St. Pierre La Vielle, **Gheel,** Roer, Ibbenburen, North-West Europe 1940, 44-45, Syria 1941, Halfaya 1941, **Tobruk 1941,** Relief of Tobruk, Gazala, Gabr el Fachri, Zt el Mrasses, Mersa Matruh,

Point 174, **El Alamein, Mareth,** Sedjenane I, El Kourzia, North Africa 1940-43, Landing in Sicily, Solarino, **Primosole Bridge,** Sicily 1943, **Salerno,** Volturno Crossing, Teano, Monte Camino, Monte Tuga, Gothic Line, Gemmano Ridge, Cosina Canal Crojssing, Pergola Ridge, Cesena, Sillaro Crossing, Italy 1943-45, Athens, Greece 1944-45, Cos, Middle East 1943, Malta 1942, Donbaik, **Kohima,** Mandalay, Burma 1943-45

Korean War
Korea 1952-53

THE HIGHLAND LIGHT INFANTRY (CITY OF GLASGOW REGIMENT)

First World War
Mons, Retreat from Mons, Marne 1914, Aisne 1914, **Ypres 1914, 15, 17, 18,** Langemarck 1914, 17, Gheluvelt, Nonne Bosschen, Givenchy 1914, Neuve Chapelle, St. Julien, Aubers, Festubert 1915, **Loos, Somme 1916, 18,** Albert 1916, 18, Bazentin, Delville Wood, Pozières, Flers-Courcelette, Le Transloy, Ancre Heights, Ancre 1916, 18, **Arras 1917, 18,** Vimy 1917, Scarpe 1917, 18, Arleux, Pilckem, Menin Road, Polygon Wood, Passchendaele, Cambrai 1917, 18, St. Quentin, Bapaume 1918, Lys, Estaires, Messines 1918, Hazebrouck, Bailleul, Kemmel, Amiens, Drocourt-Quéant, **Hindenburg Line,** Havrincourt, Canal du Nord, St. Quentin Canal, Beaurevoir, Courtrai, Selle, Sambre, France and Flanders 1914-18, **Gallipoli 1915-18,** Rumani, Egypt 1916, Gaza, El Mughar, Nebi Samwil, Jaffa, **Palestine 1917-18,** Tigris 1916, Kut al Amara 1917, Sharqat, **Mesopotamia 1916-18,** Murman 1919, **Archangel 1919**

Second World War
Withdrawal to Cherbourg, **Odon,** Cheux, Esquay, Mont Pincon, Quarry Hill, Estry, Falaise, Seine 1944, Alart, Nederrijn, Best, **Scheldt,** Lower Maas, South Beveland, **Walcheren Causeway,** Asten, Roer, Ourthe, Rhineland, **Reichswald,** Goch, Moyland Wood, Weeze, **Rhine,** Ibbenburen, Dreirwalde, Aller, Uelzen, Bremen, Artlenberg, **North-West Europe 1940, 44-45,** Jebel Shiba, Barentu, **Keren,** Massawa, Abyssinia 1941, Gazala, **Cauldron,** Mersa Matruh, Fuka, North Africa 1940-42, **Landing in Sicily,** Sicily 1943, Italy 1943, 45, Athens, **Greece 1944-45,** Adriatic, Middle East 1944

SEAFORTH HIGHLANDERS (ROSS-SHIRE BUFFS, THE DUKE OF ALBANY'S)

First World War
Le Cateau, Retreat from Mons, **Marne 1914, 18,** Aisne 1914, La Bassée 1914, Armentières 1914,

Festubert 1914, 15, Givenchy 1914, Neuve Chapelle, **Ypres 1915, 17, 18,** St. Julien, Frezenberg, Bellewaarde, Aubers, **Loos, Somme 1916, 18,** Albert 1916, Bazentin, Delville Wood, Pozières, Flers-Courcelette, Le Transloy, Ancre Heights, Ancre 1916, **Arras 1917, 18, Vimy 1917,** Scarpe 1917, 18, Arleux, Pilckem, Menin Road, Polygon Wood, Broodseinde, Poelcapelle, Passchendaele, **Cambrai 1917, 18,** St. Quentin, Bapaume 1918, Lys, Estaires, Messines 1918, Hazebrouck, Bailleul, Kemmel, Béthune, Soissonnais-Ourcq, Drocourt-Quéant, Hindenburg Line, Courtrai, Selle, **Valenciennes,** France and Flanders 1914-18, Macedonia 1917-18, Megiddo, Sharon, **Palestine 1918,** Tigris 1916, Kut al Amara 1917, **Baghdad,** Mesopotamia 1915-18

Second World War
Ypres-Comines Canal, Somme 1940, Withdrawal to Seine, **St. Valéry-en-Caux,** Odon, Cheux, **Caen,** Troarn, Mont Pincon, Quarry Hill, Falaise, Falaise Road, Dives Crossing, La Vie Crossing, Lisieux, Nederrijn, Best, Le Havre, Lower Maas, Meijel, Venlo Pocket, Ourthe, **Rhineland,** Reichswald, Goch, Moyland, Rhine, Uelzen, Artlenberg, North-West Europe 1940, 44-45, **El Alamein,** Advance to Tripoli, Mareth, Wadi Zigzaou, **Akarit,** Djebel Roumana, North Africa 1942-43, Landing in Sicily, Augusta, Francofonte, Adrano, Sferro Hills, **Sicily 1943,** Garigliano Crossing, **Anzio,** Italy 1943-44, **Madagascar,** Middle East 1942, **Imphal,** Shenam Pass, Litan, Tengnoupal, **Burma 1942-44**

THE GORDON HIGHLANDERS

First World War
Mons, Le Cateau, Retreat from Mons, **Marne 1914, 18,** Aisne 1914, La Bassée 1914, Messines 1914, Armentières 1914, **Ypres 1914, 15, 17,** Langemarck 1914, Gheluvelt, Nonne Bosschen, Neuve Chapelle, Frezenberg, Bellewaarde, Aubers, Festubert 1915, Hooge 1915, **Loos, Somme 1916, 18,** Albert 1916, 18, Bazentin, Delville Wood, Pozières, Guillemont, Flers-Courcelette, Le Transloy, **Ancre 1916, Arras 1917, 18,** Vimy 1917, Scarpe 1917, 18, Arleux, Bullecourt, Pilckem, Menin Road, Polygon Wood, Broodseinde, Poelcapelle, Passchendaele, **Cambrai 1917, 18,** St. Quentin, Bapaume 1918, Rosières, Lys, Estaires, Hazebrouck, Béthune, Soissonnais-Ourcq, Tardenois, Hindenburg Line, Canal du Nord, Selle, Sambre, France and Flanders 1914-18, Piave, **Vittorio Veneto,** Italy 1917-18

Second World War
Withdrawal to Escaut, Ypres-Comines Canal, Dunkirk 1940, Somme 1940, St. Valéry-en-Caux, **Odon,** La Vie Crossing, Lower Maas, Venlo Pocket, Rhineland, **Reichswald,** Cleve, **Goch, Rhine, North-West Europe 1940, 44-45, El Alamein,** Advance on

Tripoli, **Mareth,** Medjez Plain, North Africa 1942-43, Landing in Sicily, **Sferro,** Sicily 1943, **Anzio,** Rome, Italy 1944-45

THE QUEEN'S OWN CAMERON HIGHLANDERS

First World War
Retreat from Mons, **Marne 1914, 18, Aisne 1914, Ypres 1914, 15, 17, 18,** Langemarck 1914, Gheluvelt, Nonne Bosschen, Givenchy 1914, **Neuve Chapelle,** Hill 60, Gravenstafel, St. Julien, Frezenberg, Bellewaarde, Aubers, Festubert 1915, **Loos, Somme 1916, 18,** Albert 1916, Bazentin, **Delville Wood,** Pozières, Flers Courcelette, Morval, Le Transloy, Ancre Heights, **Arras 1917, 18,** Scarpe 1917, Arleux, Pilckem, Menin Road, Polygon Wood, Poelcapelle, Passchendaele, St. Quentin, Bapaume 1918, Lys, Estaires, Messines 1918, Kemmel, Béthune, Soissonnais-Ourcq, Drocourt-Quéant, Hindenburg Line, Épéhy, St. Quentin Canal, Courtrai, Selle, **Sambre,** France and Flanders 1914-18, Struma, **Macedonia 1915-18**

Second World War
Defence of Escaut, **St. Omer-La Bassée,** Somme 1940, St. Valéry-en-Caux, Falaise, Falaise Road, La Vie Crossing, Le Havre, Lower Maas, Venlo Pocket, Rhineland, **Reichswald,** Goch, **Rhine,** North-West Europe 1940, 44-45, Agordat, **Keren,** Abyssinia 1941, **Sidi Barrani,** Tobruk 1941, 42, Gubi II, Carmusa, Gazala, **El Alamein,** Mareth, Wadi Zigzaou, **Akarit,** Djebel Roumana, North Africa 1940-43, Francofonte, Adrano, Sferro Hills, Sicily 1943, Cassino I, Poggio del Grillo, **Gothic Line,** Tavoleto, Coriano, Pian di Castello, Monte Reggiano, Rimini Line, San Marino, Italy 1944, **Kohima,** Relief of Kohima, Naga Village, Aradura, Shwebo, **Mandalay,** Ava, Irrawaddy, Mt. Popa, Burma 1944-45

THE ROYAL ULSTER RIFLES

First World War
Mons, Le Cateau, Retreat from Mons, **Marne 1914,** Aisne 1914, La Bassée 1914, Messines 1914, 17, 18, Armentières 1914, **Ypres 1914, 15, 17, 18,** Nonne Bosschen, **Neuve Chapelle,** Frezenberg, Aubers, **Somme 1916, 18, Albert 1916,** Bazentin, Pozières, Guillemont, Ginchy, Ancre Heights, Pilckem, Langemarck 1917, Cambrai 1917, St. Quentin, Rosières, Lys, Bailleul, Kemmel, **Courtrai,** France and Flanders 1914-18, Kosturino, **Struma,** Macedonia 1915-17, **Suvla,** Sari Bair, Gallipoli 1915, Gaza, **Jerusalem,** Tell Asur, Palestine 1917-18

Second World War
Dyle, Dunkirk 1940, Normandy Landing, Cambes,

Caen, Troarn, Venlo Pocket, **Rhine, Bremen,** North-West Europe 1940, 44-45

Korean War
Seoul, **Imjin, Korea 1950-51**

THE ROYAL IRISH FUSILIERS (PRINCESS VICTORIA'S)

First World War
Le Cateau, Retreat from Mons, **Marne 1914,** Aisne 1914, Armentières 1914, **Ypres 1915, 17, 18,** Gravenstafel, St. Julien, Frezenberg, Bellewaarde, **Somme 1916, 18,** Albert 1916, Guillemont, Ginchy, Le Transloy, **Arras 1917,** Scarpe 1917, **Messines 1917, 18,** Langemarck 1917, Cambrai 1917, St. Quentin, Rosières, **Lys,** Bailleul, Kemmel, Courtrai, France and Flanders 1914-18, Kosturino, Struma, **Macedonia 1915-17, Suvla,** Landing at Suvla, Scimitar Hill, Gallipoli 1915, Gaza, Jerusalem, Tell Asur, Megiddo, Nablus, **Palestine 1917-18**

Second World War
Withdrawal to Escaut, **St. Omer-La Bassée, Bou Arada,** Stuka Farm, **Oued Zarga,** Djebel Bel Mahdi, Dejebel Ang, **Djebel Tanngoucha,** Adrano, **Centuripe,** Salso Crossing, Simeto Crossing, Malleto, **Termoli,** Trigno, **Sangro,** Fossacesia, **Cassino II,** Liri Valley, Trasimene Line, Monte Spaduro, Monte Grande, **Argenta Gap,** San Nicolo Canal, Leros, **Malta 1940**

THE CONNAUGHT RANGERS

First World War
Mons, Retreat from Mons, Marne 1914, **Aisne 1914, Messines 1914, 17,** Armentières 194, **Ypres 1914, 15, 17,** Langemarck 1914, 17, Gheluvelt, Nonne Bosschen, Festubert 1914, Givenchy 1914, Neuve Chapelle, St. Julien, Aubers, Somme 1916, 18, **Guillemont,** Ginchy, St. Quentin, Bapaume 1918, Rosières, Hindenburg Line, **Cambrai 1918,** Selle, France and Flanders 1914-18, **Kosturino,** Struma, Macedonia 1915-17, Suvla, Sari Bair, **Scimitar Hill,** Gallipoli 1915, Gaza, Jerusalem, Tell Asur, **Megiddo,** Sharon, Palestine 1917-18, Tigris 1916, **Kut al Amara 1917,** Baghdad, Mesopotamia 1916-18

THE ARGYLL AND SUTHERLAND HIGHLANDERS

First World War
Mons, Le Cateau, Retreat from Mons, **Marne 1914, 18,** Aisne 1914, La Bassée 1914, Messines 1914, 18, Armentières 1914, **Ypres 1915, 17, 18,** Gravenstafel, St. Julien, Frezenberg, Bellewaarde, Festubert 1915, **Loos, Somme 1916, 18,** Albert 1916, 18, Bazentin,

Delville Wood, Pozières, Flers-Courcelette, Morval, Le Transloy, Ancre Heights, Ancre 1916, **Arras 1917, 18,** Scarpe 1917, 18, Arleux, Pilckem, Menin Road, Polygon Wood, Broodseinde, Poelcapelle, Passchendaele, **Cambrai 1917, 18,** St. Quentin, Bapaume 1918, Rosières, Lys, Estaires, Hazebrouck, Bailleul, Kemmel, Béthune, Soissonnais-Ourcq, Tardenois, Amiens, Hindenburg Line, Épéhy, Canal du Nord, St. Quentin Canal, Beaurevoir, Courtrai, Selle, Sambre, France and Flanders 1914-18, Italy 1917-18, Struma, **Doiran 1917, 18,** Macedonia 1915-18, Gallipoli 1915-16, Rumani, Egypt 1916, **Gaza,** El Mughar, Nebi Samwil, Jaffa, Palestine 1917-18

Second World War
Somme 1940, **Odon,** Tourmauville Bridge, Caen, Esquay, Mont Pincon, Quarry Hill, Estry, Falaise, Dives Crossing, Aart, Lower Maas, Meijel, Venlo Pocket, Ourthe, Rhineland, Reichswald, **Rhine,** Uelzen, Artlenberg, North-West Europe 1940, 44-45, Abyssinia 1941, **Sidi Barrani, El Alamein,** Medenine, **Akarit,** Djebel Azzag 1942, Kef Ouiba Pass, Mine de Sedjenane, Medjez Plain, **Longstop Hill 1943,** North Africa 1940-43, Landing in Sicily, Gerbini, Adrano, Centuripe, Sicily 1943, Termoli, Sangro, Cassino II, Liri Valley, Aquino, Monte Casalino, Monte Spaduro, Monte Grande, Senio, Santerno Crossing, Argenta Gap, **Italy 1943-45, Crete,** Heraklion, Middle East 1941, North Malaya, **Grik Road,** Central Malaya, Ipoh, Slim River, Singapore Island, **Malaya 1941-42**

Korean War
Pakchon, Korea 1950-51

THE PRINCE OF WALES'S LEINSTER REGIMENT (ROYAL CANADIANS)

First World War
Aisne 1914, Armentières 1914, **Ypres 1915, 17, 18,** Gravenstafel, St. Julien, Frezenberg, **Somme 1916, 18,** Delville Wood, **Guillemont,** Ginchy, Arras 1917, **Vimy 1917, Messines 1917,** Pilckem, Langemarck 1917, **St. Quentin,** Bapaume 1918, Rosières, Courtrai, France and Flanders 1914-18, Kosturino, Struma, **Macedonia, 1915-17,** Suvla, Sari Bair, **Gallipoli 1915,** Gaza, **Jerusalem,** Tell Asur, Megiddo, Nablus, Palestine 1917-18

THE ROYAL MUNSTER FUSILIERS

First World War
Retreat from Mons, Marne 1914, Aisne 1914, **Ypres 1914, 17,** Langemarck 1914, 17, Gheluvelt, Nonne Bosschen, Givenchy 1914, **Aubers,** Loos, Somme 1916, 18, Albert 1916, Bazentin, Pozières, **Guillemont,** Ginchy, Flers-Courcelette, Morval,

Messines 1917, Passchendaele, **St. Quentin,** Bapaume 1918, Rosières, Avre, Arras 1918, Scarpe 1918, **Drocourt-Quéant,** Hindenburg Line, Canal du Nord, St. Quentin Canal, Beaurevoir, Cambrai 1918, **Selle,** Sambre, France and Flanders 1914-18, Italy 1917-18, Kosturino, Struma, Macedonia 1915-17, Helles, **Landing at Helles,** Krithia, Suvla, **Landing at Suvla,** Scimitar Hill, Gallipoli 1915-16, Egypt 1916, Gaza, **Jerusalem,** Tell Asur, Palestine 1917-18

THE ROYAL DUBLIN FUSILIERS

First World War
Le Cateau, **Retreat from Mons, Marne 1914,** Aisne 1914, Armentières 1914, **Ypres 1915, 17, 18,** St. Julien, Frezenberg, Bellewaarde, **Somme 1916, 18,** Albert 1916, Guillemont, Ginchy, Le Transloy, Ancre 1916, Arras 1917, Scarpe 1917, Arleux, Messines 1917, Langemarck 1917, Polygon Wood, **Cambrai 1917, 18,** St. Quentin, Bapaume 1918, Rosières, Avre, **Hindenburg Line,** St. Quentin Canal, Beaurevoir, Courtrai, **Selle,** Sambre, France and Flanders 1914-18, Kosturino, Struma, **Macedonia 1915-17,** Helles, Landing at Helles, Krithia, Suvla, Sari Bair, Landing at Suvla, Scimitar Hill, **Gallipoli 1915-16,** Egypt 1916, Gaza, Jerusalem, Tell Asur, **Palestine 1917-18**

THE RIFLE BRIGADE
(PRINCE CONSORT'S OWN)

First World War
Le Cateau, Retreat from Mons, **Marne 1914,** Aisne 1914, 18, Armentières 1914, **Neuve Chapelle, Ypres 1915, 17,** Gravenstafel, St. Julien, Frezenberg, Bellewaarde, Aubers, Hooge 1915, **Somme 1916, 18,** Albert 1916, 18, Bazentin, Delville Wood, Guillemont, Flers-Courcelette, Morval, Le Transloy, Ancre Heights, Ancre 1916, 18, **Arras 1917, 18,** Vimy 1917, Scarpe 1917, 18, Arleux, **Messines 1917,** Pilckem, Langemarck 1917, Menin Road, Polygon Wood, Broodseinde, Poelcapelle, Passchendaele, **Cambrai 1917, 18,** St. Quentin, Rosières, Avre, Villers Bretonneux, Lys, Hazebrouck, Béthune, Drocourt-Quéant, **Hindenburg Line,** Havrincourt, Canal du Nord, Selle, Valenciennes, Sambre, France and Flanders 1914-18, **Macedonia 1915-18**

Second World War
Calais 1940, Villers Bocage, Odon, Bourguebus Ridge, Mont Pincon, Le Perier Ridge, Falaise, Antwerp, Hechtel, Nederrijn, Lower Maas, Roer, Leese, Aller, **North-West Europe 1940, 44-45,** Egyptian Frontier 1940, **Beda Fomm,** Mersa el Brega, Agedabia, Derna Aerodrome, Tobruk 1941, **Sidi Rezegh 1941,** Chor es Sufan, Saunnu, Gazala, Knightsbridge, Defence of Alamein Line, Ruweisat, **Alam el Halfa, El Alamein,** Tebaga Gap, Medjez el

Bab, Kasserine, Thala, Fondouk, Fondouk Pass, El Kourzia, Djebel Kournine, Tunis, Hammam Lif, **North Africa 1940-43,** Cardito, **Cassino II,** Liri Valley, Melfa Crossing, Monte Rotondo, **Capture of Perugia,** Monte Malbe, Arezzo, Advance to Florence, Gothic Line, Orsara, Tossignano, Argenta Gap, Fossa Cembalina, **Italy 1943-45**

THE GLIDER PILOT REGIMENT

Second World War
Normandy Landing, Pegasus Bridge, Merville Battery, Rhine, Southern France, North-West Europe 1944-45, Landing in Sicily, Sicily 1943

THE PARACHUTE REGIMENT

Second World War
Bruneval, Normandy Landing, Pegasus Bridge, Merville Battery, **Breville,** Dives Crossing, La Touques Crossing, **Arnhem 1944,** Ourthe, **Rhine, Southern France,** North-West Europe 1942, 44-45, Soudia, **Oudna,** Djebel Azzag 1943, Djebel Alliliga, El Hadjeba, **Tamera,** Djebel Dahra, Kef el Debna, North Africa 1942-43, **Primosole Bridge,** Sicily 1943, Taranto, Orsogna, Italy 1943-44, **Athens,** Greece 1944-45

2nd KING EDWARD VII's OWN GURKHA RIFLES

First World War
La Bassée 1914, Festubert 1914-15, Givenchy 1914, Neuve Chapelle, Aubers, Loos, France and Flanders 1914-15, Egypt 1915, **Tigris 1916, Kut al Amara 1917, Baghdad 1915,** Mesopotamia 1916, 18, **Persia 1918,** Baluchistan 1918

Afghanistan 1919

Second World War
El Alamein, Mareth, **Akarit,** Djebel el Meida, Enfidaville, **Tunis,** North Africa 1942-43, **Cassino I,** Monastery Hill, Pian di Maggio, **Gothic Line,** Coriano, Poggio San Giovanni, Monte Reggiano, Italy 1944-45, Greece 1944-45, North Malaya, **Jitra,** Central Malaya, Kampar, **Slim River,** Johore, Singapore Island, Malaya 1941-42, **North Arakan, Irrawaddy,** Magwe, Sittang 1945, Point 1433, Arakan Beaches, Myebon, **Tamandu,** Chindits 1943, Burma 1943-45

6th QUEEN ELIZABETH'S OWN GURKHA RIFLES

First World War
Helles, Krithia, Suvla, Sari Bair, Gallipoli 1915,

Suez Canal, Egypt 1915-16, **Khan Baghdadi, Mesopotamia 1916-18, Persia 1918, N. W. Frontier India 1915**

Afghanistan 1919

Second World War
Coriano, Santarcangelo, **Monte Chicco,** Lamone Crossing, Senio Floodbank, **Medecina,** Gaiana Crossing, **Italy 1944-45,** Shwebo, **Kyaukmyaung Bridgehead, Mandalay, Fort Dufferin,** Maymyo, **Rangoon Road,** Toungoo, **Sittang 1945, Chindits 1944, Burma 1944-45**

7th DUKE OF EDINBURGH'S OWN GURKHA RIFLES

First World War
Suez Canal, **Egypt 1915, Megiddo, Sharon, Palestine 1918,** Shaiba, **Kut al Amara 1915, 17, Ctesiphon, Defence of Kut al Amara, Baghdad, Sharqat,** Mesopotamia 1915-18

Afghanistan 1919

Second World War
Tobruk 1942, North Africa 1942, **Cassino I,** Campriano, **Poggio del Grillo, Tavoleto,** Montebello-Scorticata Ridge, Italy 1944, **Sittang 1942, 45,** Pegu 1942, **Kyaukse 1942,** Shwegyin, **Imphal, Bishenpur, Meiktila,** Capture of Meiktila, Defence of Meiktila, **Rangoon Road,** Pyawbwe, Burma 1942-45

10th PRINCESS MARY'S OWN GURKHA RIFLES .

First World War
Helles, Krithia, Suvla, Sari Bair, Gallipoli 1915, Suez Canal, Egypt 1915, Sharqat, Mesopotamia 1916-18

Afghanistan 1919

Second World War
Iraq 1941, Deir ez Zor, Syria 1941, **Coriano, Santarcangelo,** Senio Floodbank, **Bologna,** Sillaro Crossing, Italy 1944-45, Monywa 1942, **Imphal, Tuitam,** Tamu Road, Shenam Pass, Litan, Bishenpur, Tengnoupal, **Mandalay, Myinmu Bridgehead,** Kyaukse 1945, **Meiktila,** Capture of Meiktila, Defence of Meiktila, Irrawaddy, **Rangoon Road,** Pegu 1945, Sittang 1945, Burma 1942-45

THE SPECIAL AIR SERVICE REGIMENT

Second World War
North-West Europe 1944-45, Tobruk 1941, Benghazi Raid, North Africa 1940-43, Landing in Sicily, Sicily 1943, **Termoli, Valli di Comacchio, Italy 1943-45,** Greece 1944-45, **Adriatic,** Middle East 1943-44

BATTLE HONOURS 1982

On 25 October 1983 the Secretary of State for Defence announced that the Queen had approved the following Battle Honours for the Falkland Islands campaign:

Falkland Islands 1982*
Goose Green
Mount Longdon
Tumbledown Mountain
Wireless Ridge

* Only this award to be emblazoned on Colours

E

REGIMENTAL AND CORPS
HEADDRESS BADGES

If Standards, Guidons and Colours, the rallying-points, are the symbols of corporate identity in Household and Line Regiments, then headdress badges are the peculiarly British marks of regimental and corps individuality.

The history of badges and insignia is as old as the history of armies, as both general marks of recognition and signs of rank. In Britain, long before the introduction of 'uniform' dress and longer still before the development of the regimental system, men in battle sought two levels of identification: that of friend from foe, and that of leader from led. In the lowest social order stood the infantryman or common soldier, distinguished by primitive 'field marks' such as cloth patches, ribbons, pieces of paper, or assorted flora,[1] like leaves, twigs, corn-stalks — simple serviceable objects, readily recognized by simple men. In the middle rank (often literally) came the yeoman archer identified by his distinctive weapon and often by his headdress (Shakespeare's old professional, Fluellen, speaks of Welsh archers wearing leeks in their 'Monmouth caps'). High above these, also literally, were the cavalry, the 'chivalry' of medieval times, resplendent in armour, their shields and helmets charged with armorial bearings and crests, the badges of superior rank, the marks of liege-lord and leader, instantly recognized by the led. And at the summit, in an age when kings went forth to war, the royal standard, the fleur-de-lys of France, the oriflamme of Navarre, the banner of St George.

In a period of private armies and mercenary bands, the idea of uniform dress was slow to find acceptance, and the common soldier did battle in his humble homespun (sailors continued to wear their working clothes at sea until the eighteenth century). However, as a small footnote to history suggests, the profession of arms began to take on style if not yet vivid colour. In 1614 Sir Thomas Coningsby founded a small but still surviving Hospital in Hereford for 'one Corporall and ten old Servitors', all to be 'drest alike in a fustian suit of ginger-colour, a hat with border of white and red, a soldier-like jerkyn and a soldier-like sword'.

Professionalism arrived with a vengeance in the person of Cromwell. The New Model Army, the first expression of organized militarism in a kingdom without a king, was regimented, disciplined, ruthless and universally hated. Its memory would leave an indelible mark on Parliament and people for over two hundred years. So, for even longer, would its appearance.

The red coat was Cromwell's legacy, partly as a stamp of authority and partly as the first measure of uniformity. However, with the Army organized into regiments of Horse and Foot but uniformly dressed within the two arms, a visual method of distinction became necessary, and it is from the New Model that the system of regimental 'facings' of different colours may be said to date; and has so remained to the present day. As yet the modern headdress badge in even its basic form was a hundred years away, although Cromwell's soldiers sported scarves and ribbons in their hats as further distinctive devices.

With the Restoration and the raising of the first Standing Army, the King — in the event unwisely — retained the red coat, at once soldierly and symbolic of tyrannous times. So too as the new regimental system, personal and proprietary, began to evolve, uniform facings were continued as distinguishing marks, the colour blue reserved to the King's Guards and to all Royal regiments. New styles

[1]In England the rose was to acquire a special significance, as would the Scottish thistle and the Irish shamrock.

appeared — Life Guards, Horse Guards, Horse, Dragoons, Fusiliers, Foot, even, in one instance, Musketeers;[2] new titles too, like The Tangier Regiment, The Holland Regiment, The Irish Regiment. But with few exceptions — those regiments of 'Royal' lineage — Colonels reigned supreme, decorating their Company Colours with their personal crests and armorial bearings. If the Army as yet was still feeling its way towards a true sense of individuality, at least along the road it acquired in 1694 a new pecking-order in William III's 'Roosbeck' rules of precedence. But the regiments which went to Flanders with Marlborough rode and marched under royal or ancient badges or under their Colonels' colours, their headdresses innocent of any separate or distinctive device. Until 1751.

George II's Royal Warrant of 1 July of that year ran thus:

> The front of the Grenadiers Caps [*the mitre caps of Grenadier companies in infantry regiments of the Line*] to be the same colour as the faceings of the regiment with the King's Cypher Embroidered and Crown over it; the little flaps to be Red with the white Horse [*of Hanover*] motto over it, "Nec aspera terrent"; the back part of the Caps to be Red, the turn-up to be the Colour of the Front with the Number of the Regiment in the middle part behind.

The same Warrant also laid down regulations for Colours (two, and only two — the King's and the Regimental) and forbade any Colonel 'to put his Arms, Crest, Device or Livery on any part of the Appointments of the Regiment under his Command'.[3]

The 1751 Warrant provides three milestones in one. First, it ended a century of 'proprietary' ownership; secondly, it introduced the system of consecutive numbering of Line regiments in their order of precedence; and thirdly, it introduced what may best be described as the regimental 'fingerprint'. And out of this Warrant grew the headdress badge, even if it could not yet, for reasons of uniform design, be applied to any but the tall mitre cap. The principle was extended further in Warrants and Dress Regulations of 1768 and 1796, but it did not finally take root until the introduction in 1800 of the 'shako' or peaked cap as the standard headdress of the infantry, at the instance of the practically minded Duke of York.

Until it was withdrawn in 1878 the shako went through seven different patterns, varying slightly in shape and considerably in height; but common to all was a metal plate bearing the number of the regiment or, where so entitled, royal or ancient badges as set out in a schedule to the 1751 Warrant. The original design of this plate incorporated the Royal Cypher within the Garter upon a trophy of arms. Below this central feature was the Lion of the Royal Crest flanked by the engraved device or number of the regiment, and above it the Crown. The cylinder of the shako bore Company cockades in different colours to denote a particular category such as 'grenadier' or 'light infantry', and these survive to-day in the Fusilier hackle.[4] The plate varied in size at different dates

---

[2] The original title of the 11th Foot (The Devonshire Regiment).
[3] This regulation has been relaxed in a number of modern headdress badges: among others, for example, The Duke of Wellington's Regiment, The Gordon Highlanders, The Argyll and Sutherland Highlanders, and the former badge of the 7th Dragoon Guards.
[4] The eighteenth and nineteenth century meet to-day in the tricorn and shako headdresses of the Royal Hospital, Chelsea.

according to the shape of the shako,[5] but the tendency was towards simplification and ever greater prominence to the regimental number.[6]

In 1878 the shako was replaced by a spiked blue cloth helmet not dissimilar to that worn to-day by police forces, and by a 'helmet-plate' based on the simple eight-pointed star ensigned with the Crown which had been the standard pattern since 1829. The new plate carried the regimental number within the Garter on a detachable brass 'centre'.

However, this change was to prove short-lived. In 1881 the root-and-branch reform which Cardwell had initiated nine years previously came into effect, and with it a complete transformation in the anatomy of the old 'marching regiments of Foot'. Out went the single-battalion system and the numbered séquence of infantry corps.[7] In came the Territorial Regiment of two battalions, loosely linked in pairs in 1872 but now indissolubly joined together — or so it then seemed[8] — in often unholy matrimony. The barrack rooms at Aldershot were full of strange oaths and offensive neologisms; and there were immediate side-effects.

The famous — or, according to taste, infamous — General Order 41 of 1 May (hastily amended by General Order 70 of 1 July) showed an awareness of injured pride if not an appreciation of chemical synthesis, for it hastened to set forth the principle that both partners to each marriage would endow each other with all their worldly goods — that battle honours, distinctions, honour titles, traditional rights would all be common to the new union. It was the least concession that could be made. But it begged many questions. Why, for instance, should the 39th (Dorsetshire) Foot, heroes of Plassey and proud holders of the motto *Primus in Indis*, share that special honour with the 54th (West Norfolk) Foot, which by 1757 had barely flown the nest? Conversely, why should the fledgling 54th admit the 39th to the singular distinction MARABOUT? And what, even if one honour might match the other, had Dorset and Norfolk in common?

Uniform was not a problem since General Order 41 laid down in paragraph IX that (Scottish regiments excepted) 'the uniforms of all the battalions of a Territorial Regiment will be the same' and that 'the title of the regiment will be shown on the shoulder strap'. And in the next paragraph:

The facings will be the same for all regiments belonging to the same country (Royal and Rifle regiments excepted),[9] and will be as follows:

English (and Welsh) Regiments	White
Scotch [*sic*] Regiments	Yellow
Irish Regiments	Green

It will be noted that this Order applied only to infantry regiments of the Line, and to The Rifle Brigade. Cavalry, Artillery, Engineers and Foot Guards, not

---

[5]For a short period from 1872 the Army wore the 'glengarry' in walking-out dress, necessitating a smaller plate.

[6]For much of the time, when the shako was standard issue in the infantry, the cavalry went its separate way in an extravagance of peacock plumage.

[7]The regional suffixes imposed upon the Army in 1782 had been honoured more often in the breach than in the observance. 'West Middlesex' meant little or nothing to men of the 57th 'Diehards'.

[8]'Change', wrote Goethe, 'is a restless river' — and this the Army would learn again a century hence.

[9]The 22 Royal regiments — blue; Cameronians — dark green; King's Royal Rifle Corps — scarlet; Royal Irish Rifles — light green; Rifle Brigade — black.

being included in Cardwell's original localization scheme, were left alone.

Headdress badges were another matter, for with the disappearance of numbered regiments the 1878 helmet plate and centre had become obsolete, and it is an indication of the sensitive issues raised by the process of 'territorialization' that General Order 41 maintains a discreet silence on the subject. There is plenty of evidence, however, that the publication of the Order was the occasion for long and heated argument within the Army in general, and within the new regiments in particular.[10] The answer, inevitably, was a compromise. In 1883 a new set of Dress Regulations published, under the heading 'Badges of Territorial Regiments', detailed descriptions of badges to be worn on all forms of headdress and other appointments. The 1878-pattern helmet plate was retained, but the centre now consisted of a plain circle bearing the title of the regiment and enclosing a regimental device or badge. Illustrated below is the universal plate with King's Crown (Edward VII) and examples of the new-style centres:

For the 25 senior Line regiments which had consisted of two battalions since 1858 the choice of a badge was relatively simple, and in most instances consisted of one of the devices already borne on the Regimental Colour: for example, Queen's — the Paschal Lamb; Royal Warwickshire — the Antelope; Norfolk — the figure of Britannia; West Yorkshire — the White Horse of Hanover. For those regiments which now consisted of linked (and largely unrelated) battalions the problem was more complicated, and where a compromise pattern could not be mutually agreed, one was officially — and to judge from appearances — often arbitrarily imposed. None the less, it is possible to identify certain common

[10]The question of battle honours had been covered in paragraph VIII, which laid down that 'all distinctions, mottoes, badges or devices... as borne by either of the Line battalions of a Territorial Regiment will in future be borne by both those battalions.'

denominators. All nine Fusilier badges were based on the Grenade; Light Infantry all adopted the Bugle-horn; and most Irish regiments the Harp. Others assumed 'honorary distinctions', such as the Sphinx, the Royal Tiger, the Castle and Key of Gibraltar; 'ancient badges' such as the Rose or the Dragon; or the emblems of 'honour titles' such as the Prince of Wales's Plume and ducal Coronets and Cyphers.

It is appropriate to add here a word of explanation about the Crown which surmounted the helmet plate, and which features in so many subsequent badges. It will be seen that there are a number of varying designs, but these are not, as is sometimes stated, representations of the St Edward's, Tudor or Imperial Crowns. They are purely heraldic devices, and are correctly referred to as 'King's Crown' (the domed pattern) and 'Queen's Crown' (with a 'dropped' centre).[11] The flat Victorian design was replaced by the King's Crown on the accession of Edward VII, and was retained during the three following reigns. Since 1952 the present Queen's Crown has been adopted.

There is a very English anachronism here. The Crown does not signify a 'Royal' regiment or corps. For example, The Queen's, The Buffs, The Northumberland Fusiliers, and The Warwickshire (all of which are 'Royal' regiments) formerly displayed their 'ancient badges' but no Crown; while among others, The Devonshire Regiment, The Sherwood Foresters, The East Lancashire Regiment, the Army Air Corps, the Intelligence Corps and the Army Catering Corps (none of them 'royal') wore or wear 'ensigned' badges. Like much else in the British Army, this apparent eccentricity has no documentary explanation.

Towards the end of the last century, with the adoption of new forms of headdress, the helmet plate was gradually phased out, the use of the standard star discontinued,[12] and the plate centre progressively elaborated (with frequent pattern changes) into the modern style of headdress badge. In a sense they provide a kind of pictorial history of the Army, full of curiosities, lineage clues, inventive artistry, and passing from extreme simplicity (The Manchester Regiment) to fussy elaboration (Corps of Royal Electrical and Mechanical Engineers). Several medieval insignia have survived, notably the Order of the Garter, the Cross of St George, the Prince of Wales's Plume and motto, the Dragon, the Roses of York and Lancaster and, rather less grandly, the Leek. Animals and birds abound — lions, tigers, elephants, eagles, antelopes, stags, harts, even a cat and a bear. And there are oddities.

While the former badges of The Somerset Light Infantry, The Border Regiment, and The Dorset Regiment incorporated the exclusive battle honours of, respectively, JELLALABAD, ARROYO DOS MOLINOS, and MARABOUT, the 15th Hussars did not display their even more exclusive EMSDORFF. Indeed, surprisingly few battle honours or distinctions appeared on badges: for example, WATERLOO (Royal Scots Greys), TALAVERA (Northamptonshire), ALBUHERA (Middlesex), ASSAYE (Highland Light Infantry), THE CASTLE

---

[11]The one exception is the former badge of The Rifle Brigade (Prince Consort's Own), which bore a Guelphic Crown.
[12]Some twenty-two regiments and corps retained a star in their badge, either adopted from the Orders of Knighthood or taken over from the old helmet plate.

AND KEY OF GIBRALTAR (four regiments), and EGYPT with the Sphinx (six regiments).[13] Such details are noted in the captions to illustrations, as are the often ingenious forms in which regimental distinctions have been combined in badges resulting from the post-1946 amalgamations.

In the section which follows Regiments and Corps are shown in short title and broadly in their existing order of precedence. However, where there have been amalgamations since the First World War the old and new badges are grouped together, viz: The Blues and Royals (Royal Horse Guards and 1st Dragoons), The Queen's, The Royal Anglian, The Duke of Edinburgh's Royal (Berkshire and Wiltshire) and so on. Of individual badges there are shown the present design or the last pattern worn before amalgamation. Included finally in two sub-sections are the short-lived Brigade badges and those of Regiments and Corps disbanded since 1922.

In some Regiments — for example, The Coldstream Guards, The Scots Guards, The Royal Scots, The Royal Hampshire Regiment, The Royal Berkshire Regiment — officers' badges differed or differ in design from those of other ranks (the same is true of badges worn by some non-commissioned ranks in the Brigade of Guards). For purposes of uniformity, however, soldiers' badges are illustrated throughout.

---

[13]The King's Royal Rifle Corps and The Rifle Brigade, having no Regimental Colour, incorporated a number of battle honours in their badges and appointments, as, exceptionally, did The Border Regiment.

LIFE GUARDS

The Royal Cypher within a circle bearing the title, ensigned with the Crown.

ROYAL HORSE ARTILLERY

The Royal Cypher within the Garter with motto, ensigned with the Crown.

ROYAL HORSE GUARDS

The Royal Cypher within a circle bearing the title, ensigned with the Crown.

ROYAL ARMOURED CORPS

In front of two concentric circles, barbed, a gauntlet clenched, with a billet inscribed RAC, all ensigned with the Crown.

THE ROYAL DRAGOONS (1st DRAGOONS)

An Eagle upon a tablet bearing the numerals 105. The figures refer to the 105th French Infantry Regiment, whose Eagle was captured by Captain Clarke at Waterloo.

1st KING'S DRAGOON GUARDS

The double-headed Eagle from the arms of the Emperor Franz Joseph I of Austria.

BLUES AND ROYALS

The badge of the amalgamated Royal Horse Guards and Royal Dragoons (1969), The Royal Cypher within a circle ensigned with the Crown.

THE QUEEN'S BAYS (2nd DRAGOON GUARDS)

The title BAYS in old English lettering within a wreath of laurel, ensigned with the Crown.

1st THE QUEEN'S DRAGOON GUARDS

The double-headed Eagle from the arms of the Emperor Franz Joseph I of Austria.

ROYAL SCOTS GREYS (2nd DRAGOONS)

On a tablet WATERLOO the Eagle of the French 45th Infantry Regiment captured by Sergeant Ewart.

3rd DRAGOON GUARDS

The Prince of Wales's Plume, with Coronet and motto.

ROYAL SCOTS DRAGOON GUARDS

On crossed carbines the Eagle of the French 45th Infantry Regiment upon a tablet WATERLOO.

THE CARABINIERS (6th DRAGOON GUARDS)

On crossed carbines the initials VI D.G within the Garter, all ensigned with the Crown.

4th DRAGOON GUARDS

The Star of the Order of St Patrick ensigned with the Crown.

CARABINIERS (3rd DRAGOON GUARDS)

On crossed carbines the Prince of Wales's Plume, Coronet and motto.

7th DRAGOON GUARDS

The crest of Earl Ligonier, a demi-lion issuing from a Coronet.

4th/7th ROYAL DRAGOON GUARDS

Upon the Star of the Order of St Patrick a circle with the motto *Quis Separabit?* (Who shall separate us?) and the date of the amalgamation of the two Regiments, MCMXXII. Within the circle the Cross of St George and the Coronet of the Princess Royal.

5th DRAGOON GUARDS

Within a circle bearing the motto *Vestigia nulla retrorsum* (No retreat) the White Horse of Hanover and the initials VDG, all ensigned with a Crown.

THE INNISKILLINGS (6th DRAGOONS)

The Castle of Enniskillen.

5th ROYAL INNISKILLING DRAGOON GUARDS

The monogram VDG interlaced and ensigned with the Crown.

3rd HUSSARS

On a ground the White Horse of Hanover.

7th HUSSARS

Within a circle the monogram QO reversed and interlaced and ensigned with the Crown.

QUEEN'S OWN HUSSARS

On a ground the White Horse of Hanover.

4th HUSSARS

Within a circle the Roman numerals IV with, beneath, the motto *Mente et Manu* (With heart and hand), all ensigned with the Crown.

8th HUSSARS

The Angel Harp ensigned with the Crown.

ROYAL HUSSARS

The Plume, Coronet and motto of the Prince of Wales.

QUEEN'S ROYAL IRISH HUSSARS

Within a circle the Angel Harp with, beneath, the motto *Mente et Manu* (With heart and hand), all ensigned with the Royal Crest.

13th HUSSARS

Within a circle bearing the motto *Viret in Aeternum* (It flourishes for ever) the Roman numerals XIII, all within a laurel wreath and ensigned with the Crown.

10th HUSSARS

The Plume, Coronet and motto of the Prince of Wales.

18th HUSSARS

Within a circle bearing the Honour Title 'Queen Mary's Own' the Roman numerals XVIII upon a laurel spray and ensigned with the Crown.

11th HUSSARS

The crest and motto of Prince Albert, *Treu und Fest* (True and Trusty).

13th/18th HUSSARS

A 'Z' scroll superimposed upon the monogram QMO with the title of the Regiment in Roman numerals, all ensigned with the Crown.

14th HUSSARS

The Prussian Eagle granted in 1798 in honour of the Princess Royal of Prussia, wife of the Duke of York.

20th HUSSARS

The letter H flanked by the Roman numerals XX and ensigned with the Crown.

14th/20th HUSSARS

The Prussian Eagle.

15th HUSSARS

Within the Garter the Royal Crest upon the short title XVKH and the motto *Merebimur* (We shall be worthy).

19th HUSSARS

The monogram of Queen Alexandra interlaced with the Dannebrog, or Danish Cross, bearing the date 1885.

15th/19th HUSSARS

Within the Garter the Royal Crest upon the Roman numerals XV.XIX and the motto *Merebimur* (We shall be worthy).

9th LANCERS

Upon a pair of crossed lances the numeral 9 ensigned with the Crown.

12th LANCERS

Upon a pair of crossed lances the Plume and Coronet of the Prince of Wales above the Roman numerals XII, all ensigned with the Crown.

9th/12th LANCERS

Upon a pair of crossed lances the Plume and Coronet of the Prince of Wales above a scroll bearing the Roman numerals IX - XII, all ensigned with the Crown.

17th LANCERS

A skull and crossbones above the motto OR GLORY. The badge is said to have been a tribute to General James Wolfe by the Colonel of the 17th Light Dragoons, Colonel Hale.

5th LANCERS

Upon a pair of crossed lances a circle bearing the motto of the Order of St Patrick *Quis separabit?* (Who shall separate us?). Within the circle the numeral 5.

21st LANCERS

On a pair of crossed lances ensigned with the Crown the Royal Cypher VRI of Queen Victoria as Empress of India above the Roman numerals XXI.

16th LANCERS

Upon a pair of crossed lances the numerals 16 ensigned with the Crown.

17th/21st LANCERS

A skull and crossbones above the motto OR GLORY.

16th/5th LANCERS

Upon a pair of crossed lances the numerals 16 ensigned with the Crown.

ROYAL TANK CORPS

Within a laurel wreath, a tank facing to the left and ensigned with the Crown. Below, the motto FEAR NAUGHT.

ROYAL TANK REGIMENT

Within a laurel wreath, a tank facing to the right and ensigned with the Crown. Below, the motto FEAR NAUGHT.

GRENADIER GUARDS

A Grenade.

ROYAL ARTILLERY

A gun with, above, the motto *Ubique* (Everywhere) and, below, *Quo fas et gloria ducunt* (Where right and glory lead). All ensigned with the Crown.

COLDSTREAM GUARDS

A variant of the Star of the Order of the Garter.

ROYAL ENGINEERS

The Royal Cypher within the Garter and motto, all enclosed in a laurel wreath and ensigned with the Crown.

SCOTS GUARDS

The Star of the Order of the Thistle with motto *Nemo me impune lacessit* (None shall provoke me with impunity).

ROYAL CORPS OF SIGNALS

The figure of Mercury holding a caduceus or winged staff in his hand, with Crown above. Beneath, a globe and the motto *Certa Cito* (Sure and Swift).

IRISH GUARDS

The Star of the Order of St Patrick with motto *Quis separabit?* (Who shall separate us?) and the date of the founding of the Order, MDCCLXXXIII.

WELSH GUARDS

The Leek.

QUEEN'S ROYAL SURREY

Upon an eight-pointed star the Paschal Lamb and Flag, ensigned with the Crown.

ROYAL SCOTS

The Star of the Order of the Thistle. In the centre St Andrew and Cross. Worn on a red cloth background.

BUFFS

On a ground the Dragon.

QUEEN'S ROYAL (WEST SURREY)

On a ground the Paschal Lamb and Flag.

QUEEN'S OWN ROYAL WEST KENT

Upon a scroll INVICTA in Old English lettering the White Horse of Kent.

EAST SURREY

Within an eight-pointed star, ensigned with the Crown, the Arms of Guildford.

QUEEN'S OWN BUFFS

Upon a scroll INVICTA in Old English lettering the White Horse of Kent.

ROYAL SUSSEX

The Star and motto of the Order of the Garter adopted in 1881 from the Royal Sussex Militia, upon the Roussillon Plume taken from the French at Quebec.

BORDER

A cross based on that of the Order of the Bath upon a wreath, and both upon a star. Within the cross a circle with the China Dragon and bearing the honour ARROYO DOS MOLINOS 1811, exclusive to this Regiment. On the arms of the cross 14 honours. All ensigned with the Crown.

MIDDLESEX

Within a laurel wreath the Plume, Coronet and motto of the Prince of Wales, and Coronet and Cypher of the Duke of Cambridge. Below, upon a scroll, the battle honour ALBUHERA.

KING'S OWN ROYAL BORDER

The Lion of England (King's Own) within a laurel wreath (Border), ensigned with the Crown.

QUEEN'S

Within the Garter (Royal Sussex) the Dragon (Buffs). Above, the Plume and Coronet of the Prince of Wales (Middlesex). Below, upon a scroll, the title Queen's.

ROYAL NORTHUMBERLAND FUSILIERS

On the base of a grenade St George and Dragon within a circle bearing the motto *Quo fata vocant* (Wherever fate calls).

KING'S OWN ROYAL (LANCASTER)

The Lion of England upon the title THE KING'S OWN.

ROYAL WARWICKSHIRE (FUSILIERS)

Upon a ground the Antelope with Coronet and chain.

ROYAL FUSILIERS

A grenade with, on the base, a Rose within the Garter and motto.

MANCHESTER

A Fleur-de-Lys, the badge of the old 63rd Foot. The former badge of the Regiment was the Arms of the City of Manchester.

LANCASHIRE FUSILIERS

A grenade with, on the base, the Sphinx upon a tablet EGYPT within a laurel wreath.

KING'S

Upon a Fleur-de-Lys the White Horse of Hanover. Below, the title KING'S in Old English lettering.

ROYAL REGIMENT OF FUSILIERS

A grenade with, on the base, St George and Dragon within a wreath, and ensigned with the Crown.

ROYAL NORFOLK

The figure of Britannia, traditionally awarded by Queen Anne in 1707.

KING'S
(LIVERPOOL)

The White Horse of Hanover upon a ground. Below, the title KING'S in Old English lettering.

SUFFOLK

The Castle and Key of Gibraltar within a circle inscribed *Montis Insignia Calpe* (The Arms of Gibraltar), all within a wreath and ensigned with the Crown.

ROYAL LINCOLNSHIRE

The Sphinx upon a tablet EGYPT.

ROYAL LEICESTERSHIRE

On a ground the Royal Tiger superscribed HINDOOSTAN.

NORTHAMPTONSHIRE

The Castle and Key superscribed GIBRALTAR. Beneath, the battle honour TALAVERA. All within a laurel wreath.

EAST ANGLIAN

The Castle and Key of Gibraltar upon an eight-pointed star.

BEDFORDSHIRE AND HERTFORDSHIRE

Upon the Star of the Order of the Garter a variant of the Cross of the Order of the Bath, and within the Garter and motto a Hart crossing a ford.

ROYAL ANGLIAN

The Castle and Key of Gibraltar upon an eight-pointed star.

ESSEX

Within an oak wreath the Castle and Key of Gibraltar and above it the Sphinx on a tablet EGYPT.

DEVONSHIRE

Upon an eight-pointed star a circle, ensigned with the Crown. Within the circle the Castle of Exeter.

DORSET

Within a laurel wreath the Castle and Key of Gibraltar. Above, the Sphinx upon a tablet MARABOUT, an honour exclusive to this Regiment. Below, the motto *Primus in Indis* (First in India) awarded to celebrate the battle of Plassey (1757).

DEVONSHIRE AND DORSET

The Castle of Exeter. Above, the motto *Semper Fidelis* (Ever True). Below, on a tablet MARABOUT and the motto *Primus in Indis* (First in India).

SOMERSET L.I.

Within the strings of a Bugle-horn the initials P.A. (Prince Albert) and, above, a Mural Crown superscribed JELLALABAD, a battle honour exclusive to this Regiment.

DUKE OF CORNWALL'S L.I.

A stringed Bugle-horn with, above, a ducal Coronet upon a scroll CORNWALL, all upon a red cloth backing.

SOMERSET AND CORNWALL L.I.

A stringed Bugle-horn with, above, a Mural Crown, upon a red cloth backing.

KING'S OWN YORKSHIRE L.I.

A French Horn with, in the twist, the Rose of York.

KING'S SHROPSHIRE L.I.

Between the strings of a Bugle-horn the initials KSLI.

DURHAM L.I.

Within the strings of a Bugle-horn the initials DLI ensigned with the Crown.

LIGHT INFANTRY

A stringed Bugle-horn upon a red cloth backing.

YORKSHIRE

The Cypher of Princess (Queen) Alexandra interlaced with the Dannebrog, or Danish Cross. On three scrolls the full title of the Regiment. Below, a Rose of York. Above, a Coronet. On the cross the date 1875 is that of the granting of the Honour Title.

WEST YORKSHIRE

The White Horse of Hanover on a 'wreath' or ground.

GREEN HOWARDS

Above the Roman numerals XIX, the Cypher of Queen Alexandra interlaced with the Dannebrog, or Danish Cross surmounted by a Coronet. On the cross the date 1875, being that of the granting of the Honour Title.

EAST YORKSHIRE

The Rose of York within a laurel wreath upon an eight-pointed star.

ROYAL SCOTS FUSILIERS

A grenade with, on the base, the Royal Coat of Arms.

PRINCE OF WALES'S OWN REGIMENT OF YORKSHIRE

The White Horse of Hanover upon a 'wreath' or ground.

HIGHLAND L.I.

On the Star of the Order of the Thistle a Bugle-horn bearing the monogram HLI above the Elephant superscribed ASSAYE, all ensigned with the Crown.

ROYAL HIGHLAND FUSILIERS

A grenade with, on the base, the monogram HLI surmounted by the Crown.

WELCH

The Plume, Coronet and motto, of the Prince of Wales.

CHESHIRE

Upon an eight-pointed star an Acorn within a circle.

ROYAL REGIMENT OF WALES

The Plume, Coronet and motto of the Prince of Wales.

ROYAL WELCH FUSILIERS

A grenade. On the base, within a circle, the Plume and motto of the Prince of Wales.

KING'S OWN SCOTTISH BORDERERS

Upon a Saltire, the Castle of Edinburgh with mottoes *In veritate religionis confido* (I trust in the truth of my belief) and *Nisi dominus frustra* (In vain without the Lord), all ensigned with the Royal Crest.

SOUTH WALES BORDERERS

Within a wreath of immortelles (granted by Queen Victoria to commemorate the battle of Isandhlwana (1879)) the Sphinx upon a tablet EGYPT and, below, the initials SWB.

ROYAL INNISKILLING FUSILIERS

A grenade with, on the base, the Castle of Enniskillen.

ROYAL ULSTER RIFLES

The badge of the former Royal Irish Rifles (re-styled 1920). The Angel Harp with motto *Quis separabit?* above a stringed Bugle-horn, all ensigned with the Crown.

WORCESTERSHIRE

Raised in 1694 by an officer of The Coldstream Guards, the badge is the Star of the Order of the Garter. Within the Garter, the Lion of the Royal Crest upon a tablet FIRM.

ROYAL IRISH FUSILIERS

A grenade with, on the base, the Angel Harp and Prince of Wales's Plume, all surmounted by the Coronet of Princess Victoria.

SHERWOOD FORESTERS

A Maltese Cross. Within an oak wreath a White Hart, left and right the title SHERWOOD FORESTERS, all ensigned with the Crown.

ROYAL IRISH RANGERS

The Angel Harp ensigned with the Crown.

WORCESTERSHIRE AND SHERWOOD FORESTERS

The badge of the former Sherwood Foresters above a tablet FIRM, all on the Star of the Order of the Garter.

GLOUCESTERSHIRE

The Sphinx upon a tablet EGYPT above a laurel spray. Worn as a back-badge in miniature, the Sphinx within a laurel wreath.

EAST LANCASHIRE

The Sphinx upon a tablet EGYPT above the Rose of Lancaster, within a laurel wreath, all ensigned with the Crown.

SOUTH LANCASHIRE

The Plume, Coronet and motto of the Prince of Wales above the Sphinx upon a tablet EGYPT, all within a laurel wreath.

DUKE OF WELLINGTON'S

The crest of the Duke of Wellington upon his motto *Virtutis fortuna comes* (Fortune favours the brave).

LANCASHIRE

The Plume, Coronet and motto of the Prince of Wales.

ROYAL HAMPSHIRE

Within a laurel wreath the Hampshire Rose and above, the Royal Tiger, all ensigned with the Crown.

LOYAL NORTH LANCASHIRE

The Rose of Lancaster ensigned with The Royal Crest.

SOUTH STAFFORDSHIRE

The Staffordshire Knot ensigned with the Crown.

QUEEN'S LANCASHIRE

Within an oval the Rose of Lancaster ensigned with the Crown. Below, the motto LOYALLY I SERVE from the old 81st Foot.

NORTH STAFFORDSHIRE

The Staffordshire Knot ensigned with the Plume, Coronet and motto of the Prince of Wales.

STAFFORDSHIRE

The Staffordshire Knot ensigned with the Plume, Coronet and motto of the Prince of Wales.

DUKE OF EDINBURGH'S ROYAL

Upon a Cross Pattée (Wiltshire) the China Dragon within a coil of naval rope (Royal Berkshire), and above it the Coronet of the Duke of Edinburgh.

THE BLACK WATCH

The Star of the Order of the Thistle. Upon it, within an oval bearing the motto of the Order, the figure of St Andrew and his Cross. Below, the Sphinx. All ensigned with the Crown.

ROYAL MARINES

The Globe (Eastern hemisphere displayed) within a laurel wreath surmounted by the Royal Crest. Adopted in 1923 on the amalgamation of The Royal Marine Light Infantry and The Royal Marine Artillery as a single Corps.

ROYAL BERKSHIRE

Upon a ground the China Dragon (1840-42). The officers' badge was the Dragon upon a coil of naval rope (Copenhagen, 1801).

SEAFORTH HIGHLANDERS

A Stag's Head above the motto CUIDICH'N RIGH (Help the King).

WILTSHIRE

A Cross Pattée. Upon it reversed and intertwined the Cypher of Prince Philip, Duke of Edinburgh, ensigned with a Prince Consort's Coronet.

QUEEN'S OWN CAMERON HIGHLANDERS

St Andrew and his Cross within a wreath of thistles.

QUEEN'S OWN HIGHLANDERS

The Stag's Head and motto of Seaforth Highlanders. Within the antlers a Thistle, the collar badge of The Queen's Own Cameron Highlanders, ensigned with the Crown.

2nd GURKHA RIFLES

The Plume, Coronet and motto of the Prince of Wales.

GORDON HIGHLANDERS

The Crest of the Marquess of Huntly, later Duke of Gordon. A Stag's Head above a ducal Coronet within a wreath of ivy and, below, the Lowland Scots motto BYDAND (Watchful).

6th GURKHA RIFLES

Between the handles of a pair of kukris the numeral 6, all ensigned with the Crown.

ARGYLL AND SUTHERLAND HIGHLANDERS

Within a circle the Cypher and Coronet of Princess Louise. To the left a boar's head, the crest of the Argylls, and to the right a cat, the badge of the Sutherlands. All within a wreath of thistles.

7th GURKHA RIFLES

Between the blades of a pair of crossed kukris the numeral 7, and above, the Cypher and Coronet of the Duke of Edinburgh.

PARACHUTE

Within a pair of wings an open parachute, ensigned with The Royal Crest.

10th GURKHA RIFLES

A kukri interlaced with a Bugle-horn enclosing the figure 10. Above the kukri the Cypher and Coronet of the Princess Royal.

OXFORDSHIRE AND BUCKINGHAMSHIRE L.I.

A stringed Bugle-horn.

ROYAL GREEN JACKETS

A Maltese Cross bearing a circle enclosing a stringed Bugle-horn, all within a laurel wreath. On the arms of the cross 16 battle honours from QUEBEC to PEGASUS BRIDGE. Below, a Naval Crown superscribed COPENHAGEN, 2 APRIL, 1801. Above, PENINSULA upon a tablet, ensigned with The Crown.

KING'S ROYAL RIFLE CORPS

Upon a Maltese Cross a circle enclosing a stringed Bugle-horn. On the arms of the cross 36 battle honours from LOUISBURG to THE RELIEF OF LADYSMITH. Above, ensigned with the Crown, a tablet with the motto CELER ET AUDAX (Swift and Bold).

SPECIAL AIR SERVICE

A pair of wings issuing from below the hilt of a dagger. Below, the motto WHO DARES WINS.

RIFLE BRIGADE

A Maltese Cross bearing a circle enclosing a stringed Bugle-horn, all within a laurel wreath. On the arms of the cross 16 battle honours. Below, a Naval Crown superscribed COPENHAGEN, 2 APRIL, 1801. Above, WATERLOO upon a tablet, ensigned with the Guelphic Crown.

ARMY AIR CORPS

A laurel wreath surmounted by the Crown. Within the wreath an Eagle.

GLIDER PILOT

A circular scroll surmounted by the Crown. Within the scroll an Eagle.

ROYAL CORPS OF TRANSPORT

An eight-pointed star ensigned with the Crown. Upon the star a wreath and within it the Garter, motto, and Royal Cypher.

ROYAL ARMY CHAPLAINS' DEPARTMENT

Christian. A Maltese Cross. Upon it a circle inscribed IN THIS SIGN CONQUER and enclosing a quatrefoil. All within a wreath half of oak and half of laurel and ensigned with the Crown.

Jewish. The Star of David enclosing a quatrefoil, all within an oak and laurel wreath and ensigned with the Crown.

ROYAL ARMY MEDICAL CORPS

The Rod of Aesculapius and Serpent within a laurel wreath and ensigned with the Crown. Below, the motto *In Arduis Fidelis* (Faithful in Adversity).

ROYAL ARMY ORDNANCE CORPS

The Arms of the Board of Ordnance within the Garter and surmounted by the Crown. Beneath, the motto *Sua tela tonanti* (Thundering forth his weapons).

ROYAL ARMY SERVICE CORPS

An eight-pointed star ensigned with the Crown. Upon the star a wreath, and within it the Garter, motto, and Royal Cypher.

ROYAL ELECTRICAL AND MECHANICAL ENGINEERS

Upon a lightning flash a rearing horse, with a coronet collar of Fleur-de-Lys, a chain reflexed over its back, and standing on a globe. Above, the Crown.

ROYAL MILITARY POLICE

Within a laurel wreath the Royal Cypher with Crown above.

ROYAL ARMY EDUCATIONAL CORPS

A fluted flambeau and upon it the Crown.

ROYAL ARMY PAY CORPS

The Royal Crest upon the motto *Fide et Fiducia* (In faith and trust).

ROYAL ARMY DENTAL CORPS

Within a laurel wreath a dragon's head and sword, ensigned with the Crown. Beneath, the motto *Ex dentibus ensis* (From the teeth a sword).

ROYAL ARMY VETERINARY CORPS

The figure of Chiron the Centaur within a laurel wreath and ensigned with the Crown.

ROYAL PIONEER CORPS

A rifle, a shovel and a pick 'piled'. On them a laurel wreath, all ensigned with a Crown. Beneath, the motto *Labor Omnia Vincit* (Work conquers all).

MILITARY PROVOST STAFF CORPS

The Royal Cypher ensigned with the Crown.

INTELLIGENCE CORPS

A Rose with two laurel wreaths, ensigned with the Crown.

ARMY PHYSICAL TRAINING CORPS

Crossed sabres surmounted by the Crown.

QUEEN ALEXANDRA'S ROYAL ARMY NURSING CORPS

The Cypher of Queen Alexandra upon the Dannebrog, or Danish Cross, the whole within a laurel wreath and the motto *Sub Cruce Candida* (Under the White Cross). All ensigned with the Crown.

ARMY CATERING CORPS

Within a circle an ancient Greek brazier, ensigned with the Crown. Beneath, the motto WE SUSTAIN.

AUXILIARY TERRITORIAL SERVICE

The initial letters ATS within a laurel wreath and ensigned with the Crown.

ARMY LEGAL CORPS

Behind, crossed swords. Thereon, a globe and the figure of justice. All ensigned with the Royal Crest. On the circle the motto JUSTITIA IN ARMIS.

WOMEN'S ROYAL ARMY CORPS

A laurel wreath surmounted by the Crown. Within the wreath a Lioness rampant.

GENERAL SERVICE CORPS

The Royal Arms. The same badge is also worn by officers on the General List.

Disbanded Regiments and Corps

ROYAL IRISH

The Erin Harp ensigned with the Crown.

CONNAUGHT RANGERS

The Erin Harp ensigned within the Crown.

CAMERONIANS

A Mullet from the coat of arms of the Douglas family upon a stringed Bugle-horn, within two sprays of thistles.

LEINSTER

The Prince of Wales's Plume and Coronet (from the Honour title, Prince of Wales's Royal Canadians).

YORK AND LANCASTER

The Royal Tiger. Above it the Union Rose surmounted by a ducal Coronet (Duchy of Lancaster) within a laurel wreath.

ROYAL MUNSTER FUSILIERS

A grenade with, on the base, the Royal Tiger (from the previous East India Company origin).

ROYAL DUBLIN FUSILIERS

A Grenade with, on the base, the Elephant and the Royal Tiger (from the previous East India Company origin).

ROYAL FLYING CORPS

The letters RFC within a wreath and ensigned with the Crown.

MACHINE GUN CORPS

A pair of crossed Vickers machine guns with the Crown above.

Dispersed Brigades

EAST ANGLIAN BRIGADE

The Castle and Key of Gibraltar upon an eight-pointed star.

GREEN JACKET BRIGADE

A Maltese Cross with, upon it, a stringed Bugle-horn, all within a laurel wreath and ensigned with the Crown upon a tablet PENINSULA.

FORESTER (previously MIDLAND) BRIGADE

The Sherwood Foresters' cross. Upon it, within the Garter, the Royal Warwickshire Antelope. All within an oak wreath. Above, the Royal Tiger (Royal Leicestershire).

HIGHLAND BRIGADE

A Stag's Head above the motto of Seaforth Highlanders, *Cuidich'n Righ* (Help the King) upon a Saltire.

FUSILIER BRIGADE

A grenade. On the base the George and Dragon of the Royal Northumberland Fusiliers and the Crown within a laurel wreath.

HOME COUNTIES BRIGADE

A sword pointing upwards. Upon it a Saxon Crown.

LANCASTRIAN BRIGADE

The Rose of Lancaster within a laurel wreath, ensigned with the Royal Crest.

NORTH IRISH BRIGADE

An Angel Harp ensigned with the Crown.

LIGHT INFANTRY BRIGADE

A stringed Bugle-horn.

WELSH BRIGADE

The Prince of Wales's Plume above the motto and Coronet.

LOWLAND BRIGADE

Upon a Saltire a Thistle within a circle bearing the motto of the Order of the Thistle, *Nemo me impune lacessit* (None shall provoke me with impunity).

WESSEX BRIGADE

A Wyvern upon a tablet inscribed WESSEX.

MERCIAN BRIGADE

A Saxon Crown above a double-headed Eagle.

YORKSHIRE BRIGADE

The Rose of York ensigned with the Crown.

F

A CHRONOLOGY OF POLITICAL AND MILITARY CONTROL

It is an explicit commentary on political attitudes towards the Standing Army that not until 1794 was a Minister appointed with specific responsibility for military affairs. The historic, if not the natural, reason for this singular fact goes back to the friction between Charles II and his successive Parliaments, and to the constitutional principle expressed in the Declaration of Rights. The fact that by the end of the eighteenth century the despised and derided Army had, in concert with the Fleet, laid the foundations of a great colonial empire seems to have aroused an extension of prejudice rather than an access of pride. The levers of power, controlled by numerous — and often factious — hands, had a curious origin.

At the accession of William and Mary there were two Secretaries of State.[1] One, in charge of the Northern Department, was responsible for dealings with the main Continental powers; the other, the Secretary for the Southern Department, was concerned with the Mediterranean basin, and with domestic, Irish, Army and colonial affairs (America excepted). It was a peculiarly English improvisation which depended heavily on the political complexion of the party in power, and more particularly on the character and resolution of the two incumbents (for example, Pitt the Elder, who was Secretary for the Northern Department during the great years of victory from 1756 to 1762, assumed sole control of the entire global strategy. 'I used the Duke of Newcastle's majority to carry on the public business,' he said later. It was a memorable understatement.)

After the surrender at Yorktown in 1781 and the signing of the Treaty of Paris, the system of dual control was changed (in title, if not in fact); in 1782 the Secretary for the Northern Department (Charles James Fox) became head of the new Foreign Office, and the Secretary for the Southern Department (Shelburne) the head of the Home Office, with responsibility for Irish and colonial affairs and control of the 'constitutional Force', the Militia. The Regular Army remained at the mercy of royal and ministerial whim, subject to the depredations of the Treasury and the Mutiny Act.

However, with the outbreak of war with France in 1793 and the prospect of military involvement on a scale far beyond anything contemplated during the previous hundred years, the younger Pitt at last overrode the dangerous prejudices of the past and created a separate War Department. The new Secretary of State (Henry Dundas), with Cabinet rank, was charged — albeit in vaguely defined terms — with questions affecting the military policy of the country; the size of the Army to be maintained, subject to Cabinet approval; the granting of commissions; the gazetting of promotions; the allotment and movement of troops on colonial and foreign service; and the general conduct of warlike operations.

In 1801, however, with a large part of the Army engaged in the West Indies, responsibility for colonial affairs was transferred from the Home Office to the War Department and the title of the Minister changed to Secretary of State for War and the Colonies, on the curious grounds that the two functions had become largely synonymous.

With the end of the Napoleonic War the Army entered upon forty years of political neglect and public antipathy exceptional even by the standards of the previous century. Without the pressures of a European conflict, successive Ministers — and the accompanying table shows that for the greater part they

---

[1] Officially described as 'Their Majesties' Principal Secretaries of State for Foreign Affairs'.

were nonentities — devoted most of their time to colonial affairs at the expense of matters military. Thus the outbreak of the Crimean War in 1854 found the Army under-strength and ill-equipped, its organization and administrative structure virtually unchanged since the time of the Peninsula. Most critically, it had no Wellington and no Castlereagh. It was now to pay a heavy price for the locust years.

Belatedly Lord Aberdeen's Coalition Government shook itself into activity, and within six months of the start of the campaign a number of changes were made. The incompatible partnership of military and colonial affairs was at last dissolved — finally and, as it was to prove, irrevocably — and Pitt's department of 1794 was revived, with a Secretary of State for War, charged solely with the political management and control of the Army. The antiquated and autonomous Board of Ordnance was abolished and its functions divided between the War Department and the Horse Guards, as the Whitehall office of the Commander-in-Chief was known. Similarly, control of the Militia and the Yeomanry was transferred from the Home Office, and responsibility for transport and the Commissariat from the Treasury to the new Secretary of State; and in 1857, as an earnest of good intentions, if for no better reason, the War Department was renamed the War Office. Finally, in 1863 the obsolete and often contentious office of Secretary-at-War (see below) was abolished and its duties absorbed into those of the Secretary of State.

Cardwell's arrival at the War Office in 1868 marked not only a revolution in the anatomy and structure of the Army, but a no less important one in the political and military hierarchy. Since his appointment as Commander-in-Chief in 1856 the Duke of Cambridge had used — and abused — his special relationship with the Queen to maintain a scrupulous distance between his own office at the Horse Guards and that of the Secretary of State in Pall Mall. Cardwell was quick to grasp that his proposed reforms would be ineffective, if not impossible, without subjecting the ill-defined functions of the Horse Guards to overall political control. The result, in spite of royal objections, was the War Office Act of 1870. By this measure the Commander-in-Chief and his various departments were brought under the same roof as the War Office[2] and were completely subordinated to its political head. The old ramshackle structure of the Horse Guards was reconstructed thus, the main functions falling under three convenient headings:

The Commander-in-Chief	men
The Surveyor-General of Ordnance	material
The Financial Secretary	money

Of these the Commander-in-Chief was *primus inter pares*, principal military adviser to the Secretary of State, and in charge of both the Regular Army and the auxiliary forces.

Yet in a sense the C-in-C was only nominally 'in charge'. The whole thrust of Cardwell's reforms was to subordinate the military to the political executive. If the Duke of Cambridge was in fact the principal military adviser to the Secretary of State, then precious little of his advice did Cardwell take. The Army Enlistment Act and the even more controversial Localization Scheme were by

[2]The Duke of Cambridge, despite his translation from Whitehall, continued to write his letters under the address 'Horse Guards, Pall Mall.'

any yardstick matters for 'military' decision, and both were strongly opposed by the C-in-C. Cardwell's justification for pressing ahead in spite of professional objections was an ingenious interpretation of his statutory powers — namely, that since the size and cost of the Army was regulated by Parliament through the Mutiny Act, the terms of service and the regimental structure both lay within his competence.

In the event, Cardwell seems to have treated Cambridge with some deference, although when the Army Regulation Bill which abolished commission by purchase was before Parliament he wrote to the C-in-C that if he persisted in his public opposition in the Lords, he would be required to resign. How this uneasy relationship might have developed is a matter for speculation, for in 1874 Cardwell was out of office. The new Tory Government, while accepting the principle of the main reforms, addressed itself to other matters ('six years of peace,' observed Lord Wolseley drily), and it was not until the return of the Liberals in 1880 that the Localization Scheme of eight years previously was carried through to its radical conclusion, the creation of the Territorial Force.

There followed, under successive Secretaries of State, a number of measures which, while in no way relaxing political control, transferred an even greater burden on to the C-in-C's office. For example: in 1883 the Commissariat, Ordnance and Pay Departments were placed entirely under the C-in-C; in 1887[3] the Surveyor-General's office was abolished, and the C-in-C became responsible for clothing, feeding, equipment, and pay in addition to his other military duties such as discipline and promotions; in 1888 War Office business was split between a military and a civil division, both under the Secretary of State; and in 1895 the Duke of Cambridge resigned. He had held his appointment for thirty-nine years, the longest of any tenure, but the *casus belli* seems to have come six years earlier.

In 1889 a committee was convened under Lord Hartington to consider, among other things, the relationship between the Admiralty and the War Office. Its main recommendations, both radical and prophetic, were as follows:

> The establishment of a Joint Naval and Military Council.
> The abolition of the office of Commander-in-Chief.
> The appointment of a General Officer Commanding in
>   Great Britain.
> The appointment of a Chief of Staff.
> The establishment of a permanent War Office Council.

Predictably, they found no favour with the Duke of Cambridge, and so, somewhat cravenly, they were shelved. Had they been adopted, even in part, the conduct of the South African War might have been very different.

The war led to a serious reassessment of the machinery of control,[4] and in 1903 the Esher Committee submitted its recommendations. These closely reflected the Hartington proposals, and the principal features were as follows:

> The establishment of an Army Council.
> The abolition of the office of Commander-in-Chief.
> The appointment of a Chief of Staff.

[3]In this year the title of the Duke of Cambridge's appointment was changed from 'Commanding-in-Chief' to 'Commander-in-Chief'.
[4]In 1901 a Committee of Imperial Defence was set up.

The Balfour Government accepted the Committee's report in full, and on 10 August 1904 the Army Council came into existence, constituted thus:

Secretary of State for War	Chairman
Chief of the General Staff[5]	First Military Member
Adjutant-General	Second Military Member
Quartermaster-General	Third Military Member
Master-General of the Ordnance	Fourth Military Member
Parliamentary Under-Secretary of State	Civil Member
Financial Secretary of the War Office	Finance Member
Secretary of the War Office	

Except in the special circumstances of the two World Wars, this composition did not vary, apart from an addition to the Military Members, until the major reorganization of 1964.

It was thus with a radical new system of political and military control that Richard Haldane became Secretary of State in 1905. He was to prove the most pragmatic of all holders of the office; for whereas Cardwell had concentrated on restructuring the Army to meet its peacetime imperial commitments, Haldane's reforms were designed to equip it for a Continental war. His main and, as it was to prove, crucial innovation was to form an expeditionary force of one cavalry and six infantry divisions. As a first-line reserve (Cardwell's introduction of short-service enlistment was retained) he reorganized the old Militia as the Special Reserve, and the Volunteer Force as a Territorial Army of fourteen cavalry brigades and fourteen infantry divisions based on local County Associations. It was with this revitalized military machine that Britain went to war in 1914; and it was with a very similar structure that the Army embarked for France in 1939.

After the return of peace in 1945, and in a political climate which saw a fundamental change in the balance of world power and in the very nature of war itself, the lessons were slow to be applied. The concept of a separate system of control for each of the Armed Services was no longer practical or indeed desirable, and accordingly on 1 April 1964 the three Service Ministries were amalgamated to form a single Ministry of Defence under a Secretary of State for Defence with a Chief of the Defence Staff (alternating between the three services) and a joint-service Defence Council.[6] The very titles reflect the changing world and Britain's new, post-imperial role in it.

Within the structure of the Defence Council there was an Army Board[7] under a Chief of the General Staff, which replaced the old Army Council. Political control was exercised by the Secretary of State, with a Minister of State for Defence and a Parliamentary Under-Secretary for the Army.

In 1982, however, there was a further political reorganization. Separate Ministers for each Armed Service were replaced by a new structure, so that the present Ministry consists of the following appointments:

[5]Retitled Chief of the Imperial General Staff in 1909.
[6]By Royal Warrant, brought into effect by Army Orders 21 and 22, 1964.
[7]Similarly, there was an Admiralty Board and an Air Force Board, each with its own Chief of Staff.

Secretary of State for Defence
Minister of State for the Armed Forces
Minister of State for Procurement
Parliamentary Under-Secretary of State for the Armed Forces
Parliamentary Under-Secretary of State for Procurement

In the hundred years since Edward Cardwell embarked upon his revolutionary reforms the wheel has come full circle.

But long before the appointment of the first Secretary of State there had existed an important official known as the Secretary-at-War. The origins of this office are obscure, its authority ill defined, for like many English institutions it began as a self-perpetuating paradox.

With the Militia Act of 1661 Parliament in one breath had refused to recognize the existence of a Standing Army and in the next had vested in the King 'the supreme Command of all Forces by Land and Sea'. Since the Army was held to be constitutionally illegal, a political head was superfluous; but since the royal Guards and Garrisons were grudgingly accepted, a superior office-boy was needed. One such already existed in the person of the Secretary-at-War, whose high-sounding title concealed a clerical-grade civil servant, independent of any political affiliation or control.

The first holder of the post was Sir William Clarke, and his appointment seems to have been little more than that of private secretary to the Commander-in-Chief, Albemarle. In this capacity he administered the routine business of the Guards and Garrisons, but his duties could not have been onerous, for in 1666 his daily rate of pay, including the amount for two clerks, was less than £1.

With the death of Albemarle in 1670 the office of Commander-in-Chief was briefly left vacant, but that of the Secretary-at-War began to acquire an added status and authority. This was largely self-assumed until 1676, when a Royal Warrant laid down that 'considering that we continue to issue from Ourselves some kind of Warrants and military Orders which did belong to the Office of Our late General, and which he was wont to despatch and sign ... it is our Will and pleasure that all such kinds of warrants [*viz: movements, quarterings and reliefs*] which We continue to issue shall have Our Sign Manual only and shall be countersigned by the Secretary to our Forces as by Our Command.'

By the reign of William III the Secretary-at-War was no longer merely a clerical assistant to the Commander-in-Chief, and had created a separate establishment of his own,[8] issuing orders for the King, countersigning parliamentary estimates, and handling all commissions and pay warrants. Predictably, he prospered greatly, for by 1695 the holder of the post, William Blathwayte, drew £2,000 a year, supplemented by a fee of £1,000 out of a stoppage of 5 per cent from the pay of all ranks.

In 1704, partly at Marlborough's instance, a reorganization of Army administration took place, and Henry St John, a professional politician, replaced Blathwayte. St John, although not a member of the Ministry, took charge of all military matters in the Commons. The Secretary-at-War thus ceased to be an

---

[8]The office of Adjutant-General dates from 1673, and that of Quartermaster-General from 1686.

appendage of the Commander-in-Chief[9] and his importance grew correspondingly, even if his position had no statutory authority and his duties no clear definition. So the absurd dichotomy arose whereby the ultimate responsibility for the Army rested with the Secretary of State for the Southern Department whose main duties lay elsewhere, while the detailed management of military business was conducted by the Secretary-at-War, who had no constitutional standing. It is not surprising that the victim of this state of incoherence was the Army itself.

When, after the loss of the American colonies, the functions of the two Secretaries of State were redefined, the process was extended to the office of the Secretary-at-War. With the passing of Burke's Act for Economical Reform in 1782 he was given statutory responsibility for the financial and civil business of the Army, and for the preparation of the estimates to be laid before Parliament. When supplies had been voted he transmitted them to the Paymaster-General, who was in turn responsible for their disbursement. He remained subordinate to the Cabinet, but although he was not a Cabinet Minister,[10] he could no longer deny responsibility to Parliament as his predecessors had done since the time of Henry St John. He now became in effect the link between the Sovereign and the Army, or (to be more precise) between the Sovereign and the infantry and cavalry arms, since the artillery and the engineers remained under the supervision of the Master-General of the Ordnance, who was also a member of the Cabinet. Thus the old dichotomy was replaced by a new and equally cumbersome one.

In 1811 Palmerston, appointed Secretary-at-War at the age of twenty-five, set out his own definition of the responsibilities of his office:

> The Secretary-at-War seems, indeed, to be the officer who stands peculiarly between the people and the Army to protect (*sic*) the former from the latter; to prevent their public revenue from being drained by any unauthorised increase of military establishment, and their persons and property from being injured by any possible misconduct of the soldiery; and upon him would Parliament and the country justly fix the responsibility for any neglect of this part (*sic*) of his duty.

Old shibboleths die hard; and not many Secretaries-at-War would have recognized themselves in that quaintly observed description.

None the less, the office survived the appointment of a Secretary of State, and indeed recovered much of its eighteenth-century influence when responsibility for colonial affairs was transferred from the Home Office to the War Department, and the Secretary of State increasingly neglected the military side of his duties. However, by the time of the Crimean War, amid a proliferation of separate and unco-ordinated sub-departments, the Secretary-at-War's authority was restricted to matters of finance and nothing else;[11] and even that limited field of activity disappeared when the post was merged with the newly styled War

---

[9]More precisely 'Generalissimo', the title given to the Queen's husband, Prince George of Denmark.
[10]William Windham became the first Secretary-at-War with a seat in the Cabinet in 1794, the year in which the office of Secretary of State for War was created.
[11]He was no longer a member of the Cabinet, thanks to the opposition of the Queen, who made no secret of her fears of the possible extension of civil rather than military authority in Army matters.

Office and finally abolished in 1863. What had started as an anomaly ended as an anachronism. It remains as a classic example of the political prejudice which had bedevilled the Army since its earliest days.

'Within all his realms and dominions, the sole Government, Command and Disposition of the Militia, and of all Forces by sea and land ... is, and by the laws of England ever was, the undoubted right of His Majesty; and that both or either of the Houses of Parliament cannot nor ought to pretend to the same.' Thus in 1662 Parliament conceded to the Crown the constitutional authority over an Army whose constitutional existence it refused to recognize. There can have been few more paradoxical *imprimaturs*.

Yet the principle set forth in the Militia Act has survived all subsequent attempts to rewrite the statute book. The Sovereign is, and by the laws of England ever was, the head of the armed services; today the Queen still takes pride of place in the Army List. This essential element of the royal prerogative has never been seriously challenged, whether by a hostile Commons in Stuart times, or by the anti-monarchist lobby of the eighteenth century, or when Queen Victoria declared her opinion that the Army was the personal property of the Sovereign. Nor was the principle ever in question between the decisive years 1870 and 1904, when successive governments finally established the primacy of the executive over the military.

Only rarely have Sovereigns exercised personal command in the field, and then, as demonstrated by William III and George II, with singular lack of distinction. Instead, from the raising of the Standing Army, the function of command and administration was delegated (not always wisely) to a military officer of distinction or long service, or simply a recipient of royal patronage. For over two hundred years the relationship between Sovereign and military magnate may thus be likened to that of chairman and chief executive, and this was the *modus operandi* until the resignation of the Duke of Cambridge in 1895.

The office of Commander-in-Chief has been held under various other commissions such as Captain-General, Generalissimo, General-on-Staff, and Field Marshal on the Staff, as if the word 'Commander' was held to be politically offensive. The first holder of the office was the Duke of Albemarle (Captain-General), who as George Monk had been the military instrument of Restoration. With neither political master nor counterpart, Albemarle had supreme authority, subject to the King's orders, in all matters such as the establishment of the Guards and Garrisons, the granting of commissions, the framing of Articles of War and, through Sir Stephen Fox, the Paymaster to the Forces, finance and administration.

On his death in 1670 the office was filled by the King's natural son, the Duke of Monmouth, but only when the country was involved in military operations;[12] and during the reign of James II the new King, determined to rule by force if not by consent, kept tight personal control of his growing Army.

The Revolution provided the first watershed. With the Declaration of Rights and the Mutiny Act, Parliament asserted its political control over the Standing Army and, while affirming the constitutional authority of the King, retained the right to impose a statutory limitation on its size in time of peace. Throughout

---

[12]Between its occupation and evacuation (1662-84) Tangier was treated as a separate command.

much of William's reign the country was at war with France and William assumed personal command of the Army in the field, issuing his orders through the now influential Secretary-at-War (see above); and it is from this period that the long-running serial of political and military controversy may be said to date.

In 1702 Marlborough was appointed Captain-General.[13] Perhaps unwisely, he asked the Queen to confirm his appointment for life, but she, alive to his dubious political record, administered a royal rebuff by elevating her Prince Consort to the high, but empty, office of Generalissimo.[14] Not even after Marlborough's victorious campaigns as field Commander was he rewarded with the highest military office, for in 1712 the Queen appointed the Duke of Ormonde as Captain-General.

Throughout the eighteenth century the office of Commander-in-Chief had a curious history. Successive governments seem to have considered the post not only unnecessary but positively undesirable except in time of war, so that during no fewer than fifty years at different periods the office was in abeyance. This lack of continuity is reflected in the constantly changing fortunes and vicissitudes through which a leaderless and ill-starred Army passed. The situation in 1783 illustrates the sorry pattern. In that year responsibility for financial matters and civil business (but not for military policy) was transferred to the Secretary-at-War; control of the artillery and the engineers remained as it had always been with the Board of Ordnance; and the Militia and the Volunteers came under the supervision of the newly created Home Office. In the absence of a Commander-in-Chief, the combatant bulk of the Army, the cavalry and the infantry, drifted rudderless on a sea of political indifference. The one concrete decision had been, in the previous year, to impose territorial designations on 57 numbered regiments of the Line. Little good did it do them.

However, with the appointment of the Duke of York as Field Marshal Commanding-in-Chief in 1795 a new era for the Regular Army began. The Duke had one valuable advantage — a royal connection; but he did not simply trade on the King's prerogative. He was an outstanding soldier and administrator in his own right. And he did not care much for political poodles.

He started by creating a headquarters staff through the transfer from the Secretary-at-War of the departments of the Adjutant-General and the Quartermaster-General and by the appointment of a Military Secretary. By the end of his tenure of command in 1827 he had provided his office with an establishment which lasted virtually unchanged until the appointment of Commander-in-Chief was abolished in 1904. That in the last analysis he failed to halt the demoralization of the Army after Waterloo is simply to demonstrate that political blood is a good deal thicker than military water.

An account of the bureaucratic machine which in the end defeated him makes sombre reading. The hydra-headed control at the top was bad enough, consisting as it did of the Secretary of State for War and the Colonies, the Secretary-at-War, the Home Office (Militia), the Commander-in-Chief, the Master-General of the Ordnance (artillery and engineers) and the Treasury (supply and transport). But at the end of the Napoleonic Wars there were in addition ten other offices in which the business of the Army was either conducted or obstructed: two Paymasters-General, the Comptrollers of Army

---

[13]He had already held the post briefly in 1690, before his disgrace and imprisonment in the Tower.
[14]More controversially, she also appointed Prince George Lord High Admiral.

Accounts, the Commissary-General of the Musters, the Army Medical Board, the Barrack Master-General, the Storekeeper-General, the Commissary-in-Chief, the Board of General Officers, the Judge Advocate General, and the Commissioners of the Royal Hospital (pensions). Each was independent of the other. Each addressed letters to the other. In all this welter of little Caesars there was no single fountain-head to express the collective wisdom of the Army on military problems. There was one man who had the necessary stature and charisma to have sent this monstrous regiment packing, and cleared the weeds from the Duke of York's garden. But the Duke of Wellington, as he was to demonstrate during his own years as Commander-in-Chief (1842-52), had no stomach for such a fight, and when the brickbats flew took refuge behind the iron shutters of Apsley House.

So the Duke of York was left to march alone to the top of the hill. He marched to some purpose. First he succeeded in securing control of almost all the military forces within the United Kingdom (although not of commanders abroad, who reported direct to the Secretary of State). All promotions, except those to the highest ranks, passed into his hands. He took sole responsibility for discipline, training, man-management and tactical innovation. He even won the first pay increase for private soldiers since 1702. Single-handed, he resisted the attempts of successive Secretaries-at-War to clip his wings. In the end he was submerged by weight of numbers. But arguably he was the greatest Commander-in-Chief — and the best friend — that the British Army has ever had.

After his death the slow decline continued. The number of committees and boards of enquiry into the state of the Army during the 1830s suggests a state of uneasy conscience. But while there was peace in Europe and success to celebrate in India and beyond, the country addressed itself to the more congenial climate of riot and reform. Old and tired, the Duke of Wellington watched from the wings, deeply concerned about the state of the nation's defences but caught like a fly in the amber of faded fame and glories past. It was in this climate of comfortable complacency that the country stumbled again into war.

The return of peace brought a moment for sober reassessment. It also brought the unexpected appointment of the Duke of Cambridge as Commanding-in-Chief (the gloss has no obvious significance), an office which he was to hold for thirty-nine years. He was a man of strong opinions, and the cousin of a Queen with even stronger convictions of her royal prerogative. Together they were to preside over the greatest of all transformations in the structure and control of the British Army. Neither was ever reconciled to the change. Neither was foolish enough to obstruct the quirky processes of democratic decision-making. And neither lived to see the final assertion of political purpose over military expediency. Cambridge fought a good fight, but he was no match for a man like Cardwell, and he went down with good grace, secured from total defeat by his popular esteem and by the covering fire of a very formidable lady. A small incident in his long life speaks volumes for his devotion to the Army. In 1894 a committee was convened (the third since 1870) to consider the case for closing down the Royal Hospital at Chelsea. The Duke was called to give evidence. 'I do not believe', he said, 'that Her Majesty would for one moment acquiesce in the views of your committee. This royal foundation exists to save old soldiers from dying in the workhouse and I do not propose to be party to its dismemberment.' In some disarray, the committee hastily withdrew.

It is not necessary to rehearse again the losing battle which Cambridge fought. The War Office Act of 1870, while redrawing — some might say overloading —

the parameters of his office, effectively established the political primacy of the Secretary of State. It was now only a matter of time until the old slate was wiped clean and new chalk-marks appeared.

That time came after the hard-learned lessons of the South African War. The Esher Committee of 1903, with a backward look at Prussia, if not yet a forward perception of Germany, made its proposals; and nine months later the Army Council was formed. With it (see above) the office of Commander-in-Chief, for so long a political whipping-boy, passed into history. The last incumbent, the public idol Lord Roberts, bowed out with dignity. 'He takes with him,' said the *Morning Post*, 'the nation's thanks — and prayers.' It was not alone in lighting a small candle.

So, with the new century, came the new General Staff. Under its freshly minted chief ('Imperial' was added to the title in 1909) it survived virtually unchanged for sixty years when, in the light of what Churchill called 'a perverted science' undreamed of by Edwardian reformers, the three services were amalgamated in a joint Defence Council under a single co-ordinating head, and a single responsible Minister of the Crown. *Tria juncta in uno*. It had taken a long time.

I

SECRETARIES-AT-WAR

1660	Sir William Clarke	1794	William Wyndham
1666	Matthew Locke	1801	Charles Yorke
1683	William Blathwayte	1803	Charles Bathurst
1704	Henry St John (Viscount Bolingbroke)	1804	William Dundas
1708	Robert Walpole (Earl of Orford)	1806	Gen. Richard Fitzpatrick
1710	George Granville (Lord Lansdowne)	1807	Lt. Gen. Sir J. M. Pulteney
1712	Sir William Wyndham	1809	Lord Leveson-Gower
1713	Francis Gwyn		Lord Palmerston
1714	William Pulteney (Earl of Bath)	1828	Col. Sir Henry Hardinge (Viscount Hardinge)
1717	James Craggs		
1718	Robert Pringle	1830	Lord Leveson-Gower
	George Treby		Charles Wynn
1724	Henry Pelham	1831	Sir Henry Parnell (Lord Congleton)
1730	Sir William Strickland	1832	Sir John Hobhouse (Lord Broughton)
1735	Sir William Yonge	1833	Edward Ellice
1746	Henry Fox (Lord Holland)	1834	John Herries
1755	Viscount Barrington	1835	Viscount Hewick (Earl Grey)
1761	Charles Townshend	1839	Thomas Macaulay
1762	Welbore Ellis (Lord Mendip)	1841	Viscount Hardinge
1765	Viscount Barrington	1844	Sir Thomas Fremantle
1778	Charles Jenkinson (Earl of Liverpool)	1845	Sidney Herbert
1782	Thomas Townshend	1846	Fox Maule (Lord Panmure)
	Sir George Yonge	1852	Vernon Smith
1783	Richard Fitzpatrick		William Beresford
1784	Sir George Yonge		Sidney Herbert (Lord Herbert)

1855	*Office merged with that of Secretary of State for War*
1863	*Office abolished*

SECRETARY OF STATE FOR WAR

1794   Henry Dundas (Viscount Melville)

SECRETARIES OF STATE FOR WAR AND THE COLONIES

1801	Lord Hobart (Earl of Buckingham)	1833	Edward Stanley (Earl of Derby)
1804	Earl Camden	1834	Thomas Spring-Rice
1805	Viscount Castlereagh		(Lord Monteagle)
	(Marquess of Londonderry)		Earl of Aberdeen
1806	William Windham	1835	Charles Grant (Lord Glenelg)
1807	Viscount Castlereagh	1839	Marquis of Normanby
1809	Earl of Liverpool		Lord John Russell (Earl Russell)
1812	Earl Bathurst	1841	Lord Stanley (Earl of Derby)
1827	Viscount Goderich (Earl of Ripon)	1845	William Gladstone
	William Huskisson	1846	Earl Grey
1828	Lt. Gen. Sir George Murray	1852	Sir John Pakington (Lord Hampton)
1830	Viscount Goderich		Duke of Newcastle

SECRETARIES OF STATE FOR WAR
(with subsequent titles)

1854	Duke of Newcastle	1918	Viscount Milner
1855	Fox Maule (Lord Panmure)	1919	Winston Churchill
1858	Maj. Gen. Jonathan Peel	1921	Sir Laming Worthington-Evans
1859	Sidney Herbert (Lord Herbert)	1922	Earl of Derby
1861	Sir George Lewis	1924	Stephen Walsh
1863	Earl de Grey (Marquis of Ripon)		Sir Laming Worthington-Evans
1866	Marquis of Hartington	1929	Thomas Shaw
	(Duke of Devonshire)	1931	Marquess of Crewe
1867	Sir John Pakington		Viscount Hailsham
1868	Edward Cardwell (Lord Cardwell)	1935	Viscount Halifax
1874	Gathorne Hardy (Earl of Cranbrook)		Duff Cooper (Lord Norwich)
1878	Col. Frederick Stanley (Earl of Derby)	1937	Leslie Hore-Belisha
1880	Hugh Childers	1940	Oliver Stanley
1882	Marquess of Hartington		Anthony Eden (Earl of Avon)
1885	W. H. Smith (Lord Hambledon)		David Margesson
1887	Edward Stanhope	1942	Sir James Grigg
1892	Henry Campbell-Bannerman	1945	James Lawson
1895	Marquess of Lansdowne	1946	Frederick Bellenger
1900	St John Brodrick (Earl of Midleton)	1947	Emanuel Shinwell (Lord Shinwell)
1903	H. O. Arnold-Forster	1950	John Strachey
1905	Richard Haldane (Viscount Haldane)	1951	Anthony Head (Lord Head)
1912	Col. J. E. B. Seely (Lord Mottistone)	1956	John Hare
1914	Herbert Asquith	1958	Christopher Soames (Lord Soames)
	(Earl of Oxford and Asquith)	1960	John Profumo
	Earl Kitchener	1963	Joseph Godber (Lord Godber)
1916	David Lloyd George		James Ramsden
	Earl of Derby		

On 1 April 1964 the War Office was combined with the Admiralty and the Air Ministry to form the Ministry of Defence. The office of Secretary of State for War was merged with that of Minister of Defence.

SECRETARIES OF STATE FOR DEFENCE

1964	James Ramsden
	Peter Thorneycroft
	(Lord Thorneycroft)
	Denis Healey
1970	Lord Carrington
1974	Ian Gilmour
	Roy Mason
1976	Fred Mulley
1979	Francis Pym
1981	John Nott
1983	Michael Heseltine

II

COMMANDERS-IN-CHIEF
(The office was held under various commissions)

1660	George, Duke of Albemarle (Captain-General)
1670	Duke of Monmouth (Captain-General)
1674	Duke of Monmouth (Commander-in-Chief)
1678	Duke of Monmouth (Captain-General)
1690	Earl of Marlborough (temporary)
1691	Duke of Schomberg (temporary)
1702	Duke of Marlborough (Captain-General)
1702	Prince George of Denmark (Generalissimo)
1712	Duke of Ormonde (Captain-General)
1714	*(Office vacant)*
1744	Earl of Stair (Commander-in-Chief)
1745	George Wade (Commander-in-Chief) Duke of Cumberland (Captain-General)
1757	Earl Ligonier
1763	*(Office vacant)*
1766	Marquis of Granby
1770	*(Office vacant)*
1778	Lord Amherst (General-on-Staff)
1782	Henry Conway
1793	Lord Amherst (General-on-Staff)
1795	Frederick, Duke of York (Field Marshal on the Staff)
1799	Frederick, Duke of York (Captain-General)
1809	Sir David Dundas
1811	Frederick, Duke of York
1827	Duke of Wellington
1828	Viscount Hill
1842	Duke of Wellington
1852	Viscount Hardinge (Commanding-in-Chief)
1856	George, Duke of Cambridge (Commanding-in-Chief)
1895	Lord Wolseley
1900	Lord Roberts
1904	*Office abolished on the creation of the Army Council.*

CHIEFS OF THE GENERAL STAFF
(with rank and style at date of appointment)

1904	Lt. Gen. Sir Neville Lyttelton
1908	Gen. Sir W. G. Nicholson

In November 1909 the title of the office was changed to:

CHIEF OF THE IMPERIAL GENERAL STAFF

CHIEFS OF THE IMPERIAL GENERAL STAFF

1909	Gen. Sir W. G. Nicholson	1936	Gen. Sir Cyril Deverell
1912	Gen. Sir John French	1937	Lt. Gen Viscount Gort
1914	Gen. Sir C. W. Douglas	1939	Gen. Sir Edmund Ironside
	Lt. Gen. Sir A. J. Murray	1940	Gen. Sir John Dill
1915	Lt. Gen. Sir A. J. Murray	1941	Gen. Sir Alan Brooke
	Gen. Sir William Robertson	1946	F. M. Viscount Montgomery
1918	Gen. Sir Henry Wilson	1948	F.M. Sir William Slim
1922	Gen. The Earl of Cavan	1952	Gen. Sir John Harding
1926	Gen. Sir G. F. Milne	1955	Gen. Sir Gerald Templer
1933	Gen. Sir A. A. Montgomery-	1958	Gen. Sir Francis Festing
	Massingberd	1961	Gen. Sir Richard Hull

On 1 April 1964 the three Service Ministries were combined into a single Ministry of Defence, with a Chief of the Defence Staff appointed in rotation from the three Services. From that date the senior military member of the new Army Board of the Defence Council was styled:

CHIEF OF THE GENERAL STAFF

1964	Gen. Sir Richard Hull
1965	Gen. Sir James Cassells
1968	Gen. Sir Geoffrey Baker
1971	Gen. Sir Michael Carver
1973	Gen. Sir Peter Hunt
1976	Gen. Sir Roland Gibbs
1979	Gen. Sir Edwin Bramall
1982	Gen. Sir John Stanier

SELECT BIBLIOGRAPHY

Anon

Fifteen Years of "Army Reform"
(Blackwood, 1884)

Barnett, Correlli

Britain and Her Army 1509-1970
(Allen Lane, The Penguin Press, 1970)

Biddulph, Sir Robert

Lord Cardwell at the War Office
(John Murray, 1904)

Blaxland, Gregory

The Regiments Depart
(William Kimber, 1971)

Chichester and Burges Short

The Records and Badges of the British Army
(Gale and Polden, 1900)

Childs, J.

The Army of Charles II
(Routledge and Kegan Paul, 1976)

The Army, James II, and the Glorious Revolution
(Manchester University Press, 1980)

Clode, C. M.

The Military Forces of the Crown
(John Murray, 1869)

Dunlop, J. K.

The Development of the British Army 1899-1914
(Methuen, 1938)

Farmer, John S.

The Regimental Records of the British Army
(Grant Richards, 1901)

Fortescue, Sir John

A History of the British Army, 13 vols.
(Macmillan, 1930)

Frederick, J. B. M.

Lineage Book of the British Army 1660-1968
(Hope Farm Press, 1969)

Glover, Michael

Wellington's Army in the Peninsula
(David and Charles, 1977)

Kipling, A. L. and King, H. L.

Headdress Badges of the British Army, 2 vols
(Muller, 1972, 1979)

Leslie, N. B.

The Battle Honours of the British and Indian Armies 1695-1914
(Leo Cooper, 1970)

Lloyd, E. M.

A Review of the History of Infantry
(Longman, 1908)

May, Carman and Tanner

Badges and Insignia of the British Armed Services
(A. & C. Black, 1974)

Norman, C. B.

Battle Honours of the British Army, 1662-1902
(John Murray, 1911)

Omond, Lt. Col. J. S.

Parliament and the Army 1642-1904
(Cambridge University Press, 1933)

Rogers, Col. H. C. B.

The British Army of the Eighteenth Century
(Allen and Unwin, 1977)

Scouller, Major R. E.

The Armies of Queen Anne
(Oxford University Press, 1966)

Spiers, Edward N.

Haldane: an army reformer
(Edinburgh University Press, 1980)

Swinson, A. (ed.)

A Register of the Regiments and Corps of the British Army
(Archive Press, 1972)

Thurburn, Brig. R. G. (ed.)

Battle Honours 1914-1919
(for Army Museums Ogilby Trust, 1957)

Battle Honours 1939-1945 and Korea 1950-1953
(for Army Museums Ogilby Trust, 1957)

FURTHER SOURCES

Army List
Bulletin of the Military Historical Society
Journal of the Royal United Services Institute for Defence Studies
Jurnal of the Society for Army Historical Research
Regimental and Corps Histories
Regimental and Corps Journals

INDEX

Since this book has been so designed that the various Sections are cross-referenced to THE SPINAL COLUMN on pp. 61-5, the following Index, with a few specific exceptions, is confined to general and chronological entries.